SCIENCE & FAITH
FRIENDS OR FOES?

SCIENCE & FAITH

FRIENDS OR FOES?

C. John
COLLINS

CROSSWAY BOOKS

A DIVISION OF
GOOD NEWS PUBLISHERS
WHEATON, ILLINOIS

Science and Faith: Friends or Foes?

Copyright © 2003 by C. John Collins

Published by Crossway Books
a division of Good News Publishers
1300 Crescent Street
Wheaton, Illinois 60187

All rights reserved. No part of this publication may be reproduced, stored in a retrieval system, or transmitted in any form by any means, electronic, mechanical, photocopy, recording, or otherwise, without the prior permission of the publisher, except as provided by USA copyright law.

Cover design: Josh Dennis

Cover photo: Getty Images

First printing 2003

Printed in the United States of America

Unless otherwise indicated, all Scripture quotations are from The Holy Bible, English Standard Version, copyright © 2001 by Crossway Bibles, a division of Good News Publishers. Used by permission. All rights reserved.

Scripture references marked NASB are from the *New American Standard Bible®* Copyright © The Lockman Foundation 1960, 1962, 1963, 1968, 1971, 1972, 1973, 1975, 1977, 1995. Used by permission.

Scripture and Apocrypha references marked RV are from the Revised Version of the Bible.

Scripture and Apocrypha references marked RSV are from the *Revised Standard Version*. Copyright © 1946, 1952, 1971, 1973 by the Division of Christian Education of the National Council of the Churches of Christ in the U.S.A.

Scripture references marked NRSV are from the *New Revised Standard Version*. Copyright © 1989 by the Division of Christian Education of the National Council of the Churches of Christ in the U.S.A. Published by Thomas Nelson, Inc. Used by permission of the National Council of the Churches of Christ in the U.S.A.

Apocrypha references marked NAB are from the New American Bible, copyright © 1970 by the Confraternity of Christian Doctrine, Washington, DC, and are used by permission. All rights reserved.

Library of Congress Cataloging-in-Publication Data
Collins, C. John, 1954–
Science and faith : friends or foes? / C. John Collins.
p. cm.
Includes bibliographical references and index.
ISBN 1-58134-430-9 (TPB : alk. paper)
1. Religion and science. I. Title.
BL240.3.C65 2003
261.5'5—dc21 2003004799

ML 13 12 11 10 09 08 07 06 05 04 03
15 14 13 12 11 10 9 8 7 6 5 4 3 2 1

CONTENTS

SECTION III: SCIENCE AND FAITH INTERACT

SECTION IV: CONCLUSION

APPENDICES

ACKNOWLEDGMENTS

I AM DEEPLY GRATEFUL to many people who have helped me along the way.

Thanks go to the Discovery Institute's Center for Science and Culture, for financial support and intellectual stimulus—especially to Stephen Meyer and Jay Richards.

Thanks also to the Templeton Foundation's Science and Religion Course Program, for awarding grants for my seminary course, "Christian Faith in an Age of Science." Not only the Foundation but also the students in my classes have helped me think through so many things.

The President of Covenant Theological Seminary, Bryan Chapell; the Dean of Faculty, Daniel Doriani; and the Dean of Academics, Donald Guthrie, have supported and encouraged me in many ways. I am also grateful for my faculty colleagues, who have informed me, corrected me, and prayed for me—especially Jerram Barrs, Hans Bayer, David Calhoun, David Jones, Esther Meek, Robert Peterson, Jay Sklar, Bob Vasholz, Mike Williams, and Richard Winter. It is a privilege to work with you all.

A fair number of other folks have helped in important ways, especially in giving feedback on earlier drafts of this book: David Farbishel, Mike Glidewell, Annette Homan, Kent Keller, John Pickett, Tom Ricks, Bob Rogland, David Snoke, Mark Wardell, and Doug Wiens. Others have helped through answering questions and giving advice, such as John Dishman, Mike Farley, Tim Hall, Donna Hawk-Reinhard, Phillip Johnson, Steve Jones, Rob Koons, Rich McGee, Bryonie Moon, Stephen Moshier, J. I. Packer, Nancy Pearcey, Brian Pitts, Marcus Ross, Jonathan Wells, and Kurt Wise. Others, members of an e-mail list formerly directed by Phillip Johnson, have shaped my thoughts, saved me from rabbit trails, and enabled me to understand why people hold their views.

Thanks as well go to Lane Dennis and Marvin Padgett of Crossway, who urged me to write this book.

I wouldn't like to imply that these fine folk agree with everything I say here, nor that they are responsible for any errors I have made. You'll have to ask them for their opinions.

The Lord who made and saved me, gave me a wife and children who love me, encourage me, and challenge me. They are proof that God's aim is to flood my life with blessing—as he has done so abundantly. Of my wife and children I can say with the ancient sage,

> Her children rise up and call her blessed;
>   her husband also, and he praises her:
> "Many women have done excellently,
>   but you surpass them all."

A few years ago our friend Annette Homan phoned to ask for some help in teaching science to her children. This book is the result of that phone call—so much so that at my house we call it "Annette's book." Thank you, Annette, for caring about God's truth and for pushing me to make my thoughts clear.

1

Introduction to the Questions and Survey of the Book

ONE EVENING WHEN my daughter was about two and my wife was pregnant with my son, I gave my wife a break by taking my daughter to the mall. We went to her favorite place, the pet shop, to look at all the animals. While we were there, a clerk was showing a snake—some kind of python—to two teenage boys. As these boys were trying to get up the nerve to touch the snake—all the while needling each other about who was the more manly—my daughter asked if she could pet the snake. She reached up and stroked it gently. The boys were ashamed at being shown up by a toddler girl.

Well, yes, I'm a proud father; but I have another reason for telling you this story. I find in it a parable for the way many Christians approach science: we fear it. We fear it, I think, for two main reasons: first, because we found science classes hard in school. That is something we have in common with everyone, including those who do not share our Christian commitment; but the second reason touches on our faith directly: we fear that science will somehow undermine our faith. The fact that many writers hostile to Christianity—such as Richard Dawkins and Carl Sagan—make just that point, only adds to the fear.

I think my daughter's interest in the python models true Christianity better than these common fears do. Her curiosity about the little wriggler, and her delight in touching it—which is how she feels about most animals, including bugs—were untainted by any fears or misgivings. And in this book I will argue that this is just how it ought to be: in fact, if we have a proper hold on Christian belief we will love the natural world and respect the study of it; and by it we will also come to these studies with full mental vigor, confident that God's truth can hold up under any challenge—and not only that, but also that his truth will both illuminate and enrich those studies.

But of course to support this positive view of the sciences, and of Christians' active work in them, I will have to consider just what is a "proper hold on Christian belief," and that is what I aim to do in this book. I will start by looking into some of the philosophical issues that come into play in this discussion. This is because we need to know what faith and science are, how they relate to one another, and what claims either has a right to make about "truth." My theme, which I will develop throughout the book, is that good science and good faith both need sound critical thinking.

From there I will move on to discuss the biblical teaching that most impacts our view of science: namely the teaching about creation—how the universe came into being; and about providence—how God keeps the universe in being and interacts with it, and how he expects us to interact with it. And of course this raises questions about the age of the earth, miracles, psychology, and evolution—the places that most people think of as conflicts between faith and science; so I will go on to discuss these topics.

I will finish by considering what it means to live in a created world. That is, I will outline a Christian view of the world, give some ideas about educating children in the sciences, and reflect on how Christians can impact their culture in this arena.

You can see how I have arranged the material: philosophical issues, then theological ones, then areas where science and faith interact, and finally the conclusion. Some of my students who read a draft of this book wondered why I didn't arrange it by topic—so that, for example, the chapters discussing the biblical view of the age of the earth (chapters 4–7) would lead directly into the chapter on cosmology and geology (chapter 15). My reason is that the chapters on interaction depend on a wide range of theological and philosophical discussions. But if you prefer to read the chapters in that order, go right ahead; but, whatever you do, please be sure to read chapters 2–3 first. If you're like me, you want to get to the real stuff, and skip the preliminaries; but these chapters are not preliminaries, they are crucial to my overall case.

I am writing this book for people who do not have specialist training in theology or philosophy. I think, for example, of Christian parents who want to know how their children should study science; of college students thinking about entering the sciences, or challenged in their faith by them;

of teachers and those who write books for children. I would also be pleased if any who have doubts about Christianity, because of what the spokesmen for science tell them, might read this book and find that believing in Christ is reasonable after all. Finally, I have Christian friends who are scientists, and they mostly feel that their non-Christian colleagues at work think they're crazy for their faith, and the people they share their pews with think they're suspect for their scientific work: I'd like to help them achieve some sense of peace.

This means I will restrict myself to ordinary language and keep technical terms to a minimum. (I have done without footnotes altogether. If you want to pursue things further—or to make sure that I've done my homework—I've included "Notes and Comments" for each chapter as an appendix.) But in all this I intend to *translate* the discussion for your benefit, not to *dumb it down*. Some of the issues are complicated, and we can't do justice either to them or to God or to those we love if we don't want to think them out. I aim, then, to help you do some serious thinking: but so does Jesus, who wants his followers to be "wise as to what is good" as well as "innocent as to what is evil" (Rom. 16:19; compare Matt. 10:16). As C. S. Lewis said, Christ "wants a child's heart, but a grown-up's head. He wants us to be simple, single-minded, affectionate, and teachable, as good children are; but he also wants every bit of intelligence we have to be alert at its job, and in first-class fighting trim."

You may feel that I've given you more material than you want. My defense is that I am concerned to help with *how* to think about these questions, even more than *what* to think.

When I need to discuss a disputed point of biblical interpretation, I will generally use a fairly literal translation such as the English Standard Version (ESV), or sometimes the New American Standard Version (NASB) or the Revised Version (RV). Citations of the Apocrypha/Deuterocanonical books will be from the New American Bible (NAB) or Revised Standard Version (RSV), or from the RV if I need greater literalism. Unless I mark a Bible quotation otherwise, I'm using the ESV.

I write from the standpoint of "mere Christianity": that is, I write as a Christian who shares in common with all Christians such basic convictions as: the Bible is God's special revelation to man; the ecumenical creeds (such as the Apostles' Creed, Nicene Creed, Athanasian Creed) express the Bible's teaching about Christ and the Trinity; and Christ saves his people and calls them to pursue holiness and to serve him in the church and in the world. For all that divides Christians from one another, these common beliefs give them a common cause: to combat the unbelief that riddles our contemporary world. I sympathize with the elf Haldir in Tolkien's *Lord of the Rings,* who apologized for having to treat the Fellowship of the Ring with suspicion when they entered Lothlórien: "Indeed in nothing is the power of the Dark Lord more clearly shown than in the estrangement that divides all those who still oppose him." This means that I will stick with the Bible; if I cite a church's confession, it is because it says nicely what needs to be said, not because it in itself settles the discussion.

There are a few points in the theology section where I cannot claim to speak for all believers, but have to take sides in disputes that divide them. I have generally indicated when this is so.

Don't misunderstand me: I am a loyal member of my denomination, and think its distinctives matter a great deal; but presenting them is not my goal in this book. I have found spiritual help in a wide range of Christian authors: the ardent Roman Catholics Blaise Pascal, Romano Guardini, and G. K. Chesterton; the staunch Protestants J. Gresham Machen, John Murray, and Francis Schaeffer; and the irenic Anglicans C. S. Lewis and J. I. Packer—not to mention the giants Thomas Aquinas, Martin Luther, and John Calvin. (I am sorry to say that my reading in Eastern writers is primarily limited to the exegetical writings of Chrysostom and Theophylact.) I hope to give back to the whole church something of what I have gained.

You deserve to know who I am and what right I have to write this book. I was born in the Baby Boom generation and grew up in a nominally Christian home, receiving a decent education in good public schools. I have always been interested in science, math, and languages. I was an amateur herpetologist as a teenager (I loved snakes, lizards, turtles, frogs, and salamanders; bless my mother for putting up with me), and went to MIT where I got my bachelor's and master's degrees in electrical engineering. I came to a living Christian faith during my second year there. After a few years of work I went to seminary, and then earned a Ph.D. in Hebrew linguistics (which is a "science") in a department of Oriental studies at an English university. I now teach at a theological seminary; and besides the usual classes in Biblical studies (I am at heart a grammarian of Hebrew and Greek), I also teach a class called "Christian Faith in an Age of Science." I have been studying and writing about Genesis 1–3 for several years now, and have also written a technical book on nature and miracle (*The God of Miracles*). My wife and I have two children, and at present we school them at home. As I write this, my daughter wants to be a veterinarian, and my son wants to be an inventor—both noble careers. I can't think of anything I want more than for these children to grow up serving Christ faithfully in this world.

Annette, a friend of ours, provoked me to write this one day, when she phoned us to ask what she should teach her children about fossils and the history of the earth. I had intended to write a technical book on science and faith (as I indicated in the footnotes of *The God of Miracles*), but Annette's question made me think that a book on a general level would do more good. If God wills, I'll yet write that other, more technical, book.

Section I
Philosophical Issues

2

Science, Faith, and Rationality

A Short Course in Good Thinking

The Importance of Philosophy

This chapter and the next cover some issues in the philosophy of science; but if I'm going to write about that, I'd better first defend myself against a flurry of objections. If I don't defend myself, you might easily fall prey to the temptation to skip these chapters so you can get right to the red meat. But these chapters are foundational to most of what I will argue later, so please bear with me.

Philosophers, with their endless questions and uncertainties, frustrate people in the sciences: if these philosophers had any experience in the lab, they wouldn't get so hung up over whether the scientist actually knows anything or deserves to be believed. In my six years as an undergraduate and graduate student at MIT, never did anyone official suggest that any of us would learn something worth knowing from a philosopher. So why should I think there is anything to be gained from even mentioning philosophy?

And in the Christian world there won't be a much warmer reception. Doesn't Scripture warn us not to be taken captive through philosophy (Col. 2:8)? Isn't philosophy just the wisdom of this world, which gets in the way of genuine faith (1 Cor. 1:21)?

Let me start my defense by saying that there is a difference between philoso*phy* and philoso*phers*. Philosophy is the discipline that studies how to think clearly: to know what is a good argument that deserves our agreement because it makes its point, and what is a bad argument that we should reject. If an ornithologist (a scientific bird-watcher) tells me that my favorite canary is safe with his falcon, I want to know how he knows: is it just because he's never seen his falcon go for a canary, or what? This is, as it turns out, a question in the philosophy of science: has the ornithologist made a sound conclusion? Actually, in matters of faith we have similar issues: if someone tells me I should (or should not) have my children baptized, I want to know how he arrived at his opinion. That, too, is a kind of philosophical question, one in the subject that theologians call "hermeneutics" and "theological method"; but at bottom it's all about drawing sound conclusions.

G. K. Chesterton put it well:

> Men have always one of two things: either a complete and conscious philosophy or the unconscious acceptance of the broken bits of some incomplete and often discredited philosophy. . . . Philosophy is merely thought that has been thought out. It is often a great bore. But man has no alternative, except between being influenced by thought that has been thought out and being influenced by thought that has not been thought out.

In reference to a man who responds to miracle claims with, "But my dear fellow, this is the twentieth century!" Chesterton observed:

> In the mysterious depths of his being even that enormous ass does actually mean something. The point is that he cannot really explain what he means; and *that* is the argument for a better education in philosophy.

Now if we look at it this way, we can see that what Paul warned the early Christians about was bad philosophy, namely the kind that kept people from believing that the Christian message is true. And what about the philosophy that my fellow MIT students and I despised? Is that bad philosophy too—or were we following a bad philosophy of our own? To answer that we need this chapter.

Here is my basic claim, which I intend to develop throughout this book: our conclusions, whether in science or in religious faith or in any other area, are sound only to the extent that they follow the principles of good reasoning. (Just what those principles are will come soon.) In this I am following the lead of C. S. Lewis, who observed,

> The distinction thus made between scientific and non-scientific thoughts will not easily bear the weight we are attempting to put on it. . . . The physical sciences, then, depend on the validity of logic just as much as metaphysics [philosophy] or mathematics. If popular thought feels 'science' to be different from all other kinds of knowledge because science is experimentally verifiable, popular thought is mistaken. . . . *We should therefore abandon the distinction between scientific and non-scientific thought. The proper distinction is between logical and non-logical thought.*

I put the last two sentences in italics because they sum up my case. Science and faith are "good" to the extent that they obey the rules of rationality. So the key to a solidly Christian way of thinking about science is sound critical thinking.

Now there are two groups who will disagree with this idea. Some will say that science *defines* what rationality is. The answer to that is simple: they have made a claim, and the way to decide whether the claim is true or not is to evaluate whether it makes sense. So the very claim itself has to answer to the rules for rationality. Others will say that there is no such thing as "rationality," because that is a human invention (this group is called "postmodern"). The problem with that objection is that in everyday life we know it's not true: we know that getting hit by a flying stone is bad news, and typically we take steps to avoid it; we know that some materials make better knives than others (flint is better than sand, and steel is even better). A good philosophy will start from everyday rationality and build on it, and refine it. The principles of sound thinking that come next are just such a development.

Principles of Sound Thinking

To return to my example of the ornithologist, how will I know whether I should believe his assurances about his falcon and my canary—that is, how will I know whether or not I am reasonable to believe him? And the answer is, of course, if he has followed the rules for drawing sound conclusions from his experiences. So then: what are the rules?

To begin with, we need to understand what are the parts of an argument. (I use the word "argument" to mean the process of drawing a conclusion, not the quarrels that erupt between brothers and sisters.) Then we can decide whether the parts are all in good working order.

The first part of the argument is its *data*—that is, the raw facts. What has my bird-watching friend seen his falcon eat? What has he seen it pass by even when it's hungry? A good argument has data that are honestly reported—no fudging, no editing out of inconvenient facts—and are as complete as possible. It is of course a judgment call when someone decides what is "complete enough"; in fact, that is one thing that makes science interesting, because people do not always agree in their judgment calls, and sometimes people make mistakes in them. It is often true that my data are second-hand: someone reports it and I believe it. (Much of what I know about the animal world comes from such reports—Audubon Society *Field Guides*, documentary films, and so on.) In this case my data are good if I have sound reason to believe that the source is trustworthy.

The second part of the argument is the *premises*—the things you take for granted, often without even thinking about them. Both I and the ornithologist take it for granted that falcons eat something; we also, based on our experience of falcons and birds like them, assume that they eat other animals. So some premises may seem too obvious to need stating; but we have to be careful even then: what's obvious to you may not be obvious to me, and not only because I'm thickheaded. For example, suppose someone says, "The universe started either by the Big Bang or by divine creation." He's taking for granted a number of things, such as that creation and a Big Bang are the only alternatives, and that creation *by means of* a Big Bang is not possible. He's also taking for granted that the universe exists, and that it started. Our speaker has taken these assumptions as starting points, perhaps because he has thought it through before, or perhaps because he hasn't. But in any case he owes it to you to acknowledge his premises and expose them to evaluation.

I want to introduce a special kind of premise that I call a *touchstone truth*. By this I mean the sort of thing you have to take for granted before you can even start thinking: you take for granted that you exist, that you are a self (which means that you make real choices that matter, and that when you reason soundly you come to valid conclusions), and that other selves exist and can communicate with you. (These are just examples: there may be more.) I call them "touchstones" because if they're not true then there's no way you'll know if anything else is true. It follows that if someone contradicts one of these touchstone truths, then his argument falls apart. You don't have to argue to prove that a touchstone truth is a valid premise, although you may have to show that some particular belief has the right to touchstone status. (You can see that some premises *do* need to be shown valid.)

Here is an example of why I call these premises touchstone truths: J. B. S. Haldane, a British biologist who in the early twentieth century helped develop what is now known as neo-Darwinism, said:

> If my mental processes are determined wholly by the motions of atoms in my brain, I have no reason to suppose that my beliefs are true . . . and hence I have no reason for supposing my brain to be composed of atoms.

The notion that our thoughts are determined by the way the atoms in our brains move about is called "materialism"; and if materialism is true, then I cannot know whether my thoughts are true. It also follows that my choices are the products of these atomic movements as well, so that they cannot really be called "choices" at all (who thinks a rock *chooses* to fall when I let it go?). But this means that my belief that I am a self is false. The trouble is, you have to rely on that belief to *argue* that materialism is true. So we're far more reasonable to conclude that materialism is false (or if it's true, who cares?).

The next part of an argument for us to consider is its *terms*—the definitions of the words used for the argument. We want to know if they are clear or not; if they are used consistently; and if they are standard usage for the words, or specific to one person or a small group. We have to recognize that most words have more than one meaning, and in order to know what someone is saying we have to know which meaning he is using. For example, in *Mere Christianity* C. S. Lewis has a chapter on "The Great Sin," which is pride. But, as he shows, the word "pride" has more than one meaning: the sin of pride is that of comparing yourself to others in order to prove that you're superior to them, and of wanting the world to revolve around you. But there's a "pride" that we take, say, in our parents or children or school; and if by that we mean that we "have a warm-hearted admiration for" them, that's not the *sin* of pride—though we may be boring if we talk too much about them. (We may, of course, commit the sin of pride if we use our children's talents to prove how superior we are.) We also have to be careful of taking a word that is in ordinary use and giving it a peculiar sense that no one ever uses: for example, some historians use the word "history" to mean an account of things without any reference to God. In such a case they could say, "Even though 'In the beginning God created the heavens and the earth' is not a *historical* statement, I'm not saying it didn't happen"—and this sounds to most people like nonsense.

You will find that in the chapters that follow, I keep trying to make sure we know what we mean by our terms. I realize that this may make me tiresome—J. Gresham Machen once acknowledged, "nothing makes a man more unpopular in the controversies of the present day than an insistence upon definition of terms"—but I want us to think clearly.

The fourth part of an argument is the *logic*—the process of arranging conclusions in a step-by-step sequence to produce an inference. If I add two marbles to a cup holding two marbles, it is sound logic to believe that the cup now has four marbles in it (taking as a premise that no one is interfering). If I see a hawk eating a rabbit, I infer that at least this hawk eats rabbits from time to time; but if I watch a number of hawks in different places eat rabbits, I infer that rabbit is part of their diet. (To have an idea of how big a part of their diet it is requires that I compare the number of rabbit kills to the number of other kinds of kills.) If the last cookie is missing from the cookie jar, it is reasonable to suppose that someone took it; but it is not reasonable to blame my brother, who lives two thousand miles away. To know whom to hold responsible I need to know who has been in the kitchen since I last checked, and something of the habits of the potential suspects. My children don't pinch cookies from the jar, while my wife does snack on them; so she's the most logical candidate.

There are different kinds of inference: the marble example is *deductive,* depending on the rules of math, while the hawk diet is *inductive,* making generalizations from observations. The who-ate-the-cookie example is more complicated; it is like what detectives do, and we can call it a *historical inference,* trying to explain the cause of a specific event in terms of what I know about the possible causes. We have to follow the rules for the particular kind of inference we're making.

The fifth part of an argument is its *scope*—the realm of ideas in which our inference is supposed to apply. We might also call this the *with-respect-to-whatness* of our inference. (Sometimes the best way to answer a question is with "With respect to what?") For example, if an astronomer tells you that the earth is not the *center* of the universe, his scope is the realm of physical location. If a theologian tells you that the earth is the *center* of the universe, his scope is the realm of God's attention. To say that these two have contradicted each other you have to show that they have similar scopes—and I think anyone who tries to show such a thing with these two statements is talking foolishness.

And finally, there is the *gradation of confidence*—what level of confidence I am entitled to give this conclusion in view of the data, the premises, and the kind of inference. For example, if I have seen two hawks eat nothing but rabbits, I can be confident that they eat rabbits. But if I want to be confident that hawks primarily eat rabbit, I have to watch many hawks, and see what they do when given a choice between rabbit and squirrel, and find out if hawks live where rabbits don't. In the case of adding marbles to the cup, my inference is certain provided my premise that no one interferes is solid. In the case of the missing cookie, the level of confidence to which I am entitled depends on whether I have considered all the options, and how well I know the possible suspects.

If you study critical thinking or logic you will get a list of "fallacies" to look out for. These fallacies generally have to do with failures to be careful in one or more of the components of sound thinking that we are discussing. For example, the "fallacy of equivocation" happens when we use a word without paying attention to the distinction of meanings: it is a problem in the "terms" component, and our "pride" example illustrates an equivocation if we call being "proud" of my daughter's courage when she gets a painful shot an instance of sinful pride. The fallacy called "non sequitur" (Latin for "it does not follow") is a problem in the "logic" component: if I see a hawk catching a rabbit, it does not follow from this fact that the same hawk—let alone other hawks—will not eat squirrels.

There's a Latin phrase that warns us against a very common logical mistake: *abusus usum non tollit,* "abuse does not take away proper use." The idea is that we must distinguish between the actual idea we are discussing, and the trappings that wrap around it. For example, people have used the Bible to defend the African slave trade; but the only way that fact can be a sound argument against the Bible is if defending the slave trade is part and parcel of the Bible's teaching. If defense of slavery is an abuse of biblical teaching, then we can say that defending the slave trade is inconsistent with the Bible. People have also used Darwinism to defend racism; and the only way that can be a sound argument against Darwinism is if the racism is bound up with the very essence of Darwinism. The English proverb that goes along with this is "one bad apple doesn't spoil the whole bunch": you can't refute Christianity, or Darwinism, or anything else, just by pointing to the buffoons who have used it for base purposes; you have to examine the ideas themselves. (Recall how I began this chapter by making a distinction between philoso*phy* and philoso*phers*.)

There is another kind of logic problem that we need to think about, because of how it applies to the sciences—especially to those with a historical component. Suppose you find a stone on the ground, and after looking at its sharp edges you decide that some person sharpened it. You then want to figure out why he sharpened it and how it came to be where you found it. In each of these inferences—that it was sharpened, the purpose it was sharpened for, and what train of events led to it being where you found it, your reasoning probably follows a sequence like this: you imagine a scenario, you look for reasons to support or refute that scenario, you consider other possible scenarios, and you try to support or reject each of those scenarios. For example, to decide that someone sharpened the stone, you imagine some natural process—say, wind and weather—that could have made it sharp like it is. You test that scenario by asking whether these natural processes produce such a clear pattern, and whether they would have made the stone in such an oblong shape. You don't think so—and besides, you've seen other similar stones that you know were sharpened by a person.

The key thing is that you have to give reasons to go from "I can imagine this scenario" to "this is a possible chain of events that led to this," and from there to "this is the likely chain of events." Unless you can give those reasons, you don't have the logical right to make the shift.

TESTING A TRUTH CLAIM

When I am faced with a claim that something is true, how can I know whether or not to believe it? Well, I should at least decide whether or not the argument that produced the truth claim is sound. Now, just because the argument might have some flaws in its components doesn't mean that the conclusion is untrue. For example, I have seen an argument for the truthfulness of Scripture based on fulfilled prophecy, where I disagreed with the writer's way of interpreting prophecy (which was an unargued premise for him), and therefore thought his argument was a bad one—but I still think that Scripture is true. To show that this writer's conclusion about the truthfulness of Scripture is false would require someone to show that the flaws in his argument undermine his conclusion altogether, or else to show that there is a better explanation for the data of prophecy (which doesn't happen in the case of Scripture's truthfulness).

Can we go beyond deciding that an argument is not simply false, to deciding that it is likely true? I think we can, if the argument meets the following conditions.

(a) The set of data is large enough, and the conclusion covers all of the data. For example, I have observed enough hawks and accurately reported what I have seen them eat.

(b) The argument openly says what premises must be true for the argument to hold, and offers reasonable grounds for believing those premises. For example, my premise that no one is interfering with the marbles in the cup is good if I am looking inside the cup.

(c) The argument covers the data without introducing unnecessary complicating assumptions. This is often called Ockham's razor: it means that the simplest conclusion that covers the facts is to be preferred. For example, when the cookie is missing, it is simpler to suppose one person pinched it than to imagine a UN conspiracy.

(d) The logic of the argument is sound and self-consistent.

(e) When the conclusion challenges other beliefs I hold, it shows why the other beliefs are wrong; but in any case it is consistent with my touchstone beliefs. This is just another way of saying that reasonable people don't want to hold contradictory beliefs if they can avoid it. For example, if I thought hawks ate only rodents like mice and chipmunks and then I saw hawks eating rabbits—rabbits aren't *rodents,* they're *lagomorphs,* with two pairs of upper front teeth instead of one pair— then I have to reject my previous belief. But if someone argues from brain science that my beliefs are determined by the chemical properties of my brain, than I should reject the argument, even if the advocate wears a lab coat—because it contradicts a touchstone belief.

Sometimes, though, even if my other belief is not a touchstone, I might hold on to it and reject the new conclusion. For example, if my detective work on the missing cookie leads me to conclude that a space alien pinched the cookie with a transporter beam, I may decide that my disbelief in transporter beams is strong enough to make it reasonable to reject the conclusion. If a psychologist tells me that a tendency to alcoholism is related to one's genes, and I think it is a moral issue, I have to be careful to sort out just what is and is not in conflict. (I will look at this kind of question when I discuss the human and social sciences.)

(f) It lists the possible refutations and counterarguments fairly and honestly, and answers them. For example, someone might argue that the cookie disappeared because my son broke his habit of not pinching from the cookie jar; but if his habit is well-established, and he denies having done so, and he is truthful, and I know that my wife gets hungry, then the counter explanation doesn't look promising.

(g) It helps if we can describe a way of testing it. For example, if I have concluded that hawks eat rabbits, I should be able to set up a blind in a place where there are hawks and rabbits, and see it happen. I could test the two marbles plus two marbles gives four example, too, if I wanted to—but, since it's a deductive inference, I wouldn't be testing the inference itself but instead would be testing my premise that nothing is interfering.

In the rest of this book I will put these principles to work to help us achieve good faith and good science.

But for now I want to emphasize again that this is what you do—or at least should do—every day.

A Word About Rational Christian Faith

I have stressed that good faith as well as good science needs sound rational thinking. I know that many will either not understand this just yet or will think they are reading something heretical: after all, faith is in the heart, not the head, they will say. Or they will point out that God reveals Christianity through Scripture, not through human reason. I will talk more in the next chapter about what "faith" is, and how it relates to reason. Before I move on, though, let me say a few things in clarification, so that you don't hear what I'm not saying.

To begin with, by "reason" and "rationality" I don't mean what theologians usually mean when they contrast reason with revelation: they are speaking of the process of reasoning that takes for its premise the notion that only what we can discover by study *without God's help* is reasonable. I am instead speaking of the process of thinking soundly in general. So this objection is based on failure to be clear that I use the word "reason" with a different meaning than the objector does. In fact I don't believe for a second that it is at all "reasonable" to do without God's help in understanding his world!

Another thing to clarify: I haven't at this point said anything about the role of reasoning in how we come to believe in Christ; instead I have been focusing on the responsibility every convinced Christian has, to use and develop his reasoning ability in service to his faith and life. I will come back in a later chapter to the role of rational arguments in coming to faith.

The theological discipline that studies how to use rational arguments to support faith is called apologetics. Christians don't all agree on what place these arguments should play in bringing someone to believe in God. Some say that no arguments are needed; some say that sound faith requires evidence; some say that you have to challenge the unbeliever's worldview before he can even think rightly about God.

One of the things that distinguishes these schools of thought is their answer to the question, "Where does belief in God come in?" Some say that belief in God is actually a *datum*—that is, you just know God directly, and what you need is to get in touch with that knowledge that you've been suppressing. Others say that belief in God is a *premise*—unless you take God's existence for granted, you have no basis for sound reasoning of any sort. Still others say that belief in God is an *inference*—a conclusion from a chain of reasoning—which is why you need evidence and strong arguments.

As it turns out, each of these schools of thought has something to offer—rather than "either-or" I prefer the "both-and" approach. This is because these different schools seem to mean different things by "belief in God" (an expression we'll examine in the next chapter).

3

Must Science and Faith Be At Odds?

In this chapter I will examine some of the issues in the philosophy of science that come into play when we think about the interaction of science and faith. The first of these issues is the definition of "science" as well as that of "faith." This will lead us to look at some of the questions of proper scientific method, the connection between science and knowledge, and the possible operating relationships between science and faith.

In each of these areas I will start by giving what I take to be the most common way of thinking in our culture, and show how this leads to problems if we try to analyze it. I will then offer a way of thinking that serves us better.

Defining "Science"

Would you be surprised to learn that defining "science" is actually controversial? Well, it is—because if we want to be any more informative than "what scientists do," we run into all kinds of difficulties. Philosophers do not agree on whether there is something like *a* "scientific method" that unites all the different sciences; and they also don't agree on what is the essence of science that would allow you to define it. Further, many of them disagree over the connection between "science" and "knowledge." And finally, a good definition should help us to distinguish between what *is* scientific, and what is *not*—but that creates problems because "scientific" is a power word in our culture. If you're a scientist people have to listen to you, and if you're not—well, no one wants to be dismissed as "unscientific." In a case like this, it's easy to set up a definition that sneaks in any number of philosophical premises that need to be examined. As I told you in the last chapter, I am one of those who often finds philosophers tiresome and unhelpful; but here they have a point. I think we can arrive at a reasonable definition of science, but we do need to be careful.

I recall being taught as a boy that "science" is, at its simplest, the collecting of data from observations of the world, and then the organizing of those observations in a way that leads to a generalization called a "law." The best laws are in the form of an equation that allows you to predict what will happen next. The thing that makes science so superior to everything else, I was told, is that it is "objective," which means it is free from bias and not subject to disagreement (I think of the character in Chesterton's Father Brown story who says, "I don't believe in anything; I'm a man of science"). Christian, Buddhist, and atheist will all agree that the ball traveled 25.6 meters. This makes science a safer path to knowledge than any other kind of study, such as religion or philosophy, which can never get anywhere because they are so full of disagreements: "scientific proof" is the end of disagreement.

My hunch is that this definition captures the elements of the popular view of science; it was certainly the standard view of science in my college days. The three features that stand out are the empirical nature of the work (the collection of data), the production of laws, and the objectivity (or freedom from all bias).

The big problem with this kind of definition is that it's not true to what scientists do. In the first place, we have neglected the fact that scientists are people, and no one is free of all bias—nor should they be. The search for laws actually takes for granted that such laws exist: it is biased in favor of finding mathematical regularity in nature. (I think that the biblical teaching on creation and providence make this bias quite reasonable, as we'll see later.) But even more importantly, many scientists have held to their ideas with the persistence of a bulldog even when it looked like they were wrong. Some cosmologists (physicists who study the origin and history of the universe) dislike the Big Bang theory because it implies a beginning to the universe—and such an idea is repulsive to them.

Speaking of cosmologists, Stephen Hawking, in his book *A Brief History of Time,* writes about the assumption that the universe looks the same in every direction as seen from any other galaxy, just as it does when seen from ours. He says,

> We have no scientific evidence [*note:* what does he mean by that?] for, or against, this assumption. We believe it only on grounds of modesty: it would be most remarkable if the universe looked the same in every direction around us, but not around other points in the universe!

In other words, they're biased in favor of modesty (good thing, too).

Unfortunately, for many in our culture, "bias" is a negative word, because we think it leads us to distort our view of the world, like "rose-colored glasses." As Sherlock Holmes said more than once, "It is a capital mistake to theorize before you have all the evidence—it biases the judgment." But not every bias distorts: some biases can help us decide ahead of time what is worth paying attention to and what is not. As Holmes said in another story, "It is of the highest importance in the art of deduction to be able to recognize out of a number of facts which are incidental and which are vital." I am biased against the possibility that the number of puppies in a litter has anything to do with the number of legs the father has, so I would never pay anyone money to study what the relationship is. But some biases *can* distort: people who think that all human behavior can be explained by our genes have a bias that blinds them to moral realities. So we cannot promise that "science" is without bias; and we have to assess—by critical thinking—whether that leads to sound or unsound conclusions.

The second way that the popular definition of science causes trouble is its emphasis on laws, or regularities. Some sciences do in fact concern themselves with such regularities: Newton's laws of motion, as well as quantum mechanics and relativity, are examples of laws. But what about theories of the origin of the universe, or the geological history of a mountain range, or the history of life on this planet? These are unique historical events, and what makes them interesting is exactly their uniqueness: and yet we usually group cosmology, geology, and evolutionary biology among the sciences. (We may think that these events were produced by regularities, but that is a philosophical assumption, which I will address later.) So we have to allow science to study *both* the regularities *and* the unique historical chains of cause-and-effect.

Finally, the bit about the empirical nature of the work is good, so long as we are reasonable about what data we might legitimately consider. The science writer John Gribbin, in *Almost Everyone's Guide to Science,* draws on the famous physicist Richard Feynman to get a crisp definition of science:

> That is what science, and scientific models, are all about. *If it disagrees with experiment it is wrong.*

Gribbin here limits the empirical data to the kind you can collect in an experiment—and that's clearly wrong. Does this mean that the guy who hides in a blind and watches animals to see their natural behavior, is no scientist? And what place does this have for the sciences that study unique events? Are they not sciences either? It is much better to speak of "observation" or "experience," recognizing that "experiments" are a special kind of experience (and an artificial one at that, since they purposely exclude "irrelevant" factors). It's even better to speak of observations that are "publicly accessible"—that is, anyone else can get the same data. For example, you can come over to my house and watch the birds and squirrels, and see if what I report about them is true. You can mix the same five chemicals at the same temperature, and blow up your lab just like I did mine. Mind you, this kind of data isn't the only kind there is: I know what I dreamed about last night and you only have my report. In research projects that involve this kind of data (say, to discover the connection between rapid eye movement and dreaming), the researcher really only has access to the person's *report*—and that's the part that is publicly accessible.

No one has a problem with physics, chemistry, geology, and biology being sciences (they are often called "natural" or even "hard" sciences); but what should we do about "social" sciences such as linguistics, sociology, and anthropology, or the "human" sciences such as physiology or psychology? Admittedly, people in the "soft" sciences want the social prestige that comes from being called "scientists," just as some in the "hard" sciences want to be able to exclude them as not really science; but we should look for some definition that is not part of a social strategy.

This last point brings up a further difficulty in definition. Most of us want to have some way of distinguishing between those who do legitimate work and those who don't. We'd like to be able to say that the cranks and quacks aren't "real" scientists, so that we don't have to believe them. Some people whose theories put them on the fringe (such as UFO researchers) would like to be called scientists so that we will hesitate to dismiss them. Similarly, there are many who want to keep some ideas out of the science classroom, such as any criticism of Darwinism, by calling them "religion" or "philosophy" and not "science" (and the sub-text is, if it's not science no one needs to believe it). So the scramble for the right to use the prestige title compounds the definitional difficulties.

We can find some help from the history of usage. We get our word "science" from the Latin word *scientia*. The great scholars of the Middle Ages—who built on the ideas of the Greek philosophers, especially Aristotle (who lived from 384 to 322 B.C.)—used *scientia* to speak of a particular area of disciplined and rational study, worthy of the investment of the time and energy it took to gain knowledge. These areas of study included such fields as physics, biology, mathematics, ethics, politics, grammar, theology, and what we now call philosophy. When we use the word "science" today, we tend to focus on the natural or physical sciences, such as physics, chemistry, and biology, and to leave mathematics as a tool rather than a science. The term "scientist" was apparently coined by the Cambridge philosopher-scientist William Whewell (1794–1866) and appears in his 1840 book, *The Philosophy of the Inductive Sciences,* "to describe a cultivator of science." Generally, our culture tends to treat physics, which is heavily mathematical and able to make very accurate predictions, as the prime example of "true science"; some even go so far as to make it the prime example of "true knowledge." (This explains the pressure on the "soft" sciences such as sociology to put their results in mathematical form.) Though the principles I set out in the previous chapter should lead us to resist such a tendency, we are foolish not to be aware of it.

Further, we can throw into the mix a clarification that C. S. Lewis offered:

> Strictly speaking there is, I confess, no such thing as 'modern science'. There are only particular sciences, all in a stage of rapid change, and sometimes inconsistent with one another.

Lewis correctly represents both the history of usage of the word "science" and the practice of modern scientists. He also shows why John Gribbin is talking nonsense when he says,

> Both evolution and the Big Bang (and all the rest) are based on the same principles, and you can't pick and choose which bits of the scientific story you are going to accept.

There is no reason for us to accept this before we look into the specifics, and there is every reason to suppose that this makes no sense at all. It is quite possible that the Big Bang theory satisfies the criteria for sound thinking while evolutionary theory does not—and vice versa. The hidden premise—that there is one "scientific story"—needs to be brought into the light.

A few paragraphs ago I mentioned that the medieval sciences involved disciplined and rational study. This brings up two other aspects that we normally think belong to science: *discursive reasoning* and *distantiation.* "Discursive reasoning" means that you can put your reasons into words and defend them. (This is not the only way to knowledge, of course: you can recognize your daughter's voice even if you can't say *why* you know it's hers.)

"Distantiation" means you try to put some emotional distance between yourself and the object of your study, so that you can keep your cool and think clearly. (Holmes warned Watson, "It is of the first importance not to allow your judgment to be biased by personal qualities. . . . The emotional qualities are antagonistic to clear reasoning.") We may agree with those who say there's no such thing as pure neutrality—and who would want to meet someone who had no commitments?—but we *can* distance ourselves and be self-critical. The idea is that we should be honest, and willing to follow the evidence wherever it leads. We ought further to say that this is an *ideal,* and scientists—being human—don't always meet it.

If we put all these things together, we can see that "science" typically involves publicly accessible data, discursive reasoning, and personal distantiation. We can then come up with the following definition of "science":

> A science is a discipline in which one studies features of the world around us, and tries to describe his observations systematically and critically.

Some sciences focus on the regularities (the laws), while others focus on chains of cause-and-effect that produced unique events (the histories). It helps us to group them into those that study the material world (the natural or physical sciences, such as physics, chemistry, biology, geology, astronomy), those that study human beings (the human sciences, such as anatomy, physiology, and psychology), and those that study the ways that humans interact (the social sciences, such as linguistics, textual hermeneutics, anthropology, and sociology). If we still want to use the word "science" as an umbrella for all these activities, we may, but we should be wary of the pitfalls that such a usage can lead us into.

If we describe the sciences this way, we will find several advantages for thinking clearly. The first is that it captures the empirical nature of the work, and reminds us as well that science is a human activity. It also makes the sciences subject to the rules of sound thinking.

This kind of description will also help us when we are faced with statements that begin with, "Science says . . ." We will immediately ask, "*Which* science?" And then we will move on to see that "a science" doesn't say anything; scien*tists* do. So then we can ask, "Which scientists? And have they reasoned so well that I should believe them?" This is especially helpful when someone makes a statement on behalf of all science; or when an expert in one science (say, physics) tries to speak authoritatively about some other field (say, linguistics or psychology): just because he's a scientist doesn't mean I am obligated to believe him. (Of course, if someone speaks as an expert in his own field, then I ought to pay closer attention.)

But I will be honest: this description has one big disadvantage, namely that most people don't use the word "science" that way. I think that's because most people aren't aware of the problems we have been talking about; but in any case we have to listen to them and hear what *they* mean by the words they use, and help them to see why the description here has advantages over popular usage. Because I think the popular usage leads to fuzzy thinking, I don't intend to go along with it.

In any case, the first thing to do when someone mentions science is to figure out what he means by it, and whether he has said anything sensible. For example, Sherlock Holmes called himself a scientific detective; and he meant that he was careful in his collection of information, and that he had an extensive knowledge of how things work, and that he was rigorous in his process of reasoning. Since his intent was to contrast his methods with the haphazard guesswork of the official police, he was saying something worth saying.

On the other hand, Father Brown exposed the idiocy of the American Grandison Chace, who spoke of the "science of detection," with the following critique:

> Science is a grand thing when you can get it; in its real sense it is one of the grandest words in the world. But what do these men mean, nine times out of ten, when they use it nowadays? When they say detection is a science? When they say criminology is a science? They mean getting *outside* a man and studying him as if he were a gigantic insect: in what they would call a dry impartial light, in what I should call a dead and dehumanized light. . . . So far from being knowledge, it's actually suppression of what we know. It's treating a friend as a stranger, and pretending that something familiar is really remote and mysterious. It's like saying that a man has a proboscis between the eyes, or that he falls down in a fit of insensibility once every twenty-four hours.

In this case the "scientific" approach meant that you didn't use all the information at your disposal—and if that's science, it's bad science, because it's irrational.

Defining "Faith"

If we are looking for what most people mean when they use the word "faith," I'll bet that the definition of faith in *Webster's New World College Dictionary* (4th edition) nails it:

1. unquestioning belief that does not require proof or evidence;
2. unquestioning belief in God, religious tenets, etc.

And in the list of synonyms under "belief," they say that *faith* "implies complete, unquestioning acceptance of something even in the absence of proof and, especially, of something not supported by reason."

Well, we can't expect a dictionary to be a manual of theology; but don't ever read these definitions into any biblical passage, please! I have found J. Gresham Machen's book *What Is Faith?* to be more helpful than the dictionary if we want to know the traditional Christian view of faith, and I recommend it to you.

When biblical writers (and responsible Christians) use the word "faith," they are usually speaking in one of two ways. The first sense of "Christian faith" is trust toward God because you are persuaded that he is trustworthy. The second sense is "*the* faith," that is, the set of truths that Christians believe. Let's talk about each of these in turn.

We'll begin with the first sense, "faith-as-trust." This idea of faith has two dimensions: to begin with, it is directed toward a *person;* the Bible writers tell us to believe *in* God, to trust that he speaks true words and to entrust ourselves to him. The other dimension is that it is *rational:* we become persuaded of God's trustworthiness because he gives us things to believe and reasons for trusting him. You can see why Christians think of faith as a moral matter: it goes beyond accepting certain things as true (believing *that*), to committing oneself to a person (believing *in*). This also shows why some people will not become Christian believers: they don't want to give themselves to God, and this is not a purely intellectual matter.

This leads to a subject that could take pages, but that I'll just outline: namely, that in the Bible, reasoning and knowing are functions of what it calls the "heart." When Bible writers speak of the heart, they're speaking about the center of our inner life, from which we do all our thinking, feeling, and choosing. As Proverbs 4:23 puts it,

> Keep your heart with all vigilance,
> for from it flow the springs of life.

There's much more to say, but for now we have to see that when we think and know, it is the heart at work. This means that our discursive reasoning is a function of the heart, and the other functions—our feelings, our commitments—can come into play (for better or for worse). Hence we can distinguish these different functions of the heart, but I don't think we can separate them. And this means that our heart's disposition—our loyalties, our likes and dislikes—will play a part in our thinking and knowing. I don't consider this to be a shortcoming, but it does mean we have to be honest (remember what I said about distantiation).

Therefore when it comes to faith, no sound Christian would really think that the intellectual content of his or her faith is separate from the relational commitment to God.

The Old Testament commonly appeals to the great things God has done for his people, in order to remind them of the reasons for their trust: for example, Psalm 136 lists the creation, the deliverance from Egypt, the giving of the promised land, and the constant care for his people as reasons why Israel should keep their faith in God, even in trouble. In the New Testament, Jesus says (John 10:37-38),

> "If I am not doing the works of my Father, then do not believe [or *have faith in*] me; but if I am doing them, even though you do not believe me, believe the works, so that you may know and understand that the Father is in me and I am in the Father."

No shunning of evidence here!

You see too that this faith has content: we believe that certain things are true about God. (We could probably take "mere Christianity"—to use C. S. Lewis's term—as the solid core of these truths, and we build other beliefs around that.)

We can learn a lot about faith by thinking of our trust in other people. I am sorry to admit it, but I have teased my daughter by serving her a bowl of ice cream and then picking up the spoon as if I were going to eat it myself. The first time I did it she was alarmed; but when she saw that I wouldn't really eat it—and I reminded her that I'm her daddy who loves her—she never worried about it again. And when I pulled the same trick on her younger brother, she settled him down by reminding him that it's Daddy and we don't need to worry about it.

But they have also learned that they can trust me to be looking out for their best interests, and that they can show their trust by obedience—even when they don't understand *why* I have given a command. For example, we read books as a family before bedtime—books like *The Hobbit* or *The Secret Garden.* One evening we got to an exciting part, but had to stop because it was time for the kids to go to sleep. My son was displeased, telling me that it was a cliffhanger (it wasn't as bad as he thought, though). He was focused on the short-term goal of relieving the suspense of the story; I was looking to the bigger picture of what he's like the next day if he doesn't get enough sleep. At his level of development, the bigger picture didn't mean anything to him. I found a reasonable break in the story, and asked him to trust my judgment and go to bed. To trust and obey would be rational for him.

Now God never teases us; he assures us that he always has good, wise, holy, and loving reasons for what he does—but he doesn't promise to tell us what those reasons are. Instead, because we have learned that he is trustworthy, we can take him at his word and keep on trusting him—and this means, keep on obeying his commands as we know we should.

C. S. Lewis hit the target when he said,

> Faith, in the sense in which I am here using the word, is the art of holding on to things your reason has once accepted, in spite of your changing moods. For moods will change, whatever view your reason takes.

Now let's turn to the second sense in which biblical authors use the word "faith": they speak of "*the* faith," that is, as the set of truths that Christians believe. When Paul says that he has "kept the faith" (2 Tim. 4:7), or when he wants Timothy to be "nourished on the words of the faith" (1 Tim. 4:6, NASB), this is the sense he is using. These truths are contained in the Scripture, and no serious Christian claims that he understands everything in the Scripture (for example, how the Trinity works, or the way the human and divine natures of Christ are joined); nor does he claim that he must understand them in every detail and prove them philosophically before he accepts them. Instead, the process of accepting *the* faith involves faith-as-trust: in the final analysis, I believe the Scripture because it has shown itself to be the reliable voice of the God who gave it, who is himself reliable. (That doesn't mean I don't try to understand, and to justify as well as I can, what the Bible teaches; but it does mean that I recognize my limitations.)

Now this discussion will help us because a number of conclusions follow from it. One conclusion is that faith and reason are not at odds with each other. Faith is in fact rational behavior: given who God is, and the reasons he's given for trusting him, it's unreasonable *not* to trust him. It is true that faith goes beyond what I can verify; but that's true of every kind of relational faith: when I married my wife, I trusted her claim to love me. How else could I verify it but by taking the "risk" (though I would never call it that)? Was that unreasonable? No: to have waited until I could verify her love would have been unreasonable. As Blaise Pascal observed,

> Reason would never submit unless it judged that there are occasions when it ought to submit. It is right, then, that reason should submit when it judges that it ought to submit.

Not only does reason help faith, but faith helps reason: I see my life more clearly because of my faith in God. For example, we often hear encouragements to serve the rest of humanity, and I agree that this is good, but a secular mind gives me no reason *why* it is good. As Machen pointed out,

> The [human] race is worthy of a man's service not if it is composed of mere creatures of a day, whose life is essentially like the life of the beasts, but only if it is composed of men with immortal souls.

I think most people can recognize the duty to serve others; and solid faith supplies the reason that actually energizes the service.

Another conclusion is that doubt is not always the same as lack of faith. Many of the Psalms (Psalm 73 is a good example) express deep distress over God's mysterious ways of running the world, and some people would use the word "doubt" to describe the feelings there. (There we go again: what do we mean by our words?) In the midst of this distress, however, the psalmist holds on tightly to his loyalty toward God—the Psalms are prayers and hymns after all. If we resolve our doubts of this kind—using our reason as well as our prayers and our Christian friends—our faith grows stronger. On the other hand, if by "doubt" we mean divided or wavering loyalty, then this kind of doubt is dangerous to faith (just like divided loyalty is dangerous to a marriage). This kind of doubt hasn't come from our reason, but from our emotions; and the remedy is repentance.

The last helpful conclusion that I'll mention is that our discussion shows us where confidence and assurance fit in. That is, I can be assured in my *faith-as-trust* because I am confident of the person I trust. And the solid core content of this faith does not change unless I decide the whole thing is rubbish. On the other hand, I should never claim to be so confident that I know every bit of *the faith* that I won't be willing to reconsider it. I ought to hold views on other things beyond the core content of the faith, say on baptism or predestination or church government; but how tightly I hold to these other views should be related to how well I have thought them through. (As I said before, that doesn't make them unimportant or divisive or any of those things: but we do have to keep them in perspective.)

PREMISES OF THE METHODS OF SCIENCE

Does being a scientist commit me to certain premises beyond the touchstone truths? And if it does, what are those premises? In our discussion of bias, we have seen that of course we must take for granted that we can find regularities in nature; for some of these regularities we assume that mathematical equations are legitimate descriptions. We have also seen that we are biased in favor of simpler solutions.

None of these biases is (or at least should be) controversial. But here I want to examine a few issues that should be controversial, especially because they affect the way science and faith will interact with each other.

The first of these issues is what is called "methodological naturalism." In order to understand it we can start by citing a description of science from the National Science Teachers Association (NSTA):

> Science is a method of explaining the natural world. It *assumes the universe operates according to regularities* and that through systematic investigation we can understand these regularities. The methodology of science emphasizes the logical testing of alternate explanations of natural phenomena against empirical data. Because *science is limited to explaining the natural world by means of natural processes,* it cannot use supernatural causation in its explanations. Similarly, science is precluded from making statements about supernatural forces, because these are outside its provenance. Science has increased our knowledge because of this insistence on the search for natural causes.

I have highlighted the key phrases: Science *assumes the universe operates according to regularities* and *science is limited to explaining the natural world by means of natural processes.* These statements seem to hide a very debatable premise: namely that the scientific approach to describing everything is "methodological naturalism"—we require that all our descriptions be in terms of *natural causes* only. This premise is debatable because the statement makes no distinction between the study of regularities and the study of historical events. That is, it may be a quite right, when we are studying a regularity such as the laws of motion, to assume that the steel balls always move in the same way when the forces on them are the same. (That's how we can call the right ball and pocket in a game of pool.)

But if we're talking about a historical event—well, that's a lot tougher. For example, if I see a scratch on my son's leg, I think I'm on solid ground to suppose that he scraped his leg on something hard and sharp—that natural causes can explain how the scratch got there on his skin. But should I consider his thoughts and choices a "natural process"? Well, I don't mind, so long as you don't mean "purely material process" (remember Father Brown's lecture to Grandison Chace). But the NSTA hasn't made it clear what it means by "natural process": it seems to include it under "regularity," and, as we'll see when we talk about human nature, that won't account for human reason and choice.

And what of such events as the origin of the universe, or of life? What about the parting of the Red Sea, or the resurrection of Jesus? Must we insist that science can only describe these in terms of natural processes and the orderly function of regularities? The only way this insistence is rational is if we know beforehand that only natural factors are involved. And if we don't know that—well, then such insistence is not rational, and we have no reason to suppose the story it tells is true. Under those circumstances, we have done science a disservice by wrenching it away from rationality.

So the NSTA statement involves a premise that it should have explained and defended. And to defend the premise, it would have had to make a philosophical claim about natural processes being adequate to explain everything we study—in fact that's a *theological* claim, too, since it touches on the ways we're allowed to imagine God's interaction with the world. In other words, the NSTA statement actually has made a statement about supernatural forces (it claims they're irrelevant to science), exactly what it says science may not do. It contradicts itself.

What the statement needed to say in order to be more reasonable was that the natural, human, and social sciences take natural causes as far as they can go in describing the world around us. The scientist *as a scientist* does not have to say whether God or gods were involved in the events they study. We will come back to this in our chapter on "Science, Providence, and Miracle."

You will of course notice that the NSTA statement also assumes a definition of "science" that creates problems as well: they are defining science by the methods of the natural sciences when those sciences are describing regularities. I have no doubt that they would not follow Aristotle and call ethics a science; but I cannot tell from their description whether psychology meets the criteria for a science.

I think that I can guess what the NSTA people were trying to accomplish, though: they wanted to preserve a kind of "ordinary science" that doesn't depend on whether you're a Christian, Jew, Hindu, or atheist. When you're looking at how billiard balls move, or studying quarks and leptons, or designing new drugs, your religious commitment should not affect your results—and if those commitments affect what you're willing to work on, well, that's ethics, not physics or chemistry. I suppose they also wanted to allow physicists, say, to speak about the Big Bang without having to say whether or not this is a creation event (that is, without having to commit themselves to saying the event was supernatural). This can be helpful because it keeps science from being pressed into service either in the cause of atheism or in the cause of Christian apologetics. If that's the sort of thing they were after—and anyone who's ever worked in a research lab will welcome such goals—they failed, because they overstated their position. The effort to promote *methodological* naturalism—appealing only to natural processes in your explanations—slides over into *philosophical* naturalism—the belief that natural processes are all there is.

The next issue to discuss is called *reductionism*. Reductionism is the view that, in order to explain something, you have to explain how its components work. For example, you can describe the way a virus attacks you by describing the way it gets inside your cells: its chemistry fits the chemistry of your cell membranes in such a way that it is allowed to get inside. You can then go deeper to describe the chemical bonds that produce the shapes, and the electron interactions, and so on until you get to the most elementary particles and forces. So we have explained something biological in terms of its chemistry, and have explained the chemistry in terms of its physics. (This is one reason physics is considered the science that underlies all others: it studies the things at the bottom of this ladder.)

Like naturalism, reductionism comes in both the methodological kind and the philosophical kind. The methodological kind says, as a matter of method we study the complex in terms of the simple. The philosophical kind says that at bottom, there is *nothing but* the simple components (some call it "nothing-buttery").

Even the methodological kind of reductionism can lead to foolishness. For example, you can understand the workings of my watch by talking about the physics that underlies the LCD numbers and the semi-conductor chips, but that hardly explains why the watch *tells time:* someone has imposed a pattern on the components, that makes use of the physics and makes the parts work together to achieve some goal. But this working together involves *more* than the physics of the components. So the reduction tells only part of the story, and hence the method isn't very good if what we want is the true story.

Philosophical reductionism is just what the name says: it is a philosophical position, not a scientific result or a necessary premise for science. It says that this purring cat in my lap *is really* a set chemical reactions. I say it is really a *cat,* a living structure built out of its chemical components and their reactions.

The last issue we will examine is the role of *modeling* in science. When you make a scientific description, you have to make a *model*—you decide which features of the subject you're studying are important, and which you can leave out. For example, if you are studying the motion of billiard balls on a table, you can leave out the colors of the balls. You will probably also assume the balls are perfectly round, and you might even leave out the effects of friction. It is probably reasonable to ignore these factors for the sake of having a model you can work with. If you are studying human behavior, though, you would be silly to leave out color—in American society, color has a deep impact on a person's experiences.

Reductionism, as we have seen, works by leaving the pattern out of the model it makes, and is therefore an inadequate kind of modeling. Some psychologists study the electrical and chemical reactions in the brain when people think or feel in different ways. They then go on to speak as if these thoughts and feelings *are* the electro-chemical reactions they have studied. In other words, they have made a model that leaves things out, and then have acted as if the model was all there is. There is a famous parable about a man studying deep-sea life using a net with a three-inch mesh. After bringing up many samples, the man concluded that there was no deep-sea fish that was smaller than three inches in length. Our method of "fishing"—our scientific model—sets limits on what we can find.

Our culture is obsessed with measurable things, as if that alone guaranteed objectivity. But it would be laughable to decide that, since you can't measure the strength of one's will, you can ignore it in a "scientific" description of a man.

Science and Knowledge

All of this raises the question of what the relationship is between science and knowledge. Of course some think that science is the only path to knowledge (and that is usually linked to a naturalistic worldview). There are others who deny that science produces knowledge at all—either because its basis in experiment always leaves you wondering whether you have done enough trials, or because the world is not knowable anyhow.

The big difficulty in all of this is to define "knowledge"—and that's as tricky as defining "science"! If we mean, as some do, to know something in all its details without error or precommitment, well, then, no one knows anything (except, apparently, that they don't know anything). But no one except a philosopher ever means that when he says he "knows" something or someone. I know that I am sitting here in front of the keyboard. I know that my daughter has brown hair that shows red highlights in the sun. There have been times when in talking with my children about a difficulty, I have known just why they behave the way they do. I believe it is right to say I know my wife and children—though I don't know everything about them. By that I mean that I know that they think and feel in some ways and not in others, and I can base my own behavior on these known patterns.

But let's think about some other examples. Suppose I ask my daughter if she slept well last night, and she says "yes," and I believe her. May I say that I *know* she slept well? And try this one: one winter morning I looked into the backyard and saw a hawk on the ground, stooping over and tugging at something with its beak. A couple of hours later I went outside and found dozens of feathers scattered all around where the hawk had been. I checked with the local Department of Conservation to be sure I identified the hawk rightly (it was a red-tailed). "Knowing" what I know about their eating habits (to be precise, believing the booklet that the Department sent me), I inferred that the hawk had caught and eaten a bird—probably a mourning dove or mockingbird, based on the color of the feathers. Now, then: do I *know* that the hawk ate a bird there?

When philosophers talk about knowing, they often contrast it with believing and inferring. I find this confusing because they usually don't use the words in the same way that we do in ordinary speech. So let's just think about the English verb "to know." There are four basic patterns in which we use the verb.

1. I know *that* <a> is true

Think of some sentences in this pattern: "I know that I'm sitting here"; "I know that my wife and children love me"; "I know that I don't own a dog"; "I know that a squirrel made these tracks in the snow"; "I know that the hawk ate a bird." In each case, I'm saying that I have a good reason to believe that <a> is true. There seems to be some idea of a threshold of confidence level, though: in the last sentence, if I'm not sure, I might say, "I *think* that the hawk ate a bird." This threshold varies with context—it probably depends on just how important the topic is. (It matters more to me whether my wife and children love me, than whether a hawk ate a bird, so I set the confidence bar higher for that.)

2. I know *how to do* <b>

A sample sentence would be, "I know how to cook eggs." The idea is that I have a skill, and can reliably carry out the actions needed to bring about some goal.

3. I know *<person* c>

Consider some sentences: "I know Diane"; "I know George, but not well." The idea is that I have experience of the way person <c> behaves—and that my experience is enough for me to be able to say what her likes and dislikes are, how she thinks, what principles govern her actions. The sentence "I know God"—in a Christian context—includes all this, with love and delight.

4. I know <d> *from* <e>

For example, "I know good apples from bad" means that I know what the difference is, or how to tell the difference—which makes this a variation either from pattern 1 or from pattern 2.

When we are talking about science, we're generally talking about pattern 1; so our question is, Does scientific study lead us to "know that" some statement is true—say, *that* hawks eat birds, or *that* the earth is $4^1/_2$ billion years old? What we are asking is, Does it give us good reason to believe that such a statement is true?

When we're using pattern 2 (know how to do) and pattern 3 (know a person), we're building on knowledge *that,* and taking it further.

Some philosophers, as I said, distinguish between knowing, inferring, and believing: I *know* things that I observe directly; I *infer* things when I draw conclusions; I *believe* things that others tell me. Now, I don't think this distinction corresponds to ordinary usage either, but it does introduce a useful distinction. I have no reason to doubt that lions eat wildebeests, or that bears hole up for the winter, even though I have never seen one do so. Nor do I have reason to doubt that squirrels eat acorns—even though, strictly speaking, I have only seen a few do so, and I am making a generalization. I don't doubt that Romans executed certain criminals by crucifixion. Nor do I doubt that the hawk I saw ate a bird. Am I wrong to refer to these items as "knowledge"? I don't think so, but I should recognize that there are different categories of knowledge—knowledge by direct observation (I have seen squirrels eat acorns), knowledge by believing reliable reports (others tell me they have seen squirrels eat acorns), and knowledge by inference (I conclude that squirrels in general eat acorns when they can find them).

So how can we apply these ideas to science? Well, it follows that I can say without embarrassment that I know things scientifically. I know a part of what squirrels eat; I know how to sink a billiard ball (the angle of incidence equals the angle of reflection, as I learned in high school physics). I know how the Greek and Hebrew verb tenses are used.

This also helps us to see where science fits in to the general project of knowing. Science, as I argued earlier, depends on discursive reasoning; and discursive reasoning depends on accepting touchstone truths (such as that reasoning is valid). But this means I know some things apart from discursive reasoning—I know that I exist, I know what I dreamed last night, I know my wife's voice. But also, not all discursive reasoning is science—because, for instance, the data might not be publicly accessible. When I try to figure out why I'm tired, and then realize it's because I woke up too early because I had a yucky dream and couldn't go back to sleep—well, that's all very rational, but I wouldn't call it "science." This means that we have a ladder: knowing-in-general, which includes discursive reasoning, which in turn includes science. The higher the rung, the broader is the coverage. And each lower rung is subject to the rules of the rungs above it: that is, discursive reasoning depends on things that I know directly; science depends on discursive reasoning. This shows why I have to evaluate scientific results for the quality of their reasoning; it also shows why I can't make science—or discursive reasoning—the be-all-and-end-all of knowing. Each has its place.

The common thread in the things I listed above—what squirrels eat; how billiard balls travel; how verb tenses are used—is that I can see them with my own eyes (or can accept others' eyesight) and test them in my experience. But what about things I can't test this way—such as the existence of protons and electrons, or the shape of a molecule, or the components of a distant star? These things result from a chain of inferences based on their effects—in the examples given, mostly electronic measurements. Now, this in itself isn't bad: if I see deer tracks in the woods I know by inference that a deer has gone by (unless someone is pulling a gag). So really the inference is as good as the chain of reasoning that produced it, and we're back to the features of sound thinking in chapter 2. For example, cosmologists think the universe has lots of what they call "dark matter": but the only way to detect it is by its gravitational effects (that's why they call it "dark": you can't see it). Likewise, how can we find planets around other stars, when they're too far away for us to see them? Astronomers look for wobbles in the movements of a star, assuming that the gravitational pull of a planet causes the wobble.

But things are a bit more complicated than that. Remember that science proceeds by making models; and this means that the inference takes for granted that we have made a good model. If we want to be really careful, we should say "matter behaves *as if* it were made of protons and electrons and other stuff, and I don't see any reason to doubt that it really is"; "molecules reflect X-rays *as if* they had such-and-such a shape"; and so on. If my model for the motion of billiard balls doesn't include the friction from the table (as it commonly doesn't in high school physics), then the model is not good enough for the real world.

The work of Thomas Kuhn, a historian of science, comes in here. He used the term "paradigm" for the generally accepted models of a scientific community. Most of the time scientists are filling in the details of these models, and sometimes the problems with a model get so severe that the only thing to do is to adopt a new model and chuck the old one. For example, in the Middle Ages, people thought that the earth was a sphere, fixed in the middle of the universe, and that the stars and planets were stuck in crystalline spheres that rotated around the earth. They also thought that all change took place within the orbit of the moon; outside that orbit, nothing changed. This was their model; science involved figuring out how the stars moved along the surfaces of the spheres to give us the patterns we observe. In 1572 Tycho Brahe found that a "new star" had appeared, and he called it a "nova" (that's Latin for "new": today we'd call it a supernova). This was also the age of Copernicus (1473–1543), who suggested that the earth revolves around the sun. The model that we hold today—we go around our sun, which is a star in the Milky Way, which is a galaxy among innumerable others—looks like it does a better job of accounting for the observations.

Another feature of Kuhn's notion of paradigms, though, is that paradigms don't actually get you nearer to the truth: they just gain general acceptance and set new problems for scientists to work on. The topic is too big for me to do it justice here; I've put a critical review of Kuhn's theory in an appendix to this book. For now I'll say that I don't think he's really made his case, but he has done us the service of showing how many different factors are involved when a scientific model gets accepted.

And then there is the problem of our generalizations: when can we make a sound one, and when should we refrain from making a generalization? For example: in every American presidential election since 1940, the outcome of the election is tied to whether the Washington Redskins win their last home game before the election: if they win, the party in power stays in power, and if they lose, the party out of power wins the election. The record is 100 percent, and has been since the 1940s. Since the football game comes first, we can say that it "predicts" the outcome of the election, can't we? (Some columnists complained that George Bush's campaign slacked off a bit just before the November 2000 election, and they almost lost because of it: do you suppose that the Redskins' loss that year made them too cocky about winning?)

Another example: the natives of the New Hebrides in the South Pacific observed that people in good health usually had body lice, while sick people very often did not; hence, they concluded, body lice produce good health.

Both of these generalizations are unsound, despite the force of the statistics (that is, the apparent grounding in solid empirical data). What makes a statistical generalization sound or not is the presence of an *explanation*—can we give a reason why the relationship should be so? As to the football example, no one has a reason that makes any sense, and so no sensible person will waste time looking for some deeper connection. In the case of body lice in the New Hebrides, what we know—or think we know—about body lice makes it hard to swallow; and once we think it through, we find another explanation that fits the data and is more consistent with what else we know. As Darrell Huff put it in his *How to Lie with Statistics,*

> More sophisticated observers finally got things straightened out in the New Hebrides. As it turned out, almost everybody in those circles had lice most of the time. It was, you might say, the normal condition of man. When, however, anyone took a fever (quite possibly carried to him by those same lice) and his body became too hot for comfortable habitation, the lice left. There you have cause and effect altogether confusingly distorted, reversed, and intermingled.

Of course these explanations might themselves be based on a fabric of inferences and premises, so they need to be put under the microscope, too.

Consider how we now have an international standard for telling time: the atomic clock, based on the cesium atom. James Trefil tells us,

> Every electron in every cesium atom in the universe behaves in exactly the same way, so the cesium standard is both universal and reproducible.

I expect that this claim is true—true down to thirteen decimal places, anyhow. What makes it worth believing? Has anyone actually examined "every electron in every cesium atom in the universe"? (Has anyone actually examined *any* electron?) The answer is no; but the generalization is based on a model of the atom, which is itself based on a network of inferences.

The Scottish philosopher David Hume (1711–1776) had his doubts over whether you could ever make a valid inference from your experience. He wrote,

> It is impossible, therefore, that any arguments from experience can prove this resemblance of the past to the future, since all these arguments are founded on the supposition of that resemblance. Let the course of things be allowed hitherto ever so regular, that alone, without some new argument or inference, proves not that for the future it will continue so. . . . My practice, you say, refutes my doubts. But you mistake the purport of my question. As an agent, I am quite satisfied in the point; but as a philosopher who has some share of curiosity, I will not say skepticism, I want to learn the foundation of this inference.

He's asking us to supply a reason for thinking that the world is regular and knowable by discursive reasoning. In the final analysis, we can't prove that these inferences are valid; we have to take this principle as a given in order to do anything. As a matter of fact, that's just what we all do, and we need a jolly good reason for dropping it.

Hume's doubts don't provide that good reason, and here's why. Let me quote from my own book, *The God of Miracles:*

> Hume's doubts offer no compelling reason, and his own reference to himself as an agent is the key. He has started from the wrong end of the stick. He should have begun, not with "By what right do I assume the reliability of the world and of inductive inference?" but with, "What is it about us and about the world that explains why we are such successful agents?" [He] offers an impoverished epistemology, because he suggests that the only way we "know" is either through logical deduction or through experience; he makes no allowance for the possibility that as agents created by the God who made the world we are endowed with the capacities to function in that world, and even to understand it to some extent.

There are some things you don't have to prove: in fact, the Christian message explains them better than any other system of thought does.

Even though we have a right to draw inferences from our experience, we still have to be careful. Some studies only allow us a modest level of confidence—and honesty demands that we admit it. Medical research is a good example of that. When I was a baby, doctors taught that mother's milk wasn't anywhere near as good as formula; when my children were born, though, they told us just the opposite. They were quite sure in both cases. Some researchers seem to be getting the message now: have you noticed how most new studies on the effects of different kinds of food close with "eat a balanced diet and get regular exercise"?

The approach to knowledge and science that I favor is often called "critical" or "qualified" realism—it is realism because it takes for granted that there is a real world for us to know, that we can know it, and that our scientific models can describe it accurately; and it is critical or qualified because we have to recognize the limitations of our studies and models. In a later chapter I will argue that this is the approach to knowledge that the Bible itself supports. In another later chapter, on the age of the universe, I will discuss whether critical realism is appropriate *both* for ordinary and for historical contexts.

Most working scientists embrace some kind of realism; for example, Michael Behe, a biochemist, writing in his *Darwin's Black Box,* meets head-on the idea of some that science is a game that can set its own rules (such as the methodological naturalism we already looked at):

> Most people, from ordinary taxpayers to prominent scientists, would more likely view science not as a game but as *a vigorous attempt to make true statements about the physical world.*

Or, as Machen—my hero in this chapter—put it,

> Science, in other words, though it may not in any generation attain truth, is at any rate aiming at truth.

OPERATING RELATIONSHIPS OF SCIENCE AND FAITH

Suppose Doctors Hatfield and McCoy work in a coroner's office, and they both have to give their opinion on how someone died. Imagine the following four conversations:

MCCOY (to the police captain): He's dead.

1	HATFIELD:	He died from the bullet through his heart.
	MCCOY:	No, he died from strangling.

2	HATFIELD:	He died because the bullet pierced his heart.
	MCCOY:	He died because his number was up.
3	HATFIELD:	He died because the bullet pierced his heart.
	MCCOY:	He died because someone killed him.
4	HATFIELD:	The bullet entered from the back.
	MCCOY:	No, the bullet entered from the front.
	HATFIELD:	Actually, the wound in front is the exit wound.
	MCCOY:	Oh, you're right.

These conversations illustrate the four possible relationships between two statements. In conversation 1 we are looking at a *conflict*—there are two competing claims about the same thing, and at least one of them is wrong. He died from the bullet or from strangling or from neither, but not from both. In conversation 2 we have an example of *compartmentalization*—the statements have two different scopes, and do not interact at all. There is no conflict, but McCoy isn't really doing what coroners are supposed to do. In conversation 3 we have *complementarity*—the two statements are about separate parts of the same thing, and fill out the total picture. McCoy and Hatfield might both be right, and they are both doing the coroner's work (it wasn't suicide). And conversation 4 gives us an instance of *coordination*—the two statements are about the same thing (or at least they have some overlap), and apparent conflict triggers a revision in interpretation that yields a harmony. They both saw the same things, and agreed on what they saw (wounds in front and back); but McCoy corrected his interpretation of what he saw and agreed with Hatfield.

When we come to consider which of these categories might describe statements from science and statements from Christian faith, we have to think first about whether it is possible for these statements to come into any contact at all. By that I mean, we can acknowledge that scientists try to say something true about the world we all experience. Newton's laws of motion are intended to describe the way the balls on my pool table move. But does Christian faith speak about this same world? Many people think not: they say, science is about *what* and *how,* religion is about *why;* or, science is about *facts,* religion is about *values*. By such a reckoning it is impossible for science and religion ever to conflict so long as they keep to their proper spheres; so the relationship is one of *compartmentalization.* Stephen Jay Gould calls this arrangement "non-overlapping magisteria" (NOMA).

The trouble with this view, however, is that neither those who practice science nor those who hold to Christian faith can rest content with such an arrangement. Biblical faith rests on a number of historical assertions—the universe really had a beginning (creation); Adam really did sin and bring us all with him (fall); Abram really did answer God's call, and receive promises from God (covenant); the people of Israel really did pass through the Red Sea while the Egyptians drowned; and Jesus rose from the dead (redemption). When Paul defended himself before the crowd in Jerusalem, he said that "the high priest and all the Council of the elders can testify" about his former way of life (Acts 22:5, NASB); and before King Agrippa he declared that "the king knows about these matters [the words of the Prophets and the resurrection of Jesus] . . . for this has not been done in a corner" (Acts 26:26, NASB). These things are open to investigation (historical science), even for those who are hostile. Paul also claims that the world speaks to everyone of its Creator (Rom. 1:19-20). It is at least possible that this means that a soundly scientific study of the world should support Paul's claim (we will come back to this in a later chapter). When anyone tells religion that it may not speak to matters of fact, he is making a pronouncement about the content of religion: in other words, to follow the NOMA rule means to violate the rule. And further, as usual, the question is not whether "science" can interact with these claims, but which particular science we are speaking of.

So we have to take each statement on its own. Once when my son was about three I saw a scab on his leg and asked him, "How did you get that?" He told me, "God put it there." Now if I had wanted him to affirm his belief in God's providence, I couldn't have asked for better than this. But instead I was asking for the particular chain of events that led to the wound—he fell, or was swinging a chain saw, or whatever. Now since I could say, "God put it there by designing the human skin with the properties of softness and self-healing, and by so arranging events that my son scraped his leg, and the wound began to heal," then I can say that the answer my son gave and the one I was looking for are *complementary.* They fill out the total picture.

We considered in chapter 2 the possibility that "the earth is not the physical center of the universe" conflicts with "the earth is the center of God's attention." But these statements cannot conflict—they can't even come into contact—because their scopes are so different. That is, they come from separate *compartments* of a description of reality.

From time to time people have proposed the theory called *polygenesis*—

the idea that the different types of human beings came about separately (*poly* for several, *genesis* for origin), either by separate creation or by separate evolution. This is in direct *conflict* with the most common interpretation of the biblical Adam. Some have tried therefore to reinterpret the biblical role of Adam; I think they've been unsuccessful, but we'll come back to that in our chapter on human nature. So in that case, I can either reject the biblical picture or reject the scientific theory. I will give reasons later for sticking with the common interpretation of Adam (and hence for opposing the theory of polygenesis).

On the other hand, we consider it legitimate to *coordinate* the dates of events in the Bible with the dates we gather from our studies of ancient Egypt and Mesopotamia. In the film *The Prince of Egypt* the Pharaoh is called Rameses, and, because many believing Egyptologists think that what they know about Rameses II best matches the biblical account, that's a real possibility. Again, if you read what the Old Testament books of 1 and 2 Kings say about the lengths of the reigns of different kings, you get an impression of timing that you can't harmonize with what we find in the other inscriptions from the ancient Near East. Now you could just decide that those pagans got their dates wrong; but it's better to do what most Old Testament scholars do, and learn from the dating practices of the ancient world. It turns out that there was a practice called "co-regency," where a son was co-regent (sort of a joint king) with his father as on-the-job training. Then we realize that some accounts in the Bible may use the beginning of the co-regency for the date of a king's reign, while others may use the date of the father's death. Using this we get a nice harmonization between the Bible and archaeology (a science that studies the remains of ancient civilizations).

In order to decide what the relationship is between a biblical statement and one from the sciences, we have to ask whether they are about the same thing, that is, whether they share the same scope. We will also have to decide whether they are using their words in the same way. We also need to know just what kind of communication is going on, and how it meets the needs of the first readers. There's a big difference between ordinary language and the kind of language we might use in the sciences.

Some sciences—say, chemistry—will mostly be *complementary* to the interests of our faith. This is because chemistry is primarily about the normal operations of the things it studies, and our faith is mostly based on claims about what it means to be human, and what works God has done for us in history. When the relationship is one of complementarity, that doesn't mean that the biblical view of the world is irrelevant—since, as we'll see, that view provides a set of premises that encourage scientific study, namely that the world is good, stable, and knowable, and that God made us to know the world.

Other sciences will overlap with the content of our faith: for example, when they deal with the origin of the universe (cosmology), or with the origin of man (anthropology), or with human nature (psychology). The closer we get to what it means to be human, the more opportunities we have for overlap; and, as it turns out, the more one's personal commitments come into play in scientific theories.

The sciences can play a role in our ethics. For example, the Ten Commandments tell us not to murder (Ex. 20:13). But what is a human life? Specifically, is the thing that develops in the womb a "human"—and when does it become one? There is some biblical material that helps us (say, Ex. 21:22-23; Ps. 139:13-16); however, while such passages take us into the womb, they don't decisively settle the kinds of questions we face today (say, the difference between fertilization and implantation; or, is the first brain wave important?). But fetology, the study of how the human embryo develops, does help. It shows that there is no point along the way at which the embryo "becomes human," which means that it's a human life from the get-go. Such studies helped in the process of a leading abortion advocate, Bernard Nathanson (raised as a secular Jew), becoming first pro-life and then a Christian.

CONCLUSION

Let's bring this to a conclusion. Science and faith each have a relationship to knowledge; and this means that there is the potential for them to overlap in what they speak about. In particular, if science is *defined* as "giving a naturalistic explanation for every thing and every event," then conflict is inevitable. But there is no reason that justifies defining science that way: neither from the history of science, nor from the rules of reason.

The discussion of this chapter allows us to evaluate the views of any writer or speaker who addresses how science will bear on our faith. We can ask five diagnostic questions:

1. What is his definition of "science"?
2. What is his definition of "faith"?
3. What does he think is the relationship of science or faith to knowledge?

4. What does he think is the operating relationship between science and faith?
5. What is his model of God's relationship to the world?

In most cases you'll have to tease the answers to these questions out of what he says; few authors will give you these up front.

SECTION II
THEOLOGICAL ISSUES

4

THIS IS MY FATHER'S WORLD

The Biblical Doctrine of Creation

THE FIRST BIG QUESTION of life is, Who or what made you? How we answer this basic question will decide for us what makes life meaningful or worthwhile.

The purpose of this chapter is to discuss the biblical teaching about the world as God's *creation.* Since this leads us into a discussion about how God continues his involvement in the world, we will also touch on the biblical teaching about *providence*—but the fuller discussion of that topic will come in a later chapter.

Most people, when they hear that a discussion is about "creation," assume you're talking about the days in Genesis 1 and the age of the earth. I don't believe that such issues are at the heart of the biblical teaching, but I will of course address them since they are controversial and divisive. However, I will do so in the three chapters that follow this one, and I will focus here on the conclusions from Genesis 1 and 2 that should unite all Christians. I will focus on Genesis 1:1–2:3, and leave most of the details of 2:4-25 until my chapter on human nature.

HOW MANY CREATION ACCOUNTS DOES ONE RELIGION NEED? LITERARY RELATIONSHIPS OF GENESIS 1 AND 2

We often find people referring to Genesis 1 and 2 as the "creation accounts," implying that they think these are two stories about the beginning, each having a separate origin, a different purpose, and conflicting details. I want to show you why I think that it's better biblical interpretation to see them as two accounts that support each other: Genesis 1 gives you the big picture, while Genesis 2 fills out the details of the sixth day of Genesis 1.

I don't think anyone disputes the idea that there are two narratives; what they dispute is where one ends and the other begins, and how the events of the one relate to those of the other. So let's begin our study by seeing what the boundaries are of the different stories.

To follow along, you will be best off if you use the ESV for your Bible. If you have a NASB or RV, you will be able to see most of what I'm saying, and I'll comment on the differences without getting technical.

We don't have any problem with where the first story begins: "In the beginning . . ." Nor do we have a problem seeing that it covers six days of God's work, with a seventh day being his day of rest, his Sabbath. The real difficulty is whether the first story ends with 2:3 (God resting on his Sabbath), or with 2:4a ("These are the generations of the heavens and the earth when they were created," which would round off the narrative by summing it up and pointing back to 1:1).

The second approach to division—taking the first story as 1:1–2:4a—is pretty common, among both commentaries and Bible translations such as NAB, NRSV, and CEV. The NIV and REB divide 2:4, but put both halves in the second narrative. The NKJV does not divide the verse, but makes the whole verse an introduction to the sentence that continues through verse 6.

The reasons why we should not divide the verse at all, but should treat it as a separate sentence, as ESV and NASB do, are apparent once we set it out in poetic lines:

> These are the generations
> of the heavens and the earth when they were created,
> in the day that the LORD God made earth and the heavens.

The phrase "these are the generations" appears ten other times in Genesis (5:1; 6:9; 10:1; 11:10, 27; 25:12, 19; 36:1, 9; 37:2), and each time it marks the beginning of a new section. It is reasonable to expect it to do the same here—or at least we need a good reason not to find it doing so. Further, the lines "of the heavens and the earth when they were created" and "in the day that the LORD God made earth and the heavens" actually form an elaborate mirror pattern (called a *chiasmus*):

of the heavens and the earth when they were created
a b c

in the day that the Lord God made earth and the heavens
c' b' a'

In this pattern the elements have the order a-b-c || c'-b'-a', that is, the second line mirrors the first in its order of elements. Scholars of the ancient Near East often feel good when they can show a chiasmus with two elements in a passage (a-b || b'-a'), though it may be chance rather than art that produced it. But when there are three elements, that's taken as clear evidence of art—which means the author wanted you to notice it. And what was the author telling you to do once you noticed it? He wanted you to read it as a whole thought, without breaking it apart.

Another feature shows that the author was also telling you to harmonize the two stories: the name of God in 1:1–2:3 is just "God," while in 2:5–3:24 he is "the LORD God." The name "God" is the title of the deity in his role as Creator and Ruler of the world; and the name LORD (Hebrew *Yahweh* or *Jehovah*) is his personal name, the one that he uses in entering into a relationship with humans (see Ex. 3:13-15, where God himself explains it). Now if we read this verse in cooperation with our author, we will see that he wanted us to see that "God" of 1:1–2:3 is the same being as "the LORD God" in 2:5–3:24—in other words, the covenant God of Israel ("the LORD") is the Maker of heaven and earth ("God").

There is plenty more to say about Genesis 2:5-7, and I will touch on more details in the next chapter. For now I will quote these verses from the ESV and make a few comments:

> [5] When no bush of the field was yet in the land and no small plant of the field had yet sprung up—for the LORD God had not caused it to rain on the land, and there was no man to work the ground, [6] and a mist was going up from the land and was watering the whole face of the ground— [7] then the LORD God formed the man of dust from the ground and breathed into his nostrils the breath of life, and the man became a living creature.

You can see from this version that verses 5 and 6 give you the setting for what happened in verse 7. That is, at some particular time before the rain fell on the ground to make the plants grow, while a mist (or rain cloud) was coming up and watering the land, God formed the man. As we will see when we compare these verses with Genesis 1:1–2:3, the event of 2:7, 21-22—the making of the first man and woman—is the same as that of 1:27, but told more fully. This helps us to see that the way to harmonize the two stories is to see 1:1–2:3 as the overall narrative, while 2:4-25 fills in lots of particulars of the sixth day. This will come in handy when, in the next chapter of this book, we decide what to do with the days of Genesis 1.

OUTLINE OF GENESIS 1:1–2:3

The outline of Genesis 1:1–2:3 will help us find its purpose. Without too much trouble we can see that it is as follows:

1:1-2	Preface (background actions and information)
1:3-5	Day 1 (light and darkness)
1:6-8	Day 2 (sea and sky)
1:9-13	Day 3 (land, sea, vegetation)
1:14-19	Day 4 (light-bearers)
1:20-23	Day 5 (sea animals and flying creatures)
1:24-31	Day 6 (land animals and humans)—*the longest day*
2:1-3	Day 7 (rest and enjoyment)—*no refrain*

Another way to look at the account is to see it as giving us three days of setting up locations, and then three days of making the inhabitants for those locations, followed by the day of rest:

Location	*Inhabitants*
1. light and dark	4. lights of day and night
2. sea and sky	5. animals of water and air
3. fertile earth	6. land animals (including humans)

7. Rest and enjoyment

Each of the six workdays begins with "and God said," and ends with the refrain, "and there was evening and there was morning, the *n*th day." (I know that the King James Version has "and the evening and the morning were the *n*th day" for the refrain; but this is a mistranslation, apparently inherited from the Latin version of the fourth century A.D. The Greek version of the third century B.C. had it right, and most modern translations give the correct rendering.)

The seventh day is different, because God doesn't "say" anything and he doesn't "do" anything—he's "resting"—and because there is no refrain about the evening and the morning.

What Is Genesis 1:1–2:3 About?

If we are to know how to make use of this passage, we need to know what it is about. As C. S. Lewis said so well,

> The first qualification for judging any piece of workmanship from a corkscrew to a cathedral is to know what it is—what it was intended to do and how it is meant to be used.

The first thing to say about Genesis 1:1–2:3 is that it is part of Genesis 1–3, which in turn is part of Genesis 1–11, which in turn is part of Genesis—which is the first of the five books of Moses. The books of Moses are about how God called Abram to be his friend, and promised that he would make of Abram a mighty nation—a nation that would be God's treasured possession. But the promise was never for the nation alone; it always had in mind "all the families of the earth" (Gen. 12:3). So the books of Moses are about how God fashioned a people for himself, through whom he would bring blessing to the rest of the peoples (which is what the apostles carried out).

Genesis 1–11 sets the stage for this special call to Abram. In it we learn of the one God who made everything there is (Gen. 1:1–2:3), and who had a special plan for mankind (Gen. 2:4-25). Mankind fell into sin (Genesis 3), and then began to disperse over the earth (Genesis 4–5). The stories of the flood (Genesis 6–9) and of the Tower of Babel (Genesis 11) are similar: all mankind are accountable to the same God, the very one who made the world and mankind; and with such power no one can stop him from bringing about his righteous judgment. But all mankind are his—so the plan for Abram looks forward to restoring all mankind to a right standing with God.

You will find that many writers call Genesis 1:1–2:3 a *cosmogony,* meaning a story about how the universe came to be (*cosmo-* for the cosmos, *-gony* for the origin). I would say that this description is only partly true, and really misses the point. The cosmogony part gets taken care of in verse 1 ("in the beginning God created the heavens and the earth"), and then the narrative moves on to its main point, the making and preparing of the earth as a place for humans to live. We can see this if we make the following observations.

First, let's consider the relationship of verses 1-2 to the rest of the account. I take verse 1 as describing the initial creation event. Some think it is actually a summary of the whole account, but I don't think that can work: as we'll see shortly, other Bible writers took this verse as describing creation from nothing; and if the verse is a summary of the account, then it's non-committal on whether creation took place from nothing. I prefer to go with the other Bible writers. Besides, the first day begins in verse 3 (with "and God said"), and verses 1-2 are *background*—they describe the setting of day one. The most usual function of the kind of background statement you have in verse 1 is to give an action that took place some unspecified time before the narrative actually gets under way (as in Gen. 16:1; 21:1; 24:1).

All this means that the origin of the whole show gets taken care of in one verse, and the author moves on to focus on something else.

Second, the words "heavens" and "earth" in verse 1 refer to "everything"; but after verse 2 they get narrower in their meaning: "heavens" narrows to "Sky" (see v. 8, ESV margin), and "earth" narrows to "Land" (see v. 10, ESV margin). This tells us that the author has narrowed his focus from the whole universe down to planet earth.

Third, the high point of the narrative is the sixth day (which gets the longest description), and especially verse 27, the making of mankind. You can see this by the repetitive structure of the verse: "So God created man in his own image," repeated as "in the image of God he created him," and followed by "male and female he created them": three statements of the same event. The effect of this repetition is to slow you down and make you mull over what the verse says, and what the event means. This is because mankind is the crown of God's creation week.

So the focus on the making of the earth's different environments and inhabitants reaches its peak at the making of the humans who are to rule over the whole earth. The earth is a good place for these people to live, love, work, and worship God.

IS GENESIS 1:1–2:3 SUPPOSED TO BE A HISTORICAL RECORD?

To answer this question, we have to be able to say what we mean by the word "historical." (We're back to the meanings of our terms again!) In ordinary language, "history" means "the things that happened in the past"; and therefore to say that a story is "historical" is to say that the author wants you to believe that he is telling you about events that actually took place.

We have to clarify this, because for some scholars, "history" means a narrative that does not involve God as doing anything. This is a ridiculous specialized use of a word that has a perfectly reasonable ordinary meaning, and could lead to such odd assertions as, "this account is not 'historical,' but I'm not saying it didn't happen." I think more often, though, people hear the word "historical" as meaning that the account tells you its events in just the order in which they happened, or that it's a complete record, or that there are no figurative elements in it. When we use the word "historical," though, we are not committing ourselves to anything of the sort. Otherwise, how could we call Psalm 105 a "historical" psalm—does the fact that in verses 28-36 it tells the events of the exodus in a different order than the book of Exodus does, and leaves out some of the plagues, mean that it's not "historical"? This doesn't make any sense to me, so I'll stick with the ordinary meaning of the word (the author wants you to believe that he is telling you about events that actually took place) and not read into it what isn't there.

Now then: did the author mean us to take Genesis 1:1–2:3 as history? The answer is certainly yes, for two reasons. The first is its place in the book of Genesis, a book that is concerned with historical matters: it starts the whole thing off and explains why things are the way they are. Obvious evidence for this is the genealogies that run through the book: they connect later people with those earlier ones. (For example, they tell us how Abraham came from Adam.) The second reason is, that's the way people in the same culture read it: for example, in Exodus 20:11 the Israelites' regular workweek is to be patterned after God's unique creation week. And many verses (such as Jonah 1:9; Isa. 40:26; Heb. 11:3; Rev. 4:11) refer to God as the Creator of all there is in a way that shows they think the creation events actually happened.

Now it's easy to object and say that this is "theology," not "history." I think the people who say that are recognizing some of the highly stylized features of the account—which we will take up in the next chapter—that make it hard to call it "scientific." They usually want to avoid the endless wrangling over the meaning of the days that seems to get us away from actually hearing what the text is about. I share some of their concerns, as I discussed in the previous section, but I think they're making a big mistake when they contrast "theology" with "history." Since in the Bible most theology is actually built on historical events, they're making a distinction the Bible writers would not make, and that will only spell trouble in the long run.

This is a good place to comment on two other words that some people use for this account, namely "myth" and "poetry." I'm sorry to say, again we run into trouble if we don't nail down definitions of these terms and stick with them.

Most people think of a myth as a purely fictitious story, usually featuring gods or heroes, which explains something in nature or in history. An example would be the Greek story of the nymph Echo, who was doomed only to answer and never to begin a conversation; when she wasted away for grief her bones turned into rocks—and that is why you get an *echo* in the mountains. No one—probably not even the one who first told the story—thinks that this actually happened. Other people might mean by "myth" a traditional story that may have some historical basis, but no one knows where it came from and its purpose is to explain something in nature or history—for example, a story about the origin of man. Other, more literary, people use the word for fantasy stories that touch us very deeply, such as *The Lord of the Rings*. All of these definitions really play down the historical element, and most people hear "myth" as implying "it didn't happen." (I remember the schoolchild's definition of a "fairy tale": "something that never happened a long time ago.")

So I don't think that "myth" is the best word for what we have in Genesis—even though this story does share things in common with myths, such as the purpose of explaining where we came from and why things are the way they are now. But Genesis reflects the notion that our present grows out of the past, so history matters. You could call it a "true myth," if you like—much as J. R. R. Tolkien once described the Gospels as a fairy story that has entered History—but I think you risk being misunderstood by anyone who doesn't follow your usage.

The meaning of "poetry" likewise depends on who is using the word. A linguist might mean by "poetry" a piece that uses language artistically, with things like rhythm and imaginative language; the purpose is to help you feel what the poet is describing. In ordinary language, however, "poetry" generally gives the idea of "not real" (much like the word "metaphorical"). Tolkien supplied an excellent example of the popular usage of "poetry" in his *Lord of the Rings*. In the chapter "A Conspiracy Unmasked," the hobbits Merry and Pippin have just sung a song whose refrain is, "We must away! We must away! We ride before the break of day!" In response Frodo says, "Very good! But in that case there are a lot of things to do before we go to bed . . ." To this Pippin replies, "Oh! *That was poetry*! Do you really mean to start before the break of day?"

To apply this popular usage all the time is nonsense, to be sure—after all, there are plenty of *historical* poems in the Bible (such as Deborah's Song in Judges 5; Psalms 78; 105; 106)—but that's still what people hear in this word. So, though Genesis 1:1–2:3 certainly has some "poetic" features, I will not use the word "poem" to describe it.

DOES GENESIS 1:1 TEACH "CREATION FROM NOTHING"?

Most Christian theologians have taken Genesis 1:1 as describing creation *from nothing*—that is, God didn't have to start with anything in order to make the world; he called it into being by his own powerful word. (Traditionally this is called "creation *ex nihilo,*" using the Latin for "from nothing.")

The usual way of translating verses 1 and 2 is to take verse 1 as a complete sentence, with a new one starting in verse 2:

> [1]In the beginning, God created the heavens and the earth. [2] The earth was without form and void, . . . (ESV, compare NASB, REB, NIV, KJV, NJB)

However, some Bible versions make verse 1 the introduction to verse 2:

> [1]In the beginning when God created the heavens and the earth, [2] the earth was a formless void . . . (NRSV, compare NAB, NEB).

The second translation makes it sound like God started with formless stuff and then shaped it. Part of the motivation for this translation is that there is a Babylonian story that begins in a very similar way. But the traditional translation is right and the newer one is wrong, for several reasons. First, the traditional one is what the Hebrew text actually says; you have to modify the text (be it ever so slightly) to get the newer version. Second, the traditional rendering is good Hebrew grammar: it follows the conventions for giving us an event that took place before the main story (which in this case begins in v. 3) and then telling us what the conditions were when the events in the main story got under way (that's what v. 2 does). And third, all the ancient translations (the Septuagint in Greek, the Vulgate in Latin, and the Peshitta in Syriac) take it the traditional way, and in doing so reflect the standard way that Jewish and Christian readers have read the account. This standard reading lies behind the opening verse of John's Gospel:

> [1] In the beginning was the Word, and the Word was with God, and the Word was God. . . . [3] All things were made through him, and without him was not any thing made that was made.

Genesis 1:1 declares that God created all things from nothing. But first, let me point out that some will make a bad argument for this interpretation of the verse: they think the verb "created" itself means "created from nothing." This is not true: for example, the "creation" of mankind in 1:27 is amplified in 2:7 (and 2:21-22), where we see that it was not strictly "from nothing" (the man was made using mud, the woman using a rib). You may be tempted to conclude, from the way the *ex nihilo* position has been supported with a faulty argument, that the position itself is wrong. I don't want you to draw that conclusion, so let me show you why creation from nothing really does follow from this verse, when we take the sentence as a whole. The words "the heavens and the earth" refer to everything; and "in the beginning" tells us when it happened—and in fact points to an absolute beginning. And if God created everything at the very beginning, then before the beginning there was—well, nothing.

Let's consider two other verses that also affirm creation from nothing. Hebrews 11:3 says,

> By faith we understand that the universe was created by the word of God, so that what is seen was not made out of things that are visible.

The things that are "seen" or are "visible" are material things, so this author says that the material world didn't come from preexisting material—it was the word of God that brought it into being. Then Revelation 4:11 says,

> "Worthy are you, our Lord and God,
> to receive glory and honor and power,
> for you created all things,
> and by your will they existed and were created."

If all things owe their existence to God's will, and if he created them at some point in time, then he created them from nothing.

DOES GENESIS 1:1–2:3 GIVE US A CHRONOLOGY?

In this section I want to ask whether the creation account is supposed to take up some length of time. For now I'm not asking *how much* time it took; we'll save that for the next chapter. The reason we need to ask this is because St. Augustine seems to have thought that creation took place in an instant. He took this approach because he wanted to harmonize Genesis with Sirach (Ecclesiasticus) 18:1, which in the Latin version reads "he who lives forever created all things at once." (As it turns out, this is a mistranslation: the correct translation is "created all things without exception," as modern versions have it.)

Some have appealed to Augustine to say that therefore the Genesis account is an idealized picture of creation, not describing an extent of time. That is, the "days" describe the creation *as if* it took place over a period of time, so that we can understand it; but we aren't supposed to think they were an *actual* length of time.

We dealt with part of this when we discussed historicity above. But now we need to show that God is portrayed as having taken some length of time to prepare the world as a place for mankind to live and love. This is the natural effect of the narrative form—which normally describes a sequence of events one after the other—that uses the six days with their evenings and mornings. And this is how the Sabbath commandment takes it. Exodus 20:9 tells Israel to work for six days ("over the course of six days" captures the Hebrew nuance), because God did his work for six days (v. 11, "over the course of six days").

It is straightforward to see as well that these days are presented to us as six separate periods of time, that took place one after the other—after all, they're the "first day . . . second day," and so on to the seventh day.

We have to decide whether this necessarily means that everything narrated on a given day is supposed to have taken place on that day. For example, day five includes the great sea creatures—is it possible that they are there for logical reasons (grouping with other things that live in the water), and that they could actually have appeared later? And how would we decide this? We would consider the style of the account, its purpose, and how much the account is supposed to be "confirmable" by scientific research. Since we still have to consider those issues, we'll hold this question for later.

Is Genesis 1:1–2:3 a "Scientific" Account of Creation?

If you have been with me this far, you know that I'm going to start this section, about whether the biblical creation account is scientific, with all kinds of warnings to be careful about definitions in questions like this. If "scientific" means "true," or even "superior to ordinary language," then of course we want to say yes, Genesis 1:1–2:3 is a scientific account of creation. But if instead by "scientific" we mean "suited to the purposes for which today's scientists might want to use the information," then to answer "no" helps us because it reminds us, first, that types of language—such as ordinary, poetic, scientific—are geared toward specific purposes in communication; and second, that the creation account is given for purposes other than what we call "scientific." (We might also remember that what *today's* scientists want to do could be different from what those of other times wanted to do.) We should follow the lead of John Calvin (1509–1564), who commented on the way Moses' account differed from that of the "philosopher" (what we would call a "scientist"):

> To my mind, this is a certain principle, that nothing is here [in Genesis 1] treated of but the visible form of the world. He who would learn astronomy, and other recondite arts, let him go elsewhere. . . .
>
> Moses wrote in a popular style things which, without instruction, all ordinary persons, endued with common sense, are able to understand; but astronomers investigate with great labor whatever the sagacity of the human mind can comprehend.

(This came from a man who had no doubts about the historical truthfulness of Genesis!)

So what do I mean by saying that the account is not "scientific"? Well, we notice for one thing that it paints with broad strokes: except for man, no single species of plant or animal receives a proper name; we find no details about *how* the earth brought forth vegetation, or how the animals appeared in their different environments. When it mentions plants and animals, it certainly does not use the kind of taxonomy that we're used to: the land animals, for instance, are grouped according to their relationship to a peasant farmer. The categories in 1:24 are "livestock" (animals that man can tame and put to work, such as sheep, goats, cattle, camels), "creeping things" (small creepy-crawlies such as mice, lizards, and spiders), and "beasts of the earth" (larger wild animals). The account describes things with suggestive terms, such as the "greater light" and the "lesser light" (strange names for the sun and moon, for which there were ordinary words in Hebrew).

Some scholars think the "expanse" of verse 6 (traditionally "firmament") is some kind of surface like a dome or canopy (compare NAB, NRSV, REB). And, depending on what the scholar thinks the account is for, he either takes "expanse" as an example of a primitive world-picture (the earth as a flat disk supported over the waters by pillars, with the sky as a great dome), or else as some kind of early cloud cover (which is no longer here because of the rain that produced the flood). I think both of these interpretations are misguided: we can rule out the "early cloud cover" interpretation by noticing that the "expanse" gets a name in verse 8, "Heaven," or better, "Sky" (ESV margin), It's even clearer that expanse refers to the sky because the same word appears in Psalm 19:1 and Daniel 12:3 meaning just the sky that you and I see. I don't accept the "primitive world-picture" view because I think that those who see it in the Old Testament are treating lots of figurative language as if it were to be taken "literally" (we'll see some examples of that later).

It's much simpler to take the term "expanse" as a more elevated word for the sky, describing it as it appears to us on the ground, as if it were some kind of extended surface. This is an example of what is called *phenomenological language*—describing things by the way they appear, without committing ourselves to being taken "literally." (Even the world's top astronomers can say "sunrise" without anyone gasping in shock.) Another example is the term "lights" to describe the sun, moon, and stars. The word in Hebrew usually means "lamp," and that gives us a good idea of what these heavenly bodies do in a world without street-lamps.

We should imagine that the author has used the kind of language that best suits his purpose. And this kind of description—broad stroke, majestic in its simplicity, allusive, strictly patterned—is well suited to bring out a sense of wonder and delight at the creativity and boundless energy of God. We should come away from reading the passage with a yearning that we can hardly express in words: "Oh, how fine the creation was; oh, if only I could have seen and smelled and heard all that; and oh, why does the world seem so different from that now?" That is, we are set up for the story about the beginning of human sin, and about God's plan to rescue people from their sin, which is what the rest of the Bible is about.

But if we say that the Genesis account isn't quite "scientific," we haven't said enough when we're talking about the Bible and science. The way Genesis describes God's work of creation lays a foundation for science and philosophy—for all sound thinking about the world. This is because it tells us that a good and wise God made the world for us to enjoy; and the things in the world have natures that are knowable (for example, the plants and animals reproduce "after their kind"). Our senses and our intelligence allow us to say things that are true.

What Does It Mean That the Creation Was "Good"?

Genesis 1 is well-known for the way God keeps seeing the things he made and finding them "good": the light (v. 4), the seas and land (v. 10), the plants (v. 12), the sun, moon, and stars (v. 18), the swimming and flying creatures (v. 21), and all varieties of land animals before he made man (v. 24). And then in verse 31, after God made the first humans and commissioned them to make babies and rule over the world,

> And God saw everything that he had made, and behold, it was very good.

We should try hard to feel the full force of this statement. When a Hebrew narrator says, "and behold," he's inviting you to view the scene as if from the eyes of the participants. In this case he has us see it all as God saw it, as *very good.* God, who is himself good, and the source of all goodness, has shared some of that goodness with his creation. It's as if God overflows with goodness, and wanted to put that on display through what he made. This includes both the real existence of created things and their diversity—there are so many different things with so many different properties. There is so much goodness that only one creature, or multitudes of only one kind of creature, wouldn't be enough to display it.

Then on the seventh day, God's "Sabbath," God called the work finished; he rested and blessed the day, and made it holy: that's the extent of what he "does" on his Sabbath. God puts his stamp of approval on the goodness of the creation, and, as it were, leans back and *enjoys* it.

How Did God Make the World?

Another thing that stands out about this story is the way God "says" something and then it gets done. In each case he is expressing a wish ("Let this thing happen"), and then the story tells us that the wish was carried out: God said "Let there be light," and hey-presto, there was light (v. 3), and so on (vv. 6, 9, 11, 14, 20, 24, 26). The final "and God said," in verses 28-30, introduces God's blessing on the first humans.

God says it, and then it happens—it doesn't say how long it took for it to happen, but that doesn't matter: what matters is that God's wishes get carried out. God expresses his power in the way he calls the universe into existence and then shapes the earth as a place for his human creatures to live.

Psalm 33 is a hymn that makes this thought a part of worship:

> [6] By the word of the LORD the heavens were made,
> and by the breath of his mouth all their host. . . .
>
> [9] For he spoke, and it came to be;
> he commanded, and it stood firm.

All of this reminds us that the world did not make itself: instead it's something God made with no one's help—and what a job he did!

Summary of the Doctrine of Creation in Genesis 1:1–2:3

Let's try to summarize what Genesis 1:1–2:3 teaches about creation. Based on this passage (and our discussion in this chapter), we can say that God made *all things*—

(a) *from nothing.* This means that God, and only God, is self-sufficient: the created world depends on him, but he doesn't depend on it. When he made the world, he made something different than he is, and less than he is.

(b) *by the word of his power.* This means that when God wanted something to be a certain way, he spoke a word and that's just the way it was.

(c) *in the space of six days.* This means that he spread the work of fashioning the world for us over a length of time. (The problem of deciding what the "days" mean is the subject of the next chapter.)

(d) *all very good.* This is what the creation was like at first; we will discuss later the sense in which this still applies. For now we note that sin and dysfunction are foreign invaders of God's good creation.

(e) *that it bears his imprint.* The whole creation displays to all of us something of what God is like; it helps us to know and worship him. (In a later chapter we will discuss the role this should play in how we defend Christian faith.)

In other words, this is God's world from first to last.

This, then, is the outline of the biblical doctrine of creation; and it is a key doctrine to the Christian faith—after all, the creeds call God the "Maker of heaven and earth."

What Does This Mean for Us?

Can we say what this means for us? In this chapter we have been putting together the pieces of the Christian doctrine of creation. But we have no business discussing any Christian doctrines apart from the goal of living them out. Christians claim that their doctrines describe the way things are in the *real* world.

What this means for us in our daily lives is that we need to use this doctrine of creation to form our view of the world we live in. This can apply in a number of ways, and I'll mention only a few of them.

First, it applies in the way we should worship God. The Lord, who is our Shepherd, is the Maker of heaven and earth. This truth keeps appearing in the Psalms (such as 33; 95; 100), as well as the Revelation of John (4:11), passages intended to shape and describe solid worship. In worship God calls his people into his presence, so that he can cleanse their hearts, renew their love for him, and refresh their vision of reality. The bit of reality that this teaching makes us mindful of is that this world of sound, sight, and sense is not all there is: God is the one who made it, who rules it, and who has power to keep his promises to his people.

Second, this teaching about creation helps us to put moral obedience in its true perspective. If God made us, then he also set the goal of our existence—a loving relationship with him and with one another. Now we could just say that God our Maker has the right to tell us how to live; but we would do better to take this further like the Bible does. He knows us, he knows what we need, he knows how we can achieve our purpose: which means that obedience to his moral commands is good sense. As C. S. Lewis observed,

> I am afraid that is the sort of idea that the word Morality raises in a good many people's minds: something that interferes, something that stops you having a good time. In reality, moral rules are directions for running the human machine.

And these directions come straight from the Maker.

Third, this teaching reminds us that God's creation was good (and, as we'll see, is still good). Sex, eating, owning things—these are good, and God made them to be enjoyed. Again as Lewis noted,

> There is no good trying to be more spiritual than God. God never meant man to be a purely spiritual creature. That is why he uses material things like bread and wine to put the new life into us. We may think this rather crude and unspiritual. God does not: He invented eating. He likes matter. He invented it.

This of course reinforces what I just said about morality, namely, that God's will tells us the right way to express our God-given desires for sex, food, and comfort—and sometimes this means *not* expressing them. But: if we have to forego the use of some things (and we all at times *do*), it's not because *they're* bad, but because *we* are. Nevertheless, though obedience may seem painful to us, it's never harmful.

Remembering that the creation is good also tells us that enjoying and studying that creation is a worthy task. We will see in later chapters that when God said he wanted man to rule, that meant he wanted us to rule with understanding (which means that knowledge is possible) as well as with kindness (which means that man is to be a steward of his environment).

Many of the pioneers of modern science were English clergymen; they referred to science as a fit subject for a Sabbath day—meaning that thinking about God's creation was a kind of private worship, one that complemented the public worship of the Sabbath. The hymn writer Folliott Pierpoint captured the Christian spirit well in these verses:

> For the beauty of the earth,
> for the glory of the skies,
> for the love which from our birth
> over and around us lies,
> Lord of all, to thee we raise this our hymn of grateful praise.
>
> For the beauty of each hour
> of the day and of the night,
> hill and vale, and tree and flower,
> sun and moon and stars of light,
> Lord of all, to thee we raise this our hymn of grateful praise.
>
> For the joy of ear and eye,
> for the heart and mind's delight,
> for the mystic harmony
> linking sense to sound and sight,
> Lord of all, to thee we raise this our hymn of grateful praise. . . .
>
> For each perfect gift of thine
> to our race so freely given,
> graces human and divine,
> flowers of earth and buds of heaven,
> Lord of all, to thee we raise this our hymn of grateful praise.

God made his world to be a place for us to enjoy as we love and serve him.

5

What Kind of Days Were Those, Anyhow?

Preliminaries: The Key Issues At Stake

This chapter—really, this book—got its beginning the day our friend Annette phoned us with a question: she was home-schooling as we were, and was about to teach her daughter about the earth and solar system, the dinosaurs, and so on. But what, she wanted to know, ought she to say? All Christians must sooner or later face this kind of question—what should they think of the standard "scientific" story of earth history? Is their faith in conflict with that story?

To begin our answer, we have to decide what we believe about the days in Genesis 1, and that is what this chapter is about. (Other chapters will fill out the rest of the answer.)

I must confess that writing this chapter makes me nervous. Up to now I have been self-consciously writing as a spokesman for conservative Christians in general. Now, however, I have to take up a topic that divides Christians into opposing camps.

It is mostly Protestants who dispute over the days. Because of the influence of Augustine (mentioned in the last chapter, and we'll come back to him soon), Roman Catholics don't usually have a problem taking the days as a figure of some kind. *The Catholic Study Bible* says in its note at Genesis 1:5,

> According to the highly artificial literary structure of Gn 1,1—2,4a, God's creative activity is divided into six days to teach the sacredness of the sabbath rest on the seventh day in the Israelite religion (Gn 2,2f).

Nevertheless, all those who want to use the Bible to form their thinking about science and faith—Protestants, Orthodox, and Catholics alike—must work this question through.

Many Bible-readers say that we must take the days as ordinary days; they usually add that it follows that the Bible teaches that the earth is relatively young (from about 6,000 to 100,000 years). They think that failure to read the account this way—what they are sure is the "plain sense" of the passage—compromises the authority of Scripture. (Some of them, as we'll see, go on to say that it gives away the historicity of this account, but also of many other passages as well—and even calls the deity of Jesus into question.) They believe that you need to hold to this interpretation in order to have a credible opposition to modern materialist science.

On another side are those who think that to use this passage for any "scientific" purpose is to misuse the passage altogether. By this view, the Genesis "literalists" (as they call them) not only abuse good modern science but also twist the biblical text itself.

Now throw into the mix those who don't think the days are the ordinary kind, and who are willing to allow that the earth is old like the scientists say—but who reject some scientific theories (and I'm especially thinking about evolutionary biology here).

But the problem is even worse than that: the different sides don't even agree on just what principles we can use to decide the matter: the "non-literalists" typically appeal to the sciences—especially geology and cosmology—and want to harmonize the Bible and science. Those who favor the "ordinary day" interpretation, on the other hand, say that any appeal to scientific data or theories fails to give the biblical text its rightful place of authority. In their minds, all modern sciences are under suspicion of having fallen prey to a naturalistic worldview—a worldview that finds its fullest expression in evolutionary theory.

So you can see that loads of strongly held premises underlie the different positions. I don't agree with the way many "ordinary day" folk denounce all modern sciences, nor do I agree with them that we must exclude scientific conclusions if we want to be faithful to the Bible; nevertheless I will focus on the evidence of Genesis 1–2 itself for my study. But we all owe it to one another to show how the various components of our arguments (data, premises, and so on) operate.

Here is how I will proceed in this chapter. First, I will list the features of the biblical text that our interpretation has to account for. Second, I will outline an interpretation that accounts for all of these features. And third, I will describe the wide variety of interpretive schemes that are "out there" and show why I think they fail.

Let's dispense with a few arguments that some have offered to support the ordinary day position. The first is the claim that since the vast majority of readers in the history of the church have held that the days are ordinary, so should we—to do otherwise would be unbearable arrogance. The problem with this argument is that it assumes that the "vast majority" are right, regardless of the reasons that led to their reading. After the first century, very few Christians read Hebrew at all, until about 1500; this means that this "vast majority" arrived at their reading of Genesis on the basis of the Greek Old Testament in the Eastern church, and the Latin Old Testament in the West. These translations are good in some places and bad in others, and our "vast majority" didn't have the resources to know which is which. Besides, when we consider that some of the best and brightest—such as Augustine, Anselm, and possibly Aquinas—did *not* take the days as the ordinary kind, we realize that the key question is not, "How many people read it this way?" but, "What reasons did they have for their reading?"

A second faulty argument for the ordinary day reading of the days is the claim that this is in fact the "literal" reading of the text. The trouble with that is nailing down just what we mean by "literal." In ordinary speech, to "take something literally" usually means to read it in its most physical terms, without appealing to figures of speech. For example, we say that it can't "literally" rain cats and dogs. From this it is only a short step to saying that if the days are not "literal," then they're poetic or metaphorical—which, to many, means they didn't happen. But in theology, the word "literal" has a special meaning: namely it refers to interpreting a Bible text in the sense that the author intended, as opposed to, say, the allegorical sense. That is the only meaning of the word "literal" that should carry any weight with us—"the sense the author intended." That of course puts no limits beforehand on whether the passage has in it any metaphors or other figures of speech. (Current usage adds to the confusion: now people say "literally" when they mean "in the strongest possible sense," so it *is* now possible to say "literally raining cats and dogs"!)

This means that I should bend my efforts to finding out what a good reader from the original culture would have seen in the story. Let me show you why this is different from what can be called a "literalistic" reading, which means asking, "What would I mean if *I* used those words?" One day when my son was six, he was coloring pictures in the family room. I heard him start whimpering so I asked him what was wrong. He said, "They shouldn't have labeled this a 'washable marker.' It's not." He had colored a spot with the wrong marker, so he wet a sponge to rub the blotch off his picture—and ended up wearing a hole right through the paper. He read "washable" in terms of what *he* would have meant, namely, you can wash it off the paper. The manufacturer, of course, meant you could wash it off your skin or clothing. My son, the literalist.

So we have to make a distinction between what the author of a text meant, and our interpretation of that author. (Actually, my son's experience also shows the importance of testing our interpretation against the real world. I am sure that the manufacturer meant the label to apply to the real world; and when my son's experience didn't match what he expected, he should have rethought his interpretation before declaring the text untrue. This is a good example of the *coordination* we talked about in chapter 3.)

A third faulty argument is related to the second: the claim that "the doctrine of the clarity of Scripture" is at stake. That is, the Bible must be transparent in its meaning, and this favors the "simple" reading. This argument is faulty because it actually misuses the doctrine it is supposedly upholding. I know of no responsible statement of this doctrine that claims that all parts of the Bible are equally easy to understand, or that we should prefer a "simple" reading no matter what. The clarity of Scripture is typically a Protestant doctrine; and here is how the English Puritans framed it in their *Westminster Confession of Faith:*

> All things in Scripture are not alike plain in themselves, nor alike clear unto all: yet those things which are necessary to be known, believed, and observed for salvation, are so clearly propounded, and opened in some place of Scripture or other, that not only the learned, but the unlearned, in a due use of the ordinary means, may attain unto a sufficient understanding of them.

You see that these Puritans were confident that we would find that the parts of the Bible that we need to understand and believe in order to be saved and to live well are clear. Furthermore, they don't deny that you may have to study and think to get to a right understanding—that's what they mean by "a due use of the ordinary means." The reason we have to study it out, of course, is that when someone says it's supposed to be "clear," we should right away ask, "Clear to whom?" And the right answer to that, as I argued above, is "To the original audience, and to those who share their reading competence."

That's why we have to distinguish between what the author meant, and *my* first impression from reading his work. We have to take a part of a text in the light of the whole—we should expect it to be consistent with its whole context. (So you'll see why, for example, I think we need to read Genesis 1:1–2:3 in the light of Genesis 2:4-7.) More broadly, we want to look for something consistent with the Bible as a whole.

A fourth false claim is the idea that Christians changed their interpretation of the days in order to make peace with Darwinism. As a matter of fact, most of the major interpretive options came into play before 1850—and Darwin's *Origin of Species* came out in 1859. The big factor for many in the church was the new geology that began in the late 1700s, which seemed to most to prove that the earth was much older than a few thousand years. And if someone wants to make the counterclaim, "You see, that just proves that geology is naturalistic, too," he has to come to grips with the simple fact that most of the early geologists were devout Christians who were far from being naturalistic. (That doesn't make them right: I am only trying to clear away false arguments so we can go at this with cool heads.)

Let's get something out in the open: it is certainly true that the attraction of many of the non-ordinary day views is, at least at first, the possibility of not having a conflict with scientific theories about the beginning of the universe or the age of the earth. Saying this does not make these views right or wrong. But we do need to lower the rhetorical temperature when we talk about it. For example, Charles Hodge (1797–1878), a very conservative Presbyterian theologian of the nineteenth century, wrote the following:

> It is of course admitted that, taking [the Genesis creation] account by itself, it would be most natural to understand the word ["day"] in its ordinary sense; but if that sense brings the Mosaic account into conflict with facts, and another sense avoids such conflict, then it is obligatory on us to adopt that other. . . . The Church has been forced more than once to alter her interpretation of the Bible to accommodate the discoveries of science. But this has been done without doing any violence to the Scriptures or in any degree impairing their authority.

It may be that Hodge was too optimistic about whether the geological theories of his day were the same as "facts"; it may also be that he made a mistake about whether this harmonization did any "violence" to the Bible—I'm not commenting on either at this point. (As you will see, I do dissent from his view of what happens when you "take the creation account by itself.") But let's never lose sight of the main thing: he favored harmony because he thought the biblical account was true, and he thought the Bible could be read this way without trouble. His understanding of the Bible also led him to approach science as a "critical realist." (My son with his "washable marker" should have done the same: assume that the maker wanted his label to correspond to the world of experience.)

FEATURES OF GENESIS 1–2 THAT WE MUST ACCOUNT FOR

My purpose in this section is to gather the data. I aim to find an interpretation of the days that accounts for all of the details of the text, and that does so without having to invent new grammar or to stretch word meanings. Those details of the text are the data I'm after here.

Let's start with some things that we already mentioned in the last chapter. In that chapter I showed why I think the first story is 1:1–2:3, and I laid out the flow of the story as follows:

1:1-2	Preface (background actions and information)
1:3-5	Day 1 (light and darkness)
1:6-8	Day 2 (sea and sky)
1:9-13	Day 3 (land, sea, vegetation)
1:14-19	Day 4 (light-bearers)
1:20-23	Day 5 (sea animals and flying creatures)
1:24-31	Day 6 (land animals and humans)—*the longest day*
2:1-3	Day 7 (rest and enjoyment)—*no refrain*

I also argued that the first day begins in 1:3, and that 1:1-2 is background information. The reason I gave was that each day begins with "and God said . . ." (I could have added that verse 3 is the first place the normal Hebrew narrative tense appears, but I'm trying to keep technical stuff to a minimum.) I concluded that this means that Moses describes the initial creation of everything in verse 1, which happened some unspecified time before the beginning of the first day. Then verse 2, "The earth was without form and void, and darkness was over the face of the deep. And the Spirit of God was hovering over the face of the waters," tells us what the conditions were on the earth as the "creation week" got under way. We must decide, therefore, if Moses means for us to see the creation week as the first week of the whole universe.

We have already noticed that each of the six workdays has the refrain, "and there was evening and there was morning, the *n*th day," while the refrain is missing from the seventh day. We will need to understand the meaning of this refrain, and the meaning of its absence from day seven.

We have seen that the Sabbath commandment of Exodus 20:8-11 bases the human workweek on God's workweek in the creation narrative. I have also argued that the way the commandment refers to the six days ("over the course of six days"), together with the march of the numbered days in Genesis, seems to suggest that the creation week consists of periods of time following one after another.

Beyond these things I have already touched on, there are three new items for us to consider. The first is to look in more detail at how 2:4-7 helps us to harmonize the stories of 1:1–2:3 and 2:5-25, and what follows from that. The second is how 1:14-19 (the fourth day) describes the heavenly lights: is this telling us about their *creation* or about something else? And the third is the way the Bible refers to the creation account in Exodus 20:11 and 31:17—these passages say that human work and rest is *like* God's work and rest. We have to find out just what kind of likeness Moses had in mind.

An Interpretation That Accounts for All of These Features

The fact that 1:1-2 is not part of the first day tells us that we don't have to take the creation week as the first "week" of the universe. This is not at all surprising in view of what I said about the purpose of the creation story, to describe how God prepared the earth as the ideal place for humans to live, love, and serve. The rest of the universe has a part in all that—the heavenly lights mark off the days and "seasons" (literally, "appointed times"; probably the seasons in the liturgical year)—but just how and when they took their form doesn't matter much to Moses' main picture. This means that, however we interpret the days, we have no obligation to read Moses as claiming that God began his creative work of the first day at the very beginning of the universe—or even at the very beginning of the earth. This tells us that some lengths of time don't matter to the story.

What are we supposed to conclude from the refrain, "and there was evening and there was morning, the *n*th day"? We had better notice one thing right off the bat: the order, evening followed by morning. When my son was memorizing Genesis 1:31 at the age of seven, he commented, "Isn't it supposed to be 'and there was morning and there was evening'?" He was exactly right: the order is unusual and begs us to pay attention.

Many have thought that this has something to do with the Jewish way of reckoning a day so that it runs from evening to evening. But how can it, when it only mentions evening followed by morning? Others have taken this as defining the extent of the "day": but how does that make any sense when the order is evening *followed by* morning? (Those who read the King James Bible, "and the evening and the morning were the *n*th day," have a real problem here: but, as I said before, this is a mistranslation, and modern versions have fixed it. Besides, how can an evening followed by a morning make up a day?)

So what is the significance of evening followed by morning in the ancient Hebrew world? Quite simply, it's in what falls between them, the night-time—in fact, Numbers 9:15-16 practically defines the night as the period between evening and morning, when the appearance of fire would be over the tabernacle. And what is the significance of the night-time? It's when the worker takes his daily rest: as Psalm 104:23 puts it, at sunrise "man goes out to his work and to his labor until the evening" (compare also Gen. 30:16; Ex. 18:13). This daily rest in Israel looks forward to the weekly Sabbath rest.

And what shall we make of the *absence* of the refrain on the seventh day (2:1-3)? Absence can tell us a lot; in one Sherlock Holmes story, he directs someone's attention "to the curious incident of the dog in the night-time." To the reply, "But the dog did nothing in the night-time," Holmes answers, "That was the curious incident." Now this absence does in fact draw attention to itself: as I have already argued, 2:4 introduces a new story—which, as I will argue below, is an expansion of the sixth day of chapter 1. This means that we might reasonably expect Moses to round off the first story by telling us about the end of the seventh day. That is, we might expect it if the days are ordinary ones, and if that seventh day came to an end. But supposing the seventh day didn't end—what then? Why, then there would be no refrain.

This leads me to consider the possibility that Moses wanted us to think that the seventh day had no end—that we are right now living in God's Sabbath. And I find this shedding light on a couple of passages from the New Testament, John 5:17 and Hebrews 4:3-11. In John 5, Jesus heals a man on the Sabbath, which gets him in trouble with the authorities (for healing, a kind of "work," on the Sabbath, v. 16). In reply Jesus says (v. 17), "My Father is working still, and I am working." If we want Jesus' saying to make sense, we should take it as "My Father is working on *his* Sabbath, just as I am working on *my* Sabbath"; and we can account for that most easily if we take Jesus to mean that the creation Sabbath still goes on.

This notion also helps us make sense of Hebrews 4:3-11. In verse 3 the author quotes Psalm 95:11 to the effect that unbelievers in Israel will not enter God's "rest"—and then in verse 4 he notes that God "rested" on the seventh day (referring to Gen. 2:2). In verse 8 he denies that Joshua gave the Israelites the "rest" of which he speaks, in order to keep us from taking Psalm 95:11 literalistically—the psalm is based on a historical occasion when people who left Egypt were now forbidden to enter the promised land. Instead, there is a Sabbath rest for God's people to enter: they enter God's "rest" by "resting from their works" as God did from his (v. 10). This makes good sense if "God's rest," which he entered on the creation Sabbath, is the same "rest" that believers enter—and thus God's rest is still available because it still continues.

Augustine wrote about this in his *Confessions:* God's creation Sabbath "has no evening and has no ending; you sanctified it to abide everlastingly." If the seventh day is not an ordinary one, then we may begin to wonder if perhaps the other six days have to be ordinary.

We are getting somewhere, and the other features I mentioned above lead us in the same direction. Let's go on to the Sabbath commandment, Exodus 20:8-11:

> [8] "Remember the Sabbath day, to keep it holy. [9] Six days you shall labor, and do all your work, [10] but the seventh day is a Sabbath to the LORD your God. On it you shall not do any work, you, or your son, or your daughter, your male servant, or your female servant, or your livestock, or the sojourner who is within your gates. [11] For in six days the LORD made heaven and earth, the sea, and all that is in them, and rested the seventh day. Therefore the LORD blessed the Sabbath day and made it holy."

(Some churches call this the third commandment, others the fourth. Churches also disagree on how this commandment applies to Christians. I won't get into any of those things here.) In this commandment God tells the Israelites to keep the Sabbath day holy, working for six days and resting on the seventh (along with all their households). The reason is the pattern God set in his creation week: he worked for six days and rested on the seventh. Many of the Hebrew expressions match directly to those found in Genesis 2:2-3—such as the reference to doing work, to blessing the seventh day and making it holy—so it's clear that the commandment and the narrative are connected. Now, some will say that this proves that God's workweek was six ordinary days—otherwise how could it be a pattern for a *human* workweek? But this misses two key points: the first is what we have already noticed about the creation rest being unique. The second is that our working and resting cannot be *identical* to God's—they are *like* God's in some way, but certainly not the same. For example, when was the last time you spoke and caused a plant to grow up? Rather, our planting and watering and fertilizing are like God's work because they operate on what's there and make it produce something it wouldn't have produced otherwise. Our rest is like God's, because we cease from our work for the sake of contemplating his works with pleasure.

This comes out when we look at another place where the Lord (through Moses) speaks of his Sabbath rest, Exodus 31:17. After insisting that the people of Israel keep the Sabbath, the Lord in verse 17 calls the Sabbath "a sign forever . . . that in six days the LORD made heaven and earth, and on the seventh day he rested and was refreshed." That last word in Hebrew, "was refreshed," carries the sense of getting your breath back after being worn out (see Ex. 23:12; 2 Sam. 16:14); and I can assure you that you don't want to say that God needs that kind of refreshment (see Isa. 40:28-31—God doesn't get weary). Instead we have to see it as an *analogy:* there are points of similarity between the two things, but also points of difference. (When we say "the eyes of the Lord," we don't mean he has a body with eyeballs in his head: instead we use this way of talking about how God knows everything and searches everywhere, with nothing hidden from him.) The point of similarity, the analogy, is the fact that during the creation week God was "working on" the earth to make it just right for man to live on, and this included the creative production of new things (such as plants and animals and man). In his Sabbath he is no longer doing this, but now keeps it all in being. (That doesn't rule out special works of God such as miracles and personal relationships—but we'll take that up in our chapter on providence and miracles.) It follows from this that length of time has no bearing on the analogy.

We have one last issue to address before we can draw all this together. That is the passage I partly discussed in the previous chapter, Genesis 2:5-7. These verses are the key to bringing the two stories, 1:1–2:3 and 2:5-25, together. I cannot put too much stress on why this matters. You see, we can't just read 1:1–2:3 on its own; it's part of a context, namely chapters 1–3 (and then the larger context of chapters 1–11, and then the book of Genesis, and then the Bible as a whole), and it has to fit into its context. In the NASB (compare RV) these verses read:

> [5] Now no shrub of the field was yet in the earth, and no plant of the field had yet sprouted, for the LORD God had not sent rain upon the earth, and there was no man to cultivate the ground. [6] But a mist used to rise from the earth and water the whole surface of the ground. [7] Then the LORD God formed man of dust from the ground, and breathed into his nostrils the breath of life; and man became a living being.

Now this creates a problem if we try to follow the lead of verse 4 and harmonize the two narratives 1:1–2:3 and 2:5-25 (as I argued in the previous chapter). The problem has two parts: first, it's out of step with the sequence of the days in the first story: there, God made the plants on the third day, as we find in 1:11-12:

> [11] And God said, "Let the earth sprout vegetation, plants yielding seed, and fruit trees bearing fruit in which is their seed, each according to its kind, on the earth." And it was so. [12] The earth brought forth vegetation, plants yielding seed according to their own kinds, and trees bearing fruit in which is their seed, each according to its kind. And God saw that it was good.

Now, in 2:5-6, it looks like the plants don't exist on the sixth day (when God forms the man). The second part of the problem is that 2:5-6 says that those plants weren't there because it hadn't yet rained (which is the "ordinary providence" reason for plants not being there), while Genesis 1 has them being created (which is a special situation).

So we have three options: we can (1) give up on harmonization; (2) give up on finding sequence in the days (the "literary framework" approach); or (3) look again at the Hebrew to see if we have understood it right to begin with. I don't like option (1) because, as I have said, I think verse 4 invites us to harmonize. I don't like option (2) because, as I argued in the last chapter, I think the days do have a sequence. So I prefer to try option (3) before being forced to reconsider my earlier conclusions.

The ESV of these verses provides the opening we need to argue for option (3). In that version we read,

> [5] When no bush of the field was yet in the land and no small plant of the field had yet sprung up—for the LORD God had not caused it to rain on the land, and there was no man to work the ground, [6] and a mist was going up from the land and was watering the whole face of the ground—[7] then the LORD God formed the man of dust from the ground and breathed into his nostrils the breath of life, and the man became a living creature.

Now the main difference between the ESV and the NASB—both claiming to be fairly literal translations—is that the word rendered "land" in the ESV of verses 5-6 ("was yet in the *land* . . . rain on the *land* . . . going up from the *land*") is rendered "earth" in the NASB. This Hebrew word can refer to the earth as a whole (as in 1:1-2), the region of dry land (1:10), or some particular region (as in 2:11-13). How can we decide between the two versions?

We find our first bit of help in the climate of the Middle East. In Palestine it doesn't rain during the summer, and the autumn rains bring about a burst of plant growth. So verses 5-7 would make good sense if we supposed that they describe a time of year, when it has been a dry summer, so the plants aren't growing—but the rains and the man are about to come, so the plants will be able to grow in the "land." You'll notice that verse 5 puts things in terms of what we can call "ordinary providence"—that is, the way that we're used to seeing things work. (The plants are missing, it says, because there's no rain, and no man to cultivate and irrigate—something you can see in any uninhabited area in the Middle East.) The only way that I can make any sense out of this ordinary providence explanation that the Bible itself gives is if I imagine that the cycle of rain, plant growth, and dry season had been going on for some number of years before this point—because the text says nothing about God not yet having made the plants.

We find the next bit of help we need in the fact that verses 5-6 are the setting for the events of verse 7. If we take the word "land" as "some particular land," we get a clear picture for verses 5-8: in some particular land, in some particular year, at the time of year before the rainy season began, but when the mist (or rain cloud) was rising (which may suggest the beginning of the rainy season)—that's when God formed the first human, planted the Garden of Eden, and transplanted the man there. (By the way, that also explains why ESV "a mist *was going up*" is better than NASB "a mist *used to rise.*")

Does that solve our problem? You bet it does! First, it shows us that the events of 2:5-25 happened on the sixth day of chapter 1. Second, it shows us that this is an expansion of the chapter 1 account of the sixth day—for example, 1:27 gives us the creation of the first man and the first woman together ("so God created man in his own image . . . male and female he created them"), while 2:7, 21-22 presents some amount of time between the two creations (God forms the man in v. 7, and after a while, in vv. 21-22, he makes the man sleep and shapes a rib into the woman). Third, it means we shouldn't confuse anything in 2:5-6 with the third day of chapter 1. And fourth, if we are to follow the lead of the way Moses has narrated these details—especially the bit about the cycle of seasons going on for some time—then we have to say that the length of the creation week could not have been an ordinary week: it must have been longer.

You might try to salvage the ordinary day reading of Genesis 1 by accepting the ESV rendering of 2:5-7, but suggesting that either the plants described there were different from those of 1:11-12, or that when God made the plants grow on the third day he left the particular region barren where he was to make the man. But I don't see that either of these suggestions will work. First, 1:11-12 describes the vegetation as consisting of two broad types: the lower growing varieties ("plants yielding seed") and the taller ones ("fruit trees bearing fruit in which is their seed"). This means that the plants in 2:5 ("bush of the field" and "small plant of the field") are included in the vegetation. Second, 2:5 gives us an explicit reason why the plants had not yet sprouted in the region, one that invites us to think in terms of the seasonal cycles.

Another reason not to follow this attempt to rescue the ordinary day reading is the peculiar nature of the sixth day (as many have noticed). That is, God makes the land animals, forms Adam, plants the Garden and moves the man there, lays instructions upon him, puts him through a search for "a helper fit for him" (and during this search Adam names all the animals), casts a deep sleep over him and makes a woman out of his rib. No doubt the first man was a genius, but we all still expect this to take a fair bit of time. The way the man responds in verse 23, "this *at last*" (ESV, which is a better rendering of the Hebrew than NASB "this is now"), confirms our impression of a long wait. All of this supports the view that the creation period is longer than an ordinary week. So this salvage operation fails—but, as I intend to show, that failure yields such gains that we'll be glad it failed.

So, as I said, we should take the creation week as having been longer than an ordinary week. The only ways for that to be true are if the days aren't ordinary days, or if the days have spaces of time between them.

And how should we decide which of these alternatives to follow? I think that the picture I found earlier, namely the way the account portrays God as if he were a workman going through his workweek, clears it up. On each day he works, then rests for the night; and then on his Sabbath, he rests in full enjoyment of his achievements. Similarly, in 2:7, where God "forms" the man, it's as if he were a potter working in clay.

If we put all of these things together, we see that the best explanation is the one that takes these days as not the ordinary kind; they are instead "God's workdays." Our workdays are not identical to them, but analogous. The purpose of the analogy is to set a pattern for the human rhythm of work and rest. The length of these days is not relevant to this purpose, but we have to conclude from Genesis 2:5-7 that some of them (at least) were longer than our ordinary days. How much longer we can't say, except that days 1-5 have to add up to a fair number of years in order to establish the seasonal cycle seen in 2:5-7.

I call this the "analogical days" interpretation. I claim that this interpretation accounts for the details of Genesis, and for how the rest of the Bible refers to this account. It also gives you tight agreement between the first story (1:1–2:3) and the second (2:4-25) by showing that the second amplifies just day six. Later in this chapter I will argue that none of the other interpretive schemes gets you this much. And if the only price you have to pay for all these benefits is to give up ordinary days—well, that's not too bad, is it?

WHAT ABOUT THE FOURTH DAY?

One feature of the text that I haven't dealt with yet is what happens on the fourth day: namely, that it seems that on this day God *creates* the sun, moon, and stars, even though he created *light* on the first day (v. 3). I bring this up because throughout history people have noticed this as a difficulty to be solved. I used the word "seems" on purpose: it may seem so to the English reader, but not necessarily to the Hebrew reader.

To begin with, you'll note that it doesn't say God *created* these things in any of the verses: in verse 3 God says, "Let there be light," and in verse 14 he says "Let there be light-bearers." (Our translations say "lights" in verse 14 to bring out this distinction.) This doesn't have to mean that they did not exist before, only that they are to come into view now. My evidence for this claim is the fact that the same Hebrew verb form translated, "Let there be," can be used in the phrase "*May* the Lord *be* with you" (as in 1 Sam. 20:13 and elsewhere)—and this doesn't suggest that he wasn't with you before. Likewise, "*Let* your steadfast love . . . *be* upon us" (Ps. 33:22; compare 90:17; 119:76) hardly means that it wasn't there before. In the same vein, Genesis 1:16 says that God "made" the great lights; and this Hebrew word doesn't need to mean that they didn't exist before—in fact it can mean "he worked on" something that was there already, or even just "he appointed." That is, "he *made*" is not the same as "he *created.*"

This is helpful when we remember that the lights in Genesis 1:14 are for marking "seasons"—actually, these are "appointed times" (ESV margin), when special worship celebrations are to be held (as in Ex. 13:10 and elsewhere). That is, these lights have the purpose of marking out the human calendar of worshiping God. The idea is that, whenever these actually began to be, from now on they have a particular purpose for mankind.

With this in mind, I think we can take the "Let there be light" of the first day to be God's summoning the "dawn" of the first "day," and the fourth day involves God appointing the heavenly lights to mark the set times for worship on man's calendar. This may well involve some kind of "creative" activity (and I think that it does); but even then it doesn't say that God brought these things into being at these particular times.

If we take it this way, we are relieved of a difficulty that many have tried to explain in ways that I find awkward. For example, we don't have to suppose that there was some other source of light than the sun before the first day, when Genesis says nothing of the sort. We also don't have to suppose that the sun, moon, and stars *appeared* on the fourth day as the cloud cover cleared, when Genesis says nothing about a cloud cover. We don't have to suppose that the days are not in sequence—that day four cannot be *after* day three (when plants began to grow).

Other Possible Interpretations of the Days

In this section I want to outline some of the other main interpretations of the days that are out there, and to say briefly why I don't think they work.

Of course the most common view is that these days are ordinary ones—maybe not all twenty-four hours exactly (some have thought the first day was thirty-six hours, for example), but basically ordinary. The main problems with this position are, first, it doesn't allow us to harmonize Genesis 1:1–2:3 with 2:4-25, because it cannot account for the way Genesis 2:5 says the plants hadn't grown since it hadn't yet rained. Part of one ordinary week is too short a time for this explanation to be meaningful. The second problem is that I think the overall picture of the days is analogical anyhow, just as human work and rest are analogous to God's work and rest.

Another view of historical importance is the notion that the creation week was instantaneous. This seems to have been the position of Augustine, and it derives from his interpretation of Sirach (Ecclesiasticus) 18:1, which, as we have seen already, he mistakenly took to mean, "he who lives forever created all things at once." Since God's action doesn't require any length of time, he reasoned, it must be that Moses broke the account out in days so that we could understand it. It's possible that the eminent Greek theologians Clement of Alexandria (about 150–215) and Athanasius (296–373) provided early versions of this view, but Augustine is the one who developed it. The profound theologian Anselm (1033–1109) was under its influence, and Thomas Aquinas (1225–1274) respected it but doesn't seem to have held it.

In the last chapter I gave my reasons for thinking instead that the account describes some length and sequence of time, and therefore for rejecting Augustine's view.

When the "new geology" arose in the late 1700s, two views became prominent with the aim of harmonizing the Bible and geology. The first is called the "gap theory": God made everything at the beginning, and then, some unspecified length of time later, Satan rebelled. As a result, "the earth *became* without form and void," as they argue Genesis 1:2 should read. Then the six days of the creation week—usually taken to be ordinary days—are the *re*-making of the earth after this rebellion. This view was especially prominent in the first half of the nineteenth century, but is fairly rare since then. The Scofield Reference Bible (1909) in its notes argued for a combination of this view and the next, the day-age view. The fatal weakness of the gap theory is the grammar of Genesis 1:2: it doesn't say what the gap theory needs it to say, because (1) it doesn't describe an event but a condition, and (2) the verb "was" cannot be made to mean "became" (for which there is a proper Hebrew expression).

The other view that became popular after the rise of the new geology, the "day-age" view, actually seems to have had its start before the new geology—in the 1600s in the English-speaking world. By this view the days are long ages. The arguments for this position include the fact that the Hebrew word "day" can have several meanings, such as "day-time," "period of twenty-four hours," and "period of undetermined length." Those who favor this view think that the third sense should be taken here; and some will add that, after all, "with the Lord one day is as a thousand years, and a thousand years is as one day" (2 Pet. 3:8; compare Ps. 90:4). Many of the advocates point to Genesis 2:4, "in the *day* that the LORD God made earth and the heavens," as evidence for this extended sense of "day" right here in this passage. This position was very common among conservative Christians in the nineteenth century and is still popular today. Probably the most visible advocate of this view now is the Canadian-born physicist-turned-evangelist Hugh Ross.

I think the chief problem with this position is what it does with "day": in other places, when the third sense of "day" is used, you find some qualifying expression like "the day *of the Lord*" or "the day *of wrath*." Nothing like that shows up in Genesis, and that means we have none of the normal signals for the third sense of "day." (Genesis 2:4 uses "in the day" as part of a special idiom, so it doesn't help us with the numbered days.) Besides, the day-age view became popular because it seemed to offer a nice concordance with the geological story; but (1) it's hard to believe that the biblical account and the geological account have common purposes, so harmonization is questionable; (2) it leaves us wondering what we are to do if the geological story gets revised; and (3) some think the harmonization isn't all that close anyhow.

Another view with a similar motivation to the day-age theory, which aims to avoid its problems with the word "day," is called the "intermittent day" theory. In this scheme the days are ordinary days where God was busy creating, with periods of unspecified length separating the days. This makes the days normal and consecutive: but the total creative period is longer than an ordinary week. The chief advocates of this view today are Robert Newman and Herman Eckelmann, who wrote *Genesis One and the Origin of the Earth* in 1977. I consider this view a strong possibility if only the harmony of the two stories in Genesis 1–2 is the issue, as I said above; but I don't think it does full justice to the analogical portrayal of God's workweek, so I don't think it will do. I also think that the level of harmonization it seeks with the geological story gives it the same weaknesses as I mentioned under the day-age view.

The last group of interpretive schemes I'll discuss is the "literary framework view." I consider this a group of views, unified by the idea that the days are primarily a literary structuring device to describe the creation week, and not necessarily told in the order of events. Part of the argument for this is the apparent creation of the sun, moon, and stars on the fourth day, while there was light on the first day. This is taken as evidence that Moses wasn't trying to describe the events in the order in which they actually happened. Another part of the argument is the apparent "disagreement" on the sequence of creation between Genesis 2:5-6 and Genesis 1—that is, if you take 2:5 as referring to plants on the *earth,* and hence day six (the making of man, 2:7) overlaps with day three (the making of plants).

Some scholars stop there and say that order of events and length of time aren't part of what Moses intended for you to get out of the story. Others, influenced by Meredith Kline, go further: they notice that we have careful structuring in the account, as we already noticed in the last chapter. You have days 1-3 describing the locations, and days 4-6 describing the inhabitants of the locations:

Location	*Inhabitants*
1. light and dark	4. lights of day and night
2. sea and sky	5. animals of water and air
3. fertile earth	6. land animals (including humans)

7. Rest and enjoyment

In Kline's developed view, the matching is there to tell us that days one and four are really the same events viewed from different angles; likewise days two and five, and days three and six. Kline and those who follow him strongly defend historicity for this story, but they don't think historicity and exact narrative sequence are the same thing. Some others who hold a version of the framework view think that Moses didn't care about sequence but also didn't narrate "history." By their understanding, then, we cannot find any record of these events in geology or paleontology, because the story and the science are complementary only: the real purpose of the story was to assert that the LORD was the Creator, and that the gods of the nations were powerless nothings.

I have already given most of the reasons I don't hold to the framework view. To begin with, I think the way the story describes the days, with the first, second, third, up to the seventh, implies that they followed one after the other. I think as well that the Sabbath commandment, with its "over the course of six days," implies that we have six separate days that follow one another (allowing for analogy, of course). Then, I don't see the fourth day as describing the *creation* of the heavenly lights. I have also shown how the two stories in Genesis 1–2 actually fit quite well together when we understand 2:4-7 properly. In the section on "history" in the last chapter, I showed why I agree with those who find this account to be "historical," and not with those who don't. (I do agree with Kline, by the way, that historicity and exact narrative sequence are not the same thing.)

COMPARING THE DIFFERENT VIEWS

These different interpretations of the six days of Genesis 1 have points in common as well as points of difference. For example, conservatives who hold to the ordinary day view, the day-age view, the framework view, the analogical days view, the intermittent days view, and the gap view, all agree that we can call Genesis 1 "historical" (in the sense I defined it above). The "instantaneous creation" view would probably not use that word, except as it applies to the initial creation from nothing.

The ordinary day, day-age, analogical day, intermittent day, and gap views all see the days as following one after another, while the framework view sees sequence in the days as optional at best. The ordinary day, day-age, intermittent day, and gap views take sequence very strictly, while the analogical days view allows for more reserve about it (and hence is more cautious about strict harmonization with geology).

My version of the analogical day view takes Genesis 1:1 as the initial creation, with an unknown amount of time between that and the start of the first day. This may sound like the gap view, which also has a "gap" between the first creation and the creation week. The differences, though, are striking. For example, the gap view holds that during the gap Satan led a revolt that brought the creation into a condition of chaos. My view says nothing of the sort: the formlessness and emptiness are not bad, just incomplete. Further, the gap view needs the gap to be a long one; my view says the Bible gives us no information on how long it was.

A big difference between the day-age and analogical day views is what they do for the meaning of the word "day." The day-age view appeals to the sense "period of undefined length," while the analogical days view takes the word in its ordinary meaning, but applies that meaning analogically. (This is just what we do with other analogical terms like "eyes of the Lord": we don't need a new entry in the dictionary for "eye"; we use the ordinary meaning and apply it by analogy to God.)

These different approaches to the days are not necessarily mutually exclusive: it is possible to mix elements from several views to get something even more complex. For example, the Scofield Reference Bible combined the gap and the day-age views; some who hold the framework view combine it with the day-age view or intermittent days view; and so on.

Finally, the day-age, analogical day, intermittent day, instantaneous creation, and framework views do not of themselves require us to reject the standard theories of geology and cosmology. On the other hand, none of them *requires* an "old earth" view from Genesis. Most of those who follow the ordinary day view think that this means the Bible supports "young earth creation" (some don't, but I don't see how they can be consistent).

CONCLUSIONS

This array of differing interpretations of the days can be bewildering, and you can be excused if you prefer some simplicity from the first chapter of the Bible. But I don't think it is as bad as all that, and I am convinced that the evidence points to the "analogical days" interpretation.

The evidence that points this way includes: (1) the seventh day is *not* an ordinary day; (2) the other six don't have to be ordinary days (because they're presented as God's workdays); and (3) the best way to get full agreement between chapters 1 and 2 is if the creation week is much longer than an ordinary week.

The main reason, then, that I don't hold any of these other views is that

I think the analogical days view that I have described is the best way of accounting for all the features of the text. The stalwart Presbyterian William G. T. Shedd argued for a version of this position in his *Dogmatic Theology* (1888), drawing on a number of the statements in Augustine and Anselm but also on the day-age arguments. Franz Delitzsch, in his *New Commentary on Genesis* (German, 1887; English, 1899), also held this position. (This matters to me because I hold Delitzsch to be the chief Hebraist that the Christian world has ever produced.) The prominent conservative Dutch theologian Herman Bavinck, in his *Reformed Dogmatics* (Dutch, 1906; English, 1999), also took this view; in fact this seems to have been the most common view among the conservative Dutch Protestants in the late nineteenth and early twentieth centuries.

We can't help but ask whether this leads us to a young earth or an old earth position. The answer is that we have to decide that by other factors than just what the days were: Shedd was happy with the old earth geology of his day (but not with Darwinism), while Bavinck, writing shortly afterwards, was skeptical of the geologists (as well as of Darwinism). I will take this up again in a later chapter, and get into those "other factors."

6

Other Biblical Passages About Creation

GENESIS 1–2 IS THE main biblical text on the work of creation, but it's not the only one. In this chapter I will survey some of the other creation-related texts in both the Old and New Testaments.

Old Testament

As we keep on reading in Genesis, we see that chapters 4–5 continue the story of Adam and Eve's family; this confirms our earlier idea that Adam and Eve are in fact supposed to be historical figures, and the first parents of us all. In Genesis 6–9, the story of the flood, God is not only the Creator but also the moral judge of all (see 6:6-8, where God was "sorry that he had made man on the earth," and resolved to blot him out). And in Genesis 14:19, Melchizedek refers to "God Most High" as "Possessor of heaven and earth" (not "maker," as some versions have it): he owns it all because he made it all (compare Ps. 24:1-2, where "the earth is the LORD's," because "he has founded it"). I can't help thinking of what C. S. Lewis had the senior tempter Screwtape say to his nephew Wormwood:

> At present the Enemy [God] says "Mine" of everything on the pedantic, legalistic ground that He made it: Our Father [Satan] hopes in the end to say "Mine" of all things on the more realistic and dynamic ground of conquest.

I mentioned in the last chapter that the creation Sabbath (Gen. 2:1-3) lies behind the wording of the Sabbath commandment (Ex. 20:8-11). To illustrate more fully, consider the two passages (with parallel terms highlighted):

> *Genesis 2:* [1] Thus the *heavens* and the *earth* were finished, and all the host of them. [2] And on the seventh day God finished his *work* that he had *done,*

> and he rested *on the seventh day* from all his *work* that he had *done.* [3] So God *blessed* the seventh day and *made it holy,* because on it God rested from all his work that he had done in creation.

> *Exodus 20:* [8] "Remember the Sabbath day, to keep it holy. [9] Six days you shall labor, and *do* all your *work,* [10] but the *seventh day* is a Sabbath to the LORD your God. On it you shall not *do* any *work,* you, or your son, or your daughter, your male servant, or your female servant, or your livestock, or the sojourner who is within your gates. [11] For in six days the LORD made *heaven* and *earth,* the sea, and all that is in them, and rested *the seventh day.* Therefore the LORD *blessed* the Sabbath day and *made it holy.*"

Other references to the Sabbath follow this same line; a good example is Exodus 31:12-17:

> [12] And the LORD said to Moses, [13] "You are to speak to the people of Israel and say, 'Above all you shall keep my Sabbaths, for this is a sign between me and you throughout your generations, that you may know that I, the LORD, sanctify you. [14] You shall keep the Sabbath, because it is holy for you. Everyone who profanes it shall be put to death. Whoever does any work on it, that soul shall be cut off from among his people. [15] Six days shall work be done, but the seventh day is a Sabbath of solemn rest, holy to the LORD. Whoever does any work on the Sabbath day shall be put to death. [16] Therefore the people of Israel shall keep the Sabbath, observing the Sabbath throughout their generations, as a covenant forever. [17] It is a sign forever between me and the people of Israel that in six days the LORD made heaven and earth, and on the seventh day he rested and was refreshed.'"

These passages—Genesis 2:2-3; Exodus 20:11; 31:17—use a variety of Hebrew words for the notion of "rest": in Genesis 2:2-3 the word carries the idea "to cease from activity," and is the word from which we get our term "Sabbath." In Exodus 20:11 the word is more explicitly "to rest." Exodus 31:17 uses the term from Genesis ("rest"), and adds a bold anthropomorphism, "and was refreshed"—which, if taken literalistically, would mean that God needed to get his breath back. Exodus 23:12 speaks of "rest" (the word in Ex. 20:11) and "refreshment" (the word in 31:17).

The way the terms from Genesis show up in Exodus is striking: certainly man, the image of God, is to follow the pattern set by his Maker. Indeed, this commandment is founded on the creation order—which tells us that all mankind, Jews and Gentiles alike, are at our best when we obey the principles set down here. Therefore it cannot be in anyone's best interest to set this commandment aside—though it is of course proper to ask just how it is to be applied in our day. I have already argued that the principle of analogy is what makes this commandment tick: human work and rest are *like* God's work and rest in some respects (as well as unlike in other respects); and therefore this commandment is noncommittal on the duration of the days (although it does seem to imply that they are sequential).

The creation story also lies behind the clean and unclean requirements of Leviticus. "Clean" and "unclean" are not *moral* categories—how can they be if God made everything good, including the "unclean" creepy-crawlies and birds (see Leviticus 11)? Besides, if eating the "unclean" animals is morally bad, how could God remove the restrictions as he does in Acts 10:9-16 (v. 15, "What God has made clean, do not call common") and Mark 7:19 ("Thus he declared all foods clean")? Rather, in the laws "clean" tends to correspond to "permitted" while "unclean" corresponds to "not permitted." These rules have three functions: (a) they make a distinction between Israel and the Gentiles (see Lev. 20:24-26); (b) they provide a useful metaphor for *moral* purity (as in Ezek. 36:25-27); and (c) they gave Israel a chance to apply the doctrine of creation—if God made it, he has the right to tell people how to use it. This will apply not only to food but also to sex; for example, Leviticus 15:18, 24 forbids Israelites to have sex at certain times, because it involves uncleanness—but the God who invented sex has a right to tell his people when to refrain from it.

The books of Moses remind Israel that all creation and all mankind belong to God because he made them, and that Israel's status as God's treasured possession is pure privilege (see Ex. 19:5-6; Deut. 10:14-15). There are three basic ways to apply this idea: the first is that the chosen people have special obligations, to love and serve God with unswerving loyalty (Deut. 4:19; 10:15; 29:25; 32:8-9). The second way to apply this idea is to remember that God is able to carry out his promises to prosper his people, to punish them, and to restore them from exile: he who owns everything and rules it, will make sure that it fulfills his holy, wise, and gracious plans. And the third application is the coming of salvation to the rest of mankind, who are God's creatures as well (Deut. 4:5-8).

These themes then echo through the pages of the Bible. Biblical authors aim to encourage the godly with the idea that God is fully able to deliver on his promises (for example, Ps. 136:4-9; 145:5-7; 147:4-5; 148; 65:5-13; 89:6-14; 93; 95:3-5; 121:2; 123:1; 124:8; Isa. 40:12-31; 42:5; 44:24-28; 45:7, 11-13, 18). At other times writers warn the unfaithful with the idea that nothing can stop the Creator from doing what he pleases (for example, Amos 4:13;

9:5-6; Ps. 94:8-11; Dan. 2:37-38; 4:25, 35). In a special sense God "rules" over his covenant people, but that hardly suggests that there is any limit to his power over anything in his creation. The creation tells how great the Creator is (Ps. 19:1-6; 29; 90:2; 147:4-5); and this should make it clear that to serve God is a privilege he grants to people, which does not arise out of some need he himself has (Ps. 50:1-13; Isa. 66:1-2). The bringing of salvation to the Gentiles is especially the work of the Messiah (Isa. 11:1-10; 49:5-6; Ps. 72:8-11).

One of the ways Proverbs encourages young people to seek wisdom is with the idea that by wisdom God created the world and set it up as a coherent system (Prov. 3:19-20; 8:22-31). This is the wisdom that will enter our own lives if we seek it from God. Godly living actually participates in the rationality that lies at the heart of things—and this is one reason why wickedness is called "foolish" and "stupid" (as in Ps. 92:6; 94:8-11; compare Prov. 8:32-35).

A number of passages use the story of Genesis 1 explicitly. For example, Psalm 104:5-9 is a poetic retelling of Genesis 1:9-10 (making of land and sea). In the rest of the psalm the author delights in the way God continues to involve himself in his creation: he even takes those events that we call "natural" (such as plants growing and lions catching prey) and says that *God* does them! As we'll see in the chapter on providence and miracle, natural events are every bit as much God's action as miracles are.

Another reflection on Genesis 1 comes in Psalm 8, a hymn that enables God's people to feel the wonder of the unique place God gave to man (compare Gen. 1:26-28). Using Psalm 33:6-7, 9, the people would remember some of Genesis 1, especially the way God "spoke, and it came to be." Since that's true, then God can frustrate the plans of unbelieving Gentiles and protect his people (vv. 10-22); and it's only right that all mankind worship the Creator (v. 8).

I will finish this survey of what the Old Testament says about creation by looking at some passages that some people think show a "primitive" view of the world. For example, in Exodus 20:4 (Deut. 5:8) the commandment forbids idols in the "likeness of anything that is in heaven above, or that is on the earth beneath, or that is in the water under the earth." From this some have concluded that the Bible pictures a three-decker universe, with water actually under the land. Now this simply fails to read the commandment in its context. The idea it expresses is the commonsense notion that ordinarily the water in the seas is lower than the land, and instead of "*under* the earth" we'd be better off with "*lower than* the earth" (as also in Deut. 4:18). In fact, the verse gives us the three arenas of experience for an ancient Israelite: the sky ("heaven"), the land ("earth"), and the lakes, rivers, and seas (the "waters").

Another "primitive" element in the Bible is the way the Psalms seem to say that the earth does not move: for example, Psalm 93:1 (see also 96:10; 104:5) says, "the world is established, it shall never be moved" (ESV). The Christian philosopher Nicholas Wolterstorff put it this way:

> What is coming to the surface here, of course, is the geocentric cosmology widely shared among the peoples of antiquity. The author expresses this cosmology in his discourse; it's part of what he actually says—part of the content of his discourse. But as a matter of fact the earth is moved, and we all believe that it is.

To read these verses as saying anything about *physical cosmology* means that we have to believe that such is their "with-respect-to-whatness." And that's exactly where the problem lies: these are psalms, which means that they were written to be hymns in public worship (and not treatises on natural philosophy). The Hebrew verb translated "moved" also appears in Psalm 125:1, where Mount Zion "cannot be moved," and 46:5, where the city of God "shall not be moved" because God is in her midst. When the Psalms say something "shall not be moved," they are describing some kind of stability—but physical immobility is not at all implied.

We can explain the three Psalm verses in the light of their contexts much more sensibly if we take this into account. For example, at Psalm 96:10 the commentator Franz Delitzsch said,

> The world below, hitherto shaken by war and anarchy, now stands upon foundations that cannot be shaken in time to come, under Yahwe's righteous and gentle sway. This is the joyful tidings of the new era which the poet predicts from out of his own times, when he depicts the joy that will then pervade the whole creation.

Physical cosmology is just irrelevant to the context. Psalm 104 is about the stability of the created order because God still keeps it in his care. In the same way, Psalm 93 is a song about God's rule over all things (his "reign," v. 1), and the security that this gives his people (this comes from v. 5, where the "decrees" and the "house" speak of God's covenant with Israel). Again, physical cosmology is just outside the scope of this altogether.

Now it is certainly true that scholars in the Middle Ages read these texts as "teaching" just what I am saying they don't teach, namely physical cosmology. But I claim that this is a misreading, and one that came about because the standard world-picture of Ptolemaic cosmology was firmly established long before the Christian church produced its intellectuals (Ptolemy was born about A.D. 100). In this scheme the spherical earth was at the center of the universe, surrounded by concentric spheres that contained the stars on their surfaces. Christian scholars probably didn't question the cosmology until the work of scholars like Copernicus (1473–1543), Kepler (1571–1630), and Galileo (1564–1642) became widely available: and that is small wonder, since before the work of these men there was no reason to raise any questions.

We should not doubt that the Bible typically speaks in the language of Everyman, and hence that it doesn't make much sense to look for "scientific" statements in it. But by the same token we shouldn't be looking for pre-Copernican cosmology either!

NEW TESTAMENT

The New Testament takes for granted the Old Testament view of creation. Its own passages that speak about creation touch on six themes:

(a) Christ was the one who carried out the work of creating and who continues to keep the created world going (John 1:1-3; Col. 1:16-17; Heb. 1:3, 10-12);

(b) the fact that the biblical God is the Creator shows why polytheism is wrong (1 Cor. 8:5-6; 10:26);

(c) the creation story establishes proper role relationships for men and women (1 Cor. 11:8-9; 1 Tim. 2:12-14), as well as guidance for the ethics of sex and marriage (Rom. 1:24-27; Matt. 19:4-6);

(d) the creation is good (1 Tim. 4:3-5);

(e) God created the world from nothing (Heb. 11:3; Rev. 4:11);

(f) all mankind share a common human nature (Acts 17:22-31, which we will examine in a later chapter).

Let's discuss these in turn.

The opening of John's Gospel, "In the beginning," calls to mind the opening of Genesis; likewise the claim that "all things were made through" the Word (who, as we find out, is the one who became flesh in Jesus Christ) reminds us of God "making" all things in Genesis 1. It is quite possible that John uses the very title "the Word" (Greek *Logos*) to remind us of how God "said" things in Genesis 1—since Psalm 33:6 tells us that "by the *word* [Greek *Logos*] of the LORD the heavens were made." (See also Wisdom 9:1, where God made all things by his *word* [Greek *Logos*].) John hasn't left any ambiguity about the deity of Christ, since he says "and the Word was God."

In Colossians 1:16-17 Paul asserts that in Christ "all things were created," and that "in him all things hold together"—Christ is the Creator, Sustainer, and Ruler of all there is. Likewise Hebrews 1:3 speaks of Christ "upholding the universe by his word of power"—making a point very much like Colossians 1:17. Hebrews, like the rest of the New Testament, is remarkable for the frank way in which it takes Old Testament passages about the LORD and applies them to Christ; and in particular, 1:10-12 applies Psalm 102:25-27, describing the way the LORD laid the foundation of the earth and will outlast it all, to Jesus. Jesus' deity, as established by his role as Creator and Ruler, is a doctrine of the New Testament itself; it didn't have to wait for the early church to invent it.

In 1 Corinthians Paul uses the Old Testament teaching that everything derives its being from only one God, both to agree that therefore the idols are not gods (8:4), and to endorse the notion that God owns it all (10:26, quoting Ps. 24:1). This means that meat offered to idols is not automatically off limits for the Corinthian believers—though they must not govern themselves by this teaching alone but rather must be ruled by love for their fellow Christians.

When Paul wants to show why men and women have different roles to play, he appeals to the creation narrative (1 Cor. 11:8-9; 1 Tim. 2:12-14). This is important because by grounding role differences in the very nature of things (the creation order), Paul can insist that these differences apply to all cultures and all times—which includes us! And what a valuable reminder, that Christian morality does not consist in erasing "nature" but in restoring it to its wholesome functioning! I think the idea of a "creation order" (or "nature") also underlies Paul's indictment of sexual immorality in Romans 1:24-27. I will come back to this in talking about general revelation and apologetics. And in Matthew 19:4-6 Jesus refers to the creation story—holding Genesis 1 and 2 together, by the way—as the basis for his teaching that opposes divorce: "from the beginning it was not so," he says (v. 8). The civil laws given through Moses have a purpose—but their purpose is to restrain social evil. The creation narrative tells us what marriage was supposed to be;

and to follow Jesus (and really, to follow Moses) leads to the restoring of that creation order.

Christian morality restores the creation order because that order was good at the beginning. But Paul goes on to assert, in 1 Timothy 4:3-5, that it is still good. There he reminds Timothy that God created marriage as well as different kinds of food (see Gen. 1:28-30), and that believers should receive them with thanksgiving, consecrating them by the word of God and prayer; indeed, "everything created by God is good" (v. 4, reflecting Gen. 1:31). Now, this looks like it has a problem if we want to make it agree with Romans 8:20-22, which seems to speak of the fallenness and futility of creation. I will come back to this in the chapter on nature after the fall. But for now we need to see that there must be a sense in which the natural world keeps its goodness.

I have already shown in chapter 4 that the New Testament authors held to creation from nothing. The two places that are clearest about this are Hebrews 11:3 and Revelation 4:11. In Hebrews 11:3, "by faith we understand that the universe was created by the word of God, so that what is seen was not made out of things that are visible," the author denies that what we see—the material world—came from things that are visible—preexisting stuff. Revelation 4:11, "you created all things, and by your will they existed and were created," makes it clear that all things owe their existence to God, and that he created them at some point in time—which means he created them from nothing.

In Paul's speech to the philosophers of Athens in Acts 17:22-31, he says in verses 24-27,

> [24] "The God who made the world and everything in it, being Lord of heaven and earth, does not live in temples made by man, [25] nor is he served by human hands, as though he needed anything, since he himself gives to all mankind life and breath and everything. [26] And he made from one man every nation of mankind to live on all the face of the earth, having determined allotted periods and the boundaries of their habitation, [27] that they should seek God, in the hope that they might feel their way toward him and find him. Yet he is actually not far from each one of us . . ."

Key points are that God is Maker of all things and all people, and does not depend on them for his well-being; that one man (surely Adam) is the ancestor of all mankind; that all people everywhere need God and were made to seek after him. In a later chapter we will explore how Paul's apologetic strategy should affect our own.

7

IS THE EARTH YOUNG OR OLD?

Biblical Arguments

LET'S REVIEW WHERE WE ARE. I have argued that we cannot get from the creation days any biblical position on how old the earth and the universe are supposed to be. All we can say for sure is that the beginning of the first day (Gen. 1:3) may be some unknown amount of time after the absolute beginning of the universe (Gen. 1:1), and that the creation "week" for earth (Gen. 1:3–2:3) had to be longer than an ordinary week in order for Genesis 2:5 to make any sense.

Is this all we can say? Does any other biblical passage give us a chronology? And what should we make of the reigning theories in cosmology (the Big Bang) and geology? In this chapter I will explore the biblical texts that may speak to this matter, and then in chapter 15 I will consider some of the scientific issues.

In my experience the three strongest biblical arguments for a young earth are: (a) the days of Genesis as ordinary days; (b) the genealogies of Genesis 5 and 11; and (c) the statement of Jesus that seems to put Adam and Eve at the beginning of creation (Mark 10:6 and its parallel Matt. 19:4). I have already dealt with the creation days, and therefore I will now turn my attention to the other two arguments. I will start with the Gospels and then go to the genealogies.

DID JESUS THINK THE CREATION PERIOD WAS SHORT?

In the context of answering a question on divorce in Mark 10:1-12 (paralleled by Matt. 19:1-12), Jesus bases his argument on the fact that the creation narrative sets the pattern for moral human life, and therefore it trumps a civil law (Deut. 24:1-4, with which the Pharisees challenge him) whose purpose is to restrain "hardness of heart." In verses 6-9 he says (italics added),

> [6] "But *from the beginning of creation,* 'God made them male and female.' [compare Gen. 1:27] [7] 'Therefore a man shall leave his father and mother and hold fast to his wife, [8] and the two shall become one flesh' [compare Gen. 2:24]. So they are no longer two but one flesh. [9] What therefore God has joined together, let not man separate."

The parallel in Matthew 19:4-6 reads,

> [4] He answered, "Have you not read that he who created them *from the beginning* made them male and female, [5] and said, 'Therefore a man shall leave his father and mother and hold fast to his wife, and the two shall become one flesh'? [6] So they are no longer two but one flesh. What therefore God has joined together, let not man separate."

When confronted with the Deuteronomy text, Jesus replies (v. 8), "Because of your hardness of heart Moses allowed you to divorce your wives, but *from the beginning* it was not so."

The argument for a young earth based on these texts goes like this: the phrases "from the beginning of creation" (Mark 10:6) and "from the beginning" (Matt. 19:4, 8) do not refer to the beginning of mankind but to the beginning of creation itself. Therefore, Jesus was dating the origin of mankind to a time very shortly after the initial creation of Genesis 1:1. If there is any kind of gap between the initial creation and the beginning of the creation week, or if the week itself lasts much longer than an ordinary week, then we must conclude that Jesus was mistaken (or worse, misleading), and therefore he can't be God.

If this argument is sound, I'm in trouble, because for reasons I have already given I cannot follow this reading of Genesis 1. On the other hand, I firmly believe in the traditional Christian doctrine of Christ, and tremble at the thought of doing anything to undermine it.

But the argument is not sound. It finds its credibility from the way the English "from *the* beginning" seems so definite; but the Greek is not so fixed in meaning. The same Greek expression "from the beginning" appears in the New Testament quite a number of times. When you find it without any qualification ("from the beginning," as in Matt. 19:4, 8), you have to ask, "beginning *of what?*" And the answer to that is something you infer from what the context is about. For example, 1 John 1:1 speaks of "That which was from the beginning"; I take this to refer to Christ, and hence to a "time" before the world began (as also in 2:13, 14). Then in 3:8 John tells us that "the devil has been sinning from the beginning"—possibly referring to the beginning of the world, or perhaps to the beginning of his own rebellion (compare also

John 8:44). On the other hand, in 2:7 John says, "I am writing you no new commandment, but an old commandment that you had from the beginning"—namely, from the time they began to be Christians (see also 2:24; 3:11), or from the beginning of the apostles' ministry, if 1 John 2:7 is referring to John 13:34 ("A new commandment I give to you, that you love one another: just as I have loved you, you also are to love one another").

If we apply this insight to the verses in Matthew 19, we find that they most naturally refer to "the beginning" of the human race.

The text in Mark 10 is a little harder, but not much. It has a qualifier, "from the beginning *of creation*": does that mean it must refer to the initial creation act? But it seems to me that we still have to rely on the subject of the context. For example, in Matthew 24:21 we find "from the beginning *of the world*" (compare the parallel Mark 13:19, "from the beginning *of the creation*"): since the context is about unprecedented tribulation, we are justified in seeing this as covering all of time—or at least all of the time in which humans have been around to experience tribulation. On the other hand, the total time since the absolute creation is irrelevant to Jesus' point in Mark 10:6. The most obvious "beginning of creation" for this verse is the beginning of the creation of the first pair of humans (note how Gen. 1:27 speaks of how "God *created* man"): and if we read what Jesus goes on to say about the first human marriage as a pattern for all marriages, this obvious sense is surely the right one.

So I conclude that these verses from the Gospels do not refer to the time since creation, and therefore have no bearing on the age of the earth.

THE GENEALOGIES IN GENESIS

Most first-time Bible readers can make it through Genesis 1–4 without too much difficulty; but when they hit chapter 5 they might find it off-putting with its repetitious (following ESV):

> When A had lived X years, he fathered B. A lived after he fathered B Y years and had other sons and daughters. Thus all the days of A were Z (= X + Y) years, and he died.

If these readers endure, they come to chapter 10, the Table of Nations, and then chapter 11, where verses 1-9 tell about the Tower of Babel. Then 11:10 starts up again with a genealogy that has a very similar pattern to that of chapter 5. I hope that such readers will ask what purpose these genealogies serve—and I will say something about that soon. But many readers, from first-time to experts, have supposed that one purpose is to chronicle the amount of time since the creation of mankind; all you have to do is add up the numbers. This is the way Archbishop James Ussher (1581–1656) calculated 4004 B.C. as the year of creation.

Many see this as the natural way to interpret the terms in the genealogy: for example, to "father" someone means to beget a child, doesn't it? By this reading Adam was 130 years old when Seth was born (Gen. 5:3), Seth was 105 when Enosh was born, and so on—an unbroken chronology from Adam to Abraham.

The RSV translation (among others) furthered this interpretation by the way it rendered the pattern:

> When A had lived X years, he became the father of B. A lived *after the birth* of B Y years, and had other sons and daughters. Thus all the days of A were Z years; and he died.

When it says "after the birth of B" it gives the idea that, in fact, direct descent from father to son is exactly what the genealogy is about.

The problem here, though, is that the translation "after the birth of B" is inaccurate; the ESV "after he fathered" is truer to the Hebrew. But even that doesn't really get to the heart of things.

The first thing to say about this approach to the genealogies is that, strictly speaking, this wouldn't tell us anything about the age of the *earth:* it would tell us at most what Moses thought was the time since man was created. The second thing to say about this approach is that modern study of genealogies, both in the Bible and in the Ancient Near Eastern world in general, have shown that this way of reading the genealogies is wrong. The man who got the ball rolling was William Henry Green, who defended the authenticity of the books of Moses. Out of that work came an essay on "Primeval Chronology" in 1890. Green noticed that the genealogies in the Bible have gaps: for example, in the genealogy of Jesus, Matthew tells us that "Joram *fathered* Uzziah" (Matt. 1:8, using the Greek equivalent to the Hebrew word in Genesis 5). However, if you read 2 Kings, you see that Uzziah was actually Joram's great-great grandson. Apparently "A fathered B" may mean "A fathered an ancestor of B."

We can find other examples of compressed genealogies in the Bible: for example, if we look at Exodus 6:14-27, we read that Moses was the son of Amram, who was the son of Kohath, who was the son of Levi (who was the son of Jacob): that is, you have four generations from Jacob to Moses. However, Kohath was born before Jacob took his family down to Egypt

(Gen. 46:11); and if the Israelites spent 430 years in Egypt (Ex. 12:40-41 is pretty explicit), and if Moses was 80 at the time of the exodus (Ex. 7:7), then Kohath was born at least 350 years before Moses was. That's a bit long if Kohath was Moses' grandfather (my grandfathers were born 50-55 years before I was). Not only that, but Kohath's descendants numbered 8,600 males over the age of one month (Num. 3:27-28), and 2,750 of them were between the ages of 30 and 50 (Num. 4:34-37)—and this just a month after the Israelites left Egypt (Num. 1:1). That is phenomenal fertility if Kohath was Moses' grandfather. (We'd expect a number closer to 100.)

The solution becomes clear if we look at the genealogy of Joshua, who was about half Moses' age, in 1 Chronicles 7:23-27. Joshua was the son of Nun who was the son of Elishama who was the son of Ammihud who was the son of Ladan who was the son of Tahan who was the son of Telah who was the son of Resheph who was the son of Rephah who was the son of Beriah who was the son of Ephraim (who was the son of Joseph who was the son of Jacob). That gives twelve generations from Jacob to Joshua—and I don't know if that's all of them, either.

Therefore the genealogy of Moses is compressed—that is, it doesn't list all the generations.

So the genealogies in the books of Moses are not there to give us lengths of time—in fact, no biblical author ever reckons up a length of time based on them. What is their purpose? Primarily they aim to give us the line of descent for the people they list. Hence the word "to father" can mean "to be the ancestor of," and "son" can mean "descendant." (This purpose also appears in other genealogies in the Ancient Near East, which can also contain gaps.) In addition, the genealogies in Genesis 5 hammer home to us the reign of death that came through the sin of Adam and Eve (see Gen. 3:19, and Rom. 5:14). They are selective, just as all the narration in Genesis (indeed, in all of the Bible) is highly selective—it never had as its purpose to tell you everything.

From all of this it is right to conclude that to use these genealogies to compute the length of time since the creation is a *misuse* of them, since they do not even claim to give such information. I know of no way to figure out whether there is even an upper limit to the number of possible gaps.

Conclusion: Does the Bible Have a Position on the Age of the Earth?

It wouldn't be quite true to say the Bible has *no* position on the age of the earth: it does in fact have a *lower* limit. I think we can say that the time since man was created has been *at least* 6,000 years, and that the length of the creation week before that was at least a fair number of years; and before that—who knows? But I don't think we can legitimately set an upper limit on the age of the earth from the Bible.

As I have noted before, most people think of the interpretation of the Genesis days as the focus of the biblical doctrine of creation; but really, the Bible is concerned with the doctrine that I outlined in chapter 4, and the reflections on creation that we looked at in chapter 6. In fact, the interpretation of the days and the age of the earth play virtually no role elsewhere in the Bible—though of course what we think of these issues will matter a great deal to how we look at our world, to how we practice science, and to how we commend the Christian faith to others.

8

What a Piece of Work Is Man!

Human Nature as It Was Created

"What a piece of work is a man! how noble in reason! how infinite in faculty! in form and moving, how express and admirable! in action, how like an angel! in apprehension, how like a god! the beauty of the world! the paragon of animals!" That's what Shakespeare had Hamlet, prince of Denmark, say to Rosencrantz and Gildenstern. Later in the play he says, "What is a man, if his chief good, and market of his time, be but to sleep, and feed? A beast, no more. Sure, He that made us with such large discourse, looking before and after, gave us not that capability and godlike reason to fust in us unused."

"Man is only a reed, the weakest in nature, but he is a thinking reed," noted the French thinker Blaise Pascal (1623–1662) in his *Pensées*.

Maybe we should come a couple of notches lower on the brow: my children have a Disney music video that opens with the song,

> You are a human animal,
> you are a very special breed;
> for you are the only animal,
> who can think, who can reason, who can read.

In this chapter we'll see that all these sources, the high-brow and the low, convey something true about man's nature. The Genesis account and other places in Scripture tell us where these faculties come from and how they were intended to function.

You Are a Human Animal

When we look at Genesis 1 and 2, we find that they show us ways in which people are similar to the other living things God made, and ways that they are different. Let's start with the similarities.

First, in Genesis 2:7, "the LORD God formed the man of dust from the ground and breathed into his nostrils the breath of life, and the man became a *living creature.*" Down in verse 19, the man gave names to all the animals, and "whatever the man called every living creature, that was its name." Back in the first story, 1:1–2:3, the waters had swarmed with "living creatures" (1:20), and the earth brought forth "living creatures" (1:24). So in these chapters "living creature" is a name for a body that has within it the principle of life—that is, an animal. Humans are like the other animals in this respect. Also in Genesis 2, man is formed from the ground (v. 7), and so are the other animals (v. 19). The man receives the "breath of life" in verse 7—and in Genesis 7:22 we find that all land-dwelling animals have "the breath of life" (and they all died in the flood). Back in 1:22, God blessed the swimming and flying animals, urging them to "be fruitful and multiply"—and in verse 28 God blesses the newly made human pair with similar words.

But for all the similarities, we'd better notice the differences, too—for they set mankind apart from the rest of the animal world. For example, consider how God decides to make a man (1:26):

> Then God said, "Let us make man in our image, after our likeness. And let them have dominion over the fish of the sea and over the birds of the heavens and over the livestock and over all the earth and over every creeping thing that creeps on the earth."

Scholars debate over who is the "us" that God addresses here, but I think all the evidence favors the conclusion that God is consulting with himself. Since God says "Let *us* make" in verse 26, it stands to reason that the "us" is the same as whoever creates in verse 27; and this is "God" alone. It also makes sense to suppose that the "our" of "our image" is the same as whoever's image man is made in; and in fact, verse 27 (and all other examples) says that man was made in *God's* image. So in verse 26 God talks to himself, planning it out specially, as it were—something he does for no other animal. Notice further that man is in God's image and after his likeness: whatever that means (we'll discuss it below), it's not true of any other animal. And finally, man is made to have dominion over the rest of the animal world. When we remember the purpose of the first story (see chapter 4), to show how God made the earth as a place for humans to live, love, rule, and serve, we see again that mankind is the crown of God's creation week.

The second story, 2:4–25, carries these themes forward. Even though God formed both man and animals from the ground (compare vv. 7 and 19),

God pays special attention to the man and "breathes" into him (v. 7). God forms a religious bond, a "covenant," with the first man, and holds him morally responsible in a way distinct from the rest of the animal world (2:15-17). The other animals cannot provide "a helper fit for" the man, so God has to form his mate in a unique way (2:18-25). In the process the man exercises his authority over the animals by naming them (vv. 19-20). And man alone has the capacity to sin—which, sadly, he uses in Genesis 3 (more on this in the next chapter).

These differences between us and the other animals are obvious to everyone. For example, take Laura Ingalls Wilder's story of her childhood during the pioneering days in the prairies. In *The Long Winter* she records a conversation with her father, Pa Ingalls, who has just looked at a muskrat's house and concluded that a hard winter was coming (he was right). Laura asked how he knew.

> "The colder the winter will be, the thicker the muskrats build the walls of their houses," Pa told her. . . .
>
> "Pa, how can the muskrats know?" she asked.
>
> "I don't know how they know," Pa said. "But they do. God tells them somehow, I suppose."
>
> "Then why doesn't God tell us?" Laura wanted to know.
>
> "Because," said Pa, "we're not animals. We're humans, and, like it says in the Declaration of Independence, God created us free. That means we got to take care of ourselves."
>
> Laura said faintly, "I thought God takes care of us."
>
> "He does," Pa said, "so far as we do what's right. And he gives us a conscience and brains to know what's right. But he leaves it to us to do as we please. That's the difference between us and everything else in creation."
>
> "Can't muskrats do as they please?" Laura asked, amazed.
>
> "No," said Pa. "I don't know why they can't but you can see they can't. Look at that muskrat house. Muskrats have to build that kind of house. They always have and they always will. It's plain they can't build any other kind. But folks build all kinds of houses. A man can build any kind of house he can think of. So if his house don't keep out the weather, that's *his* look-out; he's free and independent."

So we may, if we like, talk about the "animal" life of man, meaning that he has a body, needs to eat, breeds by a bodily process, is limited by time and space, and so on. But if we do speak this way, we may easily fall into a number of traps, such as taking this to imply that what we share with other animals means we *must have* descended from them (we'll take this up later); or that we are "just another" animal species; or that our animal side is "lower" than our spiritual side (or "more real," for that matter).

One way theologians and philosophers have clarified the similarities and differences is to call man the "rational animal," where "rational" includes the moral and spiritual side of man. As a matter of fact, some of the better Greek thinkers spoke in the same way. Epictetus, for example, a Greek Stoic who lived about A.D. 50–130, wrote of "body, which we have in common with the beasts, and reason and intelligence, which we have in common with the gods." Aristotle, who lived 384–322 B.C., described man as having three parts: the part that has to do with living and growing, which we have in common with the plants; the part that has senses and some form of consciousness, which we have in common with all animals; and the part that acts on reason or principle, which is distinctively human.

BODY AND SOUL

"O God, if there be a God, save my soul, if I have a soul"—so an English soldier prayed before the Battle of Blenheim in 1704. Christians, of course, know that there's a God; but what do they think about the soul?

Christians have traditionally thought that human nature is made up of two parts: the material part, the body; and the non-material part, the soul. There have been dissenters, though: some have argued that, instead, humans are made up of *three* parts, body, soul, and spirit; while others (especially in the twentieth century) have insisted that man is made up of only one part, with body and soul being the names you'd call a man depending on how you were looking at him. The traditional view is called *dualism,* because it speaks of two distinct parts; the three-part view is called *trichotomy;* and the one-part view is called *monism.* In this section I intend first to show (briefly) why a form of dualism is in fact the biblical teaching, while the alternatives are not; and second, to explore just what kind of dualism is true to the Bible. Because I aim to be brief, I know I run the risk of over-simplifying; but really, (a) I would need to write a pretty technical book to give a proper treatment of the subject, and (b) the arguments are not, once you get down to it, as difficult as people like to make them.

To establish dualism or trichotomy, we can look at three basic lines of argument: first, there are some explicit texts—both in the Old Testament and in the New—referring to man's "soul" or "spirit" as distinct from his body; second, the biblical teaching about life after death requires that the soul be distinct from the body; and third, a philosophical argument about man's moral nature leads to the conclusion that his total life is more than just his body. To show that dualism is better than trichotomy, I need to show that the Bible doesn't really support a distinction between "soul" and "spirit."

Before I go further I must say a word or two about the right way to use a word study. Almost all words in any language can have more than one meaning, and the Hebrew and Greek words we are looking at are no exception. For example, the Hebrew word *nefesh,* which is sometimes translated "soul," in some places means "breath"; in some places it means "life" or "living being"; in others it means something like "person" (even so that "my *nefesh*" is just "me"). A good word study will help us find out which of the several *possible* meanings is the *right* one in a given place. Most of those who argue against dualism in favor of monism base their argument on the fact that there are many meanings for *nefesh,* and they go on to suggest that any of these others is better than "soul"; or else they make the mistake of supposing that the *concept* "soul" is the same as the *word nefesh.*

If you stop and think about English for a second, you'll see that neither of these conclusions is worth a thing. For example, if I say that one kind of music has "soul," I certainly don't want you to think that other kinds of music have "body"! Instead I expect you to read the right meaning of the word in this context. Also, I don't have to use the *word* "soul" to talk about the *concept:* instead of "soul" I can say "that part of me that survives the death of my body," for example.

What this means is that I should look for those verses where "soul" or "spirit" really seem to be something different from the body; that is, I'm looking for verses that use *one* of the possible meanings of the words, and I'm not bothered about verses that *don't* use the meaning I'm looking for. It also means that I can look for verses where the idea is there even when the usual words are not.

(a) Explicit Biblical Texts

The Genesis creation account says very little about the components of human nature. It is obvious, as we have seen, that man, in common with the other animals, has a body; it is also clear that man has abilities and capacities quite distinct from those of the other "living creatures" that God made. We don't get much explanation, though, of whether this is because man has different parts that have different functions. Now this does *not* mean that it is impossible to find out whether there are different parts, or even whether the question is important; it only indicates that Genesis wasn't written to answer these questions. It also means that we'll have to be careful and that we'll have to cast our net much wider than these first few chapters.

In Genesis 42:21, Joseph's brothers refer to "the distress of his *soul*" when they were selling him into slavery: the soul is the inner self. Deuteronomy 6:5, where Israel is to love the Lord with all their heart, *soul,* and might, is similar. The word "spirit" can also be used for the inner self, as in Genesis 41:8, where Pharaoh's "*spirit* was troubled." This particular usage, which is common for both words in the Old and New Testaments, does not prove that the soul or spirit is something separate from the body—though it points that way, as we will see under heading (c) shortly.

There are some passages, however, that distinguish the soul or spirit from the body. For example, Psalm 31:9 says "my eye is wasted from grief, my *soul* and my body also"—which makes sense if the soul and the body are distinct. In 2 Corinthians 7:1 Paul says to the Corinthian Christians, "let us cleanse ourselves from every defilement of body and *spirit*"—indicating that "body" and "spirit" are two realms of defilement.

In Isaiah 26:9 the prophet speaks of "my *spirit* within me," which I guess means "my spirit within my body." This becomes quite clear in Daniel 7:15, where Daniel says, "my *spirit* within me was anxious"; the Aramaic expression translated "within me" is literally, "within its sheath" (ESV margin), a reference to the spirit being within the body and therefore distinct from it. Then James 4:5 says, "He yearns jealously over the *spirit* that he has made to dwell in us"—and, yes, this sentence in Greek is difficult, but the possibilities still agree on the idea of a "spirit dwelling within us." In fact, in 1 Corinthians 5:4 Paul can even say, "When you are assembled in the name of the Lord Jesus and my *spirit* is present"—when his body is absent!

Finally, consider how biblical authors describe death. In Genesis 35:18, we read of how Rachel's "*soul* was departing (for she was dying)": the soul is something that is leaving her body as it dies. Compare 1 Kings 17:21-22 in the RV, where Elijah asks that the dead boy's *soul* might return to his body; and Luke 12:20, where a man's *soul* is required of him, that is, he must yield it up to God in death. Similarly, in Ecclesiastes 12:7, at death "the dust [the body] returns to the earth as it was, and the *spirit* returns to God who gave it." In Luke 8:55, when Jesus restores a girl to life, "her *spirit* returned." When Jesus dies, he hands his *spirit* over to God (Matt. 27:50; Luke 23:46; John 19:30); Stephen, the first Christian martyr, does likewise (Acts 7:59).

These texts strongly suggest that the words "soul" and "spirit" can name something distinct from the body; but, in case anyone thinks they don't prove it, the next category should settle the matter.

(b) Texts About Life After Death

Someone might try to argue that in the passages about the soul or spirit leaving the body at death, these are just other words for the "life": thus many versions at 1 Kings 17:21-22 use the word "life." However, when we consider this further category of texts, we see that there's a "me" that doesn't cease when my body dies, which means that there is such a thing as soul or spirit.

For example, in Psalm 16:10 (quoted in Acts 2:27) the psalmist sings, "you will not abandon my *soul* to Sheol"—instead he looks forward to everlasting life in God's presence. In Psalm 49:15, "God will ransom my *soul* from the power of Sheol"; here, "Sheol" is the place where the wicked go when they die (see v. 14), and the faithful do not. In verse 19 the bad man's "*soul* will go to the generation of his fathers," which is a grim description of damnation.

Other texts do not use the words "soul" or "spirit," but they nevertheless speak of the same thing. For example, Psalm 73:24 expresses the hope of the faithful that "afterward"—that is, at the end of my bodily life—"you will receive *me* to glory." We can also see this in 1 Samuel 28, where the witch of Endor calls back the prophet Samuel from the dead to give some advice to King Saul. When Samuel appears, the author does not portray it as a demonic hoax, as some have suggested; instead, when the ghost speaks in verse 15, the narrator tells us that "*Samuel* said to Saul . . ."; and in verse 20, Saul was "filled with fear because of the words of *Samuel.*" For these passages to make any sense, there has to be a "me" to survive the death of my body.

The clearest verse in the New Testament in this category is Matthew 10:28 (parallel in Luke 12:4-5):

> "And do not fear those who kill the body but cannot kill the *soul.* Rather fear him who can destroy both *soul* and body in hell."

Other texts include the reference to the still-living "spirits" of good people (Heb. 12:23); and to the still-living "souls" of the faithful (Rev. 6:9; 20:4). In Luke 9:30-31, Jesus at his transfiguration has a talk with Moses and Elijah—men whose bodies had long been dead but whose persons—souls or spirits—were still alive. We could add to this the tale of Enoch in Genesis 5:23-24 (and Heb. 11:5-6): he lived for 365 years and walked with

God, and then he was not, for God took him. How could cutting short his bodily life be an expression of God's favor unless there was a soul to bring near to God? Elijah was "taken" as well in 2 Kings 2:9-10, using the same word as Genesis 5:24.

In Luke 23:43 Jesus says to the dying criminal who confesses faith, "Truly, I say to you, *today* you will be with me in Paradise." What can that mean but that there is a person who is not limited to the body?

Finally, we have two passages from Paul. In 2 Corinthians 5:8, he describes what will happen at his death, and why it will be a relief from the struggles of this life: "we would rather be away from the body and at home with the Lord." Similarly, in Philippians 1:23, as he anticipates his possible martyrdom, he says, "My desire is to depart and be with Christ, for that is far better." In both of these verses, Paul expects that his "self" will go into the immediate presence of Christ when his body dies.

(c) A Philosophical Argument

The third argument is what I am calling a "philosophical" one. I use that term because the Bible generally uses ordinary language rather than philosophical; nevertheless we can discern what philosophical truths must underlie biblical statements. In this case, consider the following verses from Psalm 119, that great poem of devotion to God's word:

> [20] My *soul* is consumed with longing
> for your rules at all times.
>
> [81] My *soul* longs for your salvation;
> I hope in your word.
>
> [129] Your testimonies are wonderful;
> therefore my *soul* keeps them.
>
> [167] My *soul* keeps your testimonies;
> I love them exceedingly.
>
> [175] Let my *soul* live and praise you,
> and let your rules help me.

We saw in chapter 4 that the biblical teaching on creation shows that God is self-sufficient: he's other than the creation, and greater than it is, and he doesn't depend on it at all (in fact, it's just the other way around!). Unlike us, he's not limited in any way by time or space, and he can do just what he pleases. Another way to say this is to say that God is *transcendent:* he transcends, or goes beyond, the created universe. Since God's word, in which he reveals himself to man and invites man into a committed and loving relationship (a covenant), comes from him and not from man, it too is transcendent: that's why it speaks to us across the gaps of culture and era, and draws even us into fellowship with God; that's why its morals are the same for everyone.

God's word brings us into contact with God himself; it brings us into contact with transcendent reality. And in Psalm 119, we find that the *soul* of the godly longs for, keeps, and loves that word; we find that the *soul* of the godly will experience God's salvation, will live and praise God. For this to be so the soul must have some way of receiving something transcendent; and if this is so, then the soul must be something other than the body.

Our bodies are material—made from dirt, according to Genesis 2:7—and therefore subject to the same limitations as any other material thing. In particular, material things follow material laws: a stone drops because the law of gravity makes it; and if you hold it with your hand cupped downwards, the laws of friction keep it from falling out. Your brain is a bunch of chemicals—highly organized, mind you, but chemicals still—and its cells interact with each other according to the laws of chemical reactions. But you think, you make moral choices; and in so doing you take a share in transcendence. When you think a true thought, and follow a sound argument, your brain is active, but the results of that activity are not determined by the properties of the chemicals but by something beyond (or transcendent over) those properties. When you make a sound moral judgment, and choose to do what is right, you're not just expressing what's in your genes; you're taking a share in something that transcends your bodily mechanism. All this means that your brain activity is not the *same* as your thinking and choosing; it's the *vehicle* of your thinking and choosing.

Isn't this what makes parenting an adolescent such a challenge? Their bodies are changing at lightning speed; they're in the grip of new hormones and new desires. And we try to get them to live beyond the dictates of their hormones—at the same time, I hope, as we teach them to be thankful for what God made. They must think about right and wrong, they must make moral choices even when they fly in the face of their bodies' incessant and insistent demands. That's what biblical wisdom is: skill in applying transcendent requirements to ordinary life.

Just the other night I saw a National Geographic program about the conflict between lions and hyenas: they are enemies forever, locked in a life-and-death struggle. The narrator put it this way: they are *creatures of instinct, helpless to change their destinies.* It would take something that transcends their instincts—the demands of their genes and experiences—to change them, and, in their natural state at least, they have no transcendent influence.

But you and I do, especially from the word of God. Your soul is the organ that receives the transcendence you need to effect a destiny that is full of truth, love, and moral goodness. If monism is true, then you have no capacity for transcendence, because your animal life, being governed by material laws, cannot reason or make moral choices. You may be a human animal, as the song says: but you're a *human* animal, and that's what makes the difference.

C. S. Lewis put it well when he had the experienced tempter Screwtape write to his nephew Wormwood, the junior tempter (in *The Screwtape Letters,* "the Enemy" is God; "our Father" is Satan):

> Humans are amphibians—half spirit and half animal. (The Enemy's determination to produce such a revolting hybrid was one of the things that determined our Father to withdraw his support from him.) As spirits they belong to the eternal world, but as animals they inhabit time. This means that while their spirit can be directed to an eternal object, their bodies, passions, and imaginations are in continual change, for to be in time means to change.

(d) Dualism or Trichotomy?

The trichotomist view, namely that we are made up of three elements—body, soul, and spirit—gets its impulse from the way two verses seem to distinguish between soul and spirit:

> *1 Thessalonians 5:23:* Now may the God of peace himself sanctify you completely, and may your whole *spirit and soul and body* be kept blameless at the coming of our Lord Jesus Christ.

> *Hebrews 4:12:* For the word of God is living and active, sharper than any two-edged sword, piercing to *the division of soul and of spirit,* of joints and of marrow, and discerning the thoughts and intentions of the heart.

At first glance these verses do in fact support such a distinction: it looks like the spirit and soul and body go to make up the whole person in 1 Thessalonians 5:23; and the soul and spirit should be distinct just as joints and marrow are (Heb. 4:12).

The reason we should reject the first glance, though, is that the biblical references that support a distinction between soul and body or spirit and body, as given above, seem to treat the soul and spirit as names for the same thing. That is, someone dies when the soul leaves the body and when the spirit leaves the body, and returns to life when the soul or spirit returns. The part that survives death is called the soul and also the spirit (or just the person, when these words are missing). (A second reason, which is hiding as an unstated premise, is the conviction that if the Bible comes from God it is consistent and not contradictory. If these verses imply trichotomy where elsewhere we find dualism, then I don't know how to reconcile the conflict.)

A few verses we haven't yet looked at use parallelism in such a way as to show that the soul and spirit are names for the same thing. For example, consider Isaiah 26:9 (already mentioned), addressed to the Lord:

> My *soul* yearns for you in the night;
> my *spirit* within me earnestly seeks you.

The soul yearning and the spirit earnestly seeking are the same activity, which means that "soul" and "spirit" are names for the same thing. (That's different from saying that they're *synonyms,* which I wouldn't do; but I'm not going to afflict you with my lexicographer's hair-splitting.) In the same way consider Luke 1:46-47, where Mary sings:

> My *soul* magnifies the Lord,
> and my *spirit* rejoices in God my Savior.

Again, the soul magnifying and the spirit rejoicing in God are the same activity, and thus the soul and spirit should be considered the same thing.

So what can we do about the apparent meaning of these two trichotomist verses? It's not too hard to explain 1 Thessalonians 5:23 by suggesting that it's like Deuteronomy 6:5, "love the LORD your God with all your heart and with all your soul and with all your might." Heart, soul, and might aren't separate components of man in this context, but different ways of looking at man: in character and orientation, in the inner life and appetite, and in the energy of turning motives into action. When New Testament authors add "mind" to the list (Mark 12:30; Luke 10:26), they're continuing the idea of looking at man from every vantage point. In fact, heart and soul (and mind) are probably terms for the same thing; and the effect of piling up these terms is to emphasize that it's the whole person that does the loving. With this in mind, we can see that in 1 Thessalonians 5:23 Paul is giving us a list that emphasizes that he wants God to instill holiness in the whole person, nothing excepted. (Besides, the close of a letter would be an odd place for Paul introduce fine distinctions that he hasn't even touched on in the body of the letter.)

Hebrews 4:12 is a little harder, but I'll give it a try. The word "division" has the idea of splitting up or distributing (in Heb. 2:4 it lies behind "distributed"). So the idea isn't that of "making a distinction between soul and spirit, and between joints and marrow," but instead of splitting things open and laying them bare to divine inspection.

Defining the Kind of Dualism

Christians who argue against dualism in favor of a form of monism often do so because they have perceived that some forms of dualism have led to abuses, and thus they condemn the lot. This form of argument is not sound, because the mere fact of *abuse* does not take away the possibility of *proper use;* but it does warn us to be wary of some common traps.

The form of dualism that is most liable to abuse is that associated with the French philosopher René Descartes (1596–1650). In this system the body and soul are distinct things joined in a mysterious way in the pineal gland (a small, pine-cone shaped body found behind the third ventricle of your brain; since Descartes' time researchers have found that this gland produces the hormone melatonin). Descartes' dualism tends to make the body and soul almost independent, whereas the Bible seems to see them as interacting quite closely.

The Bible doesn't get very specific when it comes to defining just what the soul is, or where the soul leaves off and the body takes over. Instead it pretty clearly presents body and soul as hopelessly intertwined; man is a body-soul *nexus,* or *tangle,* and is fully man when both are healthy.

Once we see this intertwined relationship, a thousand other things become clear. We can see why the Christian hope for eternity is in a resurrected body in a new heavens and earth. We can see why Paul can call our bodies temples of the indwelling Holy Spirit (1 Cor. 6:19), and so we must keep them pure—not just sexually, but in our eyes, ears, mouths, and hands; why lawful enjoyment of our physical nature—including sexuality—is a spiritual matter, and pleasing to God. We can see why there's a connection between our bodily health and our spiritual health, and why being over-tired commonly makes us feel spiritually dull; and why brain injuries can deprive us of spiritual capacities. We can see why Proverbs lays so much stress on the proper and prayerful use of the rod—inflicting pain in the body can bring eternal benefits for the soul (Prov. 22:15). Now we can see why our first parents' sin—a spiritual matter—made our bodies subject to decay and death. And we can see what human wholeness consists of: when we work well, love well, and worship well.

This intertwined relationship between soul and body also explains why an important part of changing our character is prayerfully *doing* the things we ought: character works from the outside in. As C. S. Lewis said in *Mere Christianity,*

> Do not waste time bothering whether you "love" your neighbour; act as if you did. As soon as we do this we find one of the great secrets. When you are behaving as if you loved someone, you will presently come to love him.

So I don't want my daughter to frown when she's crossed: I tell her the frown will work its way from her face to her heart. And I don't want her to stand with her hands on her hips when I have to correct her, because a posture of defiance will produce an attitude of defiance.

You can understand why you and your children need hugs—because you are physical beings; and your physical health will affect the spiritual. And you can appreciate why you need the sacraments, and can't expect to be spiritually healthy without them. They're like hugs from God. Could children get along well if you didn't hug them—a lot? Well, we need plenty of hugs from our heavenly Father.

I think we can also see the wisdom in the biblical material on bodily position in prayer and worship: your posture affects your attitude. Hence worshipers kneel, stand, raise their hands, lie prostrate. What is Christian public worship? It's when the Maker of heaven and earth welcomes his blood-bought people into his presence, to love them and give himself to them in a way that's not available anywhere else, to grant them a taste of what their souls yearn for. How can I give the full range of response to such an inexpressible privilege unless my whole self is involved? For example: when we confess our sins together in worship and ask for forgiveness, we ought to be humble suppliants. I know I'm usually not. Perhaps the way to begin bringing my soul into line is to make my body kneel.

We can sum it up with another quote from C. S. Lewis (*Mere Christianity*):

> There is no good trying to be more spiritual than God. God never meant man to be a purely spiritual creature. That is why he uses material things like bread and wine to put the new life into us. We may think this rather

crude and unspiritual. God does not: He invented eating. He likes matter. He invented it.

THE IMAGE OF GOD

In Genesis 1:26-27, as we saw already, we read about God's making of the first human beings (italics added):

> [26] Then God said, "Let us make man *in our image, after our likeness.* And let them have dominion over the fish of the sea and over the birds of the heavens and over the livestock and over all the earth and over every creeping thing that creeps on the earth."
>
> [27] So God created man *in his own image,*
> *in the image of God* he created him;
> male and female he created them.

As we saw earlier, being made "in God's image" and "after God's likeness" is something that distinguishes man from every other animal. But what do these terms mean?

To begin with, many of the earlier theologians thought that the "image" and the "likeness" were separate things—with perhaps the idea that one of them was lost to man in the fall of Genesis 3, while the other remains. But this won't do: first, because Genesis 1:26 uses the two expressions without any connecting word—it says "in our image, after our likeness," with no "and" to join them—and that indicates that the two expressions are talking about the same thing and help to define each other. Second, in verse 27 we just have "in God's image"—this makes the best sense if the two terms are about the same thing, and thus the author only had to use one of them in the next verse. And finally, in Genesis 5:1 we read that God made man "in the likeness of God." So the words "image" and "likeness" describe the same thing, and clarify each other; from now on I'll just use the term "image." But what is that thing they describe?

The most common answer to this question in the history of Christian theology is that the image of God is some property of human beings that shows a resemblance to God—especially the fact that each human being has reason and will, that is, the ability to know truth and to obey that truth. The theologians have often spoken of the wider and narrower sense of the image: in the wider sense, all people have the image, because they all have reason and will—though they may misuse them. In the narrower sense, the image consists of these abilities in full harmony with God—knowing things in light of how they relate to God, and feeling and choosing the things that are pleasing to God. The image-in-the-narrower-sense was lost to mankind in their fall; the image-in-the-wider-sense was badly damaged, but still remains in every person you meet. I will call this the *resemblance* view: the way that man is resembles the way that God is.

For a number of reasons that we need not examine here, many theologians in the twentieth century began to insist that the Bible doesn't concern itself with what God and man *are,* but with what they *do;* and this led them to reject the traditional resemblance view of the image of God. They replaced it in one of two ways: first, some noted that since Genesis 1:26 follows "let us make man in our image, after our likeness" with "and let them have dominion," it must be that the dominion defines what the image is. Those who argue this way find support in Psalm 8, with its famous question "what is man that you are mindful of him, and the son of man that you care for him?" (v. 4). The psalm goes on to say,

> [5] Yet you have made him a little lower than the heavenly beings,
> and crowned him with glory and honor.
> [6] You have given him dominion over the works of your hands;
> you have put all things under his feet,
> [7] all sheep and oxen,
> and also the beasts of the field,
> [8] the birds of the heavens, and the fish of the sea,
> whatever passes along the paths of the seas.

This passage, which clearly is based on the Genesis account, shows us that the key thing about man's place under God is his work of ruling (so the argument goes). We can call this the *representative* view: man is to rule the creation on God's behalf, as God's representative.

The second replacement view starts with noticing that verse 27 has three lines, and the first two state and restate that "God created man in his own image," while the third line adds something new: "male and female he created them." The addition, says this view, tells us that it is mankind as male and female that supplies the image of God—or, more broadly, man in relationship with others, and also with God. We may therefore call it the *relational* view: man is fully man in relationship to God and others of mankind.

Which of these three views—the resemblance, representative, or relational—is right? Or perhaps none of them is right, or some combination of them. Let's now look at the biblical passages and the meanings of the biblical words to see if we can draw some conclusions.

The first thing we notice is that the number of passages is fairly small, and we can group them into three categories: (a) passages that speak of mankind as made in God's image; (b) passages that speak of Christ as the perfect image of God; and (c) passages that speak of the image as the target or norm for the believer's moral transformation. We'll take these in their turn.

(a) Mankind as Made in God's Image

Genesis 5:1 looks back to 1:26-27, reminding us that God made man "in the likeness of God." Here the Hebrew uses *likeness,* not *image,* which helps us see that the two terms refer to the same thing. (When we are looking at the meanings of the Hebrew words, we'll come back to this paragraph, since v. 3 tells us that Adam "fathered a son in his own likeness, after his image.") Genesis 9:6 offers a reason for capital punishment for murderers: "for God made man in his own image."

The New Testament gives us James 3:9, where James is shocked that with our tongue "we bless our Lord and Father, and with it we curse people who are made in the likeness of God." This verse is clear that there is some sense in which other people are "in the likeness of God"—regardless of the effects of man's fall into sin in Genesis 3.

(b) Christ as the Perfect Image of God

Colossians 1:15 tells us that Christ "is the image of the invisible God," and doesn't say what that is—but the context goes on to describe his first place in creation: "all things were created through him and for him" (v. 16). Paul says almost the same words in 2 Corinthians 4:4, calling Christ "the image of God." This ties in to the third category, because the context of verses 1-6 is about seeing the glory of God in the face of Jesus Christ, and because 3:18 had said,

> And we all, with unveiled face, beholding the glory of the Lord, are being transformed into the same image from one degree of glory to another.

The repetition of the word "image" and the "glory of the Lord" shows that these verses share the same topic; and the idea is that the image, namely the way Christ is—which shows us what God is like—is the target for God's process of transforming his people.

(c) The Image as the Target for Moral Transformation

Several verses in the New Testament speak of the believer's moral renewal in terms of the image of God. For example, Colossians 3:10 says that believers "have put on the new self, which is being renewed in knowledge after the image of its creator." Here the creator of the new self is God (or maybe Christ); and the image of the creator is the measuring stick and goal of the moral renewal that God is working in his people. Ephesians 4:24 is similar: believers have been taught "to put on the new self, created after the likeness of God [literally, *created according to God*] in true righteousness and holiness."

Along these lines we find that "the image of Christ" is the measuring stick in Romans 8:29: "those whom [God] foreknew he also predestined to be conformed to the image of his Son." Similarly in 1 Corinthians 15:49, "Just as we [believers] have borne the image of the man of dust, we shall also bear the image of the man of heaven." The man of dust is Adam; the man of heaven is Christ (see v. 47); and to bear the image of one of them is to be like him (see v. 48).

Now let's consider the meanings of the words used in Genesis 1:26, "image" and "likeness." The term "image" is generally used for a solid representation of something: for example, in 1 Samuel 6:5 the Philistines make "images"—little golden figurines—of their tumors and of the mice that plague them. In Ezekiel 23:14 the wanton Oholibah (figure for Judah) "saw men portrayed on the wall, the images of the Chaldeans portrayed in vermilion"; these images were relief carvings on the wall. In Daniel 2:31-33 and 3:1 the equivalent word in Aramaic is used for colossal statues. Often the image is an idol, as in Numbers 33:52 (made of cast metal); 2 Kings 11:18; Amos 5:26; Ezekiel 7:20 (and probably 16:17).

On the other hand, "likeness" is a more general word for "resemblance," without saying what kind of resemblance is in view (you get that from the context). The word is often used in comparisons, as in Isaiah 13:4, where "as of a great multitude" is literally "the likeness of a great multitude." Likewise, see Isaiah 40:18, "what likeness" will you compare with God? (Compare also Ezek. 1:5, 10.) In Daniel 10:16, "one in the likeness of the children of man touched [Daniel's] lips"—the angelic being looks like a man. In one place the "likeness" is a carved one, "figures of gourds" (2 Chron. 4:3).

But in Genesis 1:26 we don't have the words "image" and "likeness" by themselves, we have them with prepositions, "*in* the image" and "*after* the likeness": can we find examples of our words in these combinations so that we can know what the phrases mean? There aren't many such examples, but they do help. For example, Psalm 58:4, "they have venom *like* the venom of a serpent," is more literally "they have venom *after the likeness of* the venom of a serpent." Daniel 10:16, "one *in* the likeness of the children of man" is more literally "one *after* the likeness of the children of man," and is equivalent to "one *like* the children of man." Finally, when we look at Genesis 5:1-3, which depends on chapter 1, we see that the prepositions with "image" and "likeness" are reversed:

> [1] When God created man, he made him *in* the likeness [contrast 1:26, *after* the likeness] of God. [2] Male and female he created them, and he blessed them and named them Man when they were created. [3] When Adam had lived 130 years, he fathered a son *in* his own likeness, *after* his image [contrast 1:26 *in* the image, *after* the likeness], and named him Seth.

From these examples we can see that to say "A is *after the likeness of* B" is the same as saying "A is *like* B." Further, we can see from the way the prepositions get switched around between Genesis 1:26 and 5:1-3, that "*in* the image/likeness" and "*after* the image/likeness" are pretty close in meaning, if not equivalent. We can then suggest that to say "A is *in the image of* B" is about the same as saying "A is *a concrete resemblance of* B." You can see how this makes sense of Genesis 5:3: Seth is just like Adam, and he is a concrete resemblance of him. Therefore we can paraphrase Genesis 1:26 as:

> "Let us make man to be our concrete resemblance, to be like us."

The best way to put all this together in Genesis 1:26 is to see that "in our image" and "after our likeness" are two descriptions of the same thing, and they serve to clarify each other: man is a bodily creature who is like God—and like God in ways that no other bodily creature is.

And in what ways is this man "like God"? We have no reason from the Bible to suppose that it must only be in what man *does,* as opposed to what he *is;* instead, what he does expresses what he is—just as we can draw conclusions about the way that God is from what he does. For example, in Genesis 1–2 we see God expressing intelligence in the way he has designed and prepared the world as an ideal place for man to live and love; this intelligence is coupled with energetic creativity. We see God expressing language since he *says* "Let there be . . ." From the way that God sees that the things he makes are "good," we see both that God is himself moral and that he appreciates beauty—since the word "good" covers both realms of thought.

Here we shouldn't neglect the seventh day, where God enjoys his Sabbath, blesses it, and makes it holy. Similarly God expresses his relational nature in the way he sets up a relationship with the man (Gen. 2:15-17), as well as in his concern for the man to have a mate fit for him so that he won't be "alone" (Gen. 2:18). Of course in God these features are not limited by time, space, or change—and in this respect man as a bodily creature is *not* like God.

All of this points toward a version of the resemblance view: features of man's nature resemble God's own nature. How can we get our minds around this? Think about the way you draw a picture of a scene, say a city street: you represent the street as two lines that will converge with each other, you use acute angles to represent the corners of buildings, and so on. Or imagine reducing Beethoven's Ninth Symphony for piano. The same piano key has to do the work of a number of symphonic instruments. Thus the two-dimensional picture is "in the image, after the likeness" of the three-dimensional scene; the piano piece is a scaled-down representation of the symphony. As the commentator Derek Kidner put it, man is

> an expression or transcription of the eternal, incorporeal creator in terms of temporal, bodily, creaturely existence.

Man, unlike the other animals, has the ability to reason, a will to choose what pleases him, language, a moral pointer, the ability to make and enjoy beauty, and the capacity to enter into relationships governed by love and commitment. On the other hand, we are finite, we are bounded by time, and we change (in which respects we are like the other animals). So we may say that man is an *analogy* for God.

In the first humans as they came from God's hand, these features were also thoroughly in tune with God's own holy will and pleasure—which meant that wedlock was full of bliss and harmony; worship was full of delight and fulfillment; and work was joyful and caring. Nothing in my experience matches with that, and I'm willing to bet it's the same with you. What has happened, where did all this bliss and purity go, and is there any hope for us to be healed? We'll discuss this more in the next chapter, but at least for now we can notice a few things. First, we can see why the "wide sense" and "narrow sense" of the image help us: the wide sense describes the abilities man has that are analogies to those found in our Maker, while the narrow sense describes man with all those abilities working fully in tune with our Maker, and hence that more fully reflect our Maker's own character. Second, this explains why the New Testament both calls Christ the image of God and pictures his character as the target for our own renewal and growth in grace. Christ, as perfect man, portrays the character of God as fully as man can; and he also shows us what God, in his unspeakable love, intends to make Christians into as the remedy for their current defilement. Hence we read in 1 John 3:2-3 (italics added),

> [2] Beloved, we are God's children now, and what we will be has not yet appeared; but we know that when he appears *we will be like him,* because we shall see him as he is. [3] And everyone who thus hopes in him purifies himself as he is pure.

This approach to the resemblance view does a better job of explaining what we actually find in the Bible than do the relational and representative views. To begin with, the relational view pays little attention to the words we find in Genesis, which don't express that view very clearly. Further, the grammar of the addition in Genesis 1:26, "and let them have dominion," does not favor the idea that it's explaining the image; rather, it's the form that typically expresses the result. As the commentator Franz Delitzsch put it,

> the dominion over the earth . . . is not . . . its content but its consequence.

In other words, we could have rendered God's speech in this verse,

> Let us make man in our image, after our likeness, *so that they may* have dominion . . .

And finally, we now have a way of explaining the valid insights of the other views of the image: although neither the relational nor the representative views actually tell us what they image *is,* they do show us the main *consequences* of the image of God: it is our make-up as reasoning, choosing, speaking, and beauty-loving creatures that moves us to seek relationships with God and with other people, and that leaves us incomplete without these relationships. These same abilities move and enable us to rule over the rest of the creation—God intended for us to act as his vice-regents, showing his kindness, wisdom, and justice; but even in our perversion, we're still pretty good at "ruling" (though it's more like "lording it over").

If man is composed of a body and soul, can we say in which part of him we find the image of God? Many Christian teachers have located the image in the soul—probably because of its capacity for transcendence, which makes our reasoning and choosing meaningful. I think this is a mistake, for several reasons. First, Genesis says nothing about the soul: it simply says that *man* is to be in the image and after the likeness of God. Second, the idea that man is a body-soul tangle, and the fact that he is (in the words of Derek Kidner quoted above), "an expression or transcription of the eternal, incorporeal creator in terms of temporal, bodily, creaturely existence," tells us that our bodies are an essential part of the transcription. I would prefer to say that it was man as a body-soul tangle that was to express the image of God; man's body is the specially designed *vehicle* of this expression (this includes your brain, but also your muscles, bones, and circulatory system).

The resemblance view of God's image helps us in another very important way: it gives us confidence that we can speak about God and say something meaningful. If people were made to resemble the way that God is—by transposition, mind you, as we have seen, not by exact resemblance—then it follows that we are able to say some things about God that are true, since our minds reflect something of his. But the things that we say will be analogies, not perfect descriptions of God's own being. That is, when we say that God is a "father" to his people, we mean that there is something in the way he treats his people that is like the way a good human father treats his children—and at the same time we recognize that there are some things that are *un*like a human father. The case is the same when we speak of God's jealousy or wrath or love. Therefore one task of theology is to hedge our analogical language about to keep us from drawing absurd conclusions from it. But whatever we do we must never say, "Well, it's *just* an analogy": the analogies are the only way we can speak of God at all; and the Bible has guided us in which analogies are sound, and we should follow its lead.

C. S. Lewis, in his *Letters to Malcolm,* shows us how to use these analogies in Scripture, how to use theology to keep our heads, and why we need to stick with the Scriptural analogies instead of inventing our own:

> We are constantly represented as exciting the Divine wrath or pity—even as "grieving" God. I know this language is analogical. But when we say that, we must not smuggle in the idea that we can throw the analogy away and, as it were, get in behind it to a purely literal truth. All we can really substitute for the analogical expression is some theological abstraction. And the abstraction's value is almost entirely negative. It warns us against drawing absurd consequences from the analogical expression by prosaic extrapolations. . . .
>
> I suggest two rules for exegesis. (1) Never take the images literally. (2) When the *purport* of the images—what they say to our fear and hope and will and affections—seems to conflict with the theological abstractions,

> trust the purport of the images every time. For our abstract thinking is itself a tissue of analogies: a continual modeling of spiritual reality in legal or chemical or mechanical terms. Are these likely to be more adequate than the sensuous, organic, and personal images of scripture—light and darkness, river and well, seed and harvest, master and servant, hen and chickens, father and child? The footprints of the Divine are more visible in that rich soil than across rocks or slag-heaps. Hence what they now call "demythologising" Christianity can easily be "re-mythologising" it—and substituting a poorer mythology for a richer.

ARE ADAM AND EVE OUR ANCESTORS?

Most Christians have understood the Bible to say that all mankind have descended from the first pair, Adam and Eve. The whole theological question of "original sin"—that is, the guilt and pollution all people inherit and are born with—has to do with our origin in Adam and Eve, who sinned and brought us down with them.

The way in which we inherit guilt and pollution from our first parents is a tricky subject, and one that divides Christians; but I don't intend to try to sort that matter out. Instead, in this section I want to show that the traditional understanding of Adam and Eve as the first parents of us all has a sound basis in the Bible.

To begin with, God decided to make a man on the sixth day (Gen. 1:26). As the ESV margin there points out, "The Hebrew word for *man (adam)* is the generic term for mankind and becomes the proper name *Adam.*" That is, Adam is the first *adam* ("man"). His wife Eve comes from his own body, because there was no other source for a fitting helper (Gen. 2:18-22). In Adam's delight he assigns to her the name "woman"—using the ordinary Hebrew word for a female human—and calls himself a "man"—using the Hebrew word for a male human (Gen. 2:23). Their relationship becomes the pattern for every human marriage (Gen. 2:24).

When we get to Genesis 3:20, we can nail down the impression we get from these verses:

> The man called his wife's name Eve [Life-giver], because she was the mother of all living.

Presumably this means "the mother of all people who would ever live."

And finally, in Acts 17:26-27 Paul tells the Athenian philosophers that God "made from one man every nation of mankind to live on all the face of the earth, having determined allotted periods and the boundaries of their habitation, that they should seek God, in the hope that they might feel their way toward him and find him."

This helps us understand why the Bible sees all mankind as sharing a common human nature: we all can think true thoughts and can make moral choices. It also shows why all mankind should be included in God's plan: the gospel is to go to all the world. We can also see why the moral goodness of Christ is the target that God has set for the spiritual growth of every Christian, regardless of his race or ethnic background.

We will see in the next chapter that this unity of mankind in Adam and Eve explains why their sin could be passed on to the whole human race.

The Possibility of Science

The creation account in Genesis shows why Christians should believe that science is not only possible for mankind but also a good expression of our humanity. Back in chapter 4 I noted that, even though we shouldn't call Genesis 1–2 a "scientific account," that doesn't mean that it has no bearing on science. In fact, it lays a foundation for all good science and philosophy, because it tells us that a good and wise God made the world for us to enjoy; and the things that he made have natures that are knowable (for example, the plants and animals reproduce "after their kind").

Further, because God made man in his image, our senses and our reason can allow us to say things that are true. Again, remember that I argued above that dominion is the result of man being in God's image. If we read Genesis 1 and 2 together, we can see that God made the man, put him in the Garden, made the woman, and then commissioned them to "fill the earth": that is, beginning from Eden, to work their way outwards, bringing the blessings of Eden to all the earth. That's what it meant to "have dominion" over the earth—to manage all of its creatures and resources for holy and wise purposes. For the world to be manageable, it must be—at least partly—understandable and reliable. (How could Adam work the Garden of Eden and keep it, and safely eat of the allowable fruits, if he couldn't understand how to grow what he wanted and to prune or weed out what he didn't want?) There's no reason to believe that man came from God's hand fully loaded with all the knowledge he'd ever need; no, he can learn from experience and increase his knowledge and skill. And he would need every bit of that knowledge and skill if he was to fulfill the job of making the whole earth serve good purposes as Eden did.

And man can speak about what he has learned, so that others can benefit from his experience.

This leads me to conclude that some form of what I called "critical realism" back in chapter 3 is exactly what the Bible supports. That is, there's a real world that's outside of us, and we can interact with it and learn some true things about it: that's the "realism" part. But no one can see everything, no one has been around forever, everyone is finite and limited: therefore we have to be "critical" of what we claim to know, and willing to rethink it. (Sinfulness, which we'll discuss in the next chapter, may provide even further wrinkles.)

So man as God first made him was well equipped to approach the world, to learn about it, to manage it to good purposes, and to nurture it carefully. In other words, he was ready-made to be a good scientist. When a Christian, guided by biblical morals, follows his curiosity about the world and thanks the Maker of it all for such a fascinating world, he is expressing something of God's image; and God is delighted.

9

THE GLORIOUS RUIN

Human Nature After the Fall

IN THE LAST CHAPTER we saw what a wonder the first pair of humans were. But our experience doesn't match that: new colors have come into the picture, and have changed it. The first three chapters of Genesis accomplish three important goals. They show us why the things we meet in the world work the way they do—because God made them to work that way. They show us why, on the other hand, our life in the world is so different from the idyllic life of Adam and Eve—because sin entered in and spoiled us badly. And they foster in us a relentless yearning for some kind of healing for ourselves and for the world, so that we'll submit to God's way of saving us and look forward to the day of renewal for all things.

In this chapter, then, I will outline the changes that came into human nature through the great disaster of Genesis 3, called "the fall of man." In the next chapter I will continue to explore the results of this disaster, this time focusing beyond human nature to the rest of the creation.

GOD'S ARRANGEMENT WITH ADAM AND EVE

If we read Genesis 1–2 carefully, we can see that God made the first man somewhere ("the land," 2:5), and then took the man and put him in the Garden of Eden. He then made the woman. In Genesis 2:15-17, we find out what obligations he laid on Adam:

> [15] The LORD God took the man and put him in the garden of Eden to work it and keep it. [16] And the LORD God commanded the man, saying, "You may surely eat of every tree of the garden, [17] but of the tree of the knowledge of good and evil you shall not eat, for in the day that you eat of it you shall surely die."

What is the best way to describe this relationship that God set up? I think the best term to use is "covenant." Some will object to this, either because the word "covenant" doesn't appear in this account (the usual Hebrew word for that makes its first showing in Gen. 6:18), or because they think that to be a covenant it has to have an explicit oath and ceremony of ratification (such as animal sacrifice, compare Gen. 15:7-21).

But neither of these objections holds any water. As to the first, we would be silly to insist that we could only find a particular *concept* where we have the standard terminology for it. As we'll see below, Genesis 3 doesn't use any of the standard Hebrew words for sin or transgression; but to conclude that therefore what happened wasn't a sin would be sheer nonsense. The Old Testament rarely uses the word "Messiah" for the promised heir of David; but how could we take anyone seriously who denied that Isaiah 9:6 ("For to us a child is born, to us a son is given . . .") is about the Messiah?

Consider this example: in 2 Samuel 7 (parallel with 1 Chronicles 17) we read of God's promise to David of an enduring house (leading up to the Messiah). The word "covenant" does not appear there; but Psalm 89:3, referring to this promise, calls it a "covenant" (compare also vv. 28, 34, 39), because that's what it was. That's why it shouldn't surprise us to find that the prophet Hosea (either 700 or 500 years after Moses, depending on how we date the exodus) described his generation, "like Adam they transgressed the covenant" (Hosea 6:7).

This points the way to why we may safely toss out the second objection as well. We have to be sure we know what the right definition of the word is before we can say whether a passage speaks of its idea. And the notion that a "covenant" in the Bible *must* have such elements as a formal oath and ratification ceremony is just wrong: it's wrong because it takes features of *some* covenants and says they have to be features of *all* covenants. For example, marriage is called a "covenant" in Proverbs 2:17 (an adulteress "forgets the covenant of her God") and Malachi 2:14 ("your wife by covenant"). David and Jonathan made a covenant with each other in 1 Samuel 18:3 (see also 20:8; 23:18; Ps. 55:20). The Lord made a "covenant" with Phineas and his descendants in Numbers 25:12-13, promising them a lasting priesthood. These examples show that, in the Old Testament, a "covenant" formalizes a relationship between two parties; they are to be true to the covenant by keeping their promises of loyalty and commitment. There will be consequences for keeping or not keeping those promises (benefits for keeping, punishments for not keeping). For example, in marriage a husband and wife promise to hold fast to each other in exclusive love. If they are true to their promise, they will enjoy and deepen their companionship and love; if one breaks faith, the relationship is ruined (compare Matt. 19:3-9).

So we can in fact call the arrangement of Genesis 2:15-17 a covenant: it comes from God's initiative; verses 16-17 spell out the condition pretty clearly, obedience to God's command. The punishment for breaking the command is also clear, namely Adam will "surely die" (we'll discuss just what this means shortly). The passage does not spell out the reward for faithfulness, but I think it implies it: the relationship will continue, and Adam will have access to the tree of life.

The passage also tells us very little about those two special trees: "the tree of life . . . in the midst of the garden, and the tree of the knowledge of good and evil" (Gen. 2:9). There is no reason to suppose ahead of time that these trees are "magic," as if by some power in themselves they could bestow their effects; let's look at the Bible to see if we can draw some conclusions about these two trees.

The image of "the tree of life" appears later on in the Old Testament: Proverbs 3:18, applied to wisdom; 11:30, to the fruit of the righteous; 13:12, to desire fulfilled; and 15:4, to a healing tongue. In Proverbs each of these things will help keep us on the path to life (everlasting happiness), faithful in doing the Lord's will. In the New Testament the image of eating from the tree of life appears in Revelation 2:7; 22:2, 14, 19; it's a privilege given to those who enter Paradise. I understand this privilege to be that of being confirmed in holiness forever, and therefore being qualified to stay in Paradise. So I think the simplest explanation of the tree of life is that it's some kind of sacrament that would confirm the man in his moral condition: this is why God doesn't want him to have it after his sin (3:22), because it would confirm him in his moral state of sinfulness, and this would be horrible.

To figure out what "the tree of knowing good and evil" is, we need to discover just what it means to "know good and evil." (Note carefully: it's not a tree *of knowledge,* as if knowledge were bad or even dangerous, but a tree of *knowing good and evil.*) We have to account for the fact that in Genesis 3:22 God actually admits that "the man has become like one of us in knowing good and evil," that is, that the man has come to have some property in common with God as a result of eating of that tree. In the rest of the Old Testament the expressions "*knowing* [or *understanding*] good and evil" (for example, Deut. 1:39; 2 Sam. 14:17; 19:35; 1 Kings 3:9) carry the idea of discerning between them. The best way to account for all this is to conclude with the German Bible scholar Franz Delitzsch (1813–1890) that God intended that through this tree the humans would come to know good and evil: either from above, as masters over temptation, or from below, as slaves to sin. As C. S. Lewis wrote,

> When a man is getting better, he understands more and more clearly the evil that is still left in him. When a man is getting worse, he understands his badness less and less. . . . Good people know about both good and evil: bad people do not know about either.

The pronouns "you" in Genesis 2:16-17 are masculine singular: that is, they mean "you, Adam." But if we pay careful attention to the details (and to the ESV margins) we can see that God is here treating Adam as a representative for his family and his descendants, and not just on his own. In Genesis 3:3, the woman paraphrases 2:17 to the serpent; but the pronoun "you" is now *plural:* she has seen herself included in the covenant made with her husband. But in 3:9-11, God speaks to the man alone ("you" is singular again), and in 3:19 physical death ("returning to the dust"), which comes to all people, is the sentence pronounced specifically on the man. And when this couple are driven out from the Garden, neither they nor their descendants may return; and their descendants follow them in the way they decline into sin in Genesis 4, and all of them die in Genesis 5. In 3:17 God says to Adam, "cursed is the ground because of you" (again, "you" is singular), indicating that Adam brought punishment to the rest of the creation as well.

These details of Genesis show why Paul could say in Romans 5:12-14:

> [12] Therefore, just as sin came into the world through one man, and death through sin, and so death spread to all men because all sinned— [13] for sin indeed was in the world before the law was given, but sin is not counted where there is no law. [14] Yet death reigned from Adam to Moses, even over those whose sinning was not like the transgression of Adam, who was a type of the one who was to come.

And in Romans 8:19-23 he adds,

> [19] For the creation waits with eager longing for the revealing of the sons of God. [20] For the creation was subjected to futility, not willingly, but because of him who subjected it, in hope [21] that the creation itself will be set free from its bondage to decay and obtain the freedom of the glory of the children of God. [22] For we know that the whole creation has been groaning together in the pains of childbirth until now.

Theologians call Adam a "public person": what he did he did as a representative for all mankind, and as the appointed ruler of the creation. Although sin and moral evil existed before Adam did, it had not yet entered the material creation; it was limited to Satan and his fallen angels (and the Bible tells us precious little about them or their fall).

The First Sin

Genesis 3 describes how the first humans, Adam and his wife, were untrue to the covenant, and thus brought sin into their own lives and the lives of all their children. There is so much to explore in this story, but for our purposes we will especially focus on what it tells us about human nature, about where human sin came from and how it can be healed, and about what changes it brought about in human nature.

The story tells us that a serpent led the woman into eating from the forbidden tree, and that she then gave some to her husband, who also ate. But who or what is that serpent?

It's definitely *not* just a snake, and we can see that for several reasons. First, in Genesis 3:3 the woman tells the serpent that God had said, "You shall not eat of the fruit of the tree that is in the midst of the garden, neither shall you touch it, lest you die." Then in verse 4 the serpent says to the woman, "You will not *surely* die." The serpent introduced the word "surely" here—he must have known what God said back in 2:17 ("in the day that you eat of it you shall *surely* die"). Second, the Bible does *not* fancy that animals can speak; when Balaam's donkey speaks in Numbers 22:28, it's because the Lord "opened its mouth." So the serpent is the mouthpiece for some other power; and when we consider what filth it speaks (it directly contradicts what God had said, and stirs up disobedience), we conclude that the power must be demonic. Therefore the Jewish interpretive tradition found in Wisdom 1:13; 2:24; and in John 8:44; Revelation 12:9; 20:2, that the serpent is the mouthpiece of Satan, is the best explanation.

This tempter worked by deceit: in verse 1 he raises the question, "Did God actually say, 'You shall not eat of any tree of the garden'?" He's not really asking whether God in fact said it, but whether God is reasonable since he did say it: in modern English we would say, "Can you believe that God actually said it?" He then goes on in verse 4 to contradict God's warning (as we saw above), and to suggest in verse 5 that God is stingy: "God knows that when you eat of it your eyes will be opened, and you will be like God, knowing good and evil." The implication is that these are benefits that God wants to keep to himself. The serpent never tells Eve to disobey; all he does is cast doubt on whether God's motives can be trusted, and whether he'll carry out his threats. The woman can draw her own conclusion, which she does while looking at the tree (v. 6). Is it any wonder that the Savior of mankind calls Satan "a liar and the father of lies" (John 8:44)?

Our first parents swallowed the bait and disobeyed God's command. Genesis is silent as to just how they could have done so, what it was in them that allowed them to be so taken in. Nevertheless they did it.

Yes, I said they *disobeyed;* they *sinned.* Some have observed that Genesis doesn't use words like "sin" or "disobey," and thus the story is not about what man lost by sin, but what they failed to gain because they didn't pass the test. This is an example of a fallacy we have already mentioned, confusing the presence of the thing with the presence of the standard terms for the thing. Besides, consider Genesis 3:11, where God asks:

> "Have you eaten of the tree of which I commanded you not to eat?"

"Have you done what I commanded you not to do?" is a pretty good paraphrase for "Have you disobeyed me?"

Now let's draw a few conclusions about the sin of our first parents. First, the temptation did not come from created human nature, which was good; it came from outside human nature, from a demonic enemy. The temptation made use of deceit, which then blossomed into desire, which led to disobedience.

HUMAN NATURE AFTER GENESIS 3

What impact did this sin have on the natures of our first parents, and what impact on the nature we inherit from them?

In the first place, their attitudes changed. When they had eaten, "the eyes of both were opened, and they knew that they were naked. And they sewed fig leaves together and made themselves loincloths" (v. 7). Now since they already knew that they were naked (see 2:25, "the man and his wife were both naked and were not ashamed"), this must describe a changed disposition toward their nakedness; and we can see that they went on to cover themselves. The blissful innocence of 2:25 has been shattered.

Their attitudes changed, not just toward themselves, but toward God and each other. In verse 8 they "hid themselves from the presence of the LORD God," and in verse 10 the man explains, "I heard the sound of you in the garden, and I was afraid, because I was naked, and I hid myself." Now, before they disobeyed God's command, what do you suppose they would do when they heard the sound of the LORD God in the Garden? I suspect they'd drop whatever they were doing and rush over to greet him! But not anymore: now they're afraid, because they're guilty.

Then when God questions the man and woman about what they have done, they try to shift the blame: in verse 12 the man says, "The woman whom you gave to be with me, *she* gave me fruit of the tree, and I ate." (In the Hebrew the *she* is emphatic: "*She's* the one who did it!") What he says is factual, but not complete: he leaves out his own part, and spins the account to put himself in the best light ("I'm a victim!"). Then in verse 13 the woman says, "The serpent deceived me, and I ate"—true enough, but she's left out the bit about her own cooperation.

The chaste beauty of delight in God and harmony with each other and with their own consciences has fallen in ruins. We can easily picture the situation between the pair before God met them, just the way Milton described it in *Paradise Lost* (end of book ix):

> Thus they in mutual accusation spent
> The fruitless hours, but neither self-condemning;
> And of their vain contest appeared no end.

Blame someone else, argue, and above all, avoid responsibility!

Their inner disposition was changed; and so was their good sense. When they hid themselves among the bushes to get away from God, did they really think that would work? (We might remember another bonehead, Jonah, who said in Jonah 1:9, "I fear the LORD, the God of heaven, who made the sea and the dry land"—and yet tried to flee by taking a sea voyage!) I don't think this means that Adam and Eve's intelligence was less—after all, they figured out how to sew fig leaves together to make loincloths. Instead, I think this shows that they no longer thought clearly about what they were doing; that is, their judgment was clouded.

We see further consequences in the sentences God pronounces on them in verses 16-19. In verse 16, the Lord God says to the woman,

> "I will surely multiply your pain in childbearing;
> in pain you shall bring forth children.
> Your desire shall be for [or *against,* ESV margin] your husband,
> and he shall rule over you."

Before, bearing children had been the arena of blessing: in Genesis 1:28 God blessed Adam and Eve by saying to them, "Be fruitful and *multiply,*" but now he would *multiply* (from the same verb in Hebrew) Eve's pain in childbearing. Consider also the second part about her "desire" for her husband: this sentence is almost identical to the one in Genesis 4:7, where God says to the angry Cain: Sin's "desire is for [*against,* ESV margin, is the clear meaning] you, but you must rule over it." Here in 4:7 the *desire* is the *desire for mastery.* So in 3:16 the "desire" the woman will now have toward her husband will no longer be the sweet desire for romance and closeness, but the desire for mastery: they will compete with one another for the right to be the leader.

The woman will have "pain" in her sphere of labor, and the man will have pain in his; God says to him in verses 17-19:

> [17]" . . . cursed is the ground because of you;
> in *pain* you shall eat of it all the days of your life;
> [18]thorns and thistles it shall bring forth for you;
> and you shall eat the plants of the field.
> [19]By the sweat of your face
> you shall eat bread,
> till you return to the ground,
> for out of it you were taken;
> for you are dust,
> and to dust you shall return."

In the next chapter we will look into what it means that the ground is "cursed"; for now we will notice that man's work will now be filled with pain and frustration—though at first his job was to keep the Garden and spread its influence over the whole earth, with the prospect of success (as we saw in the last chapter; compare 2:15 with 1:28). And it will end in futility: man dies, and his body returns to the dust from which God first took it (Gen. 2:7).

This will help us to understand what God meant by his threat in Genesis 2:17, "in the day that you eat of it you shall surely die." If we take "you shall die" as meaning "your body will die," as many do, we have a problem: their bodies didn't die straightaway. Was God only fooling? Or did he change his mind about the punishment? Or is it worse than that—was the serpent right when he said, "You will not surely die"?

It's none of the above, as two observations will show us. First, we have to know what the range of possibilities is for the word "die." It most often speaks of the body dying; but sometimes it speaks of what we might call "spiritual death"—estrangement from a life-giving relationship with God. For example, consider Proverbs 12:28:

> In the path of righteousness is life,
> and in its pathway there is no *death*.

Since everyone's body dies, it would be silly to think that this is talking about physical life and death: no, it's speaking about fullness of life, that is, God's care and love given to us forever; and "death" would be the opposite of that. In the same way, Proverbs 23:13-14 tells us:

> [13] Do not withhold discipline from a child;
> if you strike him with a rod, he will not *die*.
> [14] If you strike him with the rod,
> you will save his soul from Sheol.

These verses treat "not dying" and "being saved from Sheol" as the same thing; and here, Sheol means "hell" (not just bodily death, since that comes to everyone).

So which part of the word's range did God have in mind in Genesis 2:17? To answer that we need the second observation. God is a reliable character in the Bible: he means what he says. Therefore he could not have been fooling—nor should we suppose that it's easy for God to change his mind when it's a matter of justice (as it would be here). In fact, the serpent is the one who lies, who tries to undermine trust in God. Therefore we can decide which of the possible meanings of "die" God was using, by just observing what actually happened. Their bodies did not die; but they were in fact estranged from God, they were driven by fear to run from him, they had lost their innocence. In other words, they died spiritually. Their bodies would eventually die as a consequence of their sin; but this is not the main thing, or even the worst thing: the estrangement, the fear, the shame—these are what make man's fate so gruesome.

This is just how Paul speaks of death in Romans 5:12-21, which is based on Genesis 3. The "death" that came through the trespass (vv. 15, 17) is the same as the "condemnation" that came through the trespass (vv. 16, 18), and is the opposite of the "free gift of grace" and the "free gift of righteousness." Even those who receive this gift will have their bodies die; but they have been delivered from spiritual death.

When we read in Genesis 3:20-21 that the man called his wife "Life-Giver" (for, as the ESV margin says, that is what the name *Eve* probably means), and that God made them new clothing of leather, we should conclude that these two had come to some kind of repentance for what they had done, and to faith that God would find a way to forgive them. (See what I say about

Genesis 3:15 in the next chapter.) Nevertheless, they may not stay in the Garden, so out they go, never to return (vv. 22-24).

A principle of evil has now been set loose in the world God made; and it shows itself in the way Cain murders Abel and fears the vengeance of others; in the arrogant boasting of Cain's offspring (Genesis 4); in the deaths of all those descended from Adam and Eve (Genesis 5); and in the wickedness that brought the flood (Genesis 6–8). At the same time some people do have a kind of faith, as we see in Eve's name for her son Seth (Gen. 4:25); in Enoch's walking with God (Gen. 5:22); and in the life of Noah (Gen. 5:29; 6:8-9). But even those with faith still suffer, and their bodies die.

A number of verses show that all mankind suffers from this principle of evil: it is something firmly woven into the fabric of our hearts, and can only be taken away by God's own powerful work. For example, in Genesis 6:5, God saw that "every intention of the thoughts of man's heart" was only evil continually, so he brought the flood on all except Noah and his family. But even after that, as God sniffs the aroma of Noah's sacrifice in Genesis 8:21, he acknowledges that "the intention of man's heart is evil from his youth"—and that applies to you and me. Likewise Solomon, in his great prayer to dedicate the temple to the Lord, mentions as an aside, "for there is no one who does not sin" (1 Kings 8:46). And Ecclesiastes comments on the human condition: "God made man upright, but they have sought out many schemes" (Eccles. 7:29). Paul argues that all mankind, Jews and Gentiles, are under the power of sin (Rom. 3:9), and reminds believers that they were once "dead in . . . trespasses and sins," but that God had made them "alive together with Christ" (Eph. 2:1, 5).

So we can conclude: the first disobedience, called the fall of man, made our first parents guilty of breaking the covenant God had made with them. The result was that they "died": they were estranged from God, who made them, loved them, nourished them, and heaped blessings and pleasures without number upon them. This is what they brought upon themselves, but also upon their offspring. This estrangement affected man's "heart," the core of his thinking, feeling, and choosing, turning it to evil. (It also damaged his emotional and bodily health, bringing in the afflictions we're all familiar with, and often worry about.) God's purpose for mankind now is "salvation," that is, rescue or deliverance: addressing man's guilt with forgiveness (through the sacrifice of Christ), restoring people to loving fellowship with himself, and changing the disposition of the heart to one of submission.

The Christian writer G. K. Chesterton shows us how a proper grasp of this teaching sheds light on everything else:

> The Fall is a view of life. It is not only the only enlightening, but the only encouraging view of life. It holds, as against the only real alternative philosophies, those of the Buddhist or the Pessimist or the Promethean, that we have misused a good world, and not merely been entrapped into a bad one. It refers evil back to the wrong use of the will, and thus declares that it can eventually be righted by the right use of the will. Every other creed except that one is some form of surrender to fate. A man who holds this view of life will find it giving light on a thousand things; on which mere evolutionary ethics have not a word to say. For instance, on the colossal contrast between the completeness of man's machines and the continued corruption of his motives; on the fact that no social progress really seems to leave self behind; . . . on that proverb that says "the price of liberty is eternal vigilance," which is only what the theologians say of every other virtue, and is itself only a way of stating the truth of original sin; on those extremes of good and evil by which man exceeds all the animals by the measure of heaven and hell; on that sublime sense of loss that is in the very sound of all great poetry, and nowhere more than in the poetry of pagans and sceptics: "We look before and after, and pine for what is not"; which cries against all prigs and progressives out of the very depths and abysses of the broken heart of man, that happiness is not only a hope, but also in some strange manner a memory; and that we are all kings in exile.

Is Science Possible for Fallen Man?

Well, if it's true that we are fallen because of Adam, what then does the Bible lead us to expect about the possibility of good science after this disastrous fall? How can mankind, so desperately corrupted, ever hope to carry out dominion over the world? After all, science, which depends on our knowing the world, is an act of man's heart: and when the heart is bent as badly as the Bible says it is, then science must be bent, too. Perhaps this means that science done by Christians would be utterly different from that done by non-believers.

There are two kinds of people who take this approach, who think that the Bible has no respect for science done by non-Christians: there are those Christians who say, yes, we can only trust science done by Christians; scientific results from non-Christians that seem to conflict with our faith are just an expression of the rebellion of their hearts. On the other hand, there are those who despise Christianity, and use the obvious success of modern science as an argument against the Bible—since it had led them to expect that such science would be futile and it clearly is not, and therefore the Bible does not tell the true story about mankind.

We come back to some of our observations from Genesis 3. Even though Adam and Eve acted foolishly, that didn't mean that they lost their intelligence; instead it meant that their intelligence would now be used for evil purposes. After all, Adam and Eve showed creativity and skill in sewing fig leaves together to make clothing (v. 8); when God made them leather clothes in verse 21, that was because they'd need something durable for life outside the Garden. In Genesis 4 they knew how to raise sheep and crops (v. 2), while Cain's offspring were pioneers in such skills as city building, music, metalworking, and poetry (vv. 17-24).

So the Bible writers weren't surprised that "pagans" produced high cultures, as they did in Egypt, Mesopotamia, Greece, and Rome (not to mention China and Central America, which don't come into the Bible's picture at all). Of course, a stubborn heart could get in the way of drawing reasonable conclusions. For example, in Exodus 8:19, Pharaoh's counselors got the message: they could see that Moses' miracles were "the finger of God." On the other hand, "Pharaoh's heart was hardened, and he would not listen to them." When it says that his heart was hard, it's saying that he stubbornly refused to draw the right conclusion, not that he was unable to do so. We would therefore expect that man's fallenness would show itself in those areas of study where the conclusions might have some impact on one's own life—areas such as psychology or sociology, which deal with human nature and obligation.

As Benjamin Warfield wisely put it,

> Sin clearly has not destroyed or altered in its essential nature any one of man's faculties, although . . . it has affected the operation of them all. . . . No new faculties have been inserted into him by regeneration; and the old faculties common to man in all his states have been only measurably restored to their proper functioning. He is in no position therefore to produce a science different in *kind* from that produced by sinful man.

10

How "Fallen" Is Nature?

Christians often speak of the world being "fallen"; this is why there is trouble and hardship in it. For example, John Calvin (1509–1564) wrote that "fleas, caterpillars, and other noxious insects" come as part of the penalty for Adam's fall. Many others think that before the fall, no animal ate another—all were made to be vegetarians. Some go so far as to suggest that the very workings of the world are now damaged—and hence we get earthquakes, droughts, and hurricanes.

The passages used to support these views include the curses of Genesis 3; the description of the ideal age in Isaiah 11:6-9, where "the lion shall eat straw like the ox" (the idea being, this returns all animals to their pre-fall vegetarian diet); and Paul's lament in Romans 8:20-22 that "the creation was subjected to futility."

Let's take these questions in their turn, and see whether they really do teach that the processes of nature are different because of man's fall. We'll see what the passages *don't* say, but also what they *do* say, to see if we can arrive at a soundly biblical understanding of how man's fall affects the rest of the created world.

Before I start, though, I have to tell you that this is another chapter in which I cannot claim to speak for conservative Christians in general. But the reason is that there isn't a studied consensus on this topic at all. Of course I hope that I am helping to build a consensus!

The Curses in Genesis 3

Consider the following verses from Genesis 3, where God pronounces his sentences on the serpent, the woman, and the man:

> [14] The LORD God said to the serpent,

"Because you have done this,
cursed are you above all livestock
and above all beasts of the field;
on your belly you shall go,
and dust you shall eat
all the days of your life.
[15] I will put enmity between you and the woman,
and between your offspring and her offspring;
he shall bruise your head,
and you shall bruise his heel."

[16] To the woman he said,

"I will surely multiply your pain in childbearing;
in pain you shall bring forth children.
Your desire shall be for your husband,
and he shall rule over you."

[17] And to Adam he said,

"Because you have listened to the voice of your wife
and have eaten of the tree
of which I commanded you,
'You shall not eat of it,'
cursed is the ground because of you;
in pain you shall eat of it all the days of your life;
[18] thorns and thistles it shall bring forth for you;
and you shall eat the plants of the field.
[19] By the sweat of your face
you shall eat bread,
till you return to the ground,
for out of it you were taken;
for you are dust,
and to dust you shall return."

We have looked at some matters raised by this passage already in the last chapter; and now the two issues for us to deal with are: (1) do verses 14-15 tell of a change in the way snakes eat and travel, and in how people feel about snakes? and (2) do verses 17-19 tell of a change in the way the ground will produce its crops? Once we have looked at these issues, we can step back and see what conclusions we can draw for the created order as a whole.

The Penalty on the Serpent (Genesis 3:14-15)

It would be a mistake to think that verses 14-15 are about snakes at all. We saw in the last chapter that the serpent is not acting for itself; instead, it is acting as a mouthpiece for a dark power (whom the Bible elsewhere calls Satan). So we should assume that God is both sensible and just, and won't waste any effort on a kind of animal that isn't guilty. (If God made everything good, we have no reason to believe that snakes were especially suited to the work of deceiving.)

The punishment is therefore aimed at Satan. Two things about these verses show that this is so. The first is the expressions in verse 14 about eating dust and traveling on the belly: these are vivid pictures of humiliation, and that's what Moses intended to convey to us. For example, in Micah 7:17, the Gentiles who are ashamed at God's steadfast love toward his people "shall lick the dust like a serpent"—this describes their humiliation, not their diet. We find similar expressions in Isaiah 49:23 (the Gentiles will humble themselves before restored Jerusalem, and "With their faces to the ground they shall bow down to you, and lick the dust of your feet") and Psalm 72:9 (may the Davidic king's enemies "lick the dust"). Besides, I find it hard to believe that any Israelite in the desert or in Palestine would think that snakes "literally" eat dirt; it doesn't take much watching to find out what they do eat (other animals, such as mice, lizards, other snakes, and so on).

The second thing that shows that the punishment is aimed at Satan is verse 15, which has often been taken to be about the Messiah. The woman's "offspring" could be either all of them in general (the human race), or it could be one particular offspring. I believe that it is the second of these, and that the offspring is the Messiah. Most English versions, like the ESV, have said "*he* [not *they*] shall bruise your head, and you shall bruise *his* [not *their*] heel," and have been right to do so (as I have argued elsewhere based on the grammar of the pronouns). A descendant of the woman will engage the dark power in combat, and win ("he will bruise your head")—but will himself suffer a wound ("you shall bruise his heel").

I think this lies behind an important strand of the New Testament teaching on what Christ did on the cross: he fought the Devil and defeated him, for our sakes. The apostle John tells us, "The reason the Son of God appeared was to destroy the works of the devil" (1 John 3:8). Paul tells us that through the cross of Christ God "disarmed the rulers and authorities and put them to open shame, triumphing over them in him" (Col. 2:15). Hebrews 2:14-15 tells us why Christ became a man:

> [14] Since therefore the children share in flesh and blood, he himself likewise partook of the same nature, that through death he might destroy the one who has the power of death, that is, the devil, [15] and deliver all those who through fear of death were subject to lifelong bondage.

Some scholars have supposed that Genesis 3 is really about why humans deeply dislike snakes. Excuse me for saying so, but such a trivial subject really has no place in the opening chapters of the Bible, so we should at least give Moses some credit for a sense of proportion. All the details of the chapter are shouting at us that the chapter is in fact about how the enemy of our souls deceived our first parents into disobeying God, and thus led them (and all of us in them) into a condition of guilt and misery. In verse 15, God shows that the Evil One will not win in the end: instead God will bring deliverance for mankind through the Woman's Offspring.

Therefore Genesis 3 has nothing to do with the little (and big) reptiles that slither quietly along the ground. So why do many people hate snakes? Because people are sinful, snakes are secretive (and some are venomous), and we don't understand them. You can tell that I speak as someone who *does* like snakes.

"Cursed Is the Ground" (Verses 17-19)

When we read God's sentence on the man in Genesis 3:17-19, several things seem to suggest that the workings of nature have changed: first, in verse 17, God says "cursed is the ground because of you"; second, there is the reference to the "pain" (v. 17) and "sweat" (v. 19) that it will take to eat the ground's fruit; and third, the ground will bring forth "thorns and thistles" (v. 18). This is nothing like the ready cooperation of nature that we found in chapters 1–2, is it?

Before we go any further, we have to notice that each of these things has to do with the "ground": so we'd have to have a good reason to generalize this sentence to the workings of the entire natural world—say, to suppose that now increasing entropy has entered into the whole creation. Now let's consider each of these observations in their turn.

The expression for "cursing the ground" only appears in Genesis 3:17 and 5:29 ("Out of *the ground that the LORD has cursed* this one shall bring us relief from our work and from the painful toil of our hands"), which refers back to this passage. In Genesis 8:21, the Lord says, "I will never again *curse* the ground because of man"—but the Hebrew uses a different term, as indicated by the ESV margin "dishonor."

However, we find our word in Deuteronomy 28:17-18, where if the people of Israel are unfaithful to their God:

> [16] "*Cursed* shall you be in the city, and *cursed* shall you be in the field. [17] *Cursed* shall be your basket and your kneading bowl. [18] *Cursed* shall be the fruit of your womb and the fruit of your ground, the increase of your herds and the young of your flock. [19] *Cursed* shall you be when you come in, and cursed shall you be when you go out."

Then in verse 20 Moses continues, "The Lord will send on you *curses,* confusion, and frustration in all that you undertake to do"—and then he details the outworking of this in verses 38-46 (pests that eat the crops, poverty, captivity). This does not say that somehow the way the basket and kneading bowl work, or the way the people or their animals grow young is going to be distorted, or that God will create the pests: instead, these things will be the arena in which God will chastise his people.

We can understand the "pain" and "sweat" and the "thorns and thistles" of Genesis 3:17-19 by remembering the geography of these chapters. God formed the man from the dirt in some place that we don't know (2:7), then transported him to Eden (2:8, 15), where he made the woman (2:21-22). Their original commission was to work and keep the Garden (2:15), and, starting from Eden, to bring its blessedness to the rest of the earth (1:28), which they would likewise work productively. However, God sent the man "out from the Garden of Eden to work the ground from which he was taken" (3:23); that is, the man now works ground *outside* the bounds of Eden. So now, the ground that he works does not enjoy the blessings of Eden—that is, it just keeps producing the thorns and thistles it had at first, because the man has fallen from his original assignment. This means that there's no reason to think that the passage says that the ground or its plants have changed: rather, the man has changed, and God intends to discipline him. That's why, in 3:18, he will eat "the plants of the field": that's what grew naturally from the ground, apart from the influence of Eden—this is the same kind of plant that had not yet sprung up in 2:5.

All this means that Genesis does not suggest that the properties of the ground or of plants have changed as a result of man's fall, nor does it even hint that God created new creatures to trouble man; instead, God will use the properties he gave to the ground and plants and animals to discipline his sinful creatures. We saw in the last chapter that changes have come into *human* nature—pain in childbearing, other afflictions of body and soul, and death—but it does not follow that non-human nature is affected in the same way.

WHAT DID LIONS EAT BEFORE MAN'S FALL?

When God had made the first human pair, he said to them (Gen. 1:29-30):

> [29] "Behold, I have given you every plant yielding seed that is on the face of all the earth, and every tree with seed in its fruit. You shall have them for food. [30] And to every beast of the earth and to every bird of the heavens and to everything that creeps on the earth, everything that has the breath of life, I have given every green plant for food."

It is easy to conclude from this that man and the animals ate only plant material before the fall, and that none of them ate meat. In fact, many think that if animals were to kill and eat other animals, they would mar the goodness of God's original creation. Some go on to add that "death" was unknown before the fall, since it is threatened in Genesis 2:17 as a punishment.

This conclusion seems to find strong support in Isaiah's vision of an ideal age during the reign of the Messiah, in Isaiah 11:1-10. Verses 1-5 describe the "shoot from the stump of Jesse"—that is, the heir of David, the Messiah (whom he has mentioned already in chapters 7 and 9). Verses 6-10 tell us about the results of his rule:

> [6] The wolf shall dwell with the lamb,
> and the leopard shall lie down with the young goat,
> and the calf and the lion and the fattened calf together,
> and a little child shall lead them.
> [7] The cow and the bear shall graze;
> their young shall lie down together;
> and the lion shall eat straw like the ox.
> [8] The nursing child shall play over the hole of the cobra,
> and the weaned child shall put his hand on the adder's den.
> [9] They shall not hurt or destroy
> in all my holy mountain;
> for the earth shall be full of the knowledge of the LORD
> as the waters cover the sea.
>
> [10] In that day the root of Jesse, who shall stand as a signal for the peoples—of him shall the nations inquire, and his resting place shall be glorious.

Many Christians read this as a description of heaven, or at least of a golden age under the Messiah's direct rule on earth. Either way, they take it as saying that the Messiah will restore the conditions of Eden—and that includes returning the meat-eaters to their vegetarian diet (v. 7, "the lion shall eat straw like the ox").

The trouble with these conclusions is that they depend on poor interpretation of the Bible passages. Let's begin with the Genesis passages.

The first thing to say is that, even if we take Genesis 1:29-30 as *prescribing* a strictly vegetarian diet for man and beast, it only applies to land dwellers and flying creatures: that is, it leaves out everything that lives in the water. But the things that live in the water include jellyfish, starfish, crabs, trout, sea snakes, penguins, otters, orcas and seals, all of which eat other animals. So eating meat isn't ruled out for *all* animals. But as a matter of fact, there's no reason to think that Genesis 1:29-30 is either exhaustive—listing *everything* they'll eat—or *prescriptive*—"eat this and nothing else." There's no indication of a change in diet for animals anywhere in the Bible; and though we might argue that man wasn't to eat meat until after the flood (Gen. 9:3), we still can't say what *other* animals ate.

There is an inspired commentary on the way the current world order still reflects God's good creation, and that is Psalm 104. This magnificent hymn praises God for the way he made and still rules over nature, and the commentaries on the psalm agree that it takes Genesis 1 as its starting point. Its theme is one of celebration all the way through: it opens and closes with "Bless the LORD, O my soul" (vv. 1, 35); it describes the bountiful provision God makes for man and beast on land (vv. 5-23), and then exclaims in verse 24,

> O LORD, how manifold are your works!
> In wisdom have you made them all;
> the earth is full of your creatures.

Then it describes the sea and its inhabitants (vv. 25-26), and sums up the general dependence of all creatures on God (vv. 27-30): "These all look to you to give them their food in due season" (v. 27). The psalm ends with a prayer of devotion to the Lord (vv. 31-35), and the wish that the Lord might "rejoice in his works" (v. 31). The only mention of the wicked comes in verse 35:

> Let sinners be consumed from the earth,
> and let the wicked be no more!
> Bless the LORD, O my soul!
> Praise the LORD!

From this we may conclude that Psalm 104 praises God for the goodness of his creation—a creation that still works the way he designed it to work. The creation itself is still good; it is wicked people who mar the goodness of God's creation.

I said all that so I could say this: in the midst of the section that is pure celebration for the goodness of the world God made—and just before the exclamation in verse 24—we find verses 21-23:

> [21] The young lions roar for their prey,
> seeking their food from God.
> [22] When the sun rises, they steal away
> and lie down in their dens.
> [23] Man goes out to his work
> and to his labor until the evening.

The lions are the night shift, man is the day shift; each works to get food, and each depends on God's blessing for success. And notice what verse 21 says about the lions: when they "roar for their prey," they are "seeking their food from God." You and I know what they eat: antelopes and the like. The attitude seems to be, so long as they don't eat our sheep, they're just doing what God made them to do. (Likewise, in Psalm 147:9, God "gives . . . to the young ravens that cry [for food]": that is, God feeds even the carnivorous and scavenging birds.) If we think that animal death would be a blot on the goodness of the creation, we're out of step with Psalm 104.

But we have no reason to believe that the Bible teaches that no animal died before the fall. Remember, as we saw in the last chapter, that Genesis 2:17 ("for in the day that you eat of it you shall surely die") was spoken directly to Adam: its "you" is singular. Then when Eve shows that she considers herself under the same threat (3:3), the "you" is plural—but it refers still to the human couple, not to anyone else. When we further remember just what this "death" is—spiritual death, alienation from God—we see as well that this penalty is for man only (though it may have effects on the beasts, as we'll see later).

Now we can turn to the passage in Isaiah 11. I don't intend to argue for or against the various schemes Christians have for whether to find heaven or the thousand years ("millennium," Rev. 20:2-3) in an Old Testament passage. I only intend to show that such questions do not have any bearing whatever on this particular passage from Isaiah. The only question for us right now is whether we should read this passage in Isaiah as foretelling an era in which animals no longer eat meat because eating meat is contrary to the way they were first created.

To understand this passage, though, we need a sound method for interpreting biblical prophecies. Now, no traditional Christian should have any difficulty with the idea that God might reveal the future to his specially chosen spokesmen: after all, God knows the future and can make it fulfill his purposes (see Isa. 14:24-27). So God can speak of real events before they happen; but his normal manner of doing so, according to the Bible itself, is through dreams, visions, and parables (see Num. 12:6; Hosea 12:10). This means that the prophets will often describe real things using figures of speech and analogies. Isaiah himself invites us to read his prophecy this way; in the opening verse (1:1) he writes of "the *vision* . . . which he saw" (see also 2:1; 13:1).

When we want to understand a passage, we need to know something of its context. Isaiah 11:1-10 forms a unit about what will happen under the rule of the Messiah (the descendant of Jesse, the father of David, vv. 1, 10). This perfectly wise and just person will rule not only over the Jewish people from whom he comes but also over the Gentiles: verse 9 says that "the earth shall be full of the knowledge of the LORD," and verse 10 says that the peoples and nations will turn to the "root of Jesse." This ties in with other passages in Isaiah about the worldwide rule of the Messiah; in the first part of Isaiah's book, consider 2:2-4:

> [2] It shall come to pass in the latter days
>   that the mountain of the house of the LORD
> shall be established as the highest of the mountains,
>   and shall be lifted up above the hills;
> and all the nations shall flow to it,
> [3]   and many peoples shall come, and say:
> "Come, let us go up to the mountain of the LORD,
>   to the house of the God of Jacob,
> that he may teach us his ways
>   and that we may walk in his paths."
> For out of Zion shall go the law,
>   and the word of the LORD from Jerusalem.
> [4] He shall judge between the nations,
>   and shall decide disputes for many peoples;
> and they shall beat their swords into plowshares,
>   and their spears into pruning hooks;
> nation shall not lift up sword against nation,
>   neither shall they learn war anymore.

Even though this doesn't mention the Messiah, the time frame in verse 2, "the latter days," is a term for the time of the Messiah. Further, in verse 4 the LORD will "judge" and "decide disputes," while in 11:4 the Messiah will "judge" and "decide" (the same two words in Hebrew)—so 11:1-10 tells us more about how God will bring 2:1-5 to pass. Peace among the nations will come about because of the Messiah's rule.

Then we come to Isaiah 9:6-7:

> [6] For to us a child is born,
> to us a son is given;
> and the government shall be upon his shoulder,
> and his name shall be called
> Wonderful Counselor, Mighty God,
> Everlasting Father, Prince of Peace.
> [7] Of the increase of his government and of peace
> there will be no end,
> on the throne of David and over his kingdom,
> to establish it and to uphold it
> with justice and with righteousness
> from this time forth and forevermore.
> The zeal of the LORD of hosts will do this.

Here the "child" is the heir of David—clearly the Messiah—and he will extend his rule without end, and bring peace all over.

In the second part of Isaiah, we find that the Servant of the Lord (traditionally—and rightly, I judge—taken as a Messianic figure) will bring justice to the Gentiles living in the distant coastlands (42:1, 4), will be a "light for the nations" (42:6; 49:6), and will rule over Gentile kings (42:7; 52:15).

All of this leads us to expect that Isaiah 11:1-10 is a part of this expectation of peaceful, worldwide rule under the Messiah.

It looks to me like Paul read it this way, too. In Romans 15:8-12, he is showing that his own ministry to the Gentiles is part of the way in which God fulfills the Old Testament passages about the Gentiles coming to glorify God. He quotes Psalm 18:49; Deuteronomy 32:43; Psalm 117:1; *and Isaiah 11:10*. That is, he saw the faith of the Gentiles as their coming under the Messiah's rule, and he did what he could to get Jewish and Gentile Christians to "live in such harmony with one another . . . that together [they might] with one voice glorify the God and Father of [the] Lord Jesus Christ" (Rom. 15:5-6).

Well, then: since Isaiah 11:10 is the final verse of a single unit (vv. 1-10), and since the book of Isaiah speaks of the worldwide dominion of the Messiah as bringing about peaceful relationships among mankind, and since Paul saw the faith of the Gentiles as (partial) fulfillment of Isaiah 11:10, and since the prophets described future things using symbols—then it makes good sense to read Isaiah 11:6-8 as a figurative description of the peaceful reign brought in by the Messiah: it will be as startling as if wolves and lambs were to dwell together! In the historical context of Isaiah, this works extremely well: the large imperialistic nations, such as Assyria and Egypt, could easily be likened to predators, and the small countries, such as Israel (the northern kingdom) and Judah (the southern kingdom) could easily be likened to their helpless prey. In fact, within a few years of this prophecy Assyria would swallow up the northern kingdom, and soon thereafter threaten to swallow up the southern kingdom as well. Under the Messiah's reign, all peoples will love the Lord and will no longer threaten one another (see Isa. 19:19-25).

One advantage to reading Isaiah 11:1-10 this way is that it allows us to see the flow of thought: verses 1-5 describe the Messiah, the just ruler; verses 6-8 present an image of what his rule will be like; then verse 9 brings the image to a close by telling us what the image was about ("they shall not hurt or destroy"). Verse 10 sums up the whole passage by showing that the nations will be glad to have the Messiah as their ruler (which tells us that he's not going to impose his rule by force).

Another advantage to reading the passage this way is that it doesn't require us to forsake the evidence of our eyes and common sense. If you look at a leopard or lion, you are looking at a well-designed predator: the muscles, the teeth, the claws, the reflexes, are all just right for catching, killing, and eating prey. It's pretty simple to conclude that this just-rightness comes from God making them to act this way; that's why their hunting is a thing of beauty. I am reminded of C. S. Lewis's remark, "If the earthly lion could read the prophecy of that day when he shall eat hay like an ox, he would regard it as a description not of heaven, but of hell." Well, now we don't have to inflict such an abuse on the lions!

A final advantage of this reading is one that brings us back to how we read the creation account of Genesis 1:1–2:3. On the seventh day, God rested from the work of creation; but if we suppose that animals were not carnivorous before the fall, we have to explain where they got their teeth and claws from—teeth and claws wouldn't have been much good to vegetarians! Then we would have to say that God *re-created* them—violating his Sabbath from creation. I would prefer not to have to say such a thing, and now I see why I don't have to.

WHY DOES THE CREATION GROAN?

It almost seems like Paul is at odds with himself. In one place, 1 Timothy 4:4-5, he supports the Christian's right to marry and to eat all kinds of foods by reminding Timothy that Genesis 1:31 still applies:

> [4] For everything created by God is good, and nothing is to be rejected if it is received with thanksgiving, [5] for it is made holy by the word of God and prayer.

On the other hand, in the earlier book of Romans Paul wrote of how the whole creation suffers until the day of our full deliverance from the presence of sin (Rom. 8:18-25):

> [18] For I consider that the sufferings of this present time are not worth comparing with the glory that is to be revealed to us. [19] For the creation waits with eager longing for the revealing of the sons of God. [20] For the creation was subjected to futility, not willingly, but because of him who subjected it, in hope [21] that the creation itself will be set free from its bondage to decay and obtain the freedom of the glory of the children of God. [22] For we know that the whole creation has been groaning together in the pains of childbirth until now. [23] And not only the creation, but we ourselves, who have the firstfruits of the Spirit, groan inwardly as we wait eagerly for adoption as sons, the redemption of our bodies. [24] For in this hope we were saved. Now hope that is seen is not hope. For who hopes for what he sees? [25] But if we hope for what we do not see, we wait for it with patience.

Is there a way to read these two passages from Paul together?

I think there is, by paying attention to what Paul is actually saying in Romans 8:18-25. The whole paragraph is oriented toward our hope of future glory (what we call "heaven"): you can see that from the way Paul repeats the "waiting eagerly" theme in verses 19, 23, and 25; the "hope" theme in verses 20, 24, and 25; the "groaning" theme in verses 22 and 23; and the "glory" theme in verses 18 and 21 (see also v. 30). What is it that all the creation waits for? The "revealing of the sons of God" (v. 19), and the "redemption of our bodies" (v. 23). That is, it all looks forward to the time when those who have followed Jesus will be made perfectly holy in soul and body (that's what "glorification" is); until then, our being out of kilter affects the creation. And how does it affect the creation? Because God made man to rule it (Gen. 1:26), and after man's fall, man rules it badly.

The creation also groans because, as I argued already, it is the arena in which God chastises man. Hence it suffers when man is punished (as in the flood of Genesis 6–8). So the creation "waits with eager longing" for the day when this is no longer needed.

None of this, though, supports the claim that the processes of the creation themselves—the way that plants grow and die, or that animals eat and reproduce, or that chemical reactions increase entropy—are morally corrupt.

Some Conclusions for Science in a World of Fallen Mankind

Well, then, what can we say about the world that God made, and that sinful people inhabit? And what of the sciences in such a world?

First, we must affirm that God made the world a good place, and that even now it remains a good place. Therefore the sciences that study it are a noble endeavor—at least potentially; of course, people are quite capable of abusing the sciences and turning them to evil purposes.

Second, we must acknowledge that mankind has gone bad because our first parents fell into sin and brought us with them. God made us to have dominion over the rest of the world, and there is no evidence that he's taken away that responsibility. But we manage it badly, and therefore the natural world suffers from our sinful leadership.

Third, we experience pain and suffering in this world; but this is not because the world is corrupt, but because *we* are. Under God's providence, our pain might be a punishment for our sin, or it might be testing to challenge our faith, or it might be discipline for straying believers, or it might have the purpose of deepening our longing for glory. In some cases of pain and suffering we won't ever know why it came our way; God has some purpose that he doesn't share with us. In all of this God uses the creation as the arena in which he accomplishes these purposes.

Fourth, we have no biblical warrant for arguing that animal death is a result of man's fall, or that no animal ate another before then. This means that there is no *theological* objection to the possibility that fossils are the remains of animals that died before Adam was even created.

Along these lines, we can say that animal death is not part of the problem of evil. Not even when some kind of animal goes extinct is it really an *evil*—so long as it came from nature doing its own thing, and not from humans' sinful exploitation of the world. That means that when people try to argue for a young earth by saying that an old earth involves evil (especially animals dying), or when others argue against believing in God at all in view of "nature red in tooth and claw," they are making a theological mistake.

Fifth, we do have some help in dealing with the problem of evil—that is, how can God be infinitely wise, good, and powerful, when at the same time there is evil in the world? We have no reason to think that such natural things as animals preying on others, or earthquakes and hurricanes, or the law of increasing entropy, go against the will of God for his creation. However, we humans are infected with evil, which means that we don't have the sympathetic "feel" for nature that would enable us to govern it to consistently good and wise purposes. This means that we'll be out of step enough with nature that earthquakes will take us by surprise, and will go against what *we* want. Further, we also don't govern *ourselves* to consistently good and wise purposes. This means that we can easily inflict evil on others, and use the world of nature to do it. To call the existence of evil and pain a "problem" is in fact to admit that we feel that they're not right, and that the world would be better without them. But this means that we have the sense that we live in a world that was once good, and that has been spoiled; it also means that we recognize that there's a standard of rightness that is itself outside the world, and that the world we see doesn't measure up to it—and therefore we have to ask, where does that standard come from and why should it have any authority? (Christians say that it comes from God, who made the world, and who offers us salvation.) We also have to see that human sinfulness means that for God to do us good, he must heal us of our sin; and this involves pain for us.

Mind you, it may well be that man's fall *has* in fact brought trouble into the animal world—for example, it is possible that lions were not *made* to be dangerous to man, and even that man in his unfallen state could have "managed" lions in such a way that they wouldn't have messed with our flocks and herds. It's also possible that, before our first parents fell, such things as viruses and bacteria didn't affect us like they do now—our vitality is not what it once was. And please note that in this chapter I am treating nature apart from man: *human* nature has been grievously corrupted by the fall of our first parents, leading to all manner of problems in our lives. And these problems aren't just moral (having to do with our bent toward sinning); because of the body-soul tangle that we are, they include emotional and psychological troubles, interpersonal problems, as well as disorders in our bodily health.

Finally, I can say that the love for animals both tame and wild that my children and I feel, expresses something true to the best of human nature. At the same time, we have to be careful not to project onto the animals our kind of consciousness (which is what they need to have for genuine suffering). It is perfectly right for us to admire the industry of the beaver, and the graceful speed of the otter that eats the beaver. God made an endlessly fascinating world!

11

How Does God Rule the World?

The Biblical Doctrine of Providence

When my daughter was very young, and would get a cut or scrape, she would say, "God will heal it." When my son was about three, I saw a scab on his leg and asked him how it got there. He told me, "God put it there." And just recently, when the dog next door got into a scuffle with another dog and came away with some nasty cuts so that it had to go to the veterinarian, my daughter prayed that God would heal the wounded dog.

What do you think of my children? Are they victims of a simplistic picture of the world, where everything that happens comes from the direct action of God—or are they on their way to a thoughtful and wise relationship with the world that God made?

Well, the truth is, you can't tell from the words I've just given you. However, in this chapter I want to outline the traditional Christian understanding of nature, miracle, and providence—the way that God cares for the world he made. Then I'll show why I think that this view is the right way of putting together what the Bible teaches, and I'll offer some definitions that will help us as we face the problem of practicing that view in a culture that isn't very sympathetic to it. Next we'll consider—ever so briefly—some of the other views of providence that have been offered as truer to the Bible, and I'll show why I still think the traditional view is best. Finally, we'll see how all of this relates to the practice of science.

Oh, yes—along the way I'll show why I think my children have a sound understanding of the way God works in his world (largely due to their mother's wise instruction).

THE TRADITIONAL CHRISTIAN PICTURE OF GOD'S PROVIDENCE

Christians in general—regardless of their denominations—share the same basic picture of the world and the way God works in it. There are some differences, but these mostly have to do with finding the right way to put together the teaching about our free will and God's ultimate control of all things. I don't need to pursue the differences for my purposes, so I'll just let you know that they exist, that they're real and important, and that you owe it to God to think these questions through and come to some convictions about them.

We have already seen that the Bible teaches that God brought the world into existence, for his own reasons; and that he made it all very good. To say that it is "good" is to say that it shares in God's goodness: and this means that it really exists, and that its parts really do have their effects. That means that they *actually* do things, not just *appear* to do things. When I eat good food, I get stronger *because* I ate the food, and *because* it gives me strength. When I clap my hands together, I hear a sound *because* my hands have affected the air, which in turn has affected my ears. So the doctrine of creation means the creation of real things, with real properties—with the possibility of causing things.

After God's creation week, he entered his "creation Sabbath" (Gen. 2:1-3). God has finished the work of preparing the earth to be a good place for mankind to live and love, and he now enjoys his completed work, and brings people into fellowship with himself. But he's not idle: he keeps his world in being, and he *maintains* the power of created things to be causes. That is, he makes sure that plants and animals and rocks and air and everything else go on existing; and he also makes sure that they go on doing what he made them to do. Apples keep on tasting good and nourishing us because God keeps on maintaining their properties. When I strike my hands to make a sound, I can rely on God to keep my hands in being, and to keep in being their properties of causing sounds.

A traditional way of talking about the power of created things to be causes is by talking about "second causes"—they are "second" because they don't exist on their own, they depend on God who brought them into being and keeps them in being with their causal powers. But they are "causes" because God has linked the things he made into a web of cause and effect, and created things, under God, *cause* their effects.

In addition, God makes sure that everything that happens carries out his purposes; he *governs* the world. God's purposes are holy, wise, and thoroughly good; and he sees to it that, in the end, it is his purposes that stand.

Because this is God's world, he can do with it what he likes, especially when it comes to his plan of building a relationship with people such as you and me. That is, he doesn't limit himself to only the properties of the things he has made to accomplish his purposes; he sometimes works beyond those properties. This is what has traditionally been called a *miracle.* I will make it clear shortly why I don't like to use the word "miracle," but prefer "supernatural event" as a better term; but for now I'll stick with the conventional word.

Many discussions of God's providence include the terms "ordinary providence" and "special providence." Unfortunately, different authors often mean different things by these terms, so you should look carefully at their definitions. I will describe the three most common ways of using the terms.

First, some authors use "ordinary providence" for the workings of the created things according to their created properties, and "special providence" for the miracles: by this usage, the begetting of my children is an ordinary providence, while the begetting of Jesus was a special one. God was working in both events, mind you—but the "special" one is "special" because the manner of God's working is different from his ordinary manner of maintaining the created things and their properties.

A second way of using these terms is to say that an event can be a result of "ordinary providence," of "special providence," or of miracle. By this usage, what makes a special providence special is not its inner workings—that is, whether God has overridden the created properties—but the fact that it is specially suited to some need. For example, unusual circumstances kept some people away from their offices at the World Trade Center in New York City on September 11, 2001. This second manner of speaking would allow us to call these circumstances a "special providence"—and it is gratifying to hear some of these people wonder aloud what God saved them for.

The third way of using these terms is to say that events are either "ordinary providence" or "special providence," and that under special providence we can divide these into miracles and non-miracles. Again, "special" means "the people involved recognize it as specially suited to their needs"—but we have to recognize that some of these specially suited events may be the product of natural causes under God's wise guidance.

The reason why people vary in their usage of these terms is that they don't agree on what they should use to distinguish one kind of event from another: usage 1, which only allows the two categories, distinguishes events based on the way God is working in the event—that is, by his "ordinary" work of maintaining the world he made, and by his "special" work of going beyond the capacities of created things. The second and third usages distinguish events based on the way that God's purpose is visible in the events—in the "ordinary," we can't see God's governing hand, though we accept by faith that it's always there, while in the "special" God makes his presence more clear. I think each of these approaches has merit—depending on what we're talking about—"with-respect-to-whatness" again—so in my own usage I'll try to be aware of the possible confusion and ask you to pay attention to my own with-respect-to-whatness.

These, then, are the components of the traditional Christian teaching of providence: maintenance, governance, and miracle. Does this picture do a good job of following the Bible? And if so, how might we apply it to everyday life and to our practice of science?

THE BIBLICAL EVIDENCE

I am firmly convinced that if we put the biblical statements together carefully, we will find that they do in fact support the traditional Christian understanding of providence.

We have already discussed the doctrine of creation and its goodness. In the creation story of Genesis 1, we find something striking (vv. 11-12):

> [11] And God said, "Let the earth sprout vegetation, plants yielding seed, and fruit trees bearing fruit in which is their seed, each according to its kind, on the earth." And it was so. [12] The earth brought forth vegetation, plants yielding seed according to their own kinds, and trees bearing fruit in which is their seed, each according to its kind. And God saw that it was good.

In obedience to God's wish, the plants came into being. And they yield their seed "according to their kind"—that is, wheat plants yield wheat seed, apple trees yield apples in which you'll find apple seeds. And if you plant those seeds in the right soil with the right amount of water and sun, hey presto! you get wheat stalks and apple trees. And why? Because God made each plant to be the kind of thing that reproduces after its kind.

Consider Matthew 7:16, in Jesus' Sermon on the Mount:

> "Are grapes gathered from thornbushes, or figs from thistles?"

You're supposed to answer "No" to both questions. Of course not; if you want grapes, look for a grape vine; if you want figs, go to a fig tree.

Thornbushes produce thorns, and thistle plants produce thistles—don't try to eat them unless you're a donkey like Eeyore.

James 3:11-12 continues this line:

> [11] Does a spring pour forth from the same opening both fresh and salt water? [12] Can a fig tree, my brothers, bear olives, or a grapevine produce figs? Neither can a salt pond yield fresh water.

Like his master Jesus, James expects you to know the answer to his questions: "Of course not!" But he even goes further: in verse 12 he insists that a fig tree *cannot* bear olives or a grapevine figs, and a salt pond *cannot* yield fresh water. That is, each of these things *can* yield their proper products, because God made them with the properties to do so; but they *cannot* produce what they don't have the properties for.

These verses (and there are many others) show us that the Bible supports the idea that created things actually have *natures,* or properties that make them distinct from other things. It is the *nature* of wheat plants to produce more wheat plants, of fig trees to bear figs and not olives, and of salt ponds to yield salt water and not fresh. The reason is that each thing is the way God made it to be.

Nevertheless, the creation depends on God at all times; two passages we have looked at before show us that. In Colossians 1:17, we read that in Christ all things hold together; and in Hebrews 1:3 that Christ "upholds the universe by his word of his power." So the world doesn't exist or carry on by itself; Christ, who made it, is always at work holding it in being.

That explains why we find passages like Psalm 104. There we find that God makes the springs gush forth in the valleys (v. 10); he waters the mountains (v. 13); he causes the grass to grow for the livestock (v. 14); and all beasts look to him to give them their food in due season (v. 27). Some people want to read this as denying that created things have any natural powers at all; it is God who does everything directly. But this is a bad interpretation. Since this psalm takes Genesis 1 as its starting point, we should not try to make it say anything contrary to Genesis; and Genesis certainly allows us to speak of created things having natures. At the same time, it reminds us that these natures don't work on their own; they're continually dependent on God. As the commentator Derek Kidner put it,

> The psalm speaks the sober truth of God's maintenance of all life. It gives a rounded view of this by pointing to its visible and invisible operation: that

> is, at one level, the natural order and its bounty; and behind all this, the outflowing energy of God which holds all things in being.

That is, the psalm certainly endorses our view that created things have their own properties—after all, the reason God gives the water in verse 10 is so that every beast of the field can drink and slake its thirst (v. 11): in other words, because it is the nature of water to slake thirst. But the natural world isn't all there is, and it doesn't work on its own: instead God is at work keeping it going.

The biblical authors also teach that everything that happens—small or great—happens according to the will of God and fulfills his plan. For example, consider what Jesus said to his disciples in Matthew 10:29-30:

> [29] "Are not two sparrows sold for a penny? And not one of them will fall to the ground apart from your Father. [30] But even the hairs of your head are all numbered."

God not only knows about everything, he also has everything well in hand so that it does what he wants. That is tremendous comfort to believers, and that is why Jesus goes on in verse 31 to say, "Fear not, therefore; you are of more value than many sparrows." The fall of a sparrow is a "natural" event; but it is still under God's control. The apostle Paul calls God the one "who works all things according to the counsel of his will" (Eph. 1:11). Of course this presents us with a problem, namely, how does this sit with the idea that my choices are really choices and not just the programmed response of a robot? And why should I bother to pray? As I have indicated, different Christian groups answer these questions differently, but, if they want to be true to the Bible, they must confess that in the end, God's will gets the last word.

But not everything in the Bible is "natural": think of the creation of the world from nothing, for example (Gen. 1:1). How could this be the result of anything's nature interacting with the nature of something else, when there was nothing to begin with? Again, think of how Jesus was conceived, as we find in Luke 1. In verses 30-33 the angel Gabriel tells Mary that she will conceive and bear a son, the Messiah. In verse 34-35 we read:

> [34] And Mary said to the angel, "How will this be, since I am a virgin?"
>
> [35] And the angel answered her, "The Holy Spirit will come upon you, and the power of the Most High will overshadow you; therefore the child to be born will be called holy—the Son of God."

Mary's question, "How will this be?" is a very reasonable one, and she offers a very reasonable difficulty: "since I do not know a man [literally; see ESV margin]," that is, I am not doing what it takes to become pregnant. And Gabriel's reply shows that he agreed that the question was fair. He explained how: "the Holy Spirit and the power of the Most High." This conception would not be in the natural way; a power from beyond natural powers would produce it. That is why it is called *supernatural:* it is above and beyond the natural powers.

Definitions That Restate the Biblical View of Providence

I think this rapid survey of biblical teaching shows that the traditional Christian view of providence is right: namely, that we may speak of created things as having natures, and this explains why they do what they do; everything that is depends on God for its continued existence and for its causal powers; God rules everything to make sure that it carries out his holy, wise, and good purposes; and God is free to employ supernatural events to carry out his purposes. In this section I want to use these truths to support a couple of definitions that will help us to live by this doctrine, and to be obedient to it in our practice of the sciences.

I want to define two words, "natural" and "supernatural." Before I do that, let me explain why I want to use "supernatural" instead of "miraculous." The English word "miracle" has too many meanings right now. It comes from a Latin word that means "amazing," and that is the way people use it often now. I hear of how someone "miraculously" survived some disaster—what the reporter means (if he means anything at all) is that he is amazed that anyone could have survived, and doesn't know how it could have happened: he usually *doesn't* mean that it took a special work of God. Likewise, I hear of "medical miracles," which either means that the doctors don't know how it happened or that some new medical technique produces really amazing results. Neither use implies that God has gone beyond natural powers. I have a newsletter from the local conservation center, and an article describes how monarch butterflies find their way to their winter home in Mexico, and then back to Missouri. The author declares that how this can be "remains largely a mystery to science"—that is, he says, "it can truly be thought of as miraculous." When the Bible speaks, say, of the special conception of Jesus or of his resurrection, its concern is not with how amazing the thing is (it is that, to be sure!); instead, it focuses on the way in which God has gone beyond the powers of created things to produce what he wants. That's why I prefer to use "supernatural": it has a better chance of being clear.

Now for the definitions:

> *Natural:* God made the universe from nothing and endowed the things that exist with "natural properties"; he keeps those things in existence, maintaining both the properties and their power to interact with other things, in a web of cause-and-effect.
>
> *Supernatural:* God is also free to "inject" special operations of his power into this web at any time: for example, he may add objects by creation; he may cause events directly; he may enable something or someone to do what its own natural properties would never have made it able to do; or he may impose organization on some collection of natural objects—whatever suits his purposes.

I've had to pack a lot of punch inside these definitions, and I hope that as we go along it will become clear why each part is in there. For now, though, I want us to see that a number of important things follow from these definitions. First, every natural event is the work of God, as well as the work of the created things involved. For example, my daughter can say that her body has the power to heal its wounds, and my son can say that his scab resulted from the way his skin interacted with the sharp corner of the stone. At the same time, my daughter can say that God heals her wounds, because he not only designed her body to work as it does, but he keeps it and its causal powers in being, and makes sure that they work according to his design. My son can say that God made his skin and the stone in such a way that the stone cuts skin, and God was busy keeping those properties in operation when my boy was horsing around. And my daughter's prayer for the neighbor dog was good, too: God maintains the powers of the dog's body and of the veterinarian's tools.

Second, we should *not* say that a supernatural event has God more "directly" involved, while a natural event has him only "indirectly" involved. God is working directly in both kinds of events: in the natural, to maintain the natural properties; in the supernatural ones, to go beyond those properties.

Some people like to use the word "intervention" where I have used "supernatural event"; in such cases, they say, God "intervenes" in the working of his creation. Some theologians don't like this way of speaking, because it makes God sound like an intruder, and because it suggests that God is not active in ordinary or natural events. C. S. Lewis, in his book *Miracles,* outraged some fussy souls by saying, "I use the word *miracle* to mean an interference with Nature by a supernatural power."

I must admit that my mind is divided over this: if the terms "intervention" and "interference" really do give people the wrong idea about God's work in ordinary providence, then let's not use them. On the other hand, we have to recognize that the terms are *analogies*—it's *as if* God were to interfere. And analogies have their limitations, as we've already seen; but they also have their strength, namely that they make their point vividly. I don't think any believer wants to complain about the way the Bible puts things; but it constantly uses analogies for God's action. Psalm 119:126 says, "It is time for the LORD to act, for your law has been broken." Of course the psalm is using an analogy: it's *as if* God were doing nothing, but he should do something now to show the world that he honors his own law. So maybe some people need to lighten up.

Third, we should avoid a problem that some traditional definitions have brought about, when they say that in a supernatural event God works "without means." This would mean that the east wind that parted the Red Sea (Ex. 14:21) wasn't supernatural. But the same verse says that "Moses stretched out his hand over the sea"; and, if we follow my definition, we can say that the Lord used the east wind, and sent it at just the right time—which nature on its own would not have done (otherwise how would Moses have known the right time to raise his hand?).

Fourth, this gives us a way of thinking about how we can tell whether a supernatural event has taken place: not because we don't know how it happened, but because we do know the properties of the things involved, and we know they couldn't have produced the event on their own. We'll put this to good use when we get to our chapter on "Science, Providence, and Miracle"; we'll also see how we can answer some of the objections that unbelievers have raised to Christian miracle accounts.

Fifth, these definitions give us an idea of when we might expect to find a supernatural event. In speaking of supernatural events, I said "whatever suits his purposes." God's purpose in making the world was to have a relationship with mankind; and even after the sin of our first parents, he has pursued that purpose. He governs the world, natural and supernatural events alike, with this in mind. The great supernatural events of the Bible—the creation, the calling of Abraham and the deliverance from Egypt, the conception of Jesus and his rising from the dead—have to do with advancing this purpose. For God to relate to mankind, there must be a world for them to live in, and he must make people to live in it; he must call people to himself, especially since after the fall they don't naturally seek him. He must provide for their sins to be forgiven in a way that is true to his own character, which means the Son of God must take flesh and die for our sins, and rise in victory for us. If God is to speak to man, he must have messengers, and equip them with the right message, and make sure the message stays pure (this is called "inspiration"); and he must have a way of showing people who the authorized messengers are (thus prophets and apostles work miracles to show that God has appointed them). Some people have worried that talk of miracles leads to a world that is willy-nilly; but the Bible shows otherwise: its miracles are filled with purpose.

Sixth, we can see how science might relate to God's providence; but I will save that discussion for the end of this chapter.

OTHER VIEWS: ARE THEY TRUER TO THE BIBLE?

In this section I will mention three other views of God's providence that Christians have offered as being truer to the Bible, and one that you'll sometimes meet. None of these has won a wide following among Christians—and for good reason, as I will briefly show.

Occasionalism

The first of the three alternative views is called "occasionalism." According to this view, the Bible does not really allow that created things have any causal powers at all: everything comes from the direct action of God. In ordinary language—and in traditional Christian thought—we say that fire burns your skin, or that a sharp knife cuts paper. But occasionalism says that it's not biblical to say that the fire burns or that the paper cuts: instead we should say that the fire is the *occasion* for God to produce the effect on your skin that you call a burn, and the knife on the paper is the occasion for God to produce the effect of the cut paper.

One of the things that moved me to write my book *The God of Miracles* was the way so many people use the language of occasionalism to describe the laws of nature that science discovers: they say that these are really "God's usual way of working, and he may choose to work some other way if it suits his purposes." When I tell people that the philosophy of occasionalism lies behind this way of speaking, and then explain to them what occasionalism actually says, they look at me in disbelief: how could anyone actually hold such a spooky view? But occasionalism has had some pretty distinguished advocates: the priest-philosopher Nicholas Malebranche (1638–1715), the Irish bishop George Berkeley (1685–1753), the great colonial American philosopher-pastor Jonathan Edwards (1703–1758), the Dutch theologian-statesman Abraham Kuyper (1837–1920) and his admirer G. C. Berkouwer (1903–1996), and most advocates of what is called "Biblical theology" (a movement of the mid-twentieth century that stressed dynamic "Hebrew" thought over static "Greek" thought). These have generally thought that occasionalism gives the most glory to God, because it denies to the creature any credit for anything.

Occasionalists will point to a passage like Psalm 104 to support their case. Remember that, as we saw earlier in this chapter, this psalm celebrates the way that God is intimately involved in all the workings of nature. God is the one who makes the springs gush forth (v. 10), who makes the grass grow (v. 14), who provides food for the beasts (v. 27). One occasionalist author drew this conclusion from Psalm 104:

> In the interpretation of Old Testament hymns that deal with creation, the term "nature" should straightaway be eliminated. Israel was not familiar with the concept of nature, nor did she speak of the world as a cosmos, that is, about an ordered structure that is self-contained and subject to definite laws.

The passages we looked at above show that this claim is false: biblical authors did in fact portray the world in terms of "nature"—or, better, in terms of *natures* that God maintains—and saw created things as having power to cause things. In this very psalm, water quenches thirst (v. 11) and nourishes trees (v. 16), grass feeds the livestock (v. 14), wine gladdens man's heart and bread strengthens him (v. 15), and all creatures need food to survive (v. 27). That is, this very psalm, which some take to support occasionalism, actually supports the traditional Christian view that created things have causal powers!

Providentialism

The second alternative Christian view does not have its own name—at least I've never seen its advocates give it one—so I have called it "providentialism." I use that term because it is the view that everything that happens is a *natural* event, that is, everything that happens is *ordinary* providence. According to this view, things are "miracles" when they meet some special need, and when we don't understand how they happened; but they are not really "supernatural." The best expression of this view comes from a Christian biologist who, in an essay about the virgin conception of Jesus, wrote,

> Probably all miracles are susceptible to an explanation other than the supernatural.

Providentialist writers try to show that the biblical miracle stories are believable because they can provide a natural process to explain them: for example, Elijah's sacrifice on Mount Carmel caught fire because a thunderbolt struck it (1 Kings 18:38, "the fire of the LORD fell and consumed the burnt offering"); Shadrach, Meshach, and Abednego survived the fiery furnace because their clothes provided special protection (Dan. 3:27, "their cloaks were not harmed, and no smell of fire had come upon them"). Here's how one author put it:

> In such instances the event is a providential ordering of natural causes for the benefit of the people of God.

(You can see why I call it "providentialism.")

The benefits that people see in providentialism are three: first, if we can give a natural explanation for a miracle story, we make it more believable—and thus we help the cause of defending the Bible. Second, we can call things "miracles" without troubling ourselves over whether they're really supernatural. And third, we can eliminate all possibility of conflict between science and faith by making these two arenas complementary: faith tells us *that* God did something, and perhaps *why* he did it; science tells us *how*.

Many prominent writers on science and faith from the conservative Christian side are providentialists (or at least almost so: it's very hard to find one who goes all the way). For example, the British authors Donald MacKay and R. J. Berry fit in this category, as does the conservative Old Testament scholar R. K. Harrison.

The big problem with providentialism is that the Bible doesn't support it. I have already mentioned the conception of Jesus in Luke 1:34-35 (parallel in Matt. 1:18, 20). These verses make it clear that Mary's pregnancy is not ordinary, and natural processes cannot explain it (that's why Mary asked how it could happen). It came from a special act of the Holy Spirit, who is outside the web of cause and effect by which ordinary providence works. I have also mentioned the initial creation (Gen. 1:1): since there was nothing to begin with, there is no natural process to explain how the universe came to be. The resurrection of Jesus is likewise supernatural: in John 10:18, Jesus declared,

> "No one takes [my life] from me, but I lay it down of my own accord. I have authority to lay it down, and I have authority to take it up again. This charge I have received from my Father."

Jesus' authority to take his life up again—that is, to rise from the dead—comes from the Father, from outside ordinary providence.

In a later chapter I will show how we can defend the miracle stories in the Bible without losing their supernatural quality. As for the advantage of complementarity between science and faith, this isn't really an advantage if our goal is the truth: sometimes scientists base their theories on bad premises (such as a false worldview), and they need to be challenged. I will also argue later that if we don't challenge them, their theories will undermine the very basis of our Christian faith.

Oddly enough, occasionalism and providentialism agree on their definitions of "miracle": they both find the importance in the way some event is specially timed to meet a need, and to focus attention on God—and not on any supernatural quality of the event. This leads to some authors actually mixing arguments from both camps, and leaving their readers confused, because the author is confused. I call this odd because the two views are so at odds with each other: occasionalism says that there's no such thing as natural, because everything is fully supernatural. Providentialism says that since everything is really natural, there's no such thing as supernatural.

A good example of this comes from the *New Bible Dictionary* article on "Miracle." The author writes,

> Scripture does not sharply distinguish between God's constant sovereign providence and his particular acts. . . . Thus when biblical writers refer to the mighty acts of God they cannot be supposed to distinguish them from "the course of nature" by their peculiar causation, since they think of all events as caused by God's sovereign power.

This sounds occasionalist, because of its last phrase: all events are supernatural anyhow. But in the very next paragraph he goes on to say,

> The discovery of, say, causal connections between the different plagues of Egypt, a repetition of the blocking of the Jordan, or increased knowledge of psychosomatic medicine could not of themselves contradict the biblical

> assertion that the deliverance from Egypt, the entry to Canaan and the healing works of Christ were mighty acts of God.

This line of thought is most properly providentialist, with its talk of finding "causal connections" (= natural explanations).

A yawning gulf separates occasionalism from providentialism, and this author seems to be utterly unaware of it; I feel like insisting, "Choose this day whom you will serve!" (Actually, I think it would be better to follow the traditional Christian view I have outlined above.)

I suspect that people are drawn to one or the other of these two views because when they learn that the biblical Christian position is that God is at work in every event, they draw the wrong conclusion that therefore no event is "special" in any sense except how it affects me—that is, no event differs from any other in its inner workings. The occasionalist goes on to say that therefore everything is supernatural because created things have no power to cause events; the providentialist goes on to say that every event is natural if we look at one way, and providential if we look at it from the other angle. But if we follow the Bible more closely we'll see that there's no problem in saying that God is at work differently in some events.

"Open" Theism

The third alternative view of God's providence is called open theism. It takes that name because its supporters say that the future is open, and not even God knows what it will be. He certainly does not control the future: instead God and man together craft the future with their free choices. They think that this does justice to biblical statements about God changing his mind, such as Jonah 3:10:

> When God saw what they did, how they turned from their evil way, God *relented* of the disaster that he had said he would do to them, and he did not do it.

God didn't know, when he sent Jonah to Nineveh, how the people there would respond; but now that they've repented, he changes his mind about what to do to the Ninevites.

This view claims as well to offer the advantage of doing proper justice to human dignity: our choices are real, and free; not even God knows what we'll do. He knows everything that exists, but the future doesn't exist yet, so of course he doesn't know it. (You can see that, according to this view, God experiences time the same way we do.) If it were otherwise—if God knew the future—our choices wouldn't really be free.

I am sorry that I cannot go into a long and detailed discussion of this view, but that would take a book in itself! However, I will give you three reasons why I don't think you should pay it much mind.

First, it has to ignore the many Bible passages about God's knowledge and even control of the future. I have already mentioned Ephesians 1:11, where God is the one "who works all things according to the counsel of his will." I don't know what this means by the openness theory. Consider also Isaiah 45:20-21, where God says:

> [20] Assemble yourselves and come;
> draw near together,
> you survivors of the nations!
> They have no knowledge
> who carry about their wooden idols,
> and keep on praying to a god
> that cannot save.
> [21] Declare and present your case;
> let them take counsel together!
> Who told this long ago?
> Who declared it of old?
> Was it not I, the LORD?
> And there is no other god besides me,
> a righteous God and a Savior;
> there is none besides me.

The LORD, the true God, challenges the other gods to present their record for telling the future. By this test the idols are losers; he comes off the winner—and why? Because he knows the end from the beginning, and shapes every event to carry out his own purposes. There are many other such texts, but these will do to show what the problem is.

Second, if God is not in control, he cannot provide assurance to his people. But the Bible is full of assurances such as James 1:2-4 and Hebrews 12:5-11, which tell us that our trials and temptations come from God to strengthen our faith. If the openness view is true, then some of our troubles come because evil people are having their way.

And third, the openness view fails to account for the Day of Judgment. All traditional Christians agree that Jesus will return in glory, and that he'll raise the bodies of all mankind and call them to stand before him in judgment.

He will not tolerate any resistance to his will then. He will make all who love him perfect in holiness, and bring them into full enjoyment of his presence forever; they'll never ever sin again. As John says (1 John 3:2), "when [Jesus] appears we will be like him, because we shall see him as he is." Those who have opposed him, on the other hand, he will punish with everlasting fire: that is, he will impose his will on them, whether they like it or not. The Bible wants us to be certain of this future, so that we'll make every effort to be faithful to follow Jesus, and so that we'll never lose heart when it looks like evil has the upper hand. But how can we be certain of it if God has not already decided to make it happen, and if he won't do it regardless of the free choices of man?

Deism

Unlike the other alternative views I have discussed here, "deism" doesn't claim to be more biblical than the traditional view. Instead it claims to do a better job philosophically. This is the view that God made the world, but that he takes no active part in any of the events since then. Events in the world unfurl according to the laws that God instilled into nature at the beginning. Deism resembles providentialism, but it leaves out the traditional idea of God's intimate involvement in every event by maintaining the world and its parts.

The English poet Alexander Pope expressed the ruling idea well:

> the first Almighty Cause
> Acts not by partial, but by general laws.

If God did anything special, that would be to show partiality to someone. C. S. Lewis, who quoted this snippet from Pope, proceeded to demolish it by noting that it implies that there is in God a distinction that we are very familiar with: namely that between the main plan and the by-products. In Pope's view, God has a grand design for the sum of things, which cannot change; he has no freedom either to grant or to deny prayers. "The grand design churns out innumerable blessings and curses for individuals. God can't help that. They're all by-products."

Lewis points out that Pope's approach (and all deism by implication) lowers God rather than raises him. We have to deal in generalities, because our minds are finite; but God's mind is infinite, and therefore able to reduce unintended by-products to zero. "If there is Providence at all, everything is providential and every providence is a special providence"—that is, specially intended.

We can add Lewis's analysis to the simple observation that all the Bible passages that refute providentialism also tell against deism as a valid option for a biblical believer.

Providence and Science

So how does the biblical teaching about providence relate to the practice of science? We have already mentioned that the biblical teaching about creation gives a foundation for scientific study of the world, because it tells us why the world is reliable and knowable, and why we are able to understand it—God made the world as a place for us to live and to rule, and he made us with the abilities we need in order to do just that. The biblical teaching about providence adds at least three consequences to our Christian philosophy of science.

First, when we are studying the normal operations of the things around us, we are trying to learn their natures—or at least, how their natures affect other things. The nature of cats is to eat mice; the nature of a cat affects the mouse by making it disappear. The nature of a billiard ball affects the nature of the bumper pad in such a way that the angle of the ball's incidence is equal to the angle of its reflection. So the things that we call the "laws of nature"—such as Newton's laws of motion—are really the ways in which the natures of things interact. (Actually, they *approximate* these ways, since quantum mechanics has given us some refinements; but that doesn't matter for the point I'm making.)

Second, when we are studying events—that is, when we are studying a historical science, such as geology or archaeology—we will of course make our inferences based on what we think are the natures of the things involved. For example, a geologist has a model for how an ocean lays down sediment, and how that builds up over time—that is, of how the natures of silt and water and plankton and dead fish and who knows what else interact with each other to form a layer of sediment at the bottom; and he'll apply that model when he's looking at a road cutting in order to discover what sequence of events produced this pattern.

That is, in describing a historical event we have to start with the natures of the things involved. But must we assume *at the very beginning of our study* that all the events are natural? Well, you may, so long as you have a good reason to suppose that only natural factors are involved; but if you don't have a good reason, then such an assumption before you start would be silly. Now I don't imagine that supernatural factors are involved in the vast majority of geological studies. But can I say the same about, say, the history of Israel? Must I *assume* that the parting of the Red Sea came from a natural process—and if it didn't, then it didn't happen? This kind of reasoning is itself unreasonable.

I feel myself pulled apart by two horses: on the one hand, I don't want to be untrue to my faith that says God is free to do as he pleases with his creation, and I have no right to tell him to be stingy with his miracles. On the other hand, the Bible leads me to believe that the world is mostly made up of regularities that I can study—and the sciences are mostly about those regularities. Our understanding of natural and supernatural events will keep us in one piece, because it tells us under what conditions we might expect supernatural events, and it gives us a way of detecting them.

God does what he does in order to pursue a relationship with mankind: in general, the supernatural events in the Bible have to do with advancing that cause—creation, exodus, conception and resurrection of Jesus, Day of Judgment. (Do the origins of life and of man fit into this pattern? We'll take that up later.)

Our definition of a supernatural event gives us a means of detecting them as well. When the overall effect is something that the natural properties of the things involved *could not* have produced on their own, then the event is *super*natural. Joseph, the "father" of Jesus, believed that a woman *could not* get pregnant without a man's contribution. That's why he "resolved to divorce [Mary] quietly" (Matt. 1:19). The Lord must have thought Joseph to be reasonable, since he sent an angel to tell him how it had really happened, and for what purpose (Matt. 1:20-21). Joseph didn't have to know everything in order to form a sound conclusion; modern medical research only supports his reasoning. As C. S. Lewis put it,

> No doubt a modern gynaecologist knows several things about birth and begetting which St. Joseph did not know. But those things do not concern the main point—that a virgin birth is contrary to the course of nature. And St. Joseph obviously knew *that.*

In other words, a woman doesn't get pregnant without a man—unless the pregnancy is supernatural.

This isn't a matter of appealing to what we *don't* know—"I don't know how it could happen, so I'll call it a miracle"—but of appealing to what we *do* know. Good science does not work against a real supernatural event; it only brings the miracle into sharper relief.

The third consequence for science that comes from the biblical teaching about providence has to do with the fact that what we typically study is natures and their interactions. That is, in most of the sciences we study the properties of quarks, electrons, carbon rings, cats, and stars, and what effects they have on each other. Our access to things like *how* God holds them in existence, or *why* he made them and what he's using them for, and *what* he expects us to do about them, is pretty limited—at least, we won't find it out by studying the things themselves. It is the study of Scripture, as well as reason and conscience and spiritual experience, that gives us the resources to begin saying something about these philosophical questions. As the Christian philosopher Paul Helm put it,

> The exact sense in which objects which are distinct from God are yet upheld by him is difficult to get clear. . . . It should be stressed that this upholding, being metaphysical or ontological in character, is physically undetectable.

We can say similar things about purpose and duty. This doesn't mean that such things don't matter, or that we can't know something about them—but it shows that our study of them is not a *physical* science.

12

God Reveals Himself in His World

Science, Faith, and Apologetics

Back in chapter 4, in summarizing what Genesis 1:1–2:3 teaches about creation, I noted that the Bible leads us to believe that God made all things *so that the whole show bears his imprint.* In this chapter we will examine this topic in more detail, with the following questions in mind: How does the creation tell us about God? Whom does the creation tell about God? How does "science" figure in to this telling—both for the Christian believer and for the nonbeliever?

Defining Terms

There are a number of terms used to name the topics I'm looking at here; I think some of the variation comes from the fact that different people focus on different aspects of the questions I just listed. Some speak of "natural revelation," others of "general revelation," or of "creational revelation," or of "natural theology." This means we'll have to start by defining our terms.

For my general usage, I prefer to use the terms "natural revelation" and "creational revelation." By these I mean the way in which the created world speaks to us of its Creator. If we use this way of speaking, we'll be able to consider under it two separate questions: how God's world speaks to us *believers,* and how it speaks to *non*believers (and therefore how we can employ that message in our outreach to them). I think this gives us an advantage over the other common terms, namely "general revelation" and "natural theology."

Theologians have traditionally used the term "general revelation" in contrast to "special revelation": general revelation comes to all people everywhere (hence it is "general"), while special revelation is what God has specially revealed of himself in his covenant, made to his chosen people (Israel and the church).

Many have used the expression "natural theology" for the process of giving proofs of God's existence, and proofs of some features of his character (such as being all-powerful, just, and loving) based on what we see in the created world. For example, William Paley wrote his book *Natural Theology* (published in 1802), and it is the classic presentation of the "argument from design": we observe many kinds of design in the natural world, and, if we think it all through, we must conclude that a Designer is responsible for it all. He goes on to argue that from the world we can also conclude that the Designer is personal, all-powerful, all-knowing, all-present, eternal, self-existing, spiritual (not material); and that he is one (not many), and that he is generous and kind. On the other hand, some have used the term "natural theology" for the kind of true knowledge and awareness of God that a person can have (or at least has the capacity to have) just by virtue of being human and living in God's world, quite apart from the special way that God reveals himself in the Bible. This sounds a lot like "natural revelation" as the nonbeliever receives it.

The reason I prefer the terms "natural revelation" and "creational revelation" over "general revelation" is that I don't want to contrast what the natural world says with what the Bible says. Instead I want to consider just how the believer and the nonbeliever receive the message differently. The reason I prefer these terms over "natural theology" is two-fold: first, because, again, it has been contrasted with what comes through God's covenant; and second, because its history of usage is confusing.

I think it should be clear that natural revelation has a connection to the sciences and philosophy. These are the disciplines that systematically study the world and how to think about the world. On the other hand, they aren't the same thing: first, because—as we'll see—the Bible addresses itself to Everyman, not just to the learned; and this means that one need not be a scientist or philosopher to receive natural revelation. Second, the goals of the sciences and philosophy aren't limited to seeing what the creation reveals about its Creator—as we'll see in a later chapter, this even applies when the scientist or philosopher is a Christian. So the relationship is one of overlap; and this certainly means that the sciences and philosophy will speak to natural revelation.

Now, before we go on to look at specific Bible passages, we need to think about what might be the relationship between natural revelation and God's covenantal revelation in the Bible. The Christian faith has a number of components, and natural revelation can only apply to some of them: for example, it has a component of *metaphysics*—that is, basic convictions about what God is like, what the world is like, how God is active in the world, and whether we can know God and the world at all. (We covered this in our chapters on providence and on human nature.) But anyone who stopped there would not be a Christian: the Bible speaks of particular historical events in which God has been forming and protecting a people of his own—that is, it has a *redemptive-historical* component. (These include the call of Abram; the deliverance from Egypt; the dynasty of David; the birth, death, and resurrection of Jesus; and the second coming.) The Christian faith also includes an *ethical* component—principles of good behavior for those who love God and their neighbor. And it also has an *experiential* component—what it feels like to walk with God; to know his love and fatherly care; to hope for everlasting glory; to struggle with sin, fear, pain, and doubt; to love our neighbor.

So if we want to think about how natural revelation—or some scientific result—will interact with Christian faith, we have to ask, "What *aspect* of the faith are we talking about?" Mostly the interaction will be with the *metaphysical* and *ethical* components of the faith. On the metaphysical side, we'll have interaction over such issues as how we know the world; whether we can say that something must have come from God; whether we have a right to draw an inference about some sequence of events in the history of the universe—are inferences such as the Big Bang and standard geology believable, and what impact do they have on our confidence in the Bible? On the ethical side, Christian theologians have commonly distinguished between "cardinal virtues" (prudence, temperance, justice, fortitude)—which all civilized people recognize, and "theological virtues" (faith, hope, love)—which are peculiar to Christians.

The sciences might have some limited interaction with the other components of the Christian faith: say, an archaeologist might bring evidence to support (or condemn) the biblical narrative of some event. However, the thing that makes an event part of God's covenantal revelation is not just that it happened, but also the interpretation that God's spokesmen put on it—and no archaeological study will be able to speak to that at all. Or, for another example: a psychologist might argue that Christian experience is delusional (or healthy). But this kind of judgment is closely tied to premises about what healthy humanness actually is, and is therefore not strictly empirical. In this section we'll focus on how science and faith interact in the areas of metaphysics and ethics—especially since that's where the Bible itself finds the interaction.

NATURAL REVELATION IN THE OLD TESTAMENT

The Old Testament was mostly written for the people of God, to equip them to love and serve him faithfully—and, quite often, to rebuke them for the way they were so consistently indifferent to being faithful. That means that most of its natural revelation passages have to do either with the person who is already a believer, or with the member of God's people who is tempted to throw his faith over and take part in pagan religions.

Several passages in the Psalms show how the believer is to see God's greatness revealed in the creation. The one everyone knows best is Psalm 19:1-6:

> 1 The heavens declare the glory of God,
> and the sky above proclaims his handiwork.
> 2 Day to day pours out speech,
> and night to night reveals knowledge.
> 3 There is no speech, nor are there words,
> whose voice is not heard.
> 4 Their measuring line goes out through all the earth,
> and their words to the end of the world.
> In them he has set a tent for the sun,
> 5 which comes out like a bridegroom leaving his chamber,
> and, like a strong man, runs its course with joy.
> 6 Its rising is from the end of the heavens,
> and its circuit to the end of them,
> and there is nothing hidden from its heat.

The Psalms are the hymnbook of believing Israel; they form the faith of God's people by giving them the right things to sing in their public worship. In Psalm 19 the people of God sing of how the whole creation shouts to them of the Creator—the magnificence of the starry sky tells us how great, how boundlessly creative and powerful, is the God who has drawn his people into his presence. The sun—which other peoples were inclined to worship—becomes a symbol of the way the law of God relentlessly searches out the nooks and crannies of our hearts (with v. 6, "nothing *hidden* from its heat," compare v. 12: "Who can discern his errors? Declare me innocent from *hidden* faults").

Psalm 8 is a similar song:

> 1 O LORD, our Lord,
> how majestic is your name in all the earth!
> You have set your glory above the heavens.

[2] Out of the mouth of babes and infants,
you have established strength because of your foes,
to still the enemy and the avenger.

[3] When I look at your heavens, the work of your fingers,
the moon and the stars, which you have set in place,
[4] what is man that you are mindful of him,
and the son of man that you care for him?

[5] Yet you have made him a little lower than the heavenly beings,
and crowned him with glory and honor.
[6] You have given him dominion over the works of your hands;
you have put all things under his feet,
[7] all sheep and oxen,
and also the beasts of the field,
[8] the birds of the heavens, and the fish of the sea,
whatever passes along the paths of the seas.

[9] O LORD, our Lord,
how majestic is your name in all the earth!

In this hymn the believer marvels over how the God who is majestic enough to have made the heavens—not to mention the earth and all its creatures—would take any notice of mere man; but God goes further than taking notice, he "is mindful of him," he has "crowned him with glory and honor," and has "given him dominion"! This is Genesis 1 set to music. It would be easy to examine the heavens, to think of them as God's handiwork, and to reckon ourselves of little interest to a God who is that great; but, as Derek Kidner points out, "the right inference from God's ordered heavens is not his remoteness but his eye for detail."

Other psalms that celebrate the way God reveals himself in the workings of nature include Psalms 29 (God's power revealed in a thunderstorm), 93 (God's power is greater than that of the crashing sea), and 104 (God's manifold works in making and caring for the natural world reveal his wisdom and goodness). We can say, in general, that these psalms are for the believer: they invite the believer to see the world as God's handiwork and to learn of the greatness of the God who made and rules such a magnificent and intricate nature.

As we will see below, however, Paul could use these ideas—even a direct quote of Psalm 19:4—to show how nature gives testimony to all mankind about the Maker and Ruler of all.

The Old Testament has little material addressed to the person outside the people of God, to show why he should believe in the God of Israel. This is partly because the major way of commending the true God in the Old Testament era was to be the lives of the faithful people of God, as we read in Deuteronomy 4:5-6, where Moses tells them,

> [5] "See, I have taught you statutes and rules, as the LORD my God commanded me, that you should do them in the land that you are entering to take possession of it. [6] Keep them and do them, for that will be your wisdom and your understanding in the sight of the peoples, who, when they hear all these statutes, will say, "Surely this great nation is a wise and understanding people."

I think it was the repeated failure of Old Testament Israel in their faithfulness to God's covenant that explains why there is so little about going out to evangelize in the Old Testament.

The Old Testament comes nearest to arguing against the ideas of pagan beliefs, in the passages that uncover the folly of idolatry. For example, Isaiah shows the Judeans of his day, who are strongly tempted to embrace Canaanite idolatry, that the whole thing is foolish because an idol can do nothing. As he wrote in Isaiah 44:9-20,

> [9] All who fashion idols are nothing, and the things they delight in do not profit. Their witnesses neither see nor know, that they may be put to shame. [10] Who fashions a god or casts an idol that is profitable for nothing? [11] Behold, all his companions shall be put to shame, and the craftsmen are only human. Let them all assemble, let them stand forth. They shall be terrified; they shall be put to shame together.
>
> [12] The ironsmith takes a cutting tool and works it over the coals. He fashions it with hammers and works it with his strong arm. He becomes hungry, and his strength fails; he drinks no water and is faint. [13] The carpenter stretches a line; he marks it out with a pencil. He shapes it with planes and marks it with a compass. He shapes it into the figure of a man, with the beauty of a man, to dwell in a house. [14] He cuts down cedars, or he chooses a cypress tree or an oak and lets it grow strong among the trees of the forest. He plants a cedar and the rain nourishes it. [15] Then it becomes fuel for a man. He takes a part of it and warms himself; he kindles a fire and bakes bread. Also he makes a god and worships it; he makes it an idol and falls down before it. [16] Half of it he burns in the fire. Over the half he

> eats meat; he roasts it and is satisfied. Also he warms himself and says, "Aha, I am warm, I have seen the fire!" [17] And the rest of it he makes into a god, his idol, and falls down to it and worships it. He prays to it and says, "Deliver me, for you are my god!"
>
> [18] They know not, nor do they discern, for he has shut their eyes, so that they cannot see, and their hearts, so that they cannot understand. [19] No one considers, nor is there knowledge or discernment to say, "Half of it I burned in the fire; I also baked bread on its coals; I roasted meat and have eaten. And shall I make the rest of it an abomination? Shall I fall down before a block of wood?" [20] He feeds on ashes; a deluded heart has led him astray, and he cannot deliver himself or say, "Is there not a lie in my right hand?"

Isaiah appeals only to the common sense of his hearers, not to special revelation. (See also Isa. 40:18-20; Jer. 10:1-16; Ps. 115:2-8; 135:15-18, for similar appeals.)

The author of the book called the Wisdom of Solomon (in the Apocrypha or Deuterocanonicals) picked up this line of argument and used it in his day (about 100 B.C.) to help Jews who were drawn to embrace what seemed to them to be the higher culture of the Greek world—especially in Alexandria, Egypt, the intellectual capital of the day. The author of Wisdom aimed to show the folly of the false religion of that culture, without appealing to special revelation or redemptive history (something that he does appeal to in other parts of his book). This author especially takes this tack in his chapters 13–15, which he introduces with 13:1-9 (RSV):

> [1] For all men who were ignorant of God were foolish by nature;
> and they were unable from the good things that are seen to know him
> who exists,
> nor did they recognize the craftsman while paying heed to his works;
> [2] but they supposed that either fire or wind or swift air,
> or the circle of the stars, or turbulent water,
> or the luminaries of heaven were the gods that rule the world.
> [3] If through delight in the beauty of these things men assumed them
> to be gods,
> let them know how much better than these is their Lord,
> for the author of beauty created them.
> [4] And if men were amazed at their power and working,
> let them perceive from them
> how much more powerful is he who formed them.
> [5] For from the greatness and beauty of created things

comes a corresponding perception of their Creator.
[6] Yet these men are little to be blamed,
for perhaps they go astray
while seeking God and desiring to find him.
[7] For as they live among his works they keep searching,
and they trust in what they see, because the things that are seen
are beautiful.
[8] Yet again, not even they are to be excused;
[9] for if they had the power to know so much
that they could investigate the world,
how did they fail to find sooner the Lord of these things?

Most scholars agree that this line of approach lies behind Paul's apologetics that we find in Acts and Romans, which we will take up below.

Another place for natural revelation in the Old Testament is in the area of ethics: that is, the ethics of the Old Testament overlap with the ethics of other peoples. We can see this in the Ten Commandments—these share some basic principles with other peoples, and at the same time they introduce new ones. We can also see it in the way Proverbs 22:17–24:34 ("words of the wise," 22:17 and 24:23) looks like it has a connection to the Egyptian wisdom book, *The Teaching of Amenemope* (which was composed before 1000 B.C.). The trouble is that it is hard to say just what the connection is: it's probably not *borrowing,* though it seems likely that the biblical author knew of the Egyptian wisdom (Solomon reigned from about 960 B.C.). Instead the best way to put the connection is that the biblical book and the Egyptian book both come from the ancient Near Eastern wisdom traditions, with similar life conditions and ethical concerns; and that the biblical author adapted some ideas found in Egyptian proverbs to his covenantal worldview. In any case there is room for saying that the biblical writers saw an overlap between the pure ethics that God expected his own people to abide by, and the ethics held by the nations who didn't have their advantages.

NATURAL REVELATION IN THE NEW TESTAMENT

When Jesus gave his followers the Great Commission, to "go . . . and make disciples of all *nations* [= *Gentiles*]" (Matt. 28:19), he brought into effect a new situation for the outreach of the people of God: namely, to go to the Gentiles and persuade them that they must become Jesus' disciples. To persuade them means you have to find places where your way of thinking makes contact with theirs, and this can include natural revelation.

The New Testament passages that especially speak to this topic are two places in the book of Acts, and the first two chapters of Paul's letter to the church in Rome. In Acts we find examples of two evangelistic speeches that Paul gave to pagan audiences, while in Romans we find Paul's own theological explanation of how natural revelation comes to all people and leaves them without excuse before God.

(a) Acts 14:15-17: Paul in Lystra

In Acts 14:8-18, we read of how Paul and Barnabas went to a town called Lystra in the Roman province of Galatia (in what is now Turkey). It was a town where the Romans had settled Latin-speaking colonists, but which also had a native population that spoke the Lycaonian language. In Lystra Paul healed a crippled man; in verses 11-13 we find out what happened:

> [11] And when the crowds saw what Paul had done, they lifted up their voices, saying in Lycaonian, "The gods have come down to us in the likeness of men!" [12] Barnabas they called Zeus, and Paul, Hermes, because he was the chief speaker. [13] And the priest of Zeus, whose temple was at the entrance to the city, brought oxen and garlands to the gates and wanted to offer sacrifice with the crowds.

You can see that this was a Gentile crowd, with no sympathy at all for the religion of the Bible: they spoke Lycaonian, they identified Paul and Barnabas with their gods (Luke uses the Greek names Zeus and Hermes for them), and a priest of Zeus was about to sacrifice oxen to them.

Instead of enjoying steak and popularity, the conscience-driven Barnabas and Paul said to the people (probably in Greek, which they all would have understood):

> [15] "Men, why are you doing these things? We also are men, of like nature with you, and bring you good news, that you should turn from these vain things to a living God who made the heaven and the earth and the sea and all that is in them. [16] In past generations he allowed all the nations to walk in their own ways. [17] Yet he did not leave himself without witness, for he did good by giving you from heaven rains and fruitful seasons, satisfying your hearts with food and gladness."

Back in Acts 10:34-43, the apostle Peter had given an evangelistic message to a Gentile audience: to Cornelius, an Italian soldier, and his household. But Cornelius already had great respect for Judaism and believed in one God

(Acts 10:2). Here in Acts 14, however, we find the first recorded evangelistic message to an audience with no background in Judaism at all. So it's no surprise that Paul doesn't start to talk about the way Jesus fulfilled Old Testament prophecy (unlike Acts 10:43)! Paul tells them that the natural world is God's testimony of his goodness and his interest in them. That is, he appeals to natural revelation, not to special revelation (v. 17).

However, that doesn't mean that he leaves out Scripture: in good Old Testament language, he speaks of turning "from vain things [compare Jer. 10:3] to a living God [compare Jer. 10:10] who made the heaven and the earth and the sea and all that is in them [compare Ex. 20:11]." The testimony of nature was enough to show mankind that there was one God—one purpose—and not many that were often at odds with each other. In appealing to such testimony, Paul is applying the Psalms passages that we looked at above: the reason the believer receives messages about God from the natural world is that those messages are actually there, not that we put them there. Part of the evangelistic task is to awaken people to those messages that they are not attending to.

Luke doesn't tell us what Paul said further; at least Paul and Barnabas stopped the crowds from sacrificing to them. Unfortunately, soon afterward some Jews came along from other towns where Paul had been and stoned Paul (they considered him a dangerous heretic).

So we don't know all that Paul would have said to these people, but we can summarize the principle with the words of the commentator J. R. Lumby:

> God had chosen Israel only for his own people before the coming of Christ, and had given to the rest of the world no revelation of himself except what they could read in the pages of the book of nature. But that, St Paul says, spake clearly of a careful Creator and Preserver of the world.

In the next passage we get a fuller account of Paul's approach.

(b) Acts 17:22-31: Paul in Athens

Some time later than this, Paul was on the European mainland. He carried out his ministry in Philippi (Acts 16), Thessalonica (17:1-9), and Berea (17:10-13), stirring up trouble wherever he went. Leaving his fellow workers Silas and Timothy, Paul made his way to Athens, the city that had once been a major political power, that had seen the great philosophers Socrates (470–399 B.C.), Plato (about 427–347 B.C.), and Aristotle (384–322 B.C.), and which even now had a high reputation for intellectual achievement (a reputation that it continued to hold for centuries afterward).

But not everyone in Athens was as sophisticated as the philosophers, and Paul was distressed to find so many idols there (v. 16). He reasoned in the synagogue with Jews and devout Gentiles, and in the marketplace with all manner of people (v. 17). This is how he came into contact with the Epicurean and Stoic philosophers, who were unsure what to make of Paul's talk, or even whether to show him any respect at all. First let's describe these schools of philosophy.

The Epicureans were followers of a philosopher named Epicurus, who lived 341–270 B.C. They thought of "pleasure" as the chief good—particularly, having a tranquil mind, free from pain, disturbing passions, and superstitious fears about the gods and their doings. They were not atheists: to them the gods dwelt in perfect calm, and had nothing to do with the life of mankind—sort of a polytheistic version of deism. If you want to get a feel for their beliefs, you can read the poem of Lucretius (about 99–55 B.C.), *De rerum natura* ("On the Nature of Things").

The Stoics regarded the philosopher Zeno (340–265 B.C.) as their founder; they were called "Stoics" because Zeno taught under a colonnade (Greek *stoa*) in Athens. They thought the highest good was to live consistently with nature, and the highest expression of nature was reason or design, the principle that combined the elements to produce the universe. Their idea of God was that he was the soul of the world. The Stoics considered the rational side of man to be better than the emotional, and sought a kind of contentment in which they did not have the feeling of wanting some material thing. At their best they showed great moral earnestness and a high sense of duty. The *Discourses* of Epictetus (about A.D. 60–140) are a good example of this kind of teaching. (But I think Mr. Spock in the 1960s television program "Star Trek" might help most of us picture them better.)

Many of both the Stoics and the Epicureans would have agreed with Paul's dislike for the idols in Athens, though for different reasons. As we look at Paul's speech we will see that there may be other points of agreement, as well as key differences. They brought Paul to the Areopagus (Mars' Hill) to give an account of himself. The Areopagus was the council that held jurisdiction over matters of morals and religion. Now, Paul was not a prisoner here, since in verse 33, after he is done, he is free to go; so we probably should not call this a trial. These men wanted to know what Paul had to say. What an opportunity, and what a challenge! In the marketplace, Paul had conversed with Epicureans and Stoics; now he was before this august body, which would have included representatives of other distinguished schools of philosophy, such as the followers of Plato and Aristotle. Here is what Paul told them (Acts 17:22-31):

> [22] "Men of Athens, I perceive that in every way you are very religious. [23] For as I passed along and observed the objects of your worship, I found also an altar with this inscription, 'To the unknown god.' What therefore you worship as unknown, this I proclaim to you. [24] The God who made the world and everything in it, being Lord of heaven and earth, does not live in temples made by man, [25] nor is he served by human hands, as though he needed anything, since he himself gives to all mankind life and breath and everything. [26] And he made from one man every nation of mankind to live on all the face of the earth, having determined allotted periods and the boundaries of their habitation, [27] that they should seek God, in the hope that they might feel their way toward him and find him. Yet he is actually not far from each one of us, [28] for
>
> "'In him we live and move and have our being';
>
> "as even some of your own poets have said,
>
> "'For we are indeed his offspring.'
>
> [29] "Being then God's offspring, we ought not to think that the divine being is like gold, or silver, or stone, an image formed by the art and imagination of man. [30] The times of ignorance God overlooked, but now he commands all people everywhere to repent, [31] because he has fixed a day on which he will judge the world in righteousness by a man whom he has appointed, and of this he has given assurance to all by raising him from the dead."

At the mention of the resurrection of the dead (v. 31), some mocked, some wanted to hear more, and some believed—all in all, a normal response to Paul's evangelism. There is no reason to suppose, as some do (based on 1 Cor. 2:2, written to the church Paul founded just after these events), that Paul afterward regretted his "philosophical" style, and went back to the simpler appeal to Christ and his cross.

We might outline Paul's speech in this way:

1. *Starting point (vv. 22-23):* All people—including Athenians—have a religious instinct, an inborn urge to worship some god. So Paul is going to tell them the truth about what they've already been yearning for.

2. *The truth about God (vv. 24-29):* The God who made the world and us is too great to be worshiped through idols.

3. *The right response (vv. 30-31):* Now is the time to respond to the true God. To "repent" (v. 30) means to call the former way of life sin. The resurrection of Jesus (v. 31) proves that God has the power to judge the world; and it also shows God's approval of Jesus.

The first two points of the speech (vv. 22-29) aim at establishing what I have called the metaphysical basis for Christian belief—namely, that there is a God who made us for himself, and the world shows that he is too great to be found as part of the world itself. The Stoics (and perhaps other philosophers) would have taken this as common ground; the Epicureans, however, with their view of the gods' indifference to human affairs, would have to change their minds in order to accept that we exist to seek after God.

The third point of Paul's speech (vv. 30-31) is what Michael Green has called "the specifically Christian content of the sermon." Another way to put it is to say that in verse 30 Paul goes from the metaphysical part to the specifically redemptive-historical and experiential parts—that is, he speaks of events (the resurrection of Jesus and the last judgment) that advance God's purpose for mankind to know him, and he calls people to respond to these ideas with repentance (and I suppose at his follow-up meetings he would tell them to become disciples of Jesus).

Most scholars recognize that Paul uses quotes from Greek poets in his speech. Now to the Greeks, unlike to us, "poets" were teachers of religion and morals, so Paul is interacting with views that his hearers would have respected.

As the ESV margin points out, the first part of verse 26, "In him we live and move and have our being," comes from the hand of Epimenides of Crete, a famous holy man of the sixth century B.C. The original ran something like this:

> They fashioned a tomb for you, O holy and high one—
> The Cretans, always liars, evil beasts, idle bellies!—
> But you are not dead; you live and abide forever,
> For in you we live and move and are.

The last line is what Paul used here (he used the second line in Titus 1:12). The argument of the poem goes like this: the people of Crete have built a tomb for Zeus (God, as the Stoics saw) and show it to visitors; but Zeus cannot be dead, since our living depends on him. That is, since we are alive, that must mean that he is, too, since without him we would not be.

The second quote of verse 26 comes from Aratus (early third century B.C.), and resembles something written by Cleanthes—the man who succeeded Zeno as the leader of the Stoics—in his *Hymn to Zeus*.

As F. F. Bruce pointed out,

> The Zeus of these Stoic poets is of course the *logos* or world-principle which animates all things. Their language, however, is largely adaptable to the God of revelation. By presenting God as Creator and Judge, Paul emphasizes his Personality in contrast to the materialistic pantheism of the Stoics.

And as Michael Green adds,

> Paul is using heathen poets to preach biblical doctrine, namely that personal beings owe their origin and significance, their life and everything, to a personal creator God.

But Paul does not leave out Bible quotes altogether; behind the thoughts in verses 24-29 lie allusions to Exodus 20:11; 1 Kings 8:27; Isaiah 66:1-2; Psalm 50:7-15; Isaiah 42:5; Genesis 1:26-28; and Deuteronomy 32:8. Paul has stitched together a string of Bible phrases to show that only the Christian message, rooted in the Old Testament and its doctrine of the creation, answers the needs that we all find in ourselves and that the better philosophers have already expressed. We can also see how Paul's approach is similar to that found in the Wisdom of Solomon, as we mentioned already; for example, Wisdom 13:5 says,

> For from the greatness and beauty of created things
> comes a corresponding perception of their Creator.

In the book of Acts most of the speeches are evangelistic—in fact, we don't find any "in-church sermons" at all! For example, in 2:14-41, Peter speaks at the first Christian Pentecost; in 3:12-26, Peter speaks at the temple; in 4:8-12, Peter and John speak before the Jewish ruling council; in 8:26-40, Philip explains Isaiah 53 to the Ethiopian; in 10:34-43, Peter speaks to Cornelius and his household (paving the way for Gentiles to become Christians without becoming Jews first); in 13:16-41, Paul speaks in the synagogue in Pisidian Antioch; and here in 17:16-31, Paul speaks before the Areopagus. These messages have their similarities and differences, mostly depending on the audience. Most speeches come to people with some background in the Old Testament and Judaism (we might call them "churched"); this one, 17:22-31, has Paul speaking to a group of people with little or no Bible background (we might call them radically "unchurched"). If we compare these speeches we can see that there's an overall plan for the message, but no one-size-fits-all presentation.

The overall plan for the message would be something like this:

(1) *There is a God who made us for himself, and what's wrong with us is that we don't know him.* With both kinds of audiences—Jews and Gentiles—the apostles used the Old Testament to establish this point: the Jews accepted its authority, and needed to see that Jesus was the Messiah; the Gentiles did not accept its authority, and hence the apostles showed that it answers to what people already know of themselves and the world, and that it shows *why* we feel the way we do.

(2) *God will one day judge all of us:* it will be a judgment that is *moral, perfect,* and *inescapable.*

(3) *The resurrection of Jesus proves that he is the one who will judge us, but also that through him we can be delivered from judgment.* In a Jewish setting this will especially be geared to proving God's favor toward Jesus (because the cross was a cursed death). In a Gentile setting it is especially proof of God's power: if he can raise the dead, he can certainly judge the world (who can stop him?), and he can change *me,* as I know I need!

(4) *You must make a personal response:* you yourself need forgiveness and a new life, and you can have it, by turning to Jesus and becoming his disciple.

And where would natural revelation come into play in such a plan? In Acts it comes in especially in point (1), what I have called the metaphysical part; but in theory it could also come in to support point (3), the ethical part. In the next section we will look at two passages from Romans, and see that Paul thought so too.

(c) Romans 1:18-21: God Revealed Through Nature

The apostle Paul wrote his letter to the Roman church in about A.D. 57, something like six years after he spoke in Athens. Paul did not found the Roman church, so Romans is different from most of his other letters. His purpose for this letter was to enlist the Roman Christians' support for his mission to the west (1:11-14; 15:23-29). He wanted more than money from them, he wanted their earnest prayers that would come from their fully identifying with his mission. Most of the details in Romans come from this purpose: Paul must show how all mankind, Jew and Gentile, needs the gospel, and how that gospel puts people right with God (chapters 1–5). He must show how that gospel of forgiveness bears the fruit of growing holiness in the lives of believers, even though they still struggle with sin, and that God will not forsake those who so struggle (chapters 6–8). He must address the question of the Jews and their place in God's plan for the world (chapters 9–11), and lay out his vision of the life of a faithful church that has Jews and Gentiles in it (chapters 12–15).

Paul wanted the Roman Christians to see this mission—indeed every kind of outreach—in the light of God's plan to include people from all races in his people, as he foretold in the Old Testament; that's why, in 15:8-12, he quoted Bible passages that invite the Gentiles to join the song of praise.

At the beginning of this theology for his mission, Paul wrote the following, to show why God has a right to hold mankind accountable for their failure to know and love him (1:18-23):

> [18] For the wrath of God is revealed from heaven against all ungodliness and unrighteousness of men, who by their unrighteousness suppress the truth. [19] For what can be known about God is plain to them, because God has shown it to them. [20] For his invisible attributes, namely, his eternal power and divine nature, have been clearly perceived, ever since the creation of the world, in the things that have been made. So they are without excuse. [21] For although they knew God, they did not honor him as God or give thanks to him, but they became futile in their thinking, and their foolish hearts were darkened. [22] Claiming to be wise, they became fools, [23] and exchanged the glory of the immortal God for images resembling mortal man and birds and animals and reptiles.

The connectors between sentences, such as the word "for" that begins 19, 20, and 21, allow us to see what Paul is saying: the truth that men suppress (v. 18) is what can be known about God, which is plain to all, because it comes through the things God has made (vv. 19-20). That is, the world itself gives some kind of testimony to its Maker, and if mankind doesn't receive that testimony, it's because they are suppressing the truth—the problem isn't with the testimony that the world gives, it's with people.

Paul certainly stands in line with the psalms that celebrate the way the creation displays the greatness of God. But, as we saw already, the Psalms are songs for the believer to sing, to celebrate what they see (or at least to know they ought to see). Now, the unbeliever is at fault for not seeing the same things. This implies that Paul thought that the testimony was objectively there, and failure to receive it was due to a problem with the human heart. The wonder of being a believer is that our eyes are opened to see what's really there!

But at the same time, the apologetic approach that we saw in the book of Wisdom also comes into play: if the testimony is there, perhaps the evangelist can help people to see that testimony, to stop suppressing it for a moment. People suppress the testimony because it points them to God; but if they can face the fact that God made us for himself and offers us forgiveness and new life, perhaps they won't keep on suppressing it. (And if they do keep on suppressing it, the moral consequences are chilling, as the rest of Romans 1 describes.)

In other words, this passage from Romans is not just the theological explanation of why people need the gospel; it is also part of Paul's reason for the kind of apologetic he used in Acts 17.

It looks to me like the particular kind of apologetic that Paul has in mind is a version of what many call the "argument from design"—an argument employed by other Jews of his day, as well as by the Stoics (them again!). For example, Paul says in verse 20 that God's "invisible attributes, namely, his eternal power and divine nature, have been clearly perceived, ever since the creation of the world, in the things that have been made." In Paul, the word "power" typically means "power made known by being expressed": compare, for example, the power expressed in Jesus' resurrection (Rom. 1:4), and in the way the gospel brings salvation (v. 16). Here, Paul is saying that the way the world is makes God's power visible to all mankind. Does he go further and suggest that the actual features of the world are part of that expression of power? I think so, and I'll show why from another first-century Jew, who used the same word to make a similar point; I will also mention the Stoics.

The Jewish scholar Flavius Josephus (A.D. 37–95) was from a priestly family and was a commander of a Jewish army when the Jews rebelled against the Romans in A.D. 66. He went over to the Romans, however, and came under the protection of Titus, the Roman commander who eventually became emperor. Josephus defended himself against the charge of being a traitor; but he also defended the Old Testament to cultured Roman audiences. In one of his writings Josephus says that Moses represented the one true God as "knowable to us by his *power.*" That is the power God expressed in his work of creation, not in his works of redemptive history. The way we perceive that power is through the intricate features of the world itself. The Stoics likewise held that,

> The rule of the [divine] *logos* is discernible in the works of the cosmos. . . . Anyone who recognizes the ordered coherence of the cosmos will . . . join in praise to the deity.

The basic point, then, is that the way the creation is points to a Creator. Since this is a testimony that comes to all people, they are all left without excuse if they don't seek after God because of it.

(d) Romans 2:14-16: God's Testimony in Every Heart

In order to show that all people need the gospel because God holds them guilty and they need his forgiveness, Paul must show that all people know—or should know—of God's existence; but also that all people know—or should know—something of God's just character. He made the first point in the verses we looked at, and the second point he makes in 2:12-16:

> [12] For all who have sinned without the law will also perish without the law, and all who have sinned under the law will be judged by the law. [13] For it is not the hearers of the law who are righteous before God, but the doers of the law who will be justified. [14] For when Gentiles who have not the law by nature do what the law requires, they are a law to themselves, even though they do not have the law. [15] They show that the work of the law is written on their hearts, while their conscience also bears witness and their conflicting thoughts accuse or even excuse them, [16] on that day when, according to my gospel, God judges the secrets of men by Christ Jesus.

Paul is speaking of those "without the law" and of those "under the law" (v. 12)—that is, of Gentiles who have not received a special gift from God, and of Jews who have. The issue is that nevertheless both types of people know full well that they are guilty of wrongdoing. They will both be answerable to God at the judgment, since the same God made them. God is just to judge them both by his standard, since the Gentiles, unschooled by the Law of Moses as they are, still show that the law is at work on their hearts, through the witness of their conscience. We may speak of the "law of nature" and the "Law of Moses" if we like; but we must remember that the same God is author of both.

When Paul says in verse 14 that the Gentiles "by nature do what the law requires," he is not referring to instinct, nor is he suggesting that it comes apart from education; instead, he means "by nature" in contrast to "by the covenant and the Holy Spirit."

Of course none of this suggests that such Gentiles will come off as innocent on the great day of judgment; by the works of the law no flesh will be justified in God's sight (3:20). Instead, it shows that God is just in holding all mankind guilty.

This speaks to what I have called the ethical component of the Christian message: even people outside the privileges of God's covenantal revelation can perceive some of it. On this point, as on so many others, C. S. Lewis has put it best:

> It is far from my intention to deny that we find in Christian ethics a deepening, an internalization, a few changes of emphasis, in the moral code. But only serious ignorance of Jewish and Pagan culture would lead anyone to the conclusion that it is a radically new thing. Essentially, Christianity is not the promulgation of a moral discovery. It is addressed only to penitents, only to those who admit their disobedience to the known moral law. It offers forgiveness for having broken, and supernatural help towards keeping, that law, and by so doing re-affirms it.

When Lewis mentions "forgiveness for having broken the law," he is referring to what I have called the redemptive-historical component of the faith—the things God has done to open a way for us, such as the death and resurrection of Jesus. When he mentions "supernatural help towards keeping the law," he is referring to what I have called the experiential component of the faith—the work of the Holy Spirit in the believer's heart.

Faith and Reasons

If we follow Paul, we must say that there is some truth about God that comes to all people by virtue of being human and living in the world that God made. Knowing that truth would not "save" anyone; but if anyone is to receive God's salvation, he has to start with that truth.

Paul's approach shows us how we can commend our faith to those who don't believe it. His strategy assumes two things: first, that there are things that we all know, and that we take for granted in all we do, and that we have to find a way to account for if we want to have a responsible philosophy of life. (These things would include the facts that: everyone yearns for God; people can reason and make valid moral judgments; the world is regular and understandable.)

The second thing Paul's strategy assumes is that our hearts' commitments affect the way we account for these things that we all know; and we have to expose those commitments themselves to view to see ways in which we suppress the truth.

This ties in to what we said earlier about how all our knowing is done with our "heart"—with that center of our personal life that thinks, feels, and chooses. If our basic loyalties are out of whack, that can't help but affect the way we think; but that doesn't mean that *all* our thinking is bad or unreliable. It does mean, though, that we may resist some conclusions because of where they may lead.

A good example of this comes from the story "Winnie-the-Pooh and Some Bees." Pooh wants to raid a bees' nest for honey, but the nest is up in a tree, so he borrows a balloon from Christopher Robin to fly to the nest. Pooh tries to disguise himself as a cloud, but the bees are suspicious and begin to fly all around him; when one lands on his nose, he calls out to Christopher Robin:

> "I have just been thinking, and I have come to a very important decision. *These are the wrong sort of bees.*"
>
> "Are they?" [said Christopher Robin.]
>
> "Quite the wrong sort. So I should think they would make the wrong sort of honey, shouldn't you?"
>
> "Would they?"
>
> "Yes. So I think I shall come down."

Pooh's reasoning is strongly influenced by his desire not to get stung by these suspicious bees—that is, his reasoning is a function of his heart.

C. S. Lewis was an excellent example of an approach to apologetics that reflects Paul's; another was Francis Schaeffer. (I think Blaise Pascal would have been, too, had he lived long enough to write his apologetic, of which his *Pensées* are just the scrap notes.) Jay Budziszewski, a recent writer on natural law, could have been describing the strategy when he wrote:

> Our point of contact with nonbelievers is established by God himself. That point is general revelation, which "penetrates the very mind of man even

> in his revolt" so that his conscience bears witness despite himself. Natural law is but the moral aspect of this penetrating arrow.
>
> First [in apologetics] we must know what is known already, then we must know how this knowledge is repressed; first we must learn the heart's inscription, then we must learn its devices. . . .
>
> From this perspective, most modern ethical thinking goes about matters backwards. It assumes that the problem of human sin is mainly *cognitive*—that it has to do with the state of our knowledge. In other words it holds that we don't know what's right and wrong and are trying to find out. But natural-law theory assumes that the problem is mainly *volitional*—that it has to do with the state of our will. It holds that by and large we know what's right and wrong but wish we didn't, and that we try to keep ourselves in ignorance so that we can do as we please.

Schools of apologetics have debated whether the Christian evangelist should focus on the evidences and arguments, or on the resistance of the human heart. But who ever said it should be *either-or*? Surely we should use *both-and.*

Science, Natural Revelation, and Apologetics

So how do the sciences fit into this picture? In other words, what is the connection between what the sciences tell us and natural revelation?

The answer to that depends on what we think the sciences are doing, and whether we think they are producing something that we can call "knowledge." Most people, I know, think "scientific knowledge" is the surest kind there is; but we have to be careful here, as I hope you can see from all we've discussed so far.

In the ancient world the sciences were part of philosophy—that is, they were part of the overall effort to understand the world, and that effort allowed people to ask questions about things such as meaning, purpose, God, and ethics. Up until the nineteenth century, in fact, the term for "scientist" was "natural philosopher." When we use today's terms, we might be tempted to forget that scientists are people with hearts and worldviews, so we must begin by remembering this obvious but easily overlooked fact.

The sciences raise all manner of questions about the world in which we live. Why is there something instead of nothing? Why is it that we can understand the world, and describe it with something so rational as mathematics? Why can we make inductive inferences—making generalizations from our observations, when we haven't tested *every* instance (as we saw in figuring out the diet of hawks, back in chapter 2)—and why are so many of these inferences reliable? How great is the universe, and could it have caused itself or does it require a cause? Why should the universe be so well suited for our enjoyment?

The sciences also study the features of human nature that apply to all people—and these include reason, conscience, and the religious instinct. Are secular or soul-denying theories of human nature adequate to account for what we see in ourselves and in our fellow man?

And what of the design evident in the world we see? Are there purely physical laws that would explain why the universe came into being? Would organic chemicals by themselves have formed a living creature? Is man's reason, conscience, and will a simple development of what we find in other animals, or is it of a different kind altogether?

One area where the sciences can serve apologetics is in the argument from design. This argument has several parts. First, there is the fact that the universe is so well suited to support our lives here on earth—and is not suited, apparently, to support life anywhere else. The second part is that there are features of the world for which a purely natural explanation is not adequate, as I mentioned above. But it's very important to distinguish between "*there is no* natural explanation for this" and "*I can't think of* a natural explanation for this." The sciences may show us that there is a natural path from some things to others—for example, there may be a natural or evolutionary path from the basic canine to the varieties of canines in the world today, the foxes, wolves, jackals, and dogs. At the same time the sciences may bring the gaps into sharper focus—much as modern genetics bring the miraculous nature of our Lord's conception into clearer focus. I will develop some of these ideas in later chapters.

The Christian should welcome the fullest rigor in studying these questions; but he will also want to be as careful as he can when it comes to integrating the answers into a view of life, because he knows how the heart can affect the way we think.

So the sciences, properly used, can help to clarify the metaphysical and ethical parts of the Christian message.

13

Caring for God's World

The Biblical View of the Environment

In this chapter I will survey some of the key Christian teachings about the environment. I am keeping to my overall plan, namely the role of the sciences in Christian thinking; and this means I can't pursue every aspect of a Christian view of the environment, worth our while though it may be. It doesn't take long before our discussion of such matters crosses over from the natural sciences into ethics; and, as a matter of fact, I think that's the main heading under which this topic belongs. So I will be content to outline the foundation for ethics, largely by drawing together material we have already looked into.

It is common to blame Christianity for the environmental problems that we face today—after all, it's the biblical mandate to exploit the earth and its resources, isn't it? Unbelievers will say this, of course; but sometimes it seems that there are Christians who think this way, too. James Watt, a committed Pentecostal Christian, was President Reagan's first secretary of the interior, coming to office in 1981. During his first appearance before the House of Representatives, someone asked him about his view of preserving the environment for future generations. He replied, "I do not know how many future generations we can count on before the Lord returns"—a remark that was widely reported as implying that he thought Jesus would return pretty soon, so we didn't have to worry about it very much. (As it turns out, the press took this remark out of context and badly twisted what Watt actually did say.)

The Original Plan

In the creation story of Genesis 1, God declares that one of his purposes for making mankind is for them to "have dominion over" the other creatures of the earth (Gen. 1:26); and after he made the man and woman he blessed them and bade them (v. 28),

> "Be fruitful and multiply and fill the earth and subdue it and have dominion over the fish of the sea and over the birds of the heavens and over every living thing that moves on the earth."

I have already argued that we should read Genesis 1 and 2 together, and that if we do so we will see that the order of events is: God made the man, put him in the Garden, had him name the animals, made the woman, and then commissioned the man and woman to "fill the earth": that is, beginning from Eden, to work their way outwards, bringing the blessings of Eden to all the earth. That's what it meant to "have dominion" over the earth—to manage all of its creatures and resources for holy and wise purposes.

This original purpose, or mandate, takes for granted that mankind was itself holy and wise, as they came from God's hand. But a Christian recognizes that the sin of our first parents brought new features into the picture, and hence this mandate is far from an encouragement to strip and exploit the earth.

Some people have thought that the command in Genesis 1:28, "subdue," encourages man to exploit the world; some have called it "military terminology." But this overlooks two factors: first, the context is that of man in his pristine condition, not as an overlord; and second, the strong term "subdue" is used, as the commentator Franz Delitzsch pointed out, "because this dominion requires the energy of strength and the art of wisdom."

THE MODIFIED PLAN

The first human pair sinned, as we have seen already. God punished them by sending them out from the Garden; they will not be able to spread Eden's blessings to the rest of the earth. I explained earlier that we should take this to mean that the properties and processes of the world will now be part of God's disciplinary plan for sinful mankind.

Further, human nature has become sinful from that time onward. Before the flood, God declared that "every intention of the thoughts of [man's] heart was only evil continually" (Gen. 6:5); while after the flood, "the intention of man's heart is evil from his youth" (8:21).

Though I don't much care to say that "nature is fallen"—because that is too easy to misunderstand—I can accept it in the sense that *in man,* its appointed head, the natural world is fallen—because man does not provide for it the headship that God made it and man for.

This will mean that man will conduct himself with evil motives and foolish planning. He will use the good things God made for evil: stones and wood to make weapons to murder; sexuality to commit adultery; male strength to dominate and abuse women and children. And with motives like that, he can't expect to have a sympathetic feel for his environment, a love for its beauty and well-being—let alone compassion for his fellow man!—as his guiding principles.

So it's no surprise that people foul their environment and show little respect for its beauty. It's also no surprise that people make so many mistakes and bring on themselves so many unforeseen consequences when they try to use their resources.

A simple example is the mongoose. In India the mongoose gained a reputation for skill in killing snakes—especially snakes in the cobra family. (Rudyard Kipling made them famous in the West with his story "Rikki-Tikki-Tavi" in his *Jungle Books.*) Someone got the bright idea of importing them to the West Indies in the New World, to take care of the dangerous snakes found there. Unfortunately, these snakes are vipers, not cobras—they strike differently and the mongoose doesn't risk his life in fighting them. Instead the mongoose is now a pest, preying on birds (including the domestic ones). Oops.

So now the natural world suffers at the hand of man.

The World Still Serves Man

Man has sinned and has departed from his original task; but he is still the head. Psalm 8 is based on the story of Genesis 1, and sees man's dominion still in effect:

> [3] When I look at your heavens, the work of your fingers,
> the moon and the stars, which you have set in place,
> [4] what is man that you are mindful of him,
> and the son of man that you care for him?
> [5] Yet you have made him a little lower than the heavenly beings,
> and crowned him with glory and honor.
> [6] You have given him dominion over the works of your hands;
> you have put all things under his feet,
> [7] all sheep and oxen,
> and also the beasts of the field,
> [8] the birds of the heavens, and the fish of the sea,
> whatever passes along the paths of the seas.

In the same way, Psalm 104 celebrates how the world keeps on working, including to serve man:

> [21] The young lions roar for their prey,
> seeking their food from God.
> [22] When the sun rises, they steal away
> and lie down in their dens.
> [23] Man goes out to his work
> and to his labor until the evening.
> [24] O LORD, how manifold are your works!
> In wisdom have you made them all;
> the earth is full of your creatures.

Francis Bacon (1561–1626) wrote in favor of the way the scientific enterprise in his day showed a new empirical emphasis. He wrote a book called *Novum Organum Scientiarum* (*The New Tool of the Sciences*) in 1620, in which he said,

> Man by the Fall fell at the same time from his state of innocency and from his dominion over created things. Both these losses can even in this life be partially repaired; the former by religion and faith, the latter by arts and sciences.

But, as a matter of fact, man never *lost* his dominion; instead, he has *defiled* it. Nevertheless, Bacon's idea still has merit: by arts (works of craftsmanship) and sciences we learn how to govern nature, to make created things do our will. The reason this becomes a matter of ethics, however, is that we must decide whether our will is right and just—we must govern *ourselves* by God's will.

But man's dominion over nature is not the only theme we find in the Bible. In the Psalms we find an appreciation for the beauty of the created world. Now there are two kinds of "beauty," and we find them both in the Bible. There is the "user's" perspective—the grass grows for the livestock and the ground yields wine to gladden man's heart, oil to make his face shine, and bread to strengthen his heart (Ps. 104:14-15).

At the same time there is another kind of beauty, one that has nothing to do with usefulness to us. In the same Psalm 104, we find the poet celebrating springs where wild donkeys quench their thirst (v. 11), fir trees for the storks to live in (v. 17), mountains for the wild goats and rock badgers to find home and shelter (v. 18), prey for the lions (v. 21), and, in the sea, Leviathan (probably the whale) playing (v. 26). The world is a delightful and fascinating place, expressing God's creativity in so many ways; and these expressions are delightful, even if we never get to use them or even see them.

Consider, for example, a few verses from Proverbs 30:

> [18] Three things are too wonderful for me;
> four I do not understand:
> [19] the way of an eagle in the sky,
> the way of a serpent on a rock,
> the way of a ship on the high seas,
> and the way of a man with a virgin. . . .
>
> [24] Four things on earth are small,
> but they are exceedingly wise:
> [25] the ants are a people not strong,
> yet they provide their food in the summer;
> [26] the rock badgers are a people not mighty,
> yet they make their homes in the cliffs;
> [27] the locusts have no king,
> yet all of them march in rank;
> [28] the lizard you can take in your hands,
> yet it is in kings' palaces.
>
> [29] Three things are stately in their tread;
> four are stately in their stride:
> [30] the lion, which is mightiest among beasts
> and does not turn back before any;
> [31] the strutting rooster, the he-goat,
> and a king whose army is with him.

Certainly the author wants to convey a lesson about human behavior, and this is clear from the last line of each of these lists—verses 19d, "the way of a man with a virgin," and 31b, "a king whose army is with him." But we shouldn't miss the sense of wonder that runs through the lists of natural things. This man has looked into the sky and felt awe at the flying eagle; he has admired the way ants, rock badgers, and locusts are fitted to get along in their places; he has enjoyed watching lions, roosters (or magpies or greyhounds, see ESV note), and he-goats strut.

The final aspect of the creation to speak of is man's relation to the animals. According to Genesis 9:2, every wild animal now fears man—and with good reason: man will not only use the animals for food, he will also inflict cruelty on them. This cruelty, too, defiles man's dominion.

The Sabbath commands require that farm animals be allowed to rest, as well as the farm hands and family (Ex. 20:10; 23:12). God gave man the right to *use* the animals, but not to *abuse* them.

Hence we also have a number of verses that require people to be kind to their animals. For example, Deuteronomy 25:4 forbids an Israelite farmer to muzzle his ox while it is treading grain; and Proverbs 27:23-27 encourages the wise person to "Know well the condition of your flocks," which means to pay careful attention to keeping them well. This is more than just good management for oneself; it is a moral matter, as Proverbs 12:10 makes clear:

> Whoever is righteous has regard for the life of his beast,
> but the mercy of the wicked is cruel.

Kindness to an animal expresses righteousness; and this is because God himself cares about animals. Note how, in Jonah 4:11, God rebukes Jonah for not caring about Nineveh; God mentions the people first, and then throws in the animals to boot!

> "And should not I pity Nineveh, that great city, in which there are more than 120,000 persons who do not know their right hand from their left, and also much cattle?"

When Jesus healed on the Sabbath, the Jewish leaders accused him of breaking the commandment. His reply shows that for him showing kindness to those in distress—to animals and to man—was being true to the very spirit of the Sabbath (Matt. 12:11-12):

> [11] He said to them, "Which one of you who has a sheep, if it falls into a pit on the Sabbath, will not take hold of it and lift it out? [12] Of how much more value is a man than a sheep! So it is lawful to do good on the Sabbath."

Stock animals that are dangerous to man—and even to other stock animals—must be restrained or put down (Gen. 9:5; Ex. 21:28-32, 35-36). Animals are decidedly *not* for man's sexual use (Ex. 22:19; Lev. 18:23; 20:15-16).

Ordinarily, man will leave wild animals to themselves—except that some might be game for the hunt. Even there, however, there are limits. In Deuteronomy 22:6-7 we find a curious law:

> [6] "If you come across a bird's nest in any tree or on the ground, with young ones or eggs and the mother sitting on the young or on the eggs, you shall

> not take the mother with the young. [7] You shall let the mother go, but the young you may take for yourself, that it may go well with you, and that you may live long."

There is some discussion among the specialists on just what motivates this law; but in any case, it puts a stop to greed and to shortsightedness. (Compare Leviticus 22:28, forbidding Israelites from killing animals and their young on the same day; and Deuteronomy 20:19-20, which forbids Israelites from cutting down fruit trees to make siege works.)

Problems come when the predators take a liking to mutton, in which case a faithful shepherd will kill the wild beast (as David tells, in 1 Sam. 17:34-36, that he did). Otherwise, they, like we, wait on God for their food. As Psalm 145 puts it, in a passage celebrating God's abundant goodness:

> [15] The eyes of all look to you,
> and you give them their food in due season.
> [16] You open your hand;
> you satisfy the desire of every living thing.

As C. S. Lewis wrote in his *Reflections on the Psalms,*

> The thought which gives these creatures a place in the Psalmist's gusto for Nature is surely obvious. They are our fellow-dependents; we all, lions, storks, ravens, whales—live, as our fathers said, "at God's charges," and the mention of all equally redounds to [God's] praise.

Ethical Considerations for the Environment

Let's briefly summarize some of the ethical issues we have to face if we want to act in a Christian manner toward the world in which we live.

Man is still the ruler of his environment. That is, he is responsible toward God for understanding the world God made, and managing it for holy and wise purposes. This means that the world is there for us to use, but to use thoughtfully. Being a litterbug isn't responsible—nor is the dumping of toxic waste.

We will discuss the purposes of science in a later chapter; but certainly, one of those purposes is to understand the world God made so that we can manage that world for the service of man. That will enable us to know how to use the things we find; but it will also enable us to know how to avoid doing damage (or else how to clean up our mess).

The Christian faces a constant tension between *using* nature and *enjoying* it: for example, should we build houses on this patch of woodland or leave it wild? There is no simple way to decide every case, except to say that we want to find ways to preserve both sides of the tension.

We will injure our own souls if we allow ourselves to be indifferent to the beauty of a wild scene, because we will never be able to sing the Psalms with integrity. Beauty is good in itself; but it is also a key factor in refreshing our spirits. The Scottish pastor William Still (1911–1997) wrote:

> It is a growing conviction with us that holiday time, which is a necessity to those who would maintain a busy life efficiently, needs to be a time of rest, and re-creation. No environment offers more hope of this than that which gets back as nearly as may be to nature. . . . For there is no doubt about this, to those who have the Word of God and store it in their minds and hearts, there is no place where it does its deepest work so well as in close contact with nature.

Still went on to cite a poem from the High Church Anglican John Keble (1792–1866):

> There is a book, who runs may read,
> which heavenly truth imparts,
> and all the lore its scholars need,
> pure eyes and Christian hearts.
>
> The works of God, above, below,
> within us and around,
> are pages in that book, to show
> how God himself is found.
>
> The glorious sky, embracing all,
> is like the Maker's love,
> wherewith encompassed, great and small
> in peace and order move.
>
> The dew of heaven is like thy grace:
> it steals in silence down:
> but, where it lights, the favoured place
> by richest fruit is known.
>
> One name above all glorious names,
> with its ten thousand tongues
> the everlasting sea proclaims,
> echoing angelic songs.

Two worlds are ours; 'tis only sin
forbids us to descry
the mystic heaven and earth within,
plain as the sea and sky.

Thou who hast given me eyes to see
and love this sight so fair,
give me a heart to find out thee,
and read thee everywhere.

SECTION III
SCIENCE AND FAITH INTERACT

14

SCIENCE, PROVIDENCE, AND MIRACLE

THE GERMAN NEW TESTAMENT scholar Rudolph Bultmann (1884–1976) was famous for his program of demythologizing Christianity so that modern people could accept it. He wrote,

> It is impossible to use the electric light and the wireless and to avail ourselves of modern medical and surgical discoveries, and at the same time to believe in the New Testament world of spirits and miracles. We may think we can manage it in our own lives, but to expect others to do so is to make the Christian faith unintelligible and unacceptable to the modern world.

This spirit shows up in the work of the Jesus Seminar; in the introduction to their *Five Gospels* they write,

> The contemporary religious controversy, epitomized in the Scopes trial and the continuing clamor for creationism as a viable alternative to the theory of evolution, turns on whether the worldview reflected in the Bible can be carried forward into this scientific age and retained as an article of faith. . . . The Christ of creed and dogma, who had been firmly in place in the Middle Ages, can no longer command the assent of those who have seen the heavens through Galileo's telescope.

These people are saying that the "modern scientific outlook" has shown that the biblical picture of the world is false. (This uses the "conflict" model of science-faith interaction.) If we want to maintain some form of Christian faith for ourselves and others, they say, we had better revise it and remove everything that offends that modern outlook.

The principal way in which this modern outlook has supposedly undermined the biblical worldview is in the doctrine of providence. In particular, this outlook has done away with any special or supernatural events; it has called the reliability of natural properties into question; and it has sharpened the traditional problem of evil.

As a committed traditional Christian I don't accept this line of reasoning for a second. Instead I ask, just what is this "modern scientific outlook," and what authority should it have in what I believe? Is the *outlook* something separate from the *practice* of science itself—must you have the outlook in order to be a good scientist?

I think that what we have covered so far should equip you to think through these questions pretty well. For now I want to focus on showing that the kinds of claims that lie behind these proposed revisions to Christian faith depend on fundamental misunderstandings both of the biblical material and of the scientific theories of our day.

MODERN SCIENCE AND THE SUPERNATURAL

Bultmann thought that things like electric lights, radios, and modern medicine were a refutation of the biblical picture of the world. In his mind, the biblical picture of "spirits and miracles" was superstition, which the sciences have shown to be false.

It is astonishing that anyone could get away with writing this. First, he has misrepresented the biblical picture of the world, confusing it with the animistic type. (This leads to a misunderstanding of the history of science as well.) Second, he has misunderstood what the sciences may and may not prove. Let's give a better account of these things than Bultmann did.

Recall from chapter 11 what we found to be the main parts of the biblical picture of the world and God's action in it—there are "natural" events and "supernatural" ones. I defined these terms in this way:

> *"Natural":* God made the universe from nothing and endowed the things that exist with "natural properties"; he keeps those things in existence, maintaining both the properties and their power to interact with other things, in a web of cause-and-effect.
>
> *"Supernatural":* God is also free to "inject" special operations of his power into this web at any time: for example, he may add objects by creation; he may cause events directly; he may enable something or someone to do what its own natural properties would never have made it able to do; or he may impose organization on some collection of natural objects—whatever suits his purposes.

If we want to talk about what the scientists have enabled us to do with electricity or medicine, we are talking about their study of the *normal operations* of electricity and human anatomy. That is, these people have studied *natural* operations, and have made use of what they have learned. How does this say anything about whether *supernatural* events have happened or are even possible? You can study the motions of billiard balls all day long, and make beautiful charts and graphs; but this tells you what happens *so long as no one interferes*. You won't know at all from this kind of study whether someone might in fact snatch up a cue stick and tap one of the balls.

The sciences behind these advances in technology are like the study of the billiard balls; they cannot tell you whether there will be any interference—that's a job for another science (in the example, the "other" science is the study of human behavior).

But Bultmann and those who agree with him seem to think that the sciences have proven that the universe is a closed system—that is, that it is sealed off from any interference from outside the web of cause-and-effect. I think this is what they would call the modern scientific outlook. But how could a study of natural events prove that the world is shut off from the supernatural? That's a job, not for the natural sciences, but for theology.

Further, Bultmann, in misunderstanding the biblical picture, has confused it with an animistic picture of spirits living in every tree and causing every event; the spirits act out of either malice or caprice. But this is the view of paganism, not of Christianity; and the better Greek philosophers rejected it, too. In fact, it is the advance of Christianity that has pushed back such animism—and this is what fostered the development of the sciences. So Bultmann actually got the order of things backward, too!

In saying this, I certainly don't want to downplay the roles of "spirits" such as angels and devils. They are a part of the biblical picture; but they hardly get rid of things like "nature": instead they, like any other agents, have to make use of the natures of things (or, in some cases, override them) to accomplish their purposes.

As a matter of fact, the sciences can help us to identify a supernatural event. Let's go back to my billiard ball example. If you have studied the motion of these balls, you will conclude things like, "A ball will travel in a straight path (unless something applies a force in another direction)." If you're careful enough, you can say how much speed a ball will lose as it drags along the table.

Well, suppose you know where a ball started and which direction it was going; and then suppose someone tells you that it hit the cushion in some place other than along a straight line. You would check your informant to be sure he was reliable, of course; and if he turned out to be trustworthy, you would check the table to be sure it was still smooth and that the path was clear. If all was still well on that score, you would then invoke the "unless" clause in your law of straight motion. You would say, "the nature of the ball and the table are such that I expected the ball to hit here; the ball actually hit five inches to the right; therefore someone knocked the ball off course."

In the same way, you may conclude that an event was *super*natural when it exceeds or overrides the natural properties of the things involved. We know how babies come into the world; and if Mary told the truth about her pregnancy, then Jesus was begotten in a supernatural way. We know that dead bodies don't get up, walk around, talk, eat fish, and pass through doors. If Jesus did these things after he died, then his resurrection was a supernatural event.

I suspect that something else lurks behind Bultmann's claim—namely, the idea that there once were things that people thought had to be supernatural, but now the sciences have shown to be natural. If you go to Mount St. Helens in Washington state, for example—where there was a volcanic eruption in 1980—you will find a museum telling you about the native Americans and their relationship to the mountain. Some of these tribes thought that the mountain was a place where the spirits dwelt, and eruptions and earthquakes told people how the gods felt. A modern geologist might explain the mountain in terms of natural processes—plate tectonics and all the rest of it. He can't say the gods didn't *use* the natural processes, only that they didn't override these processes. These processes are part of the ordinary operation of the world.

But do such considerations apply to biblical events? No, since the biblical stories focus on specific historical events, not on the ordinary operations of the world.

This does remind us of the dangers of what is sometimes called the "God-of-the-gaps" fallacy: when we come upon some object or event for which we can't think of a natural explanation, we appeal to a supernatural one and call it a "miracle." We might even use it as evidence for a supernatural worldview. Then a scientist comes along with a natural explanation and the "miracle" sounds pretty ordinary; and what then happens to our belief in God? The trouble came from basing our belief on what we *don't know,* on a gap in our understanding of things. (It also comes from a loose use of words like "miracle," meaning "something whose cause I don't understand," as I indicated in chapter 11.)

But when we decide something is supernatural because what we *do know* about the things involved shows us that their properties never would have brought this about, we're talking about a real gap. Now we're talking about a gap between the properties of those things and the result we observe, not just a gap in our understanding. This will not fall foul of the God-of-the-gaps objection.

Now the biblical supernatural events I mentioned above—Jesus' conception and resurrection—display just this kind of gap between the properties and the results.

However, someone might carry the objection further: how do you know you should believe the people who tell you the stories about supernatural events? The Scottish philosopher David Hume (1711–1776) is famous for advancing this kind of objection. He claimed that testimony is *never* good enough to establish *any* miracle claims. His reasons were:

(1) You never have enough witnesses of the right kind—in his words, "of such unquestioned good sense, education and learning; of such undoubted integrity; of such credit and reputation."

(2) People are gullible and love stories of the fabulous.

(3) Such tales typically originate "among ignorant and barbarous nations."

(4) Other religions claim miracles, so the competing claims cancel one another out.

There are books devoted to answering Hume's arguments, and I recommend Douglas Geivett and Gary Habermas, *In Defense of Miracles* (1997) and C. S. Lewis, *Miracles: A Preliminary Study* (2nd edn., 1960), as well as my own *God of Miracles*. Here I'll just make some brief comments.

I have to wonder what grounds Hume has for calling into question the sense, learning, integrity, and reputation of the people who wrote the Bible. Is it perhaps *because* they report supernatural events? If so, then the argument is circular: because the very question is whether such events are believable, and we're deciding ahead of time that they're not if we doubt someone *just because* they report such events. I think that if we pay close attention to the Bible authors we will find that they certainly have the good sense and discriminating judgment that you'd want from a witness, as well as an unswerving commitment to honesty. In fact, the Bible itself makes careful discernment a high priority, since a prophet has to show that he can tell the future (Deut. 18:15-22; see also 13:1-5, which requires Israel to put even miracle workers to the test for their teachings). The early Christians did, as a matter of fact, reject a number of stories that claimed to be about miracles that Jesus and the apostles worked—because they didn't believe these stories. So we have no good grounds for calling these people ignorant or gullible.

So anyone who claims that we can just dismiss the biblical testimony has failed to come to grips with the facts about these authors; and now we're back to grappling with the "real gaps" that they report. How you tackle these gaps depends on what else you believe, and what kind of person you are.

SCIENCE AND RELIABLE NATURAL PROPERTIES

Traditionally, Christians have believed that God makes sure that everything that happens serves his purposes. They haven't always agreed on a lot of the details in how God brings this off, but at least they have been at one with this overarching statement. Some philosophers have used the name "determinism" for this view, since God's plan determines what happens, and nothing takes him by surprise.

There are at least two ways to reject that belief. The first is to say that nature is a closed system that follows its own inexorable laws. The model of the universe that some have followed in order to make this point was that of a great machine that allowed no outside interference. In theory, at least, by this model if you knew where everything was at any given time, and how fast it was moving and in what direction, you could predict every future event with perfect certainty. This kind of philosophy is called "determinism," because physical laws determine everything.

If you've been with me all the way, you can see two problems straightaway. The first is the clash in terms: that is, we have two viewpoints called "determinism," and we have to wonder whether they mean the same thing. Perhaps the means by which God brings off his purpose is through the inexorable physical laws?

The answer to this question, which is no, actually brings us to the second difficulty: the physical kind of determinism leaves no room for anyone's purpose or reason—not yours or mine, not even God's. It leaves out human purpose and reason, because it says that the motion of the atoms in your brain is what determines your thoughts and choices—and this takes away the possibility that you might partake of something transcendent, like truth. In other words, it is *physical causes* that produce your thoughts, not *reasons*—or Reason—in which case you have no reason to think your thoughts are true. But physical determinism leaves out God's purpose and government, too, since it says that physical laws alone govern everything—which means that God cannot inject any supernatural events.

Therefore physical determinism and Christian providential determinism have quite different scopes, and are different things altogether. Generally, Christian theologians have not wanted to say just *how* God governs the world, only *that* he does so.

But a theory of twentieth-century science has called into question even physical determinism. That theory is called quantum mechanics. (I will say a few words about another theory, chaos theory, below.)

Quantum mechanics uses some very sophisticated mathematics, but its basic concepts are not all that difficult. For now let's think of electrons orbiting around the nucleus of an atom; physicists discovered that those electrons can't be just anywhere, instead they have specific orbits. These orbits are sometimes called "energy levels," because each orbit corresponds to a definite amount of energy in the electron. Further, if an electron is to go to a higher orbit, you have to add a definite amount of energy; and if it drops to a lower orbit, it loses a definite amount of energy. These jumps in energy come in fixed amounts, or quanta, with no in-betweens. Physicists have also found that other quantities, such as the rate at which an electron spins, come in quanta as well.

But the funny part comes when you try to measure where an electron is or where it's going. It turns out that you can't know *both* where it is *and* how fast it's going with perfect precision. The better you know one, the worse you know the other. This is called the uncertainty principle.

The funniness doesn't leave off there, though. Remember that I said you could picture electrons orbiting around the nucleus; I suppose you thought of planets orbiting around a star. That's the model of an atom they taught us in school; but it's not the model any physicist holds today. Instead of a well-defined orbit, electrons have a probability function: that is, where the electron is at any time is not determined by laws but is a matter of probability. These probability functions change with each orbital (or energy) level.

Quantum mechanics is a theory that applies to matter at its smallest level, the level of electrons, protons, neutrons, quarks, and so on. And some people think that the theory tells us that matter, at its most basic level, seems to behave, not by laws, but by chance. (But just what do they mean by "chance"? See the "Notes and Comments" for more on this.). But that's an interpretation of the theory, not the theory itself: it's better to say that the theory puts a limit on our ability to predict the behavior of some things at this smallest level.

There are several lines of interpreting what this theory tells us about the world: some say that the chance is just that, and reality is ultimately random. Another line of interpretation focuses on the uncertainty principle, and says that the electron has neither position nor speed *until you measure it:* the measuring device is what produces position and speed. This is called the Copenhagen Interpretation (after Niels Bohr of Denmark). Some go even further than this and say that it is the mind that interprets the reading on the measuring device that produces the reality.

Another interpretation, called the many worlds hypothesis, says that all the possible values of position and speed are actually realized—but in different universes running in parallel. We just happen to be living in the universe in which the particular values we observe are realized. Of course we can never detect these other universes, so we can't "prove" this interpretation true or false. But it does seem awfully messy.

Another interpretation denies that quantum mechanics describes reality at all: it just describes how we can make use of the world successfully. This is a version of what is called instrumentalism.

Still another interpretation, which is gaining acceptance, holds that the particles we are used to studying are not the fundamental thing: instead the fields described by the mathematics are the main thing, and the particles pop out of those fields. The fields are deterministic (that is, predictable), while the particles can be unpredictable.

And finally, there is the view that the uncertainty we observe is not genuine randomness but the limits of our ability to know and measure. Robert Hazen and James Trefil, in *Science Matters,* take one version of this tack. As they put it,

> You see a book by bouncing light off it, and the light has a negligible effect on the book. You "see" an electron, on the other hand, by bouncing another electron (or some other comparable bundle) off it.

The measurement can't help but affect the thing being measured, and thereby comes our uncertainty. (I am told that this interpretation, once widely touted, isn't very popular with specialists anymore.)

So: is there a world "out there" (that is, independent of us) for us to experience, or is it coming into being because we experience it? I doubt that any physical test could ever distinguish between these two options. My own hunch—and it's not much stronger than that—is that quantum mechanics is a model, and that it shows what the world *acts like* at the lowest level; but that we may well have reached the limits of our ability to know things with more precision than what quantum mechanics allows.

But in any case quantum mechanics in itself—as opposed to the interpretations that some might try to put on it— does not undermine the traditional Christian picture of a world with knowable natural properties behaving in a predictable and understandable way, under the rule of a wise and holy Creator. This is true for at least two reasons.

First, however spooky quantum theory may sound, it is highly mathematical: and this shows that the world is still intelligible, since that's just what mathematics is for.

Second, we experience the world at a much larger scale than the one quantum mechanics describes. And at this level, "ordinary" physics—Newton's laws and all that—describes everything quite well. So we experience the world at a level that combines all the tiny quantum effects, and all the goofiness gets washed out. As John Polkinghorne put it,

> Quantum theory must produce the same goods in the large-scale domain as those of Newtonian mechanics which works so well.

A physicist friend tells me that we have to qualify this statement a little, since there are certain areas of study, such as what they call "superconductors" and "superfluids" (both of which occur at temperatures close to absolute zero), where quantum mechanical effects show up on the large scale. So we should say that *usually* quantum mechanical effects wash out on a large scale.

And we note finally that quantum mechanics in itself says nothing about freezing God out of the world system. In other words, even if we want to say that *physical* determinism is not true, we have said nothing worth saying about *providential* determinism.

Chaos Theory

Why is it so hard to predict the weather? One answer is that the system that produces weather is so extremely complex that no one can know enough about it to be sure of what will happen next. In fact, someone once said—maybe a little tongue-in-cheek—that, for all we know, a butterfly flapping its wings today in Singapore will make it rain next week in Texas.

The weather results from what is now called a "chaotic" system. This doesn't mean that the whole thing is actually random; instead it's a technical term for the kind of system that has two basic properties: first, the output is a nonlinear function of the input; and second, the output is *very* sensitive to small changes in the initial conditions.

Let's explain that. A linear system is one where, say, if you push three times as hard, you get three times as much output. A nonlinear system doesn't follow that law—for example, if you push three times as hard and get nine times the output (following a square law). Many natural things are nonlinear. If you bend a twig, you can get a smooth arc up to a point; then it snaps. However, this is not chaotic, because it doesn't meet the second requirement.

The "initial conditions" are what you start with. James Trefil offers the following illustration:

> Think of an experiment in which you drop little chips of wood close together into a river. If the river is deep and smoothly flowing, then chips dropped near each other will stay together as they are swept downstream. And if you double the distance between the chips at the point where they're dropped in, they'll be twice as far apart downstream as they would have been had you not increased the distance. This is an example of a linear, predictable system.
>
> Now imagine that instead of a deep river, we drop wood chips into a whitewater rapids. Two chips dropped near each other on the upstream side of the rapids will, in general, be far apart when they get to the other end, and there will be no simple linear relationship between how far apart they were at the beginning and at the end.

The chips in the rapids make a chaotic system, because the slightest change in how far apart you drop the chips makes for a huge difference on the other side. You probably could not get the same result twice, except by luck.

For practical purposes, chaotic systems are unpredictable because we cannot measure the initial conditions of the system accurately enough to be able to predict the exact behavior, and often the nonlinear mathematics are so unmanageable that our uncertainty in measurement does us in.

The weather, as I said, is a chaotic system. You can't measure all the factors that produce weather—the temperature at all altitudes, the air pressure, the wind speeds, the ground temperature and rate of cooling, and so on—with enough precision to be sure what it will all do next week. (You might not even *know* all the factors that contribute, and the one you leave out could make a difference.)

We would make a mistake if we thought that the fact that there are chaotic systems in the world works against *providential* determinism. In principle, if it were possible to know all the details of the initial conditions and the exact features of the equations, we could predict the outcome. Chaotic systems are limited by our ability to know such things; but if God knows everything, it's no big challenge for him to know everything about a chaotic system, down to the last detail. Actually, chaotic systems are *physically* deterministic as well.

Uncertainty, Miracles, and Human Freedom

Some Christian thinkers have been glad of the apparent uncertainty that quantum mechanics and chaos theory have found in the world. If the world isn't such an irresistible mechanism after all, they reason, then there is room both for miracles and for human freedom. They think this way because quantum mechanics and chaos theory take away the idea that events produce their outcomes inexorably: there's room for other options, for God's freedom and for man's.

I would like to discourage Christians from reasoning this way, because I see some very basic misunderstandings of Christian doctrine and philosophy at work in this way of thinking. At its heart, it's confusing freedom with unpredictability.

God governs the world by keeping things in being, so that they have their natural effects; and also by doing supernatural things, which bring about results that are different from the natural effects. God doesn't have to work within the natures of the things he made—not even the quantum natures (assuming that quantum mechanics is true).

The thing that makes a supernatural event different from a natural one is that the supernatural event is ruled by something other than nature. For the cells of a dead body to stay dead is natural; for those cells to come back to life is not just an unexpected event, it is one that takes supernatural power. So physical unpredictability isn't even the right way to think about supernatural events.

Those who want to find room for human freedom in physical uncertainty are probably thinking that the brain and the mind are so closely connected that they may as well be the same thing. Your thoughts *are* your brain patterns. But then physical determinism means there's no reason to think that our thoughts are true, as we saw earlier. But physical indeterminacy doesn't help us either. To say that a thought is true is *not* to say that nothing determines it; rather it is to say that something *beyond the physical* determines it. I reason that two marbles plus two marbles in the cup makes four marbles in the cup because Reason, not brain chemistry, governs my thought. But that's nothing like saying the chemistry is uncertain; it's instead saying that something else *uses* the chemistry to express the thought.

Actually, as I already observed, appeals to quantum uncertainty wouldn't help us anyhow, since the uncertainty applies to a scale that is too small to have an effect on my brain chemistry.

I don't believe anything will explain our ability to think true thoughts and to grasp moral truths except our soul; nor do I think anyone needs to explain everything that happens only in terms of physical causes.

PROVIDENCE AND THE PROBLEM OF EVIL

The Christian doctrine of providence says that God's purpose has the final say in whatever happens, and that this purpose is holy, wise, and good. The two most dangerous arguments against Christianity have always been the claim that we can explain everything without referring to God (what I call "the problem of the redundant deity"), and the claim that the existence of evil in the world means that God's will is not supreme—either God is not all-powerful, or else he is not all good and wise, and therefore God in the traditional sense does not exist ("the problem of evil"). Christian apologists have dealt with these arguments for ages: the famous "five ways" of Thomas Aquinas (1225–1274)—five kinds of arguing for God's existence—speak to the first objection, for example.

In this section I want to explore briefly the way that the sciences seem to present us with the problem of evil, and thus seem to make it impossible for us to hold the traditional Christian doctrine of purposeful providence. Some examples would include (I'm sure you can add some others):

(1) The vastness of space seems to suggest that the universe is indifferent to us.

(2) The vastness of space says that it is unbearably arrogant to think that any heavenly being should care about our lives.

(3) The history of life on earth—the strange and fascinating creatures that have lived here but are now extinct, such as the dinosaurs—shows that the universe is wasteful.

(4) The ways that some animals are parasites on others—such as wasps that lay eggs inside caterpillars, which then hatch into parasites on the caterpillars—shows that the universe is cruel.

(Some people would include all kinds of animal predation whatever, but I have already argued why I don't consider that a problem. You'll notice as well that I have not included anything in this list about man's inhumanity to man, or about undeserved suffering. That is because the sciences don't really sharpen this part of the problem at all—it has always been hard.)

The reason why these and similar objections don't really overthrow our view of God's providence is that they rest on a profound misunderstanding—one that many Christian believers suffer from as well. Here's the nub: the Christian doctrine of providence is not something we dreamed up based on what we observe in the world: instead, it comes from the way God has revealed himself in his saving deeds in history, and has shown himself worthy of our trust. If he then tells us that he is working all things for the good of those who love him (as in Rom. 8:28), then we take him at his word.

As C. S. Lewis put it,

> There is, to be sure, one glaringly obvious ground for denying that any moral purpose at all is operative in the universe: namely, the actual course of events in all its wasteful cruelty and apparent indifference, or hostility, to life.
>
> At all times, then, an inference from the course of events in this world to the goodness and wisdom of the Creator would have been equally preposterous; and it was never made.

There's nothing irrational about this kind of trust, mind you: we are like children with a parent. The parent knows best, but the children don't have the ability to understand it all. For example, we all have taken our kids to the doctor for shots. The shots hurt, but they do the child good. The wise and rational child will trust his parents and submit to the procedure in the hope that one day he'll understand.

So being wise is not the same as grasping the reasons behind it all. J. I. Packer, in his book *Knowing God,* shows that this is in fact what the biblical book of Ecclesiastes teaches about God's wisdom and ours:

> The truth is that God, in His wisdom, to make and keep us humble and to teach us to walk by faith, has hidden from us almost everything that we

> should like to know about the providential purposes which he is working out in the churches and in our own lives. . . .
>
> What is this wisdom that He gives? As we have seen, it is not a sharing in all His knowledge, but a disposition to confess that He is wise, and to cleave to Him and live for Him in the light of His word through thick and thin.

But at the same time our heavenly Father gives us reassurances of his love and care—in the word and sacraments at church, in answers to our prayers, in experiences of his provision. But I don't suppose that any of these can *prove* our doctrine to the unbeliever. Such a person needs instead to think about how his human experiences of love and his craving for meaning point to his Creator; how his own sinfulness cuts him off from the Creator; and how God has provided a way of receiving forgiveness through Jesus Christ.

This gives us a perspective from which to think about the four examples I mentioned above. In fact, I would argue against these objections that a lot depends on just how you look at the facts. For example, in a later chapter we'll consider "the anthropic principle"—the discovery that the universe is finely balanced to support life here on earth, and perhaps nowhere else—and this leads to the conclusion that God has paid attention to an incredible amount of detail just so we could live here and now. So of course we should ask why he has done so—but the universe as physics sees it won't tell us.

This perspective also gives me the freedom to say that I don't know why some things are the way they are. Maybe parasites serve some good purpose; but though I might speculate about a few possibilities, I'm just guessing. But that doesn't mean that there's no purpose—it only means I haven't seen it yet. This should not be a barrier to Christian belief when we consider the many good reasons we have for trusting God.

15

How Old Is the Earth?

Cosmology and Geology

NOW IT'S TIME TO take up the next area where science and faith may interact, namely the age of the earth and of the universe. To discuss these topics we will describe two sciences: *cosmology,* the study of the origin, history, and form of the universe; and *geology,* the study of the origin, history, and form of the earth.

Everyone has some contact with these sciences, even if it's just an informal one. If you gaze up at the night sky you see countless stars. Along with being taken by their beauty, you might easily wonder how many of them there are, how far away they are, what they're made of, and how they got started. You're on your way to the study of the cosmos. If you walk by a rocky cliff, or drive by a cutting through a hillside, you notice that the rocks are in layers. You might wonder how these layers got there, why they're different, and how long it took to lay them down. On some hillsides the layers aren't straight—so you wonder whether they got twisted somehow—and if so, how. Now you're thinking about the history of the earth.

Straightaway you can see that at least two of our topics from earlier in this book will come into play: the first is the theological question of whether the Bible takes a position on the age of the earth and universe; and the second is the philosophical observation that the sciences we are dealing with are *historical* sciences—they use the things we see now and work backwards, trying to infer what chain of events must have brought this about. We will see that there are other issues as well, in both philosophy and theology—issues such as whether we should be realists in our scientific reasoning about the past, and whether we can accept the idea that God may have created something to *look* older than it actually is.

At bottom, there are two theological concerns that drive most Christian thinking about these sciences. The first is the question of *time*—how much of it does the Bible allow for? These sciences claim that the universe and earth have been around for great stretches of time. I have already shown in my discussion of the days of Genesis 1:1–2:3 and related matters, that I don't think the Bible has much to say about length of time, either for the history of the earth or for the history of the universe. Hence I will argue that this should not be a major issue for Christians. I will also discuss your options if you don't agree with me.

The second theological concern is much tougher to handle but reaches much more deeply into the vitals of our faith. This has to do with what we may call the *metaphysical* side of the theories—that is, what do they say about the way God and the world relate to each other, and whether God may govern the world according to his purposes (which includes bringing about supernatural events). If the theories presuppose a world-picture that is hostile to the Christian one, or if their conclusions support such a picture, then we Christians will have problems with the theories.

Here is my plan for this chapter. First, I'll present the main theories of the sciences we are considering. Then I'll offer a Christian assessment of them, in three parts: I'll discuss scientific realism and appearance of age approaches; then I'll discuss the relationship of Big Bang cosmology to the moment of creation; then I'll discuss whether modern geology is compatible with Christian faith. Finally, I'll say a few words about what cosmologists call "the anthropic principle."

COSMOLOGY AND THE BIG BANG

Cosmology is the science that studies the origin of the universe, together with its history and physical structure as a whole. It's related to *astrophysics,* which focuses on the physics of stars and space, both in their inner workings and in their interactions with each other. It's also related to *astronomy,* which especially focuses on observing the way the bodies in the heavens move about. I would expect universities to group cosmology and astrophysics under the physics department, while they may well put astronomy in "earth and planetary sciences" (at least that's what mine did).

Cosmology is a science, so all that it covers is interesting for its own sake; but it also raises some very basic questions about the universe and our place in it, such as, How did it all begin? and, Why are we here to observe it? and, Are we alone?

When it comes to how it all began, most cosmologists today hold to some form of what is called the "Big Bang" theory. (The name, as we'll see, was not intended as a compliment.) The different forms of this theory disagree over a number of important questions, but none of them matters much for our purposes—unless we think (which I do not) that the disagreements undermine the basic theory so badly that it can't be true. Here is a very simplified outline of what these theories have in common, based on the writings of the physicists John Polkinghorne and Ian Barbour:

> About 15 billion (15 x 10^9) years ago, space, time, and the universe began when the initial singularity—all the matter and energy compressed into a point with zero dimensions—suddenly began expanding unimaginably rapidly. (Theorists disagree on how rapidly, and how the rate has changed over time.) After the first three minutes, atomic nuclei could form, yielding helium and hydrogen; after about 500,000 years, the lighter elements could be formed. After about a billion years of expansion, the stars and galaxies began to form, in which the heavier elements were produced. Some of these stars have died and some have scattered their matter—this is how the basic building blocks for biological systems became available. About 4½ billion years ago planet earth was formed, condensed out of cosmic clouds. Biological life first appeared on earth about 3–3½ billion years ago.

The last two sentences show how the cosmological theory slides over into the history of the earth and its life. In fact, most of the time when someone presents the cosmological theory, he goes from the Big Bang to life on earth. For example, Polkinghorne has an engaging description of the Big Bang and how the stars developed—the first 10 billion years after the beginning—and then continues:

> As a second generation of stars and planets condensed, on at least one planet (and perhaps on many) the conditions of chemical composition, temperature and radiation were such that the next new development in cosmic history could take place. A billion years after conditions on earth became favourable, through biochemical pathways still unknown to us, and utilizing the subtle flexible-stability with which the laws of atomic physics endow the chemistry of carbon, long chain molecules formed with the power of replicating themselves. They rapidly gobbled up the chemical food in the shallow waters of early earth, and the three billion years of the history of life had begun.

Now it's perfectly understandable, of course, to draw the link between the Big Bang and us: how else can we get people to spend money studying the skies unless we convince them that it touches on our lives here and now? On the other hand, there is no *necessary logical* connection between these topics, and I will treat them separately. One may be true and the other false, or both true, or both false—but we should take each on its own merits and not allow one to borrow prestige from the other.

What is the history of these cosmological theories? In 1917 Albert Einstein (1879–1955) used his theory of General Relativity to provide a mathematical model for a "static" universe—namely one in which the galaxies are not moving away from each other. What the astronomers observed didn't fit that model, since there was evidence that the galaxies were in fact moving away from each other. Then in 1927 Georges Lemaître, a Belgian Jesuit who had studied astrophysics in Cambridge, published a paper that solved Einstein's mathematical equations with an expanding universe. But this had consequences: an expanding universe would then have a beginning! As science historian John North tells it in his *Norton History of Astronomy and Cosmology*,

> If the Universe really is expanding, does this not mean that there was a time in the past when it was a small compact mass? Friedmann's [a Russian scientist who held similar views to Lemaître] and Lemaître's models seemed to allow for this possibility. But was an expansion from an 'initial singularity' not simply an illusion created by the mathematics? Lemaître had been ordained abbé in 1923. His science had strong theological relevance for him. An initial singularity was not something to be avoided, but a positive merit, a token of God's creation of the world.

Other physicists took up the idea and developed it; Einstein himself came to accept the astronomers' conclusion that the universe is expanding. Perhaps the critic of this theory who is the best known to non-physicists is Fred Hoyle, who strongly opposed any model that gave the universe a beginning. He is the one who coined the name "Big Bang" sometime around 1950: he meant it as a term of contempt, but it has stuck. It isn't very accurate for what the theories hold—they carry no notion of some primeval atom, fireball, or what-have-you, exploding outward into empty space; instead, they say that space itself is expanding, along with the matter in it.

The Big Bang class of theories didn't become dominant until the mid-1960s, however. About mid-century a couple of researchers made a prediction: the radiation from the early history of the universe should still exist, showing a temperature of about 5° Kelvin. (That's very cold, since 0° Kelvin is absolute zero, the coldest temperature possible, equivalent to –273° Celsius or –459° Fahrenheit. The Kelvin degree is the same size as the Celsius degree.) Then in 1965 Arno Penzias and Robert Wilson, two physicists at Bell Telephone Labs, found a background radiation in space, equivalent to that of a 3° Kelvin body. This suited the prediction once the necessary allowances were made; and now the case for a Big Bang is pretty strong.

There are three main lines of evidence that look like they support some kind of Big Bang model as the best historical inference for the universe we see today. They are:

(1) In the 1920s Edwin Hubble (1889–1953) discovered that light from other galaxies was coming to us with a lower frequency than the one proper to the stars' elements: this is called the "red shift," and is due to the Doppler effect when a body is moving away. This then suggests that the universe is expanding, because the galaxies are moving away from us (and from each other).

(2) The equations of General Relativity, when solved, imply that the universe has a beginning (t=0, a first moment of time, when everything was compressed into a point with no dimensions).

(3) The background radiation of the universe is that of a 3° Kelvin body, and this is consistent with the after-effects of the initial "bang" 10–20 billion years ago.

Since I am not a cosmologist, I have no way of knowing whether the technical details of the Big Bang theory are sound or not. My own reading of Genesis means that I have no problem with the amount of time the theory calls for. The conclusion from these three lines of evidence seems to be fair, so far as I can tell. As long as we recognize that it's a theory in physics, I see no reason to reject it. I say this because this kind of theory can't tell us *why* we're here, only *how* we came to be here.

Geology and the History of the Earth

Geology is the science that studies the earth. Its different topics include what the earth is made of and how the rocks and minerals are formed; the processes that shape the surface of the earth (wind, water, weather, and so on); and how the earth has developed over time. Geologists might apply their science to earn money, say, by finding oil, water, or minerals, or by giving advice on whether ground is suitable for buildings.

There are two broad areas of geology: *physical geology,* which is concerned with the processes that operate on or beneath the earth and the materials that make up the earth; and *historical geology,* which studies what things happened in the history of the earth, and when. (In practice, mind you, geologists don't make rigid divisions between the two areas.) It is primarily in historical geology that people have found a conflict with the Bible, and that is where I'll focus here.

To understand the modern theory of how and when the earth was formed, we have to see it in the context of the way the solar system was formed. An earlier star had exploded in a supernova, scattering matter through a huge stretch of space. Most of the matter was hydrogen and helium, but there were traces of heavier elements, too. This matter formed a thin, swirling cloud of gas, and over time the gas thickened because the atoms drew nearer together by the force of gravity. At the center of this cloud, hydrogen and helium gathered in enough density to begin the fusion reaction, and our sun was born—somewhere between 4.6 and 6 billion years ago.

The matter in the outer portions of the gas cloud began to condense to form rocky masses, which bashed into each other and fused, and eventually became the planets, moons, and assorted other objects, all orbiting around the sun. This bashing still goes on—when meteors fall to earth, for example. The main job of assembling the earth ended about $4^1/_2$ billion years ago.

The earth has a solid inner core, made up mostly of iron and nickel. Around that is an outer core, mostly molten iron. Next comes the mantle, and on top of that is the crust—that's where we live. The top part of the mantle, together with the crust, is called the *lithosphere* (the "rocky sphere"). The lithosphere is broken into plates, and their movements and interactions (such as one plate sliding under another) are held to be responsible for most of the geological features of the earth, such as mountains, and most of its activities, such as earthquakes. Geologists think that 250 million years ago, all the land was one great continent, called Pangaea. This broke up about 200 million years ago, and eventually the continents we know developed. (And there may well have been previous break-ups and joinings that produced Pangaea.)

Modern historical geology was born in the eighteenth century as natural philosophers began to study fossils and the layers of rock that you can see on any outcropping. They began to wonder what caused the layers and the patterns by which the layers were deformed in places. Most of the early geologists were *catastrophists,* meaning that they appealed to great catastrophes to explain these features. These catastrophes could involve water or volcanoes, and the geologists were divided into competing schools of thought as to which was the more important. Some of the geologists held that the catastrophes could have had a supernatural cause—such as the great flood in the time of Noah. Others, who accepted that the biblical flood story was true, nevertheless looked for more "natural" causes, such as water underneath the earth.

The Scotsman James Hutton (1726–1797) proposed a new way of discerning the earth's history: by reasoning based on observations of the current behavior of nature. If you drive on the highway past a cutting into a hillside, you can see that the exposed rocks are in layers. Hutton came up with a theory to explain how these layers and their shapes were the result of erosion, then sedimentation (like a modern beach), and upheavals to form hills and mountains.

As the nineteenth century dawned, almost all geologists accepted that the earth had been around for longer than 6,000 years, because the processes that formed rock layers were slow. They continued to disagree over how much catastrophe was involved. In 1830, however, Charles Lyell (1797–1875) published his *Principles of Geology,* and promoted the doctrine called *uniformitarianism.* According to this doctrine, we may explain the past history of the earth entirely in terms of processes we now see in operation, without any appeal either to obsolete processes or to supernatural events. This doctrine tended to favor processes that are slow and uniform as the right kinds of explanation in geology.

Lyell's form of uniformitarianism really amounts to deciding ahead of time what kinds of causes a scientist may look for: and of course, this is only sound if you know ahead of time that these are the only possible causes. That is to say, the strong form of uniformitarianism, which some have called *substantive uniformitarianism,* is a philosophical position about the way the world is, not a scientific conclusion from a study of the world itself. Lyell's kind of uniformitarianism carried great weight in the nineteenth century but is not widely held today.

For example, consider how geologists now explain how the terrain of eastern Washington state got its current form. This terrain is full of what are called "channeled scablands" and "coulees": dry stream channels cut through the top soil and underlying basalt; many of these channels cross local drainage divides, well above the level of the modern drainage. Geologists had assumed that these were the remains of ancient streams. However, in the early 1920s J. Harlen Bretz argued that instead the evidence suggests that the scablands channels resulted from a catastrophic flood. As David Alt and Donald

Hyndman put it in their *Northwest Exposures: A Geologic Story of the Northwest* (1995),

> That conclusion aroused a vigorous storm of outraged protest from geologists wedded to the conventional view that the modern landscape is entirely the work of *weak forces and slow processes operating over long periods of time*. They accused Bretz of catastrophism, widely considered the worst and most offensive of all possible geologic heresies. He grimly pleaded guilty as charged, while vehemently adhering to his views. But he could not explain where his catastrophic flood had come from, and that was an embarrassing problem.

Then J. T. Pardee, who had in 1910 described Lake Missoula (a lake trapped by a glacier near Missoula, Montana), showed that the lake had drained suddenly—and there we have the source of the flood. As Alt and Hyndman tell it,

> Pardee published his results in 1943. Another 30 years of controversy followed before very many geologists would agree that the evidence really did tell of catastrophic floods. J. Harlen Bretz survived his detractors and lived to see most geologists finally convinced that his unpopular flood really did happen.

If you visit the Grand Coulee Dam, you can see a film that presents this theory as a fact. Nowadays catastrophic floods are an allowable explanation for many features of the landscape—there is even a catastrophic explanation for how the Black Sea was flooded from the Mediterranean.

During the nineteenth century there were many proposals for how old the earth is, ranging from a few million years to many billions. The reason there were so many proposals that ranged so widely is that there was no agreed basis for the estimates: some went by rates of erosion, others by the rate that the ocean changes its salt content, others by the rate at which limestone forms by sedimentation, others by the rate at which the earth would have cooled from its initial molten state. Toward the end of the nineteenth century, geologists were beginning to agree on an estimate of around 100 million years. Then in the 1890s the scientists Wilhelm Roentgen (1845–1923), Henri Becquerel (1852–1908), and Marie Curie (1867–1934) and her husband Pierre Curie (1859–1906) discovered radioactivity (as the Curies named it), and in the first few decades of the twentieth-century techniques for dating rocks based on the decay of radioisotopes were developed.

The accepted modern method for estimating the age of the earth uses radioactive decay as its basis. It proceeds by assuming that the earth and the oldest meteorites were formed as closed systems at the same time, and therefore the age of the earth is the age at which these oldest meteorites were formed. (The process of plate movement that I described above has recycled and destroyed the oldest rocks of the earth itself.) Geologists now generally agree that the best estimate for the age of the earth and meteorites is about $4^1/_2$ billion years old.

According to the on-line pamphlet of the U.S. Geological Survey, *Geologic Time,* by William Newman,

> The age of 4.54 billion years found for the Solar System and Earth is consistent with current calculations of 11 to 13 billion years for the age of the Milky Way Galaxy (based on the stage of evolution of globular cluster stars) and the age of 10 to 15 billion years for the Universe (based on recession of distant galaxies).

Realism, Anti-Realism, and Appearance of Age

Before we can decide whether to accept the theories of the cosmologists and geologists, we have to decide something even more basic: can we accept *any* theory from a historical science as a true account of what happened? That is, are we allowed to be *realists* when it comes to the theories of the historical sciences? (You may remember that back in chapter 3 I used Michael Behe's description of science as "a vigorous attempt to make true statements about the physical world.")

Here are the possible ways of thinking about the great lengths of time required by these historical sciences, assuming we think the Bible is true:

(1) The Bible doesn't set any upper limit on how long the earth has been around, and we can be either realists or anti-realists for this historical inference.

(2) The Bible teaches that the earth and universe are "young" (less than, say, 100,000 years old), and the evidence from the natural world supports this, so long as we interpret it properly.

(3) The Bible teaches that the earth and universe are young, but historical inferences are unreliable.

(4) The Bible teaches that the earth and universe are young, but were created with an appearance of age.

Option 1 doesn't *require* us to be realists—but most who hold it are realistic. Option 2 supports scientific realism, but, based on the Bible, it insists that the scientists have not interpreted the natural world properly. In this case, they must expose the biases and bad reasoning involved in the standard scientific models. Options 3 and 4 are anti-realistic, because they say that the physical evidence will never allow us to make a sound inference about what happened.

Which of these options should you hold? It all depends on how soundly based they are. You have to examine the claim about what the Bible teaches, as well as whether a Christian should be realistic or not. I have already given you my reasons for rejecting the claim that the Bible teaches a young earth; hence you know I favor option 1. If you don't see it this way, then you will take one of options 2–4.

Back in chapter 3 I argued that, in general, we should support realism for historical inferences. In one of the Sherlock Holmes stories, Holmes says, "In solving a problem of this sort, the grand thing is to be able to reason backwards." Even though the story is fiction, we easily recognize that this principle is a valid one. But it takes for granted that we can make true inferences by working backward—that is, it takes realism for granted.

The Bible also supports realism in making historical inferences, so long as the reasoning is sound. In Deuteronomy 21:1 we find a law for when "someone is found slain, lying in the open country, and it is not known who killed him." This implies that you can tell from a corpse whether the person died from natural causes or from murder, and that, in some cases, you can tell who did the deed. Further, in order to be able to distinguish between natural and supernatural events, historical inference has to be valid: otherwise, if ordinary causes are just as hard to account for as extraordinary ones, how would anyone be sure that an event was supernatural? When Pharaoh's magicians declare to him (Ex. 8:19), "This is the finger of God"—meaning that the miracles that Moses has done go beyond any of their power, and testify to a power behind Moses that is greater than that of their gods—they are drawing a true conclusion from the chain of events they observe. And further, the way Paul commended Christian faith in his speeches to Gentiles (as we saw in chapter 12), where features of the world and ourselves cry out for a Creator, requires some kind of realism: otherwise how could we trust such an argument?

So the question for a Christian is not whether we can be scientific realists in drawing historical conclusions *in general.* The question is whether *in the specific case* of the history of the universe and of the earth we can be realists—or at least, whether the inferences people have drawn are sound. After all, it is possible that a sound inference is available but that people have missed key evidence, or that they don't realize how much they don't know, or that their premises make the conclusion more believable but the premises are wrong. It's also possible that, in some particular case, there just isn't enough evidence to be sure of our conclusion.

This leads me to think that if you believe that the Bible teaches a young earth, then you should follow either option 2 or 4 from my list above—you shouldn't claim that historical inferences are by their nature unreliable (which is what option 3 requires).

I don't have the impression that option 2 is really available to you. Under this position, a reasonable person—even if he is not a Christian—studying the cosmos should conclude that the whole show started a pretty short time ago. But none of the young earth creationists that I have spoken with holds this view because of the physical evidence. Indeed, two advocates of the young earth position, Paul Nelson and John Mark Reynolds (in *Three Views on Creation and Evolution*), admit:

> Recent creationists should humbly agree that their view is, at the moment, implausible on purely scientific grounds. . . .
>
> In many cases, young earth creationists would need decades of fully funded research just to begin to get a grasp on a new way of looking at the mountain of current data.

Not all young earth creationists agree with this assessment, but support for it comes from two unexpected places. First, the organization Answers in Genesis (a strongly young earth group) has published at their website a paper, "Arguments we think creationists should NOT use" (it would have been better if they had said "NO LONGER use"). This article in effect retracts many of what used to be the standard arguments of the young earth movement, such as "moon dust thickness proves a young moon," "wooly mammoths were snap frozen during the Flood catastrophe," "the Second Law of Thermodynamics began at the fall," the Paluxy tracks, and several others. I am glad that this group aims to be so honest, and am sad that other young earth outfits haven't quite caught up with them.

The second line of support comes from a book by young earth astronomer John Byl, *God and Cosmos* (2001). Byl documents problems with the Big Bang theory, but he is unable to say that the theory has been defeated. In the end he has to resort to anti-realism for cosmological theories—including those that are compatible with the Bible (which means *his* reading of the Bible, generally in the King James Version, which he doesn't really examine critically).

Hence Nelson and Reynolds have given a fair account of the current state of the evidence. This doesn't make their project impossible, but it shows why, at least for the time being, you should be pretty skeptical of anyone who claims that he has found a way to carry it off.

What of option 4, the appearance of age approach? One of its best-known advocates was Philip Gosse, who wrote a book called *Omphalos* (1857). *Omphalos* is Greek for belly button: if Adam had one, he was created with an appearance of age. The usual objection to this approach is that it amounts to saying that the creation sends a deceptive message—that is, it says that God created the universe to look a way that isn't true. Another objection is based on starlight: it takes billions of years for light to get here from far-away parts of the universe (which means that the events that sent the light took place an apparent billions of years ago). Should we believe that God created this light in mid-flight—actually, virtually the whole way here?

Those who hold to this approach, though, have several replies. First, consider the water-turned-into-wine of John 2:1-11. No doubt it tasted just like properly aged wine—that is, Jesus made it with an appearance of age. Hence, so the claim goes, anything that results from a miracle may appear to be older than it actually is.

Further, the advocates say, the universe would be sending a deceptive message only if God had not told us—in the Bible—its true age and origin.

In addition, the advocates of appearance of age would say that the purpose of the universe is to support human life, and that therefore the rest of its history doesn't matter—hence God could have created a "mature" universe.

These replies don't really make the whole approach acceptable to me, and let me tell you why you shouldn't buy it, either. Let's begin by noting that these approaches got their start in the nineteenth century, and basically for the same reason as the day-age interpretation of the Genesis days. That is, Gosse and those like him agreed that the physical evidence really did point to an earth that was much older than his reading of the Bible allowed; but he offered a different explanation from the day-agers for how the evidence came to look this way. The day-agers said it looked this way because the earth really is old; Gosse said it looked this way because God made it to look old. It was an attempt to preserve both the Bible interpretation and the physical science.

This, by the way, shows why one common approach is actually at odds with itself. Some will try to combine appearance of age with young earth evidences—that is, mixing and matching bits of options 2 and 4. If the earth was made with an appearance of age, then evidences for its young age don't matter. And if the evidence from nature actually leads to a valid young earth inference, then the earth wasn't created with an appearance of age. So young earth believers really should choose which of options 2 and 4 they prefer (or else provide an argument for a fifth option).

Second, I don't think the reference to the miracle of John 2 will work. First, all we know about the wine is that it had the effect of good, mature wine; we have no idea what it would have looked like under molecular analysis. But even more, we have nothing in Scripture that suggests that *all* miracles result in the appearance of age; and the universe is on a bit bigger scale than a jug of wine, isn't it? And it's the whole universe that looks old. That leads me to the next point.

Third, as I argued in chapter 12, the biblical writers expected people to reason from aspects of the creation to the existence of a creator: Paul said that God's "eternal power and divine nature, have been clearly perceived . . . in the things that have been made," for instance (Rom. 1:20). For such reasoning to be sound, we must assume that valid reasoning about the creation—even apart from special revelation—is possible. If the whole universe is dripping with evidence of its createdness by means of the Big Bang, then to say that this is a wrong conclusion does in fact look to me like the universe is giving false testimony.

Yes, I know that this last argument assumes that the physical evidence supports the Big Bang theory, and that the "uncaused beginning" interpretation of it is sound—as we will discuss below. But the person who supports the appearance of age approach isn't in a position to dispute this—he's disputing whether we should take this inference from the physical evidence as true. If he thinks that the physical evidence points to some other theory, then he's sliding over into option 2, with a kind of scientific realism. But if that's his real argument, we're no longer disputing over whether this particular brand of anti-realism, appearance of age, is the right approach.

Some would say that to have starlight created in transit isn't really deceptive, since otherwise we would never know what's out there in the rest of the universe. The trouble is that this approach requires more than that; it requires that God has simulated events that never happened. For example, in 1572

Tycho Brahe observed a supernova (a massive explosion of a star that leads to an increase in its brightness); in 1604 Galileo observed another one. These stars are millions of light-years away—which means that the events took place an apparent millions of years ago. If these explosions didn't really happen, then starlight-created-in-transit begins to look like it is in fact deceptive. Isn't it much simpler just to suppose that the events really happened?

At the end of the day, people resort to appearance of age approaches in order to be true to the Bible. But such approaches seem so extreme that they should be a last resort, almost an act of desperation. And if the Bible doesn't say what the advocates think it says, then no one has to use these means to stay faithful to Scripture. (In fact, I think the desperate nature of this line of thinking should have warned us that something was wrong. In the Sherlock Holmes story "The Priory School," Watson cries, "Holmes, this is impossible." Holmes replies, "Admirable! A most illuminating remark. It *is* impossible as I state it, and therefore I must in some respect have stated it wrong.")

So, then, if you still think the Bible requires you to believe that the earth and universe are young, you are left with option 2. But you should take this line with the humility that Nelson and Reynolds suggest (in the quotes I gave above).

IS THE BIG BANG THE SAME AS THE ABSOLUTE BEGINNING?

If the Big Bang really happened, is it the same as the moment of creation? Does it provide us with a proof that the universe came from nothing, with no natural cause?

In order for us to tackle these questions, we have to answer some others that are more basic. First, we need to consider whether the doctrine of creation from nothing means that the universe had a beginning in time. Second, we need to consider whether this doctrine leads us to believe that it's possible for scientific study to detect such a beginning, and whether such a "proof" is helpful to Christian faith. Third, we have to discuss whether the Big Bang theories actually offer such proof.

Let's take these questions one by one. Does the doctrine of creation from nothing imply that the universe had a beginning in time? The answer seems pretty clear to me: certainly it does. When Genesis 1:1 says "in the beginning," it refers to the beginning of the material universe. Further, when Revelation 4:11 says, "for you created all things, and by your will they existed and were created," it likewise implies that there was a moment at which it all began.

We have to remind ourselves of these things—which seem pretty obvious to me—because some theologians deny that the doctrine of creation from nothing is about a historical event. Instead, they say, it is about the facts that the world is different from God, that it depends on God for its existence, and that it is understandable to us. By this thinking, the doctrine is there to teach us certain attitudes toward the world, such as respect for it and care for other creatures, and not to tell us about any event that began it. It is quite rare for *any* biblical doctrine to be primarily philosophical rather than historical—what of the resurrection of Jesus, for example?—and, as I have already argued, this doctrine is rooted in a historical event. Of course the Bible's doctrines aim at instilling attitudes in us—but they do that by telling us truths about the world God made.

The second question is whether we should think that scientific study can detect the beginning. I'm not sure that the Bible speaks to that one way or the other. When Thomas Aquinas discussed the beginning (in his *Summa Theologiae,* I.46) he first argued (first article) that philosophy cannot prove that the universe had *no* beginning; he then argued (second article) that philosophy cannot prove that it *did* have a beginning. That means that he thought that the Bible, not philosophy (which included science), is what tells us that the world had a beginning. But Thomas was dealing with the state of philosophy in his day, and he warned his readers,

> And it is useful to consider this, lest anyone, presuming to demonstrate what is of faith, should bring forward reasons that are not cogent, so as to give occasion to unbelievers to laugh, thinking that on such grounds we believe things that are of faith.

He was concerned that we might say we have proven something, but that it might turn out that our proof was faulty—and then unbelievers will say that our faith is as bad as the "proof" we offered.

Aquinas, as usual, displays great wisdom, and we are wise to pay him careful heed. He could easily appeal to Hebrews 11:3, "*By faith* we understand that the universe was created by the word of God, so that what is seen was not made out of things that are visible"—by *faith,* not by *sight.* On the other hand, he hasn't shown that empirical science *can't* uncover the first moment—instead he has shown that the kinds of philosophical arguments offered in his day were inadequate and unnecessary for the believer. As Christian philosopher Peter Kreeft remarks in his notes on this section of Aquinas,

> The scientific evidence seems to have refuted the "Steady State" and confirmed the "Big Bang" pretty conclusively, thus also confirming once again that faith and reason never really contradict each other.
>
> Article 1 shows that we cannot prove that the world is eternal; Article 2 shows that we cannot prove by philosophy alone that it is not. Philosophical reasoning leaves both options as logical possibilities. Divine revelation (and today perhaps also scientific data) resolve the question; philosophy does not.

So we don't *need* the proof—but why should we balk at it if it's on offer?

The last question is whether the Big Bang really does offer a proof of a beginning to the universe. From the time of Lemaître onwards, people have thought that it does. Some of those who are now using it for that purpose are the astrophysicists Hugh Ross and Robert Newman, and the multi-talented philosopher-theologian William Lane Craig.

It's no surprise that they would do so. The theory, as it has been typically given, presents us with an absolute beginning to the entire cosmos—and a beginning that has no cause from within the universe itself. As Ernan McMullin put it,

> If the universe began in time through the act of the creator, from our vantage point it would look something like the big bang cosmologists are now talking about.

On the other hand, some very visible physicists have done what they could to remove this uncaused beginning notion from the theory. The most notable of these is Stephen Hawking, who in his *Brief History of Time* (1988) made his "no-boundary proposal" available to the general public. It depends on some sophisticated mathematics, using "imaginary time" (an "imaginary number" is what you get when you take the square root of a negative number). By such means he gets rid of what physicists call the "initial singularity" (the singularity, where the mathematical description breaks down, supports the uncaused beginning interpretation).

Hawking is quite clear as to what motivates his proposal: under his proposal, he says,

> there would be no singularities at which the laws of science broke down and no edge of space-time at which one would have to appeal to God or some new law to set the boundary conditions for space-time.

He's also honest about where the idea comes from:

> I'd like to emphasize that this idea that space and time should be finite without boundary is just a *proposal:* it cannot be deduced from some other principle.

William Lane Craig has analyzed Hawking's proposal, and shows why we shouldn't follow it. He points out that "imaginary time is physically unintelligible." That is, Hawking introduces imaginary time as a mathematical device, but then treats it as if it corresponds to physical reality—which it can't. Some mathematical problems can have two solutions: one that is physically real, and one that isn't. The mathematics won't tell us which one we can believe—only our experience of the world can do that. Craig mentions an example:

> Five men and a monkey are marooned on an island with nothing to eat but coconuts. They decide to divide the coconuts into five equal lots and to give the remainder to the monkey. But during the night, the first man wakes up and decides to take his share at that time. After dividing by five he finds he has one coconut left over, which he gives to the monkey. After he falls asleep, the second man does exactly the same, and after him the third man, and so on. In the morning they all wake up and, saying nothing about the night's activities, divide the remaining coconuts into five equal lots and find again one left over for the monkey.

The puzzle is: What is the smallest number of coconuts at the beginning? The answer is 15,621; but, as a matter of fact, –4 is an equally correct answer (mathematically)! Mathematics can't decide the answer: rather, our knowledge of the world—namely that there's no such thing as a "negative coconut"—tells us which answer is right.

Hawking admits,

> Only if we could picture the universe in terms of imaginary time would there be no singularities. . . .
>
> When one goes back to the real time in which we live, however, there will still appear to be singularities.

As Craig observes,

> Thus, Hawking does not really eliminate the singularity. He conceals it behind the physically unintelligible artifice of imaginary time.

Another way of getting around the initial singularity of the Big Bang is to appeal to quantum fluctuations in a vacuum. In the words of Robert Hazen and James Trefil (*Science Matters*),

> One point to note is that there is no problem in principle with creating matter from a vacuum. Matter is just another form of energy, and can be produced if the energy input is balanced by something else. For the universe that "something else" could be negative energy in the gravitational field. If this were the case, creating the universe would be like digging a hole—you'd have a pile of dirt (visible matter) balanced by a hole (the gravitational field). *The process is miraculous only if you ignore the hole and insist that matter appeared "from nothing."*

The last sentence shows the religious concern behind the theory. There's nothing special about the universe or about us; as one physicist put it, "Perhaps the universe is just one of those things that happens now and again."

Craig has argued against this approach as well, and has shown why "vacuum fluctuation models have now been abandoned even by some of their original expositors." The full story is too technical for me to summarize here, but at its heart is the observation that the "vacuum" the theory requires is not a real vacuum:

> A quantum mechanical vacuum is a sea of continually forming and dissolving particles, which borrow energy from the vacuum for their brief existence. This is not "nothing," and hence, material particles do not come into being out of nothing. Popular presentations of these models often do not explain that they require a specially fine-tuned, background space-time on the analogy of a quantum mechanical vacuum.

John Maddox, editor of the British science journal *Nature,* wrote an editorial entitled "Down with the Big Bang" (August 10, 1989), in which he denounced the Big Bang theory because it supports creationists. He foretold, "it is unlikely to survive the decade ahead." His prediction was wrong, though many challenges have come and gone; but what of his philosophical analysis?

Craig thinks that "the Big Bang model dramatically and unexpectedly" supports the biblical doctrine of creation from nothing—that is, he agrees with Maddox's philosophical analysis of the Big Bang. Because I am not a physicist, I am unable to be as confident as Craig is that this model will survive all challenges to it. At any rate we can certainly say that the model is quite compatible with the biblical doctrine, and the sciences have therefore done nothing to disprove the doctrine. In the meantime we can be sure that there will be a steady stream of further challenges to this model—both because that's what scientists do and because this particular model raises the kinds of ultimate questions that get under some people's skin.

ARE THE GEOLOGISTS WRONG?

Speaking generally, the main opposition to the geological story I outlined above comes from the young earth creationists. Their objections fall into three main categories. First, they say that modern geology ignores Scripture. Second, they say that modern geology is controlled by uniformitarian premises. And third, they say that the dating techniques, such as radiometric dating, are unreliable. Let's take these objections one by one.

First, it is true that modern geology does not depend on Scripture (it isn't true that it ignores it, though: many works cite James Ussher's chronology for the world). But this is a far cry from saying that it sets itself in opposition to the Bible. In fact, most of the pioneering geologists in early nineteenth-century England were pious Anglicans—some were clergy. It would only be right to say that geology opposes Scripture if we were sure that Scripture *requires* us to believe that the world is young—and the early geologists thought the Bible gave room for other possible interpretations.

We should also note that the main ideas of a long geologic timescale were well in place before the time of Darwin's *Origin of Species* (1859). Hence the common way of calling old earth geology "evolutionary" is misleading—as we'll see when we talk about biological evolution and the meanings of words.

Second, if we want to talk about uniformitarianism, we have to decide what kind of uniformitarianism we are speaking of. Many young earth creationists have pointed out that the 1980 eruption of Mount St. Helens in Washington state gave all manner of evidence that some processes can go really fast. Therefore, uniformitarianism, which stresses slow processes and small forces operating over long periods of time, is not adequate for what we actually see in the world. For example, John Whitcomb and Henry Morris, two of the leaders in the contemporary young earth creationist movement, say,

> And how do we know that miracles and divine intervention contradict natural law? Why, of course, because our experience shows and our philosophy postulates that "all things continue as they were from the beginning of the creation" [the words of the scoffers in 2 Pet. 3:4]! This is what we call

> our "principle of uniformity" which asserts that all things even from the earliest beginnings can be explained essentially in terms of present processes and rates.

You can see in this passage that Whitcomb and Morris take the principle of uniformity to be the strict Lyellian kind, and that they take this to exclude the possibility of supernatural events (that is, to be deistic).

In my section above on the standard geological story, I mentioned Lyell and his brand of strict uniformitarianism, called *substantive uniformitarianism*. This is where we would get an insistence on slow processes, with no catastrophes. I have already shown that modern geology does not follow the strict uniformitarianism of Lyell.

Instead, geologists distinguish the *substantive* kind from the *methodological* kind of uniformitarianism. The substantive principle of uniformity says that the geological processes have run at the same rates, and at the same intensities, throughout the history of the earth. The methodological kind of uniformitarianism says that these rates and intensities may have varied over the course of the earth's history—which means that dramatic upheavals (catastrophes) may well have happened. This is the principle of uniformity that is most widely spread among today's geologists, and it makes no comment whatever on the possibility of miracles or of the biblical flood.

Christian faith is not in the least opposed to the idea that nature is basically uniform—in fact, this is just what we insist on. That's how we can say that the great events of salvation history are *super*natural, and not simply natural. In fact, it is the uniformity of natural properties that gives us the means to recognize supernatural events—when the effects go beyond what the natural properties could have caused.

So, *methodological* uniformitarianism is reasonable. But there's more: to identify catastrophic events in the past, you have to use it! Even the most devoted advocates of what is called "flood geology"—the kind of young earth creationism that appeals to the biblical flood to explain most geological features—try to show how the physical processes of the flood would have caused the various things we see in the world, such as the Grand Canyon. In other words, they assume that the same physical properties we see today were operating back then, though their rates and intensities may have been different at times. That is, as Christian (old-earth) geologist Davis Young put it, "modern Flood catastrophists are really proceeding on the same principle as do modern uniformitarian geologists."

All of this leads to the conclusion that the kind of uniformitarianism that governs modern geological study is an asset to it—that's a long way from it being a fatal flaw.

The third objection to the geologists' view of the earth's age is that the dating techniques are unreliable. Let's clear away some rabbit trails by focusing on radiometric dating. I say this because some young earth creationists have pointed out that catastrophic events—for example, the Mount St. Helens eruption in 1980—make much faster geological changes than were previously thought possible. Modern geologists grant this, but this makes no difference when it comes to dating rocks. Geologists consider that using radioisotopes provides the most reliable dates for the rocks, and they therefore don't rely on supposed rates of geological changes from volcanoes and other things that shape a landscape.

Quite simply, it doesn't look like the critique of radiometric dating—at least as young earth creationists have offered it—holds much promise for unseating this technique.

Steven Austin is chairman of the geology department of the Institute for Creation Research (ICR), and one of the leading young earth geologists. In ICR's *Impact* series (in 1988 and 1992) he has argued that radiometric methods yield bad results when applied to various rocks in the Grand Canyon. Brent Dalrymple of the U.S. Geological Survey (USGS) is generally acknowledged as one of the leading experts on geological dating—his book *The Age of the Earth* (1991) is considered the standard in the field. In 1986 Dalrymple wrote a booklet called *Radiometric Dating, Geologic Time, and the Age of the Earth: A Reply to "Scientific" Creationism* (an Open File Report from the USGS), and in 1992 he wrote a short pamphlet called "Some Comments and Observations on Steven Austin's 'Grand Canyon Dating Project'," specifically in reply to the *Impact* articles.

Austin set out to undermine confidence in what he called "the great ages claimed by evolutionists for the earth's rocks." He argued that if you take the same procedures used to date one set of rocks in the Grand Canyon—a deeply buried lava flow called the Cardenas Basalt—and apply them to lava flows that are known to be more recent than these, you get the recent rocks being older than the deeply buried ones. This calls into question the reliability of any dates based on radioisotopes.

In Dalrymple's 1992 reply, he asserts "radiometric dating methods have been tested time and time again by competent geologists and physicists over the past three decades. They work remarkably well and there are countless examples" (and he refers to his 1991 book as supplying further discussion). He then gets down to the nub:

> Do radiometric methods always work? The answer to that is yes, provided that the physical and chemical conditions necessary for the proper functioning of the methods have not been violated.

He then argues that Austin has not ensured that the proper conditions were met—particularly in his choice of data for the argument. Austin drew on data from a 1974 article by W. P. Leeman, but did not accurately represent Leeman's own report. Dalrymple concludes,

> Leeman's data and the K-Ar [potassium-argon, used for radiometric dating] ages of the lava flows tell us quite clearly that these lavas are not cogenetic, that the conditions necessary for a valid isochron have been violated, and, therefore, that any apparent isochron is not to be trusted. . . .
>
> In summary, I can't really tell what Steven Austin is doing with his western Grand Canyon data. They keep changing and he never provides enough information to do an independent evaluation of important things like the isochron fit. In addition, he is ignoring what I and others have told him about using lava flows that are demonstrably not cogenetic, and he is ignoring Leeman's data, which clearly indicates that the rough correlation between the Rb and Sr [rubidium and strontium, also used for radiometric dating] isotopic ratios reflects time-integrated radioactive decay in the source rock(s), and not in the lava flows.

Well! There are plenty of technical details on both sides, and I don't pretend to know how to assess them. However, I am confident in saying that Dalrymple has played fair with people he disagrees deeply with—he has read Austin's material and measured it against reasonable criteria for a technical work. He found it wanting because it did not meet the criteria. It therefore doesn't look to me like Austin's claim to call into question radiometric dating should carry much weight with us.

I conclude, then, that I have no reason to disbelieve the standard theories of the geologists, including their estimate for the age of the earth. They may be wrong, for all I know; but if they are wrong, it's not because they have improperly smuggled philosophical assumptions into their work.

THE ANTHROPIC PRINCIPLE

I want to finish this chapter by noting a huge benefit that comes to our faith from modern cosmology: it is called "the anthropic principle." This refers to the fact that the physical properties of the universe are finely balanced to support life here on earth—and perhaps nowhere else. Some researchers also call this the "fine tuning" of the universe.

Consider some of the constants in physics, for example. If the gravitational force constant were larger than it is, then stars would be too hot and would burn up quickly and unevenly; if it were smaller than it is, then stars would remain so cool that nuclear fusion would never get going—and then the stars could never have produced any heavy elements (since the first elements were hydrogen and then helium; we depend on elements heavier than that, such as carbon). If the electromagnetic force constant were either larger or smaller, then you wouldn't have good chemical bonds. If the rate at which the universe is expanding were greater than it is, then galaxies couldn't have formed; if it were smaller, then the universe would have collapsed back in on itself before any stars were formed. If the speed of light were greater than it is, then the stars would be too luminous; if it were smaller, then the stars would not be luminous enough. The list goes on and on—Hugh Ross lists twenty-five "design parameters" for the universe, and another thirty-two parameters that a galaxy-sun-planet-moon system needs to support life. These even include how old the universe is—if it were older than it is, there wouldn't be any of the right kind of star in the right burning phase in the right part of the galaxy to be our sun; if it were younger, the right kind of star wouldn't have formed yet.

The cosmologists who have put these things together have expressed their surprise at how fit the universe is for life on our planet; I could fill several pages with their comments, but will have to be content with just a few of them. For example, the physicist Paul Davies has said,

> It is hard to resist the impression of something—some influence capable of transcending spacetime and the confinements of relativistic causality—possessing an overview of the entire cosmos at the instant of its creation, and manipulating all the causally disconnected parts to go bang with almost exactly the same vigour at the same time, and yet not so exactly coordinated as to preclude the small scale, slight irregularities that eventually formed the galaxies, and us.

The relationship between gravity and the weak nuclear force is in a perfect balance, which has kept the universe expanding at its "comfortable" rate. According to Davies, the two forces must be tuned to each other with the accuracy of one part in 10^{60}. This, he tells us, "is the accuracy a marksman would need if he wanted to hit a one-inch target at the other end of the universe—twenty billion light years away." And, as the Christian physicist Alan Hayward points out,

> This discovery helps to answer the question that has puzzled many Christians: if God is mainly interested in our little planet, then why did he create this whole vast universe? Apparently it is all there for a purpose. Many of the elements in our own bodies were probably created in some long-vanished star, in a remote corner of the galaxy, thousands of light years away.

Well, then, perhaps we might use this for apologetic purposes—if the universe is so finely tuned, doesn't that support the idea that God *designed* it for us? We have to be careful, though; as John North notes in his *Norton History of Astronomy and Cosmology,* the conversation between Alan, a believer, and Stephen, a doubter, would go something like this:

> *Alan:* Only by God's good grace do we inhabit a Universe perfectly suited to our needs, that is, satisfying the conditions necessary for our existence.
>
> *Stephen:* God may well be responsible, but at all events we should not be surprised that we encounter conditions suited to our existence. If they did not exist, we should not exist.

Stephen's reply says we need not be surprised at the universe we live in. On the other hand, Alan doesn't have to leave off talking. As William Lane Craig pointed out, Alan could answer:

> Suppose you are to be executed by a firing squad of 100 trained marksmen, all of them aiming rifles at your heart. You are blindfolded; the command is given; you hear the deafening roar of the rifles. And you observe that you are still alive. The 100 marksmen missed!
>
> Taking off the blindfold, you do not observe that you are dead. No surprise there: you *could not* observe that you are dead. Nonetheless, you should be astonished to observe that you are alive. The entire firing squad missed you altogether! Surprise at that extremely improbable fact is wholly justified—and that fact calls for explanation. You would immediately suspect that they missed you on purpose, by design.

At the very least, then, we are quite justified in our feeling of surprise, even of awe, at the way the universe is—and this feeling links up with our other reasons for believing in the God who reveals himself in the Bible. So that means that the anthropic principle isn't a knock-down argument for the existence of God—how could it be, since it only touches on what I called the "metaphysical" part of our faith—but it is one part of a larger argument. This particular part adds the element of wonder to the whole discussion; it helps us to enter into the spirit of Psalm 8 with a renewed thrill of delight:

[1] O LORD, our Lord,
how majestic is your name in all the earth!
You have set your glory above the heavens.
[2] Out of the mouth of babes and infants,
you have established strength because of your foes,
to still the enemy and the avenger.

[3] When I look at your heavens, the work of your fingers,
the moon and the stars, which you have set in place,
[4] what is man that you are mindful of him,
and the son of man that you care for him?

[5] Yet you have made him a little lower than the heavenly beings,
and crowned him with glory and honor.
[6] You have given him dominion over the works of your hands;
you have put all things under his feet,
[7] all sheep and oxen,
and also the beasts of the field,
[8] the birds of the heavens, and the fish of the sea,
whatever passes along the paths of the seas.

[9] O LORD, our Lord,
how majestic is your name in all the earth!

16

Where Do Animals Come From?

Biological Evolution and Darwinism

LOOK AT ANY ANIMAL you like—a dog or cat, or a canary, or even a grasshopper or butterfly. I'll bet you admire the way it's built, the way it's just right for its own lifestyle. Think of how monarch butterflies migrate to Mexico every year; of how bats use "aerial sonar" to find moths and avoid landing on you; of how the sharp eyesight of the hawk allows it to soar so high and see so much.

The science of "natural history" is born as your wonder leads you to describe how these creatures live, eat and get eaten, breed, and contribute to their environment. But your wonder can't leave you there; you will go on to ponder *how* these animals came to be this way. Did God make their ancestors just the way the present ones are? Or did they change from the way they were first made? Or did God have anything at all to do with how they were first made?

The "theory of evolution," as it is called, is one attempt to answer questions like these. Of course—rightly or wrongly—this is probably the most visible arena of "conflict between science and religion." We have theologians telling us that the theory is evil, and that it produces all manner of evils—such as racism and loss of public morality. We have science educators telling us that it's *science,* and therefore we ought to believe it and adjust our faith accordingly. The science popularizers fall into two camps—one camp that says that our faith is compatible with evolution, so long as our faith is complementary with the science, and the other that says that the science proves that our faith is wrong.

Conservative Christians have not spoken with one voice on the topic of evolution. Many have accepted it because it's widely accepted as science, and therefore they have a theistic version of the theory of evolution. Others have fought against it with all their might, because they believe it cannot be squared with either the Bible or science. Of these fighters, perhaps most accept some version of the young earth approach to cosmology and geology. And then there are still others who don't like what people try to do in the name of evolutionary science, and aren't sure whether it's the theory or its abuse that leads to these results. My aim in this chapter is to point the way to a consensus for Christians.

If we're going to assess the main ideas of this theory, we should first understand just what the theory claims and where it came from. Then we can consider how it impacts Christian belief and whether it deserves our consent.

WHAT DOES DARWINISM CLAIM?

The view called "Darwinism"—after Charles Darwin (1809–1882), who proposed its key features—dominates in biology today. For example, in the St. Louis Zoo you can find a display of an African wild goat that lives in the desert. This goat has pads on its feet that enable it to walk easily on the sand and rock of the desert; but that isn't what the placard says: instead, it tells us that the goat's ancestors *developed* these footpads to adapt to the desert environment. The zoo explains the pads in terms of development because they—like most zoologists today—assume that evolution is true.

The word "evolution" has a number of possible meanings, and that leads to some confusion when we discuss this topic. Let's try to sort out the different meanings and what they do or do not imply.

Neutral sense. The basic meaning of the word *evolution* is "a process of change over time." This basic sense makes no claims about what caused this development; nor does it claim that what developed is better or worse than the starting point. For example, you can talk about the "evolution of the English language" and simply mean that the language has changed. Cosmologists speak of the "evolution" of stars or of the whole cosmos, meaning that they change over time.

Neutral sense in biology. When we apply this basic meaning to biology, we are saying that the creatures we see today are related to creatures that lived long ago, the ones whose fossils we dig up. We are also saying that the differences between the modern creatures and the fossils come from changes that the descendants have inherited. For example, most scholars think that the Australian dingo developed from domestic dogs that early human settlers brought to Australia; they "evolved." That is, some of those dogs got loose, and the ones best suited to the environment bred; as a result of this breeding the dingo, which is well-suited to wild Australia, came into being. At the same time, we can find authors who speak of the way the domestic dog "evolved" from the wolf. That is, people took the young of wild wolves, and bred the ones that had the features they liked best; as a result, the domestic dog came into being, with features distinct from the wild wolf. These two examples show that when we use the word this way we're making no claim about *how* the changes took place: in the case of dingoes, they came about by natural processes, while in the case of dogs, they came about by selective breeding (that is, by interfering with nature).

Evolution-as-the-big-picture. If either of these first two senses were all the word *evolution* ever meant, nobody would fuss over it. But when biologists refer to the "theory of evolution," they mean something much more ambitious; in the words of the National Association of Biology Teachers (NABT), which operates in the United States:

> The diversity of life on earth is the outcome of *evolution:* an unpredictable and natural process of temporal descent with genetic modification that is affected by natural selection, chance, historical contingencies and changing environments.

This definition of evolution claims to explain why *every living thing* we see is the way it is. In case you miss what they mean when they call the process a "natural" one, they add another point:

> Natural selection . . . has *no specific direction or goal,* including survival of a species.

The reason they said this is to rule out any possibility of finding a purpose behind evolutionary changes. An earlier edition of this statement called the process of evolution "unsupervised, impersonal, unpredictable and natural"—and after a storm of protest the first two adjectives were dropped. But the basic principles remain.

You will notice that the statement speaks about "the *diversity* of life on earth," meaning that evolution assumes that we start the process with living things. Biologists don't always agree on whether the origin of life itself should be included under the discussion of evolution. The NABT statement doesn't mention that at all. On the other hand, John Maynard Smith's classic book *The Theory of Evolution* (1993) has a whole chapter on "The Origin and Early Evolution of Life"—with a section called "Prebiotic Evolution." The science popularizers Robert Hazen and James Trefil, in their book *Science Matters* (1991), wrote:

> Most scientists agree about one aspect of evolution. Life seems to have arisen in a two-step process. The first stage—chemical evolution—encompasses the origin of life from nonlife. Once life appeared, the second stage—biological evolution—took over.

As we will see, Charles Darwin himself had a divided mind on the topic—but, as I intend to show, the same premises and principles that underlie the modern theory of "evolution-as-the-big-picture" also point toward the process that generated life being a "natural" one.

You will also notice that the diversity of life on earth includes you and me. That is, if the theory is true, you—including your personality, your beliefs, and whatever soul you might have—are "the outcome of evolution." You are the product of "an unpredictable and natural process," which had "no specific direction or goal." We will especially want to consider how such a conclusion might impact our Christian faith.

HOW DID DARWINISM DEVELOP?

The French natural philosopher Jean-Baptiste Lamarck (1744–1829) was the first to give a general theory of biological evolution. In 1800 he argued that the simplest life forms had arisen spontaneously (that is, without God's special action) from matter, and that all other forms of life had developed from them. In his 1809 book *Philosophie Zoologique,* he tried to explain this development as due to two factors: first, a "power of life" that pressed toward increasingly complex animal classes; and second, the pressure of environment. This second feature is what people today most remember about Lamarck's theory: an animal's environment causes it to acquire characteristics, which it then passes on to its young. For example, the ancestors of modern giraffes would stretch their necks to feed on the leaves of trees; they passed their stretched necks on to their offspring, who passed even more stretching on to theirs. Darwin himself did not reject this feature—he just didn't make it very prominent.

Lamarck's views didn't win much acceptance in his day. One of the greatest of the contemporary earth scientists, Georges Cuvier (1769–1832), for example, pointed to the absence of transition forms among the fossils. Nevertheless a Lamarckian treatise, *Vestiges of the Natural History of Creation,* appeared in Britain in 1844. The author remained anonymous, but historians agree that he was Robert Chambers (1802–1871); he rightly anticipated that he would stir up controversy. The ideas were rejected by both scientific and religious scholars, but it did put the subject of biological evolution before the English-speaking world.

The tide turned, however, when Charles Darwin (1809–1882) published *The Origin of Species* in 1859. The book went through six editions, the last coming out in 1872. As we can see, Darwin was not the first scientist to argue for some form of biological evolution. Darwin made his name by describing a way it could have happened. Putting it briefly, he started by noticing that any species will have within it small variations between individuals—say, some will be bigger, or greener, or faster. He then supposed that in the wild, creatures produce more offspring than can possibly survive—that is, the offspring are competing for scarce resources. *Natural selection* was Darwin's name for the process in which individuals better suited to their environment survive and pass their traits on to their offspring. He used the analogy of selective breeding: for example, you get a border collie by breeding those dogs that have the features you want in a shepherd dog, and then breeding those young that have the traits you want, and so on; you try to keep dogs with traits you don't want from breeding and passing on those features.

This has become known as "the survival of the fittest." Darwin didn't use that term at first, but by his sixth edition he did, borrowing it from the philosopher Herbert Spencer (1820–1903).

Darwin's *Origin* fits the ironic definition of a classic—a book that everyone praises but no one reads. I think everyone should read it and see how he develops his argument, and try to understand why it came to be so popular. Darwin was skillful in his rhetoric: for example, he wrote as if the only possible opponents to his theory would be those who held to what he called "the immutability of species"; he didn't allow that opposition might come from some other quarter.

Many of the leading scientists of Darwin's day—including those most familiar with the evidence, such as biologists and geologists—rejected his theory. But Darwin had some very capable advocates and defenders, such as T. H. Huxley (called "Darwin's bulldog"). So his theories eventually won out.

Nevertheless, people still recognized that there were unsolved problems. Actually, Darwin himself was pretty honest about some of them: for example, in his chapter 6 he addresses what he took to be some of the strongest objections to his theory. First, he admitted that the fossil record gave no support, since transitional forms—that is, the steps between the ancestor and the later species—were exceedingly rare. He replied,

> I believe the answer mainly lies in the record being incomparably less perfect than is generally supposed.

Second, he tackled the question of how creatures with peculiar habits and structures could have arisen by the accumulation of small changes—"for how could the animal in its transitional state have subsisted?" For example, how could a meat-eating land animal develop into one that lives in water? He replied,

> It would be easy to show that there now exist carnivorous animals presenting close intermediate grades from strictly terrestrial to aquatic habits; and as each exists by a struggle for life, it is clear that each must be well adapted to its place in nature.

Note that he didn't claim that the forms we now see actually *are* the transitional species; he only said that they give evidence that such transitions would have been able to get along in similar environments. And this illustrates a rhetorical move in the book that became dominant, and that still dominates much of the discussion of evolution: by saying "I can imagine a scenario that led to this result," Darwin shifted the burden of proof to those who disagree with him. He no longer had to show that his scenario is likely, or even possible—instead his opponents now have to show that it couldn't have happened this way. And if they can't, well then, they have no grounds to object to the theory. He resorted to the same tactic in discussing the *Galeopithecus,* or flying lemur, which earlier biologists had thought to be a bat, but which in Darwin's day was considered an insectivore. He said,

> Although no graduated links of structure, fitted for gliding through the air, now connect the Galeopithecus with the other Insectivora, yet *there is no difficulty in supposing* that such links formerly existed, and that each was developed in the same manner as with the less perfectly gliding squirrels; each grade of structure having been useful to its possessor.

Here Darwin has clearly shifted the question: it is now, "Is there any difficulty in supposing such a sequence?" and not, "Is such a sequence likely or even possible?" Apparently the fact that we can suppose the sequence is what makes it possible.

The third objection is how "organs of extreme perfection and complication," such as the eye, could have developed; as Darwin put it,

> To suppose that the eye with all its inimitable contrivances for adjusting the focus to different distances, for admitting different amounts of light, and for the correction of spherical and chromatic aberration, could have been formed by natural selection, seems, I freely confess, absurd in the highest degree.

But he then proposed a scenario by which it "could have happened." As to the problem of how the whole process got started, he dismissed it:

> How a nerve comes to be sensitive to light, hardly concerns us more than how life itself originated.

But if he wanted to support the shift from "I can imagine that it happened this way" to "I have a right to believe it could have happened this way," then "how it happened" is just the question he ought to answer (but never did).

As the last quote indicates, Darwin did not pretend to know how life got started. In fact, he did not claim what is now called "universal common descent"—namely, that all things now living are descended from the same primitive life form—although it is clear that he would have liked to support this. He wrote in his concluding chapter,

> Therefore I cannot doubt that the theory of descent with modification [Darwin's favored term for what we now call *evolution*] embraces all the members of the same great class or kingdom. I believe that animals are descended from at most only four or five progenitors, and plants from an equal or lesser number. . . .
>
> We must likewise admit that all the organic beings which have ever lived on this earth may be descended from some one primordial form. But this inference is chiefly grounded on analogy, and it is immaterial whether or not it be accepted. . . .
>
> There is grandeur in this view of life, with its several powers, having been originally breathed by the Creator into a few forms or into one.

I will not suggest that Darwin was dishonest in this last remark, but he certainly hoped to be able to supply a completely natural explanation even for the origin of life. This is clear from a letter he wrote in 1871 (and remember that the sixth edition of the *Origin* came out in 1872):

> It is often said that all the conditions for the first production of a living organism are now present which could ever have been present. But if (and oh! what a big if!) we could conceive in some warm little pond, with all

> sorts of ammonia and phosphoric salts, light, heat, electricity, etc. present, that a protein compound was chemically formed ready to undergo still more complex changes, at the present day such matter would be instantly devoured or absorbed, which would not have been the case before living creatures were formed.

Darwin was not an atheist, but at heart he was a Deist.

The modern theory of evolution is not actually Darwinism, however; it is "neo-Darwinism." Darwin's theory could not explain where variations could come from, since Gregor Mendel's (1822–1889) theory of inheritance—worked out in the 1860s—was not widely known until about 1900. In the 1920s and 30s, however, scientists such as the British J. B. S. Haldane (1892–1964), made use of advances in genetic theory since 1900, which explain how traits can be passed on, and how mutations can enter the gene pool. They also incorporated views on biochemical evolution or "abiogenesis" (origination of life from non-living matter), which reminds us of Darwin's "warm little pond." Further, they no longer found the selective advantage to be in the individual organism improving its own fitness for survival. The modern focus is on how an organism succeeds in passing on its genes. Neo-Darwinism is the view that the NABT statement supports, and it has eliminated all reference to special or creative divine activity.

Neo-Darwinism is today's ruling theory of biological evolution-as-the-big-picture. That shows that the two things, neo-Darwinism and evolution-as-the-big-picture, do not have to be the same thing: neo-Darwinism is a subset of big-picture-evolution. This shows us that we have to be careful: for example, we may think that neo-Darwinism is false, or at least far from established; but that doesn't mean that big-picture-evolution must automatically fall with it, since there may be some other subset that provides a better theory. On the other hand, if neo-Darwinism is the best that big-picture-evolution has to offer, and it is flawed, then big-picture-evolution is also in trouble. Similarly, if big-picture-evolution is fundamentally opposed to Christian faith, then so is neo-Darwinism.

HOW DOES NEO-DARWINISM IMPACT CHRISTIAN FAITH?

The great difficulty in deciding just how "evolution" interacts with Christian faith is the wide variety of definitions for that word. In the nineteenth and early twentieth centuries a number of influential Christian figures accepted some kind of "evolution" (or "development," as they usually called it) as having happened; but they commonly had in mind "guided evolution"—for example, that God established the natural properties of matter so that it would follow his plan; he supervised the process, bringing things together at the right time; and he carried out supernatural operations at key places—such as the forming of the first man.

But guided evolution is not Darwinism, nor is it neo-Darwinism. Charles Hodge (1797–1878), a very conservative Presbyterian theologian at Princeton Theological Seminary in New Jersey (at that time a bastion of theological conservatism in America), discussed just this point in his *Systematic Theology* (published 1871–1873), and at more length in *What Is Darwinism?* (1874).

In October of 1873 Hodge attended the meeting of the Evangelical Alliance in New York. In one session he listened to scientists who were committed Christians discuss whether "the doctrine of development" (as evolution was called) was consistent with Christian faith. On hearing one of the scientists say that it was, Hodge rose to speak:

> I rise simply to ask Mr. Brown one question. I want him to tell us what development is. That has not been done. The great question which divides theists from atheists—Christians from unbelievers—is this: Is development an intellectual [perhaps he meant *intelligent*] process guided by God, or is it a blind process of unintelligible, unconscious force, which knows no end and adopts no means? In other words, is God the author of all we see, the creator of all the beauty and grandeur of this world, or is unintelligible force, gravity, electricity, and such like? This is a vital question, sir. We can not stand here and hear men talk about development, without telling us what development is.

Later at this meeting, the devout Presbyterian layman John W. Dawson, principal of McGill University and a leading geologist, gave a paper that sought to harmonize recent archaeological finds with the Bible. The topic of development came up again, and someone asked Dawson "whether there is any necessary antagonism between the Darwinian system and the Christian religion." Dawson replied that it would "require a treatise" to answer the question, but he briefly stated that he considered Darwinism "only one branch" of the materialistic speculations exemplified by Herbert Spencer's doctrine of evolution, and not based on adequate scientific evidence.

Hodge again rose to speak.

> My idea of Darwinism is that it teaches that all the forms of vegetable and animal life, including man and all the organs of the human body, are the result of unintelligent, undesignating forces; and that the human eye was

> formed by mere unconscious action. Now, according to my idea, that is a denial of what the Bible teaches, of what reason teaches, and of what the conscience of any human being teaches; for it is impossible for any such organ as the eye to be formed by blind forces. It excludes God; it excludes intelligence from everything. Am I right?

Dawson answered that although Darwin would probably not admit as much, "his doctrine logically leads to that conclusion." Dawson continued that Darwin's theory conflicts with the Bible, "especially with respect to man," and that it is not a result of scientific induction but a merely hypothetical alternative to the doctrine of creation.

This is the background to Hodge's verdict in his work, *What Is Darwinism?* that Darwinism is "atheism." His actual words follow a quotation of Asa Gray, a botanist and one of the leading Christian supporters of Darwin in America. Gray had written,

> If Mr Darwin believes that the events which he supposes to have occurred and the results we behold around us were undirected and undesigned; or if the physicist believes that the natural forces to which he refers phenomena are uncaused and undirected, no argument is needed to show that such belief is atheistic.

Hodge pounced on Gray's statement, and concluded his book:

> We have thus arrived at the answer to our question, What is Darwinism? It is Atheism. This does not mean, as before said, that Mr Darwin himself and all who adopt his views are atheists; but it means that his theory is atheistic, that the exclusion of design from nature is atheistic.

Historians will continue to debate whether Hodge was right in his nineteenth-century context; but that is not what we should focus on. The question for us is whether Hodge's analysis properly applies to the *neo*-Darwinism that reigns today. And I think that the answer is yes.

Neo-Darwinism claims to have a thoroughly natural explanation for everything there is—for life, the universe, and everything. A theistic advocate of this theory would have to say that the natural events are God's action by way of "ordinary providence"—that is, that God designed a universe so well that he could simply keep it in being and it would go on to generate life, and eventually us. One such advocate is Howard Van Till, a physicist from Calvin College. In the British journal *Science and Christian Belief* he wrote,

> Most modern biological theorizing regarding the formative history of life on our planet presumes the possibility of some historical scenario that proceeds *from molecules to mankind along a continuous pathway of natural phenomena.*
>
> By 'continuous pathway' we here mean an unbroken succession of natural processes and events not interrupted or blocked by physical, chemical or biological gaps of the sort that would require occasional bridging by 'miraculous divine interventions' or by any other 'special' divine activity.

Van Till thinks that the Christian doctrine of the goodness of creation supports what he calls "a doctrine of Creation's functional integrity"—that is, that when God made the world he built into it all the capacities it would ever need, without any tinkering, to produce all that God wanted it to produce. If we were to find special divine activity in the history of the earth or of life's development—why then, that would imply that God was an incompetent craftsman. (That allows Van Till to enjoy tweaking the noses of "special creationists" by calling them heretical.)

Van Till is certainly right that "modern biological theorizing"—that is, evolution-as-the-big-picture, with neo-Darwinism as its most common representative—presumes that you get from molecules to mankind by a purely natural process. He thinks that they are right to *presume* it—which means that they don't have to *prove* it. But Van Till is dead wrong that the Christian doctrine of creation supports this presumption.

Back in chapter 4 we saw that Genesis 1 gives us a "historical" account of the creation week in the sense that it tells us things that really happened. Even though we wouldn't call Genesis 1 a "scientific" account, we can still find in it a basis for sound philosophy and science. One feature in particular stands out for our purposes: the way in which God expresses a wish ("let such and such a thing happen"), and then the wish is carried out. We saw this feature in Genesis 1:3, 6, 9, 11, 14, 20, 24, and 26. Genesis 1:2 tells us that the Spirit of God—a supernatural agent—was present. All of this means that we should not be surprised to find "gaps" in the natural history of the creation—gaps due to God's special or supernatural actions.

Further, the creation of the first man leads us to expect a gap; Genesis 1:26-27 reads,

> [26] Then God said, "Let us make man in our image, after our likeness. And let them have dominion over the fish of the sea and over the birds of the

heavens and over the livestock and over all the earth and over every creeping thing that creeps on the earth."

> [27] So God created man in his own image,
> in the image of God he created him;
> male and female he created them.

The term "create" describes a supernatural action; and the "image of God" that we discussed in chapter 8 refers to capacities that are distinct from those of any other animal.

The Scripture would lead us to expect, therefore, that God had been specially active, not only in the beginning of the various forms of life—which was what Darwin allowed, but neo-Darwinism (including its theistic forms) excludes even that—but also at the origin of mankind. How specific, though, does the Bible get?

For example, what should we make of the language about "kinds" in Genesis 1:11-12, 21, 24-25? Let's cite the verses themselves to see just what they say (italics added):

> [11] And God said, "Let the earth sprout vegetation, plants yielding seed, and fruit trees bearing fruit in which is their seed, *each according to its kind,* on the earth." And it was so. [12] The earth brought forth vegetation, plants yielding seed *according to their own kinds,* and trees bearing fruit in which is their seed, *each according to its kind.* And God saw that it was good.
>
> [21] So God created the great sea creatures and every living thing that moves, with which the waters swarm, *according to their kinds,* and every winged bird *according to its kind.* And God saw that it was good.
>
> [24] And God said, "Let the earth bring forth living creatures *according to their kinds*—livestock and creeping things and beasts of the earth *according to their kinds.*" And it was so. [25] And God made the beasts of the earth *according to their kinds* and the livestock *according to their kinds,* and everything that creeps on the ground *according to its kind.* And God saw that it was good.

Some suppose that these verses teach that each of the species we see today is the result of separate creative (or supernatural) acts, and that little or no change of a basic type is possible. I suppose you can find creationists who actually say this—but the claim pretty commonly comes from the pens of those who oppose creationism. For example, this is how Darwin type-cast his opponents: "he who believes that each being has been created as we now see it." Ian Barbour, one of the most important scholars of science and religion in the late twentieth century, wrote:

> Previously it had been assumed that the forms of all living things were fixed when they were created. The order of nature was thought to be essentially static and unchanging.

Now as a matter of fact these claims from Darwin and Barbour (and others) are historically wrong. Among others Carolus Linnaeus (1707–1778), the Swedish botanist who did so much to promote our modern system of classifying living things, and a committed Christian, did not hold this view.

More importantly, though, the view does not directly follow from the Bible itself, and that for three reasons. First, the biblical text simply says that these first plants bore seed according to their kinds, and that the first animals were created according to their kinds. It does not say that these are the only "kinds" there ever were or ever could be. Second, it is notoriously difficult (notorious at least among Hebrew scholars, anyhow) to define just what the word "kind" means: in any case it doesn't mean the same as "species" (that's too narrow and technical a meaning), it's more like "category." And third, to take the verses as a taxonomic statement is to misread the with-respect-to-whatness of the Genesis creation story. This story is in terms of the everyday experience of an ancient Israelite: wheat grains produce more wheat plants, barley produces more barley, and so on. (Note that it doesn't say that camels breed more camels, but that's no matter—Moses doesn't have to draw us a picture for us to get the idea.) Things work the way they do because God intended them to do so. This doesn't mean that under some circumstances you can't get varieties of wheat so different that they're different species—in fact it doesn't comment on the topic at all.

To summarize, then, by this reading of Genesis 1 I will expect to find some level of discontinuity in the family trees of the different sorts of living things. To put it another way, I will be very skeptical of claims that they all descended from a common ancestor. It is left for scientific study to discover just where the breaks are—so long as that study doesn't start off by presupposing that natural processes are the only factors that could be involved. (Oddly enough, that brings us closer to Darwin's "four or five progenitors" for animals, and "an equal or lesser number" for plants—but with a twist, to be sure!)

And what of mankind? Does the Bible allow that we are descended from animal ancestors? A great deal depends on what you mean by "descended"—

if you mean "with only ordinary natural factors in operation," then certainly the answer is no. The image of God in man is the result of special divine action, and not a development of the powers of any other animal—at least, that's what Genesis 1:27 implies. This is directly contrary to Darwin's view:

> In the future psychology will be securely based on the foundation already well laid by Mr Herbert Spencer, that of the necessary acquirement of each mental power and capacity by gradation. Much light will be thrown on the origin of man and his history.

Similarly, Ian Barbour—who supports neo-Darwinism—wrote:

> Previously, humanity was sharply distinguished from the rest of nature. Since Darwin, humanity has been understood to be part of nature, the product of a common evolutionary heritage.

The theologian Gerald Bray put all this very well from a Christian perspective:

> So much of the modern struggle against evolution is due to the subconscious realisation that what matters about man is that which distinguishes him from the animal world, not that which unites him to it. Even if some form of evolutionary theory can eventually be proved to be correct, it will not be able to explain what we call 'personhood', because personhood is the image of God in us.

In the nineteenth century some scholars who recognized this issue suggested that the *body* of Adam had developed by natural selection, and that the sole supernatural action was God giving him a *soul* (in which dwelt the image of God). I think this kind of thinking comes from a failure to understand both the image of God and the nature of the body-soul relationship that I discussed in chapter 8. There I argued that man is a *body-soul nexus,* and that this nexus displays the image of God; that is, the body, with its brain, muscles, bones, blood, and so on, is a necessary part of the display. This means that God couldn't have just injected a soul into an ape's body—he would have had to do some pretty significant upgrades to that body for it to be able to support the soul!

Well, then, someone might say, suppose that's just what happened: the "dust" of Genesis 2:7 ("the LORD God formed the man of dust from the ground") was actually the body of some ape or hominid, which God then transformed to be the vehicle of the image of God. I can commend this view as recognizing what must be involved in being human, and in preserving the distinction between man and other animals—a distinction that results from supernatural action.

I can even see how someone might defend this from the meaning of the word "form" in Genesis 2:7—since in Jeremiah 1:5 the same word is used for the natural process of child development in the womb: "before I *formed* you in the womb I knew you." J. Oliver Buswell—a very conservative Presbyterian—was right when he wrote,

> The Hebrew word means to form, but gives no specifications as to the process by which the forming was accomplished. The result is all that is specified.

I said that I can commend this approach, and that I can see how one might defend it; but I didn't say I agree with it. I am inclined to take the "dust" of Genesis 2:7 in its ordinary sense of "loose soil," that is, it wasn't a living animal when God started to form it into the first man. I think this makes the best sense in view of the way "the man *became* a living creature" after the operation—that is, he wasn't a *modified* living creature. So: this alternate view does justice to the supernatural origin of man; but, taking one thing with another, I find it easier to believe that Adam was a fresh creation rather than an upgrade of an existing model.

Therefore, when the National Association of Biology Teachers says that "evolutionary theory . . . is necessarily silent on religion and neither refutes nor supports the existence of a deity or deities," they are on shaky ground. If our religion strictly follows the complementarity model for the relationship of faith and science, as we discussed earlier, then the NABT may be right; but as soon as our faith claims that the Bible has the right to speak about matters of history (including our origin), or about the special status of mankind, then it is at odds with "evolutionary theory" as it is usually taught—namely, with neo-Darwinism.

Is Neo-Darwinism Credible?

Many sensitive Christians will tremble at my last sentence—if our faith is at odds with science, they may say, then our faith is in trouble: it must adapt or die. But really, our faith is not in conflict with *science*, but with a particular set of beliefs held by many in *one particular science*. So the question is, Does that set of beliefs derive from *good scientific practice*? I want to summarize why I think the answer is no.

To begin with, we have to make a distinction between two reasons I might not hold some belief. In the first case, I might not believe something if it's "not proven"—that is, even if I don't know that it's false, I don't have grounds for saying it's true. In the second case, I might not believe something because I think it's false.

Consider this example. In the Winnie-the-Pooh story "In Which Pooh and Piglet Go Hunting and Nearly Catch a Woozle," Piglet joins Pooh on a winter day as Pooh is following some tracks in the snow. Pooh does not know what made them, but believes that some animal did it. As they follow the tracks, Piglet suggests that they come from a woozle; and Pooh replies,

> "It may be. Sometimes it is, and sometimes it isn't. You never can tell with paw-marks."

As they continue the search they find that another set of tracks has joined the first one, so they conclude that another woozle (or whatever it is) has joined the first. As it turns out, they are actually following their own tracks around a clump of trees without knowing it; and Piglet gets more and more nervous about meeting a woozle, and eventually runs home. Piglet took his own first suggestion seriously, and acted as if it were the truth—whereas it was actually *not proven* (and wouldn't have been until they met either the woozle or some indisputable sign of him). Under such circumstances—when the belief that a woozle had made the tracks was not proven—Pooh's "sometimes it is, sometimes it isn't—you never can tell with paw-marks" was more rational than Piglet's fear. After Piglet ran away, however, Pooh hears from Christopher Robin, who was sitting on a tree branch and saw everything, the story of how he and Piglet had circled the clump of trees. Then Pooh fitted his paw into one of the tracks, and saw that they were his own, just as Christopher Robin said. He now had reason to think that the belief that a woozle had made the tracks was false:

> "I have been Foolish and Deluded," said he, "and I am a Bear of No Brain at All."

Well, yes, but at least he changed his mind when he saw that his earlier belief was shown to be false. So he was rational in this case, as well.

Let us grant that it is possible that some parts of neo-Darwinism are right—say, that animals today are descended from animals that lived long ago, and that there has been some process of evolutionary change. The question is, however, Is the grand theory as a whole worth believing? Well, if it depends on claims that haven't been proven, we can say that it hasn't been proven true. And if it depends on things that are likely to be false, then we can say that the theory is likely to be false.

What, then, is the evidence that is supposed to prove that neo-Darwinism is the true story of the history of life on earth? The basic lines of evidence for this theory are:

(1) the fossil record shows that living things today are the products of descent with modification from earlier living things;

(2) all living things use DNA to encode their characteristics and to pass them on to their offspring;

(3) there are documented cases of descent with modification in the natural world.

In addition to these empirical arguments, there is also the feeling that neo-Darwinism can explain so much about the world, and about us. It is this feeling of intellectual satisfaction that is one of the chief selling points of the theory. The last paragraph of Darwin's *Origin* conveys this in language that approaches poetry:

> It is interesting to contemplate a tangled bank, clothed with many plants of many kinds, with birds singing on the bushes, with various insects flitting about, and with worms crawling through the damp earth, and to reflect that these elaborately constructed forms, so different from each other, and dependent upon each other in so complex a manner, have all been produced by laws acting around us. These laws, taken in the largest sense, being Growth with Reproduction; Inheritance which is almost implied by reproduction; Variability from the indirect and direct action of the conditions of life, and from use and disuse: a Ratio of Increase so high as to lead to a Struggle for Life, and as a consequence to Natural Selection, entailing Divergence of Character and the Extinction of less improved forms. Thus, from the war of nature, from famine and death, the most exalted object which we are capable of conceiving, namely the production of higher animals, directly follows. *There is grandeur in this view of life, with its several powers, having been originally breathed by the Creator into a few forms or into one;* and that, whilst this planet has gone cycling on according to the fixed law of gravity, *from so simple a beginning endless forms most beautiful and most wonderful have been, and are being, evolved.*

One of the reigning ideas of the nineteenth century was the sense of history—namely that things have changed over time. And Darwin's theory (or the neo-Darwinian version) claims to provide what the National Association of Biology Teachers calls "a rational, coherent and scientific account of the taxonomic history and diversity of organisms"—namely, by saying that everything we now see is the product of these basic laws that Darwin identified. That is, it goes beyond the description that a leading textbook on genetics gives:

> In the remote past, a few very simple forms existed, and these have become transformed and differentiated into the many, highly organized and diverse forms we observe today.

Neo-Darwinism claims to have discovered, not just *that* "these have transformed and differentiated," but *how* they did so: namely by "an unpredictable and natural process of temporal descent with genetic modification that is affected by natural selection, chance, historical contingencies and changing environments," in the words of the NABT.

We must be clear on this: if you believe that God "controlled" the process of evolution, you need to define "controlled." Do you mean that he made sure it led to the results he intended? How did he "make sure"? If you mean that he determined the laws by which the natural process operated, and preserved them in ordinary providence *all the way,* then you can be called a "theistic neo-Darwinist." But if by "controlled" you mean that God *added* anything to the natural process—which would amount to supernatural actions—whether at the beginning to get the ball rolling by creating life, or along the way, say by adapting an ape's body to be the vehicle of a human soul, then even if you call yourself a "theistic evolutionist" you don't hold to the "official" version of the story. In fact, if you're in this second category, then you're on the same side of a gaping philosophical chasm as I am.

You probably know that one of the things that makes neo-Darwinism troublesome to many religious people is precisely its claim to explain so much. You find Richard Dawkins—perhaps the world's most visible promoter of "Darwinism-as-atheistic-theory-of-everything"—saying that "Biology is the study of complicated things that give the appearance of having been designed for a purpose," and implying that a scientific biologist will remove that "appearance" of design and purpose by giving a thoroughly natural explanation for it all. He goes on to say,

> Although atheism might have been *logically* tenable before Darwin, Darwin made it possible to be an intellectually fulfilled atheist.

This is because the theory provides a law-based mechanism by which everything is the way that it is—there is no longer any reasonable or scientific basis for bringing God in to explain anything.

Theistic neo-Darwinists object to the way people like Dawkins have used a theory in science to disprove religion—they think that it is just wrong to bring the two realms into conflict, since they are complementary in their scopes. I have already commented on this point at the end of the last section, so I'll say no more on it.

Let me start, then, with examples of neo-Darwinism being "not proven." This is important, because we often read that, since neo-Darwinism is "science," then schools should not subject it to critique. But if the theory doesn't have the evidence to prove that it's true, then it doesn't have the right to such a privileged position.

Let's take the list of evidences I mentioned earlier, and start with the claim that the fossil record shows that living things today are the products of descent with modification from earlier living things. Now I am not a paleontologist (that's what people who study fossils are called), so I don't intend to dispute much about the fossil record. But if my experience with other kinds of reasoning backward from evidence that doesn't tell us how it got there is any guide, then I don't see how we can say that the fossil record actually *shows* this in a way that leaves no room for doubt. We have the remains of ancient animals from different times, and someone has to draw the line that connects the dots—and to do that, he has to know that the line belongs there. But supposing we say that these lines "work"—what do we mean by that? We would have to mean that they give us a reasonable set of links.

But neo-Darwinism claims more than that you can draw the lines: it claims that the animals traveled along those lines by purely natural processes. Suppose, for example, you could show that the ancient fossil bird *Archaeopteryx* really did descend from reptiles, and that this really does show that birds developed from reptiles. To show that neo-Darwinism is true, though, you have to show that this development took place entirely without any divine interference. That's a pretty tall order.

Further, you have to do this all over the shop. You can't just show that dogs and cats descended from an ancient proto-carnivore, and that snakes descended from legged reptiles, and so on; you have to show that vertebrates—creatures with a spinal cord—descended from invertebrates; and you have to show that it all took place entirely by natural processes.

That is, you have to do more than just connect the dots. But at least you have to be able to draw the connecting lines; and that raises the question, can you? George Gaylord Simpson (1902–1984), a leading evolutionary biologist, pointed out that one of the most striking features of the fossil record is that most new kinds of organisms appear abruptly:

> They are not, as a rule, led up to by a sequence of almost imperceptibly changing forerunners such as Darwin believed should be usual in evolution. A great many sequences of two or a few temporally intergrading species are known, but even at this level most species appear without known immediate ancestors, and really long, perfectly complete sequences of numerous species are exceedingly rare. Sequences of genera immediately successive or nearly so at that level (not necessarily from one genus to the next), are more common and may be longer than known sequences of species. But the appearance of a new genus in the record is usually more abrupt than the appearance of a new species; the gaps involved are generally larger, that is, when a new genus appears in the record it is usually well separated morphologically from the most nearly similar other known genera. This phenomenon becomes more universal and more intense as the hierarchy of categories is ascended. Gaps among known species are sporadic and often small. Gaps among known orders, classes, and phyla are systematic and almost always large.

Now, don't hear what I'm *not* saying. It is quite possible that the lines that paleontologists draw do in fact represent lines of descent; and it is also quite possible that, say, we have a good story from *Eohippus* to the modern horse. It is possible that further work will uncover more fossils that fill in some of the blanks. When I looked at the skeleton of a seal in a museum in Seaside, Oregon, not long ago, I found it easy to believe that it had developed from a land-dwelling carnivore. So I am not saying that I disbelieve what the paleontologists tell us about their fossils.

What I am saying is, "So what?" We're not asking whether the fossils support *some* kind of biological evolution—I'm willing to allow that they do; we're asking whether they prove neo-Darwinism (or any other sort of evolution-as-the-big-picture). And really, how *can* they? At best we can say that they are compatible with that theory; but then again, they're compatible with other theories as well. But if that's how it is, then we can't say that they prove neo-Darwinism; in other words, the fossils leave the theory in the category of "not proven."

Actually, though, neo-Darwinism may be in worse shape than just "not proven" when it comes to the fossil record. There are serious difficulties in crossing some of the gaps that standard evolutionary theory says have been crossed: for example, to get from a reptile to a bird you need to develop a scale into a feather; to get from an amphibian to a reptile you need to develop a different kind of egg; to get from a fish to an amphibian you need to develop a whole new kind of lung. Remember that Darwin had said, regarding the transition from insectivore to flying lemur (*Galeopithecus*), "there is no difficulty in supposing that such links formerly existed." Well, being able to suppose they existed is different from saying that they actually did; and then the question is, did Darwin (or neo-Darwinists) underestimate the difficulty in supposing such links?

Let's move on to the second line of evidence, namely the way that all living things use DNA to encode their characteristics and to pass them on to their offspring. Now in itself, this could imply that God used a good idea over and over again—especially since he intended his creatures to reproduce. (All engineers that I have talked with can understand this—in fact they warm to it.) Or it could imply that—in Darwin's scenario—the several forms into which the Creator breathed life at the first were all made on similar plans. Or it could imply that life originated only once—whether by special action of God or by the course of nature—and that everything else descends from that first life form. In other words, this feature, too, does not decide between several possible theories.

Usually, though, when this is given as evidence for neo-Darwinism, the idea is that we now have a plausible mechanism for descent with modification: that is, through natural selection working on small genetic changes. The genetic changes come either from a mutation in the DNA—that is, somehow the information in a stretch of DNA gets modified, and therefore that bit of DNA now tells the cell to make a different protein—or else from recombination—that is, somehow a stretch of DNA gets spliced into a different place than where it belongs. These processes do in fact occur and produce changes in the offspring—many small, others catastrophic. Therefore, we are told, evolution proceeds by building on countless changes in DNA: that tiny percentage that leads to more successful reproduction is passed on to the offspring, and the rest are weeded out.

The trouble with this, again, is that it does not show *that* this is the way it happened; it allows us to say that we can imagine a scenario by which it happened. That is, it doesn't *prove* that neo-Darwinism is the true story. The evidence may be compatible with neo-Darwinism, but we can hardly say that it *supports* the theory until we can show just how the whole process worked without any divine tinkering with the DNA.

The basis of life in DNA is also given as evidence for the way life originated. Here is what science popularizers Robert Hazen and James Trefil write in their book *Science Matters:*

> The molecular makeup of life provides compelling evidence for evolution from one single cell. All life is built from the same small subset of organic molecules. All of earth's living things, from slime mold to tea roses to humpback whales, have the exact same DNA-based genetic code, with the molecules following right-handed (never left-handed) spirals. Of all the hundreds of different possible amino acids, only twenty different types form all proteins in every organism. It is reasonable to argue that some or all of these chemical oddities arose in the first cell and have been locked in ever since. If more than one cell had arisen independently, then life would surely possess more than one chemical vocabulary.

So, they say, the whole show started with one cell (as Darwin had hoped: "into a few forms, *or into one*"), and DNA shows this. But how did it happen? Hazen and Trefil speak honestly for everyone when they write,

> We do not know how life arose from the primordial soup. This remains the greatest gap in our knowledge of the development of life. Many scientists believe that millions of years of random mixing and shuffling of molecules culminated in the appearance of one living cell—an object that could consume surrounding chemicals to make exact copies of itself. We can't say for sure when that pivotal event occurred, but some of the earth's oldest rocks, about 3.6 billion years old, show evidence of one-celled life. Suddenly it was a whole new ball game on planet earth.

Here is a place where neo-Darwinism really fails to account for the evidence. Everyone agrees on how DNA functions: it is a system for coding and storing information (the information is the specific makeup of proteins that the cell manufactures), as well as for retrieving that information and sending it to the protein-making factories in the cell. But if what it stores is information, then the message cannot itself be a property of the system. For example, the English behind the words on this page doesn't come from the paper and ink that carry the words—it comes from me, and not from the paper. In the same way, the information doesn't come from the DNA or the chemicals that make it up—and this means that something imposed the information on the DNA. And a natural process can't do that, because a natural process just works by the properties of the things involved, and information *transcends* these properties.

To say, then, that a natural process produced an information system is a contradiction in terms, which means it's nonsense. And not even the theistic neo-Darwinist, who says that God made the natural process so that it would produce the information system (after all, he says, God can do anything he wants, can't he?), has any advantage—because the doctrine of God's omnipotence means that God can do everything he *wants* to do. God cannot make two plus two equal five. As C. S. Lewis put it so well,

> Omnipotence means power to do all that is intrinsically possible, not to do the intrinsically impossible. . . . Meaningless combinations of words do not suddenly acquire meaning simply because we prefix to them the two other words 'God can.' It remains true that all *things* are possible with God: the intrinsic impossibilities are not things but nonentities.

Nature—even Nature under God—is not enough to get the ball of life rolling.

The third line of evidence for neo-Darwinism is that there are documented cases of descent with modification in the natural world. Darwin used the example of selective breeding of domestic animals—such as pigeons—to show how a principle of selection can lead to some trait or other becoming common in a population.

A famous example comes from what are called "Darwin's finches," a group of finch species in the Galápagos Islands (in the Pacific Ocean, about six hundred miles west of South America; Darwin visited there in 1835). Peter and Rosemary Grant studied the finches on one of the islands in the 1970s and found that changing conditions, such as a drought, could lead to differing sizes of beaks being predominant. That is, apparently natural selection favored birds with some characteristics over others. Over time, they suppose, you can get new species of finches—solely by natural selection operating on variations in the population.

Now, let us suppose for the moment that this account is true. (There are, to be sure, some difficulties—for example, when the conditions became rainier, the beak sizes returned to their earlier range. But never mind that for now.) What does it tell us? That it is possible to imagine a scenario in which small changes pile up, and new species arise from this piling up. Is this enough to support the evolution-as-the-big-picture story of neo-Darwinism? No, it is not. These changes can be called "micro-evolution," that is, variations within a basic type. Neo-Darwinism needs these micro-evolutionary changes to build up so that they produce major innovations—say, for the offspring of an invertebrate to develop a spinal cord—that is, to yield "macro-evolution."

And here is where the evidence fails to *prove* neo-Darwinism—in fact, it leaves a lot of room for doubting the neo-Darwinist story. Surely the theorists owe it to us, not simply to assure us that such things *can* happen, but to show us that they *have* happened? But this takes us back to the fossil record and its imperfections.

In sum, then, we have plenty of room to say that neo-Darwinism is in the category of "not proven." Much of what the advocates offer as proof is really scenarios: they want us to imagine a chain of events that, they say, *could* have happened (and therefore *must* have happened?) to yield what we see today. But you have to do some serious work to justify the move from "I can imagine this having happened" to "this could possibly have happened"—let alone to "this is likely to have happened." One reason why I called Darwin "skillful in his rhetoric" is that I think he recognized this problem; and he dealt with it by dropping a lot of phrases like "there is no difficulty in supposing that such links formerly existed," and "how a nerve comes to be sensitive to light, hardly concerns us more than how life itself originated." He said that he could envision such a sequence; and he shifted the burden of proof to those who would doubt it. That's a clever move, and it worked.

But we can go further than simply saying that the theory isn't (yet) proven. We can identify some places where it must be false. I have already mentioned the origin of life—this is not a part of *Darwinism,* as I have said, but it is a feature of *neo-Darwinism.* Natural processes are not enough to explain where life came from. The other crucial place where neo-Darwinism runs into trouble is the origin of mankind. That is, the properties of mankind are such that no amount of piled-up changes under purely *natural* processes will be good enough to explain where those properties came from.

Those properties include the things that I called the (wide-sense) image of God. Back in chapter 8, I argued that "man, unlike the other animals, has the ability to reason, a will to choose what pleases him, language, a moral pointer, the ability to make and enjoy beauty, and the capacity to enter into relationships governed by love and commitment."

Let me take just a couple of these human properties. For instance, when you reason, you are taking part in something that transcends your bodily life—and if you're not, then you have no reason to call it reasoning. As the philosopher Paul Helm put it,

> If I am physically determined to think as I do, if these physical conditions are sufficient for me to have a certain belief, then the relation between that belief and any evidence there may be for it is purely coincidental.

The ability to reason—about truth and moral goodness—and to act on that reasoning comes from something that has been *added* to nature. We do not find it in the other animals; they are "creatures of instinct, helpless to change their destinies."

Consider as well the human capacity for language. If someone had taken my blonde-haired and blue-eyed son away from me before he was three, and raised him in the middle of Africa, he would have grown up speaking the local language *as his mother tongue*—and virtually no English at all. This is because all human languages share certain features in common, and the human brain is uniquely tuned to learn one or more of them. I didn't really have to teach my children to speak English—the only way I could have prevented them from learning it would have been to keep them away from all English-speaking company. Their brain mechanism was such that day-to-day exposure was all they needed.

Compare that to any animal you like, no matter how intelligent. We hear of gorillas and chimps being taught sign language; but the reports are exaggerated. The animals' handlers think they've learned language, but linguists typically don't agree. For example, John Maynard Smith wrote the first edition of his classic *The Theory of Evolution* in 1958, and the third edition came out in 1975. He wrote in the final chapter,

> Since the chimpanzee Washoe has been taught to use deaf-and-dumb sign language, it is no longer possible to assert that there is some peculiar feature of human language forever inaccessible to animals—not that this will stop some people asserting it.

Then in 1993 Cambridge University Press published the book in its *Canto* series, with the 1975 text unchanged but with a special preface from the author. There he wrote,

> I have been persuaded by my colleagues in linguistics that there really is something peculiar about the human capacity to talk, and that there is a deep difference between the proto-language spoken by the chimpanzee Washoe, and by very young children, and the language of adult humans. The difference lies in grammar.

That difference—grammar—is also what makes the difference between the chimp and those young children: the children have the built-in equipment to learn the grammar of their surroundings, while the chimps do not.

In other words, to call the human capacities of reason and language an extension of what we find elsewhere in the animal world—which is what you must do if you're a neo-Darwinian—is to make an incredibly big mistake.

The National Science Teachers Association (NSTA) declares,

> There is no longer a debate among scientists over whether evolution has taken place. There is considerable debate over how evolution has taken place.

This declaration suffers from several problems: to begin with, it comes hard on the heels of two paragraphs that describe "evolution in the broadest sense"—and then proceeds to claim that *biological* evolution-as-the-big-picture is on the same sure footing as the history of the cosmos and the geological history of the earth. In other words, they seem to be confusing different senses of the word "evolution," and acting as if showing that the universe has changed over time (that is, using what I called the neutral sense of evolution) is the same as showing that biological evolution-as-the-big-picture is also true. This is bad logic coupled with sloppy use of terms.

The second problem is that it implies that because scientists no longer debate something, neither should we doubt it if we want to be rational people. But the question must be, *why* do they no longer debate it? Have they followed the rules of sound thinking? It looks to me like they have not. In fact, neo-Darwinism is not just a statement about change over time; it includes the claim that natural processes acting alone are enough to produce everything we see. When the NSTA tells us that "evolution, as in any aspect of science, is continually open to and subject to experimentation and questioning," they *don't* mean that this fundamental commitment to a natural-process-only kind of explanation is open to questioning. In other words, this commitment is a philosophical *pre*commitment—and not an inference from the data of the sciences.

EVOLUTION AND "PROGRESS"

Before we finish, I should say a few words about a common misunderstanding of the modern theory of evolution, namely that it necessarily means progress from simple to complex. That is, I want to distinguish "evolution"—a theory in biology—from "evolutionism"—a philosophical theory about progress.

The confusion between the two is no surprise. The English word "evolution" comes from a Latin word meaning "to unfold," and in the nineteenth century meant "progressive development" (it had earlier been used of the way an embryo develops). Although Darwin didn't use this term, he certainly held to a view of progressive development, as he says at the end of the *Origin:*

> And as natural selection works solely by and for the good of each being, all corporeal and mental endowments *will tend to progress toward perfection.*

But modern neo-Darwinism rejects this progressivism. For example, J. B. S. Haldane, one of the founders of the neo-Darwinian synthesis, wrote:

> We are therefore inclined to regard progress as the rule in evolution. Actually it is the exception, and for every case of it there are ten of degeneration.

And the NABT states that natural selection "has no specific direction or goal, including survival of a species."

Nevertheless, in popular speech we will continue to encounter the "progressive" view along with the biological theory. C. S. Lewis called it a "myth"—a great story that fires the imagination and puts life into perspective. This view of progress came earlier in the nineteenth century than the biological theory of Darwin—perhaps the view made the biological theory more credible. That does not say the theory is untrue (though I have given reasons to say as much in the rest of this chapter). At any rate it explains why some people will hold on to the theory: as Lewis put it,

> In the popular mind the word 'Evolution' conjures up a picture of things moving 'onwards and upwards', and of nothing else whatsoever. And it might have been predicted that it would do so. Already, before science had spoken [that is, before 1859], the mythical imagination knew the kind of 'Evolution' it wanted. It wanted the Keatian [from John Keats, 1795–1821, an English poet] and Wagnerian [Richard Wagner, 1813–1883, a German composer] kind: the gods superseding the Titans, and the young, joyous, amorous Siegfried superseding the care-worn, anxious, treaty-entangled Wotan. *If science offers any instances to satisfy that demand, they will be eagerly accepted. If it offers any instances that frustrate it, they will simply be ignored.*

SUMMARY

So where are we at this point? I have argued that traditional Christian faith opposes, not *all* ideas of evolution, but biological evolution-as-the-big-picture, with neo-Darwinism as its best representative. The reason my faith opposes it is that my faith leads me to believe that life and mankind—to mention the two most solid examples—result from special or supernatural works of God; while on the other hand, neo-Darwinism claims to have found an unbroken pathway from molecules to mankind, along strictly natural lines. Not only do these two ways of thinking make conflicting claims, but also neo-Darwinism stems from a philosophical commitment to a naturalistic view of the world, which excludes what has been called "design." (I will take up this last point in more detail in the next chapter.)

Sometimes people want to contrast faith and reason or faith and science, as we've seen before: but genuine Christian faith makes us want to be true to reason, and to reason well in science. It's not my faith that denies reason and that reasons poorly from the world: it's neo-Darwinism. The reason I don't believe the neo-Darwinian story, then, is not just because of my Christian commitment: it's also because my Christian commitment makes me want to do the best I can in thinking about the world.

At this point a common reply is to say, "Well, the theory might have some of the problems you say it does, but since you're offering nothing in its place I have every right to stick with it." But this is not at all a reasonable way to proceed. To begin with, I will offer an alternative (as discussed below). But even if I weren't—or if my alternative weren't good enough—that is not a good reason for holding on to a defective theory. That's like saying, "Having a bad theory is better than having no theory at all"—which is silly, because holding fast to a bad theory closes the mind. Whatever happened to saying, "I don't know how this came about"?

Many Christians, in seeing the clash between their faith and neo-Darwinism, have supposed that therefore their faith endorses a kind of "creation science." I won't use that term, since it's already taken: most people take it to mean science whose purpose is to show that the earth is young (as their interpretation of Genesis leads them to believe), and that the amount of biological evolution is quite small.

This kind of project depends entirely upon their intention to be true to what they think is the meaning of the Bible, and for that I commend them. I have interviewed a number of creation scientists, and none of them came to his view by way of the physical evidence—in fact, they would say that their biblical insight has given them the right perspective for looking at the evidence.

I have given you my reasons for not following this take on Genesis, and for not being bothered by biological evolution as such (just so long as it's not the whole story). So I do not urge you to support "creation science," but something different: something that has been called "intelligent design." That will be the topic of the following chapter.

17

Is Intelligent Design a Dumb Idea?

Answers to Objections

I CLOSED THE PREVIOUS chapter by telling you that I favor "intelligent design" over neo-Darwinism (including its Christian forms), as well as over what has traditionally been called "creation science." Now I want to describe just what this approach actually is—and what it is *not,* as well—and see how it stacks up against the most important objections to it.

Such American organizations as the National Association of Biology Teachers, the National Science Teachers Association, and the National Academy of Sciences, which are concerned with the teaching of science in public schools, have warned us not to be taken in by what they call "creationism" of any sort—whether it's the young earth kind, or the more sophisticated intelligent design movement. They can draw on an impressive array of philosophers, scientists, and even theologians, to support this warning. They also believe they have several key court decisions on their side.

Who is involved in this new movement in favor of intelligent design? As a movement it probably got its big start in 1984, when Charles Thaxton, Walter Bradley, and Roger Olsen published *The Mystery of Life's Origin: Reassessing Current Theories.* These three—competent scientists who accept an old earth—reviewed the state of origin-of-life biology and concluded that the special work of a Creator was the best explanation for what we know. In 1986 an Australian molecular biologist, Michael Denton (who is not a Christian), published *Evolution: A Theory in Crisis,* which surveyed Darwinism and neo-Darwinism and argued that the evidence actually does not support them. Then in 1991 Phillip Johnson, a professor of law at the University of California at Berkeley, published *Darwin on Trial,* in which he assessed the evidence for Darwinism in the light of the rules for sound arguments. Johnson concluded that the reason that so many scientists hold to

Darwinism is not the force of the evidence but the philosophical assumptions they make about science and about the world—namely that all scientific explanations must involve natural causes only, and that we can find such natural explanations for everything we study. Johnson has succeeded in collecting around him an array of people who are very bright, well-educated, independent-minded, articulate, and unafraid to speak up to challenge the reigning views. These include Michael Behe, a biochemist at Lehigh University, whose 1996 *Darwin's Black Box: The Biochemical Challenge to Evolution* made a big splash—big enough, anyhow, to get negative reviews in leading scientific journals, and to get Behe on the public television talk show circuit. Other prominent members of the movement are equally impressive: for example, William Dembski (a Ph.D. in mathematics and one in philosophy), Stephen Meyer (a Ph.D. in philosophy of science), Paul Nelson (a Ph.D. in philosophy of biology), and Jonathan Wells (a Ph.D. in developmental biology).

The opponents of intelligent design are afraid it will come to be treated as a valid part of science, and they're convinced that it doesn't deserve such a privileged place. They think that to accept intelligent design would be a dumb move on our part, because it really is a dumb idea.

It doesn't look like the intelligent design people will be easy to stop—they're speaking at major international conferences, writing books, debating the best spokesmen for Darwinism, and even getting featured in establishment newspapers like the *New York Times* and the *Los Angeles Times*.

Advocates of neo-Darwinism want to paint the intelligent design movement as "anti-evolution"—but that is a drastically over-simplified picture. Rather, the movement is out to challenge the worldview of naturalism, which it sees as dominating the sciences, and through the sciences, dominating the culture. (This, by the way, is why intelligent design is not limited to biology.) Let's see if we can first understand what its advocates mean by "design," and then we'll go on to look at the arguments against their view.

WHAT IS "INTELLIGENT DESIGN"?

I hope you have had the thrill of looking at a living creature—whether it's yourself or a friend, or your dog or cat or goldfish, or the birds and flowers in your backyard—and feeling a sense of awe and admiration. Just watch how a big cat (or even a house cat) moves when it's after its prey; watch a bird flap its wings and take off, or a hawk glide as it catches an updraft. Look at the patterns in a spiderweb, or the life cycle of the cicada.

Mixed in with that awe is curiosity: how come they work that way? They act as if someone *designed* them so to act. And what of humans? Where do we get these mysterious capabilities for reason, for speech, for variety of music, and even the curiosity we have about the world around us?

We normally consider science to be a valid tool for answering questions like this. (I for one think that science is at its best when it's the search for truth.) Darwinism (and neo-Darwinism) is one way of answering the questions, by saying that they are all the products of natural processes. Most of the support for neo-Darwinism today comes with a claim about what valid science is: namely, that it must appeal only to natural causes, and that it assumes an unbroken chain of natural causes from beginning to end.

Intelligent design theory is another way of answering these questions: it says, at its simplest, that it is legitimate to have as a part of our tool-kit for scientific explanations of things we meet in the natural world, the option to say that they were "designed."

Now it's very important to be clear just what we mean by that. There are at least two different kinds of design, and we must be careful to keep them apart.

The first kind of design is what we can call *design of properties*—that is, the material was produced with certain properties that suit some purpose. For example, we produce steel from iron, so that it has such properties as hardness and resistance to rust. We produce plastics so that they are light in weight, or can be molded into shapes, and so on.

When people use the anthropic principle that we discussed at the end of chapter 15, they are in effect saying that the universe shows evidence that God designed it to have the properties that it does, so that it would support our life here on earth. You can find so many statements from cosmologists about this that we don't really have to think that this is all that controversial. If someone holds to theistic evolution (in its fullest sense, anyhow), he thinks that God also designed the world to have the properties it would need in order for life to begin and to develop as it has done.

Adherents of intelligent design of course agree with this; but they go on to add another kind of design, which I will call *imposed design:* this is what happens when you impose a structure on some object (or on a collection of objects) for some purpose; but the structure and the purpose don't come from the properties of the objects—instead they make use of those properties.

A good example of "imposed design" would be the chair you're sitting on: the wood, metal, and plastic didn't arrange themselves, someone *imposed* the arrangement on them, for a reason (so that you could sit on it, I suppose).

Another example is Stonehenge: you know those stones didn't arrange themselves, someone *imposed* that structure on them (for who knows what purpose). This example shows that we don't have to know the purpose in order to see the imposed design—in fact, the designed thing doesn't even have to be in a state of good repair! Of course, once we decide that design has been imposed, we wonder what for—and we wonder who did it.

The intelligent design movement has argued that the world of biology presents us with cases of imposed design, and that good science ought to be free to talk about them. For example, Michael Behe, in *Darwin's Black Box,* wrote about what he called "irreducible complexity": that is, we find complex systems in the biological world that need a minimum number of working parts already in place before the whole system works. One of his favorite examples is the flagellum (a whip-like tail) that certain bacteria use for swimming around: it's just like a rotary engine, and has a paddle, a rotor, and a motor. Each of these must be in place and doing its part for the system to have any function at all. This presents a serious problem if you try to explain the origin of the flagellum in Darwinist terms, namely by the gradual development of the individual parts, perhaps for some other purposes, which then led to the lucky combination that we find now. Behe argues that, for some systems in the cell, the better explanation for how they got there is that some designer imposed the structure. (As a scientist, Behe does not go on to claim that the designer must be God—though as a Christian who has other reasons for his faith, he of course believes that God is ultimately responsible for the design.)

Another instance of imposed design would be the very origin of life itself, as I discussed in the previous chapter. Also, the way that DNA works, as a message-bearing medium (also discussed in the previous chapter), can be called the product of design: indeed, if it *does* carry a message, then the message cannot be the product of the chemicals that make up the DNA, or else it is not a message at all. Another area where design might be involved would be where the diversity of life-forms (say, the phyla) comes from; and still another would be the origin of human beings with their unique abilities for reason, language, and morality.

All these examples are opposed to evolution-as-the-big-picture, as the National Association of Biology Teachers (NABT) described it: "an unpredictable and natural process of temporal descent with genetic modification that is affected by natural selection, chance, historical contingencies and changing environments." It is also opposed to the theistic version of the theory that Christian physicist Howard Van Till argues for: a "historical scenario that proceeds from molecules to mankind along a continuous pathway of natural phenomena."

Intelligent design as a program, however, takes no position on whether all living things come from a single ancestor—although many of those who favor this kind of design doubt that natural processes alone, once life got started, are enough to explain *everything.* The intelligent design movement also takes no position on the age of the earth, or on how one should apply Genesis (or any religious text) to science. In fact, the intelligent design movement is not explicitly Christian.

To identify a case of imposed design, you have to find a gap between what we see and the processes we know about that might have produced what we see, and you have to show that natural processes alone are not enough to bridge the gap. That is, there is a gap between the arrangement of the big stones in Stonehenge, and the properties of the stones and their environment (such as wind, rain, and earthquakes). There is a gap between the message-bearing function of DNA and the properties of the chemicals that make it up. There is a gap between human capacities for reason, language, and morality, and what we find in every other animal. From these gaps we conclude that it took some kind of special action, done by an agent, to bridge the gaps.

What Would Make Intelligent Design a "Dumb Idea"?

Well, if that's what intelligent design is, what would make it a dumb idea? I have culled a fair number of objections from many sources, and grouped them into the broad areas of theology, philosophy of science, and biological research itself. In this section I'll present them, and in the next I'll see what reply we might make to the objections.

(a) Theological Objections to Intelligent Design

It is just repackaged creation science. The first theological objection is that intelligent design is just repackaged "creation science" (which means young earth creationism and biblical literalism).

You can find plenty of examples of this objection, but I'll take just a few. For example, consider what the NABT says in its "Statement on Teaching Evolution":

> Whether called "creation science," "scientific creationism," "intelligent-design theory," "young-earth theory" or some other synonym, creation beliefs have no place in the science classroom.

The National Science Teachers Association (NSTA) has a similar list of "synonyms," and the National Academy of Sciences (NAS) says

> In this booklet both these "Young Earth" and "Old Earth" views are referred to as "creationism" or "special creation"

—even though the booklet only addresses the young earth variety! All of these organizations mention various court cases that have ruled against the teaching of creationism in public schools, as a further reason why intelligent design has no place in a science classroom.

It's NOT young earth creationism! The next theological objection is just the opposite: intelligent design is *not* young earth creationism. This can come from two sides. Those who oppose any idea of creation (or at least of allowing it to have a place in science) will say, "Intelligent design is inconsistent. Why don't they go all the way and affirm a literal reading of Genesis?"

On the other hand, people who favor young earth creationism as the only allowable approach will also oppose intelligent design, because it doesn't take a stand on the age of the earth. In their view there's no difference between the Big Bang theory and naturalistic evolution of life.

It shows a wrong view of God's action in the world. The third theological objection comes from those religious people who think that intelligent design, with its hunt for gaps, down-plays God's action in the ordinary or natural events of the world. Aren't those ordinary events just as much God's action as the extraordinary? And if we say that something is the product of "design," does that mean that other things were *not* designed? Doesn't Christian faith teach that God designed everything?

And if we say that there are gaps, haven't we really called God a slouch because he didn't make a world with all its capacities built into it?

It's just the "God-of-the-gaps." The fourth kind of theological objection comes from people who think that all the gaps in our scientific descriptions of things are simply due to ignorance; as science progresses, it will shrink those gaps. For example, once we didn't know what causes earthquakes, now we have a better idea. The "God-of-the-gaps" problem comes when we say that a gap must be due to some special activity of God, but then science comes to understand the natural mechanism and it seems that God has been crowded out of his universe. It's even worse if people base their belief in God on these gaps, which have now disappeared: have their reasons for believing in God also disappeared? Wouldn't it be better to take by faith that God is involved in *every* natural event, and leave the *how* to the scientists?

(b) Philosophical Objections to Intelligent Design

You shouldn't mix theology with science. A philosopher might suggest that a further problem comes when we try to make science conform to our theological beliefs. We often hear that theological and scientific explanations are supposed to be *complementary:* that is, they answer different questions (say, *why* versus *how*). For example, when my wife tells my daughter, "God will heal your cut," she is not trying to give an explanation that would compete with how a doctor would describe the cells and the way they repair themselves. Instead she's saying that all that work of the cell happens because it all comes from God and he governs it. Well, the philosopher might say, *all* scientific and theological statements must be complementary in the same way.

It's not "science." Another kind of philosophical objection is the view that intelligent design is simply outside the bounds of science. Science, we are told, must confine itself to natural explanations for everything it encounters. For example, this comes from the NSTA position paper:

> Science is a method of explaining the natural world. It assumes the universe operates according to regularities and that through systematic investigation we can understand these regularities. The methodology of science emphasizes the logical testing of alternate explanations of natural phenomena against empirical data. *Because science is limited to explaining the natural world by means of natural processes, it cannot use supernatural causation in its explanations.* Similarly, science is precluded from making statements about supernatural forces, because these are outside its provenance. Science has increased our knowledge because of this insistence on the search for natural causes.

The NAS booklets are very similar. In fact, the NAS quotes the biologist Ernst Mayr on the nature of science:

> Most scientists assume that there is historical and causal continuity among all phenomena in the material universe, and they include within the domain of legitimate scientific study everything known to exist or to happen in this universe.

That is to say, they take it as the definition of science that it offers natural-process-based explanations, and that it assumes that such explanations will apply to every event.

(c) Scientific Objections to Intelligent Design

It's not there to be found. Richard Dawkins is a professor at Oxford, and is probably the world's most visible advocate of neo-Darwinism, which he takes to be proof that reality is purely naturalistic. Here is how he defines biology in his book *The Blind Watchmaker:*

> Biology is the study of complicated things that give the appearance of having been designed for a purpose.

In other words, biologists have the task of removing the appearance of design and replacing it with a purely naturalistic explanation (which is what he thinks science is).

A variation on this objection comes from those who point to examples of what they call "bad" design. For example, the human eye has a blind spot—how could an intelligent designer have put such a thing together? And what of the panda's thumb, which is not a true thumb but is thought to be a bone that has been pressed into service for helping the panda strip the cover off of bamboo. Stephen Jay Gould wrote:

> If God had designed a beautiful machine to reflect his wisdom and power, surely he would not have used a collection of parts generally fashioned for other purposes. . . . Odd arrangements and funny solutions are the proof of evolution—paths that a sensible God would never tread but that a natural process, constrained by history, follows perforce.

Appeal to intelligent design stymies scientific progress. Those who voice this objection say that if you identify design you stop scientific research. Once you say that DNA is the product of design, you no longer ask for natural explanations of how it came to do that. Richard Dawkins is more colorful; he dismisses Behe's book by saying that the declaration of design is just the result of laziness. If Behe were a real scientist he'd get off his lazy behind and find the naturalistic explanations for the objects he studies! How, Dawkins wonders, can anyone so lazy get tenure at an American university?

A further criticism along these lines is that intelligent design proposes no new research projects—that is, to figure out the evolutionary story from mussel to man is exciting science because it's full of unsolved problems. How does accepting intelligent design further our study of the natural world?

ARE THESE OBJECTIONS VALID?

Well, now, these sound like pretty heavy objections. Let's assess them to see if they have any weight.

(a) Theological Objections

Let's take the theological objections first. First, the notion that intelligent design is just repackaged "young earth creationism" is laughable. The movement, as I said, has no position on the age of the earth. Since such leaders in the movement as Walter Bradley and Michael Behe have clearly stated that they think the geologists are right, it comes as a shock to find this objection repeated so often. I can't tell if those who identify the two approaches know that they're different or really think that they're the same. I think the plan is to label intelligent design as "creationist"—which they think is the same as "flat earther"—and to dismiss them without further ado.

In any case, to refer to court cases, such as the ones that overturned the "equal time for creation" laws in Arkansas and Louisiana, is a big mistake, since those laws dealt only with the demand for young earth creation science in the public schools. Intelligent design doesn't fit that category, and the American courts have made it clear that schools may allow critique of neo-Darwinism, so long as its basis is empirical science.

As to those who object that now we're *not* being literal, I would refer them to the discussion of Genesis and creation in this book. I have argued there that faithfulness to the Bible does not require that we believe the earth to be young. That doesn't stop the Bible from giving a true and historical account; it just tells us that the length of time is not on the list of things that Genesis is concerned about.

A more important objection is the one that says that intelligent design shows a wrong view of God's action in the world. Now, we've already seen that, biblically, it's quite proper to talk about natural processes, and that in situations like this—the ordinary function of God's creation—God's activity is that of maintaining the order of what he made. We should not appeal to any special divine action in a context like that.

However, there are also unique events that *do* involve special divine activity—things like the creation, the exodus from Egypt, the virgin birth of Jesus, and the resurrection of Jesus. In these events, the natural, created factors doing what God made them to do are not enough to explain what happened; God has added something to the mix. I do not expect ever to find that medical studies can show us how dead human bodies have in themselves the ability to rise from the grave; if it happened, it's because it was a *super*natural work. And this means that no one would ever be rationally justified in insisting that only natural factors are valid for describing what happened.

So the theological issue is not whether God may work in his world this way, but whether the Bible suggests that God did this at all; and, in my judgment, the Bible does represent him this way—as I've already discussed. Now, if you think about what's involved in the origin of life, you can see how this would be so. Biologists generally agree that what we have in DNA is *an information coding system*—it carries a message that tells a cell what kinds of proteins to make, and when. And for it to carry a message, the message cannot be an outgrowth of the medium—just as the message in this book doesn't arise from the ink and paper. To say that a *natural process*—which is governed by laws and the natural properties of the things involved—produced *an information system*—which is governed by something outside the components that make it up—is actually a contradiction in terms. And even God can't make that happen! As C. S. Lewis put it (in *The Problem of Pain*),

> Omnipotence means power to do all that is intrinsically possible, not to do the intrinsically impossible. . . . Meaningless combinations of words do not suddenly acquire meaning simply because we prefix to them the two other words 'God can.' It remains true that all *things* are possible with God: the intrinsic impossibilities are not things but nonentities.

On the other hand, we should confess that some people do in fact talk as if you can say "this is designed, and that isn't"—or as if you can only say that God is active when you identify supernatural events. The manner of speaking is sloppy—but it hardly breaches the basic position. It simply means we have to be more careful to be clear which sense of "design" we're using, and which kind of divine activity we're talking about.

This takes us to the objection that intelligent design is just "God-of-the-gaps": and instead of promoting religious belief, in the long run it undermines belief because it relies on gaps that science will eventually eliminate.

But to that I reply that there are gaps and then there are gaps. By that I mean, *some* gaps are due to our ignorance and *other* gaps are due to the properties of the things themselves. For example, suppose you don't know anything about geology, and you want to explain the 1980 Mount St. Helens eruption. Suppose that since you don't know the physical causes, you feel quite justified in saying "it must have been God's judgment on someone's sin." But then a geologist comes along and tells you about plates, and lava, and so on; he gives you the physical mechanism that brought about the eruption. Does this undermine faith? Does this sweep away the declaration of divine judgment? It does, to the extent that your faith depended on *not know-*

ing a physical mechanism. This was simply a gap due to ignorance, and an example of "God-of-the-gaps."

On the other hand, consider Stonehenge. I don't think anyone can credibly challenge the universal human reaction to that thing, that, "it was designed!" We recognize that there's a huge difference between, on the one hand, the complex arrangement of Stonehenge—which could not have come about by the properties of the rocks that make it up—and, on the other, the rock formations you find in Utah, which we are content to ascribe to the wind, weather, and geology. That is, we recognize that there's a gap between the natural properties of the rocks in Stonehenge (and its environment), and the highly structured configuration we find them in; and no new knowledge about rocks is going to change that. There is no question about whether we are rational when we declare, "Imposed design!" when we see Stonehenge. These gaps are detectable discontinuities, because they rely on the actual properties of the things involved.

Remember how, in the chapter on God's providence, we discussed the difference between the scientific study of normal operations and the scientific study of specific events. We expect that the normal operations of the things God made involve God upholding their natural properties and their interactions; and therefore we don't appeal to any special divine action for such things—not even for the things we don't understand. For example, if some new medical treatment accomplishes wonders, we shouldn't call it a "miracle" just because we're amazed at how well it works. In that chapter I also mentioned the newsletter from the local conservation center, which has an article about the flight of monarch butterflies to Mexico, and then back to Missouri. The author says,

> How this natural event came into being, how the monarchs know which way to go, and how these fragile creatures are able to survive this long journey remains largely a mystery to science. It can truly be thought of as miraculous.

The gaps in these two examples are gaps in our knowledge—we don't know how the things work. But since these are aspects of the proper functioning of the world God made, we should make no appeal to special divine action to explain how they work. To make such an appeal would be to commit the "God-of-the-gaps" mistake. (That doesn't mean that we can't find imposed design in how the things came to be, which is a historical question, as we'll see.)

In the study of historical events, we generally expect that most events in nature are the result of natural properties doing their thing. I'm limiting this to "nature"—meaning the world apart from God and man—at this point. In the study of human events, we have to be more careful (because in some events God is specifically pursuing man through supernatural means). So, for example, in considering why some species went extinct, or why an earthquake happened—or even why the tight end made that incredible catch—we'll talk about ecology, or plate tectonics, or wind speed and athletic ability, without looking for anything supernatural. Probably the gaps in our explanations are gaps in our knowledge.

But are *all* gaps simply gaps in our knowledge? How would you know that ahead of time? To say that they all *must* be gaps in our knowledge, and that there are no gaps due to properties, is itself a major fallacy: the only way to be sure is to go out and look. If we have an instance in which everything we know about the natural properties of the things involved tells us that they *could* not have produced the effect, then we have every right to consider whether the event might be supernatural. In particular, Christians have made much of the context of the event—namely a context in which God is pursuing relationship with his people—as a crucial factor as well. (That's why, say, the exodus from Egypt is supernatural while Hannibal's victories over the Romans in Italy need not be.)

The popular Christian writer G. K. Chesterton wrote the following:

> No philosopher denies that a mystery still attaches to the two great transitions: the origin of the universe itself and the origin of the principle of life itself. Most philosophers have the enlightenment to add that a third mystery attaches to the origin of man himself. In other words, a third bridge was built across a third abyss of the unthinkable when there came into the world what we call reason and what we call will.

These bridges across the abyss of the unthinkable involve gaps due to natural properties, not due to ignorance: they are candidates for *imposed design.* I don't see how there's any difficulty in detecting this design by scientific research. They further tie into God's purposes of pursuing relationship with mankind—making a place for man to live; life, so that living things could inhabit the place; and man himself with unique capacities.

(b) Philosophical Objections

Let's move on to the philosophical objections. The first was that all theological statements are *complementary* to scientific ones. The proper reply to this is, *Says who?* Christianity doesn't accept that: it's founded on an empirical claim, namely the resurrection of Jesus. Anyone could test the claim: the tomb was either empty or not; his body actually walked around or it did not. The apostle Paul was even willing to say, "if Christ has not been raised, your faith is futile and you are still in your sins" (1 Cor. 15:17). So the Christian message is hardly afraid to make empirically testable claims. The only question is, does it make them about this particular topic?

This philosophical objection is actually a companion to the "God-of-the-gaps" objection I discussed just above, because it assumes that there are no real gaps due to natures, only gaps in our knowledge. But again, how could anyone know that before they actually go out and look?

A second philosophical objection is that design is not properly part of science. But the answer is, *Why not?* Isn't it rational and scientific to identify design in Stonehenge? If we insist that "science" can only deal with natural explanations, then we're trying to win by controlling the definitions. Why can't we just say that "science" is "the disciplined and critical study of the world around us"? If we insist that, for some particular historical event, only natural-process-based explanations will count as science, the only way that can be rational is if we already know beforehand that natural factors are the only things involved. But what if we *don't* know that? Then we have no rational right to insist on natural explanations only in science—unless, of course, we're willing to make science independent of the rules for reason. (And who wants to go *there?*)

Besides that, we might point out that when Richard Dawkins says that the purpose of biology is to disprove design, he's admitting that the question of design is actually on the table for science. He thinks that science will disprove design; but it's just possible that when we try to disprove it we might fail. The only way to *ensure* that we don't fail is to make the commitment to disproof a worldview *pre*commitment—which is just what Dawkins does.

Perhaps, though, what the objectors really mean is that it's not the duty of scientists to say where things come from, and therefore that scientists shouldn't say that the cause of a gap is *super*natural. If that's what they mean, then we don't have a problem—so long as that also means they are committed to full disclosure about the difficulties. As it turns out, the NSTA statements and NAS booklets are *not* committed to this kind of honesty: they specifically discourage teachers from discussing the problems that a purely naturalistic evolutionary theory has, and dismiss all those problems as being due to lack of knowledge—sooner or later, they assert (by faith, mind you, not by sight), we'll fill in those gaps. But—just speaking for myself—I would have a lot more respect for someone who comes out and says, "Here is a problem that on the face of it is incompatible with my theory: I have no idea how you can get information out of natural processes, but I'm unwilling to draw any conclusions from that," rather than someone who says, "I know by faith that we'll solve it, so don't question my theory."

(c) Scientific Objections

Now let's turn to the objections to intelligent design from the empirical study of living things. As we have seen, Richard Dawkins says that to refer to design is actually futile, because it's not there to be found. Well, here's where we need to put up or shut up. Let me just catalogue a few phenomena, from our earlier discussions, that intelligent design explains better than natural-process-only-ism does:

- the information-bearing function of DNA;
- the existence of irreducibly complex systems in cell biology (such as blood-clotting);
- the inability to show how the kinds of small-scale adaptive changes that we all recognize (such as finch-beak variation in the Galápagos Islands or the peppered moth color variation in England) can account for large-scale variations (such as the origin of new phyla), or for where finches, moths, and biologists come from in the first place;
- human ability to reason and make moral choices.

Indeed, as J. B. S. Haldane—whom I have mentioned previously as a key figure in formulating neo-Darwinism—acknowledged,

> If my mental processes are determined wholly by the motions of atoms in my brain [that is, if my activity of thinking is entirely explicable by the natural properties of my brain, which it must be if intelligent design is false], I have no reason to suppose that my beliefs are true. They may be sound chemically, but that does not make them sound logically. And hence I have no reason for supposing my brain to be composed of atoms.

Each of us daily bumps into a profound argument for the existence of intelligent design.

We also saw that some people claim that science disproves intelligent design because they have found cases of *bad* design. The showcase example is the human eye. The trouble is that they're confusing things that differ. You'll note from my definition of imposed design I said nothing about whether the design is "optimal" as opposed to jury-rigged. The "intelligent" part of intelligent design means that an intelligent agent imposed design on something, and we can find evidence of it if we're willing to be honest as we look at the natural world. It says nothing about whether we might think the design was "intelligent" in the sense that we would have done it the same way.

Further, intelligent design does not of itself oppose some kinds of evolution—even by natural selection working on random variations; it just says that this can't be the whole story. Therefore if some feature of an animal is "odd" or "funny," it's possible that it came about by natural processes.

But even more critically, you can only say that these are bad design if you know what they were designed *for*—and that's a pretty tall order. When I was an engineer, we learned about optimizing—that is, designing a system to do the best job it could do. But you always optimize *with respect to something*. For example, when you design a radar system, you want to make your system sensitive enough so that you keep the number of missed detections to a minimum (a missed detection is when you fail to detect something when it's there); but that means that you will increase your number of false detections (a false detection is when you say something is there when it isn't). Since any system has to trade off between these two kinds of error, you have to decide which is more important for your particular system. So if you want to prove that something is not an optimal design, you have to say optimal with-respect-to-what. As a matter of fact, your eyes and mine work pretty well for their purposes—so I don't see how we have any right to call it a bad design. (Should scientists have to learn some engineering as well as philosophy?)

And finally, what of the claim that any appeal to intelligent design halts scientific progress? After all, once you say something is designed, you stop looking for explanations, don't you? Well, my first reply to this is, *So what?* Who wants to spend a dime on research into how the rocks of Stonehenge *got themselves* into the shape they're in now? So, certainly, some lines of study will get closed off, and that's all to the good. Now we can give our attention to things like: How do the properties of those rocks support the design—or would some other rocks have been better? How did they get those stones there? Who were those people and when did they build Stonehenge, and why?

But further, I don't think we need to worry that declaring that we have found imposed design is going to stymie progress. After all, science is a human activity, and human beings are just the kind of ornery beings who take pleasure in disproving other people's claims. So such claims will undergo severe review.

What we actually need is a set of criteria for detecting design, something a bit more rigorous than intuition. In fact, it's an advocate of intelligent design, William Dembski, who's done just that (in his 1998 book *The Design Inference* and elsewhere). The intelligent design program has actually *advanced* science.

This shows that the claim that intelligent design does not further research or promote our understanding of the natural world is also wrongheaded. I think that those who make this objection mean that it doesn't give us a fully natural story from beginning to end—but who wants one if it isn't true? Besides, I can think of an evolutionary research program that makes plenty of sense: namely, to see if we can figure out what natural gaps might look like in the world of living things, and then to see if we can find just where they are. We can locate two of them at least, as Chesterton noted—the origin of life and of us; are there any others?

CONCLUSION: IS PROHIBITING INTELLIGENT DESIGN A DUMB IDEA?

So now we can come back to our original question: *Is intelligent design a dumb idea?* We have a clear definition of it, so we know what we're talking about. We have considered some of the standard objections to it from the fields of theology, philosophy of science, and biology itself. None of those objections is compelling; in fact, when you look at them carefully, they actually show that to eliminate intelligent design from the scientist's toolbox of explanations would itself be a dumb idea.

I think the difficulty, one that we all feel, is just the one that we encounter when we look at Stonehenge. Now that we know it's designed, we go on to ask, who designed that thing, and what did they design it *for?* And what of ourselves: if we were designed, who designed us, and what were we designed for?

18

Science and the Argument from Design

In an earlier chapter I argued that it's very reasonable to consider intelligent design as an option for explaining some historical process. When we use the name "intelligent design," we raise a question, though: what is the connection between intelligent design in science and the traditional "argument from design" that Christians have used? To put it another way, is the purpose of intelligent design in science to prove that God is there and that he made us?

In this chapter I want to take up some of these issues. We'll proceed by trying to define just what the argument from design is, and then by looking at its history. Then we'll see if the argument is any good, and finally we'll consider what role science should have in the argument nowadays.

What Is the Argument from Design?

In order to define just what the argument from design is, let me give you a few samples of design-type arguments that believers have offered. Let's begin with the Wisdom of Solomon in the Apocrypha (or Deuterocanonicals), where in 13:5 we find a summary:

> For from the greatness and beauty of created things
> comes a corresponding perception of their Creator.

Some time later, the Apostle Paul wrote, in Romans 1:19-20,

> [19] For what can be known about God is plain to them, because God has shown it to them. [20] For his invisible attributes, namely, his eternal power and divine nature, have been clearly perceived, ever since the creation of the world, in the things that have been made. So they are without excuse.

Now we fast-forward to Thomas Aquinas (1224–1274), who in his *Summa Theologiae* included the argument from design in his "five ways" of proving that God exists:

> The fifth way is taken from the governance of the world. We see that things which lack intelligence, such as natural bodies, act for an end, and this is evident from their acting always, or nearly always, in the same way, so as to obtain the best result. Hence it is plain that not fortuitously, but designedly, do they achieve their end. Now whatever lacks intelligence cannot move towards an end, unless it be directed by some being endowed with knowledge and intelligence; as the arrow is shot to its mark by the archer. Therefore some intelligent being exists by whom all natural things are directed to their end; and this being we call God.

And finally, listen to William Paley (1743–1805), who wrote the classic *Natural Theology* (published in 1802):

> Contrivance [another word for design], if established, appears to me to prove every thing which we wish to prove. . . . Now, that which can contrive, which can design, must be a person. These capacities . . . require that which can conceive an end or purpose, as well as the power of providing means and directing them to their ends. . . . Wherever we see marks of contrivance, we are led for its cause to an intelligent author. . . .
>
> The marks of design are too strong to be gotten over. Design must have had a designer. That designer must have been a person. That person is GOD.

What are the common threads of all of these arguments? First, they assume that you can know true things about the world; second, they assume that you can intuitively see in the world evidence that it didn't just happen to be the way that it is; third, they argue that you can go from "it didn't just happen" to "some*one* made it happen," and that this leads you to God as the ultimate cause of the world.

The Christian philosopher Peter Kreeft points out that this argument is an aspect of a larger argument—that is, Aquinas's five ways together form a cosmological argument, where we reason from the features of the world to a God who must be responsible for it. There must be a First Mover for motion; there must be a First Cause, itself uncaused, to cause the existence of everything else. Of all of these, as Kreeft notes, the argument from design is "probably the most popular and instinctively obvious of all arguments for the existence of God."

All of these arguments focus on the creation as such—that is, they leave out the works God has done specifically for the sake of redeeming his people (such as the "miracles"). That makes for an important limitation on what this kind of argument can prove, as we'll soon see.

What Is the History of This Kind of Argument?

The Greek philosopher Plato (about 427–347 B.C.), in his *Laws,* when asked how you could prove that the gods exist, argued that the order and arrangement of the world must be due to the work of a soul or mind:

> In the first place, the earth and sun, and the stars and the universe, and the fair order of the seasons, and the division of them into years and months, furnishes proofs of their existence.

Plato defined atheism in terms of the belief that the world and everything in it result from the purposeless motions of material elements. He was specifically opposing Greek philosopher-scientists who tried to account for the order of nature by means of purely mechanical principles.

Aristotle (384–322 B.C.) was a student of Plato, but afterward came to differ with his teacher on important issues. Even so, he echoed Plato's view of design:

> . . . so those who first looked up to heaven and saw the sun running its course from its rising to its setting, and the orderly dances of the stars, looked for the craftsman of this lovely design, and surmised that it came about not by chance but by the agency of some mighty and imperishable nature, which was God.

He took the view that anyone who looked fairly at the world would

> surely reason that these things have not been framed without perfect skill, but that there both was and is a framer of this universe—God.

You can see the strong opposition to chance as the source of the world's order, as in Plato.

The Stoic philosophers, who came after these two, adapted this line of argument to make it even more purpose-oriented. As Robert Hurlbutt, III, in his historical study of the design argument, *Hume, Newton, and the Design Argument,* put it,

> The Stoics showed in detail how plants and animals, and the parts and organs of plants and animals, are connected by means-end relationships. They related things in particular to man, finding utility in practically everything. . . . The Stoics most assuredly did consider man to be at the very apex of the hierarchy of beings, and felt that the rest of the universe was geared to his benefit.

These schools of Greek philosophy influenced the author of Wisdom, who came from Alexandria, Egypt, a major center of learning in the ancient world. We have seen already how Wisdom and Paul expressed the argument—closer in form to Plato and Aristotle than to the Stoics; Aquinas's form, with its stress on purpose, owes a great deal to the Stoic form.

Coming to the modern period, we turn to Isaac Newton (1642–1727). Newton is best known for his laws of mechanics and gravitation, and his calculus; but he actually wrote a great deal of theological material—though very little of it was ever published (lucky for him, since he wasn't fully orthodox in his view of Christ). Though the first edition of his *Mathematical Principles of Natural Philosophy* (1687) says nothing about his religious views, in 1692–1693 Richard Bentley began exchanging letters with him, and Newton wrote:

> To make this system, therefore, with all its motions, required a cause which understood, and compared together, the quantities of matter in the several bodies of the sun and planets, and the gravitating powers resulting from thence; the several distances of the primary planets from the sun, and of the secondary ones from *Saturn, Jupiter,* and the earth; and the velocities, with which these planets could revolve about those quantities of matter in the central bodies; and to compare and adjust all these things together in so great and variety of bodies, argues that cause to be not blind and fortuitous, but very well skilled in mechanicks and geometry.

In a later work Newton referred also to "the first contrivance of those very artificial parts of animals, the eyes, ears, brain, muscles, heart, lungs, midriff, glands, larynx, hands, wings, swimming bladders, natural spectacles, and other organs of sense and motion" as well as "the instinct of brutes and insects" as further "effects of nothing else than the wisdom and skill of a powerful ever-living agent." In Newton's age it was becoming more important to use science to support the design argument.

David Hume (1711–1776) was a skeptical Scottish philosopher who tried to cast doubt on the Christian faith. He contended that a sensible person would never believe stories of miracles (including in the Bible), and that moral standards were not much more than preferences. In his *Dialogues Concerning Natural Religion,* posthumously published in 1779, he attacked the design argument, on three main fronts. First, he argued (using the character Philo as his spokesman) that the *analogy*—that is, the inference from world to God is like that from artifact to craftsman—isn't good enough:

> If we see a house, Cleanthes, we conclude, with the greatest certainty, that it had an architect or builder because this is precisely the species of effect which we have experienced to proceed from that species of cause. But surely you will not affirm that the universe bears such a resemblance to a house that we can with the same certainty infer a similar cause, or that the analogy is here entire and perfect. . . .
>
> Thought, design, intelligence, such as we discover in men and other animals, is no more than one of the springs and principles of the universe, as well as heat or cold, attraction or repulsion, and a hundred others which fall under daily observation. It is an active cause by which some particular parts of nature, we find, produce alterations on other parts. But can a conclusion, with any propriety, be transferred from parts to the whole? . . .
>
> And will any man tell me with a serious countenance that an orderly universe must arise from some thought and art like the human because we have experience of it? To ascertain this reasoning it were requisite that we had experience of the origin of worlds; and it is not sufficient, surely, that we have seen ships and cities arise from human art and contrivance.

The things that we are familiar with are only parts of nature, and the analogy needs to go from them to cover the whole of nature.

The second front of Hume's attack on the design argument was what we might call *locality*—that is, the universe is so big, and we only know something about such a little part of it, that the inference of design is too great a leap. His character Philo says,

> When nature has so extremely diversified her manner of operation in this small globe, can we imagine that she incessantly copies herself throughout so immense a universe?
>
> A very small part of this great system, during a very short time, is very imperfectly discovered to us; and do we thence pronounce decisively concerning the origin of the whole?

Hume's third line of attack was to assert that *nature is enough.* We have already seen that his character Philo called thought, design, and intelligence "one of the springs and principles of the universe, as well as heat or cold, attraction or repulsion, and a hundred others which fall under daily observation"—that is, they're part of nature. He also says,

> For aught we can know *a priori,* matter may contain the source or spring of order originally within itself, as well as mind does.

Many thought that this attack was the final defeat of the argument from design; but just a quarter of a century later we find William Paley (1743–1805)—a Cambridge academic who left teaching to pastor a country parish—writing his *Natural Theology* (published in 1802). Paley begins his book with one of the most famous analogies of all time:

> In crossing a heath, suppose I pitched my foot against a *stone,* and were asked how the stone came to be there, I might possibly answer, that for anything I knew to the contrary it had lain there forever; nor would it, perhaps, be very easy to show the absurdity of this answer. But suppose I had found a *watch* upon the ground, and it should be inquired how the watch happened to be in that place, I should hardly think of the answer which I had before given, that for anything I knew the watch might have always been there. Yet why should not this answer serve for the watch as well as for the stone; why is it not admissible in the second case as in the first? For this reason, and for no other, namely, that when we come to inspect the watch, we perceive—what we could not discover in the stone—that its several parts are framed and put together for a purpose, *e.g.* that they are so formed and adjusted as to produce motion, and that motion so regulated as to point out the hour of the day; that if the different parts had been differently shaped from what they are, or placed after any other manner or in any other order than that in which they are placed, either no motion at all would have been carried on in the machine, or none which would have answered to the use that is now served by it.

Paley goes on to describe the intricacies of the watch, and then says that under such circumstances we must conclude that someone formed it for the very purpose that we find it fulfilling.

He then notes that the conclusion is secure, even if we never knew anyone capable of making a watch; or if the watch didn't always work right; or if there were parts of the watch whose function we didn't know yet; or any of five other counterarguments.

The rest of the book is dedicated to showing that the world and many things in it are just like that watch, with a list of the parts of human bodies, animals and all their details, plants and their features, elements, and stars and planets. From all of these he says we should conclude that God, the Designer, is personal and good, and that there is only one.

The amount of sophistication, detail, and subtlety in Paley's work is magnificent, and I can only recommend that you read his book for yourself. In this section, though, I cannot do him justice.

It seems pretty likely that Paley wrote with Hume and his lot specifically in mind, and that his purpose was to overwhelm such skeptics with examples. Many of those who have written about Paley think he was successful—and this includes the philosopher Elliott Sober, who thinks that Darwin overturned Paley.

This brings us to Charles Darwin (1809–1882). Those who think of Darwin primarily as a scientist may be surprised to learn that he was strongly influenced by Paley's way of thinking—that is, there is a strongly philosophical element in Darwin's work. In the years between Paley's book and Darwin's *Origin of Species* (1859), philosophers paid more and more attention to the design of the laws of nature, more than to specific cases of what I earlier called *imposed* design; and Darwin even included a statement to this effect from a treatise on natural theology, at the beginning of his book:

> But with regard to the material world, we can at least go so far as this—we can perceive that events are brought about not by insulated interpositions of Divine power, exerted in each particular case, but by the establishment of general laws.

Most writers on the subject would say that Darwin undermined the Paley-esque type of design argument. According to the usual way of describing it, Paley had put forward countless examples from the biological world that you just could not account for except by way of imposed design. Then, however, Darwin came along with his theory of natural selection and provided a natural-process based explanation for how these features came about. The most that design could claim, by this understanding, was that God had designed the properties and the laws governing the process—and Darwin, by the way, was content with that kind of design.

Strictly speaking, it's actually more complicated than that: many of Paley's examples seem to be saying, "I cannot imagine a natural scenario that could have produced such phenomena"; while Darwin replied, "But I can." Darwin described variation plus natural selection as a mechanism that *could have* produced these structures; as I have already noted, he never supported the shift from *imaginable* to *possible,* much less to *plausible* or *probable.* Instead he argued, "I cannot see why it could not," shifting the burden of proof; and he offered no empirical tests for the proposed possibility.

Once you limit design to the laws that govern the world, you set yourself up for the obvious question: why talk about God at all? In fact, you get the problem of the redundant deity—one of the two atheistic arguments that Aquinas considered to be really dangerous. He described it like this:

> What can be fully accounted for through fewer principles is not produced through more. But it seems that all things that appear in the world can be accounted for fully through other principles, when it is supposed that God does not exist, because those that are natural are reduced to a principle that is nature, but those that come from intention are reduced to a principle that is human reason or will. Therefore there is no need to suppose that God exists.

Or, as Carl Sagan put it more crisply, there's nothing left for a Creator to do—which means we need not suppose he ever had anything to do with starting the whole show. Christian Darwinists tried to keep the idea of designed laws alive; but Charles Hodge saw the banishment of imposed design differently—when he declared Darwinism to be atheism, he was thinking of atheism pretty much along the lines of Plato, as I mentioned at the beginning of this section.

Was Hodge right? I think so. Darwin allowed for designed laws, but as he wrote:

> I am inclined to look at everything as resulting from designed laws, with the details, whether good or bad, left to the working out of what we might call chance.

The details make all the difference, though. It looks to me like George Gaylord Simpson takes the logical next step when he writes,

> Man is the result of a purposeless and natural process that did not have him in mind.

Therefore we can see why Richard Dawkins could say (as I cited him earlier),

> Although atheism might have been *logically* tenable before Darwin, Darwin made it possible to be an intellectually fulfilled atheist.

This shows why biology has become bound up with the success or failure of the design argument.

Therefore it's no surprise that Michael Behe put it this way:

> Darwinism is the most plausible unintelligent mechanism, yet it has tremendous difficulties and the evidence garnered so far points to its inability to do what its advocates claim for it. If unintelligent mechanisms can't do the job, then that shifts the focus to intelligent agency. That's as far as the argument against Darwinism takes us, but most people already have other reasons for believing in a personal God who just might act in history, and they will find the argument for intelligent design fits with what they already hold.
>
> With the evidence arranged this way, evidence against Darwinism does count as evidence for an active God. . . . Life is either the result of unintelligent causes or it is not, and the evidence against the unintelligent production of life is clearly evidence for intelligent design.

Is the Argument Any Good?

If someone asks us if the argument from design is any good, we should ask right back, good for what? Can it prove that Christianity is true? No, since it excludes God's works in the history of redemption. Rather, it's mostly concerned with what in an earlier chapter I called the "*metaphysical* part" of the Christian faith, namely our basic convictions about what the world is like, how God is active in the world, and whether we can know God and the world at all. If the design argument is valid, it shows that the world bears the marks of imposed design, which raises the question of who imposed it and why. Must the designer be God—that is, omnipotent? That depends on where we find the design, and it also depends on what we mean by omnipotent. Let's see if we can first set up a design argument that is true to what the sciences we have looked at are saying.

An up-to-date design argument would start with the anthropic principle we looked at briefly in our chapter on the age of the earth. The universe is just right to support our life right here and right now—and, so far as the evidence now points, is not suited to support life anywhere else. What's more, our minds are well suited to understand the universe. This shows why Hume's argument of locality doesn't work: because the anthropic principle looks at the universe as a whole.

As we have already seen, there are ways to try to get around this. For example, someone will say, "Well, if the universe weren't this way, we wouldn't be here to speak about it." Another angle is to suppose that all *possible* universes exist, and we just happen to live in the one that we *can* live in. We have already seen that there are ways to reply to the first part of this. As to the second, it's enough for now to notice that people who go this way are imagining an unlimited number of other universes, which we will never be able to observe. That's an act of desperation, which would only be worth doing if we had no alternative. Is belief in God really so bad that we have to go to these lengths to avoid it? (Well, it may be to some—because if there is a God, there may be a purpose and a judgment to which we all must answer; or else because they can see no satisfying answer to the problem of evil.)

We then move forward to the biological side of things: life and mankind show all the signs of being the results of imposed design. Now we have a reason to abandon the efforts to explain away the anthropic argument—we have these further evidences of imposed design, that make our gut reaction to the fine-tuning of the universe even more plausible.

Once you have evidence of imposed design, the question screams out at you: who imposed it, and why? And then you find something in your own heart that answers to that: a yearning for purpose and meaning, for a life that endures, for moral transcendence. "You have made us for yourself, O God, and our hearts are restless until they find their rest in you," as Augustine put it in his *Confessions*. And why do we have this sense inside of us that something is wrong with us and with the world—a sense of sin and a need for forgiveness and help? From here we're in a position to talk about the specific ways in which God has revealed his saving purpose for mankind.

The design argument touches us because it builds on a common experience—that of wonder at the world around us. We look at the night sky; we look at the animals God has made; we look at mankind—and we marvel at the beauty and intricate patterns we see. Can there be a purpose? Other good arguments are similar: the moral argument appeals to everyday experience of right and wrong; the argument from desire appeals to the deepest yearnings of our heart.

By the way, when we put it this way, we see that one of the common complaints against the design argument no longer holds. That is the claim that the argument has nothing to do with Christian piety—at best all we get from it is a form of deism (God started the whole show and then left it to run on its own). In Darwin's day, this claim may have been possible. Darwin, who was basically a deist, could allow for designed laws and for a Creator who at the beginning breathed life "into a few forms, or into one," and then bowed out. But now—let's just assume for now that the modern story is true; if it's not, we'll worry about that when we see the proof—we look at the origin of the universe some 15 billion years ago, and the origin of the earth some $4^1/_2$ billion years ago, and the origin of life on earth some $3^1/_2$ billion years ago, and the origin of man in the recent past. God has been imposing design over a longer course of time than just the very beginning!

The counterarguments to this argument from design may involve the effort to show that there is a natural explanation for all these things. Efforts like this miss some key points, as we have seen. Another counterargument is to say, "Well, this doesn't tell us *who* the designer is." With that I agree—that's why you can't stop with the "design" part of the argument.

And then there's the counterargument that these instances of design don't establish the Christian God as the designer, because they don't prove that the designer is omnipotent. All we can conclude is that the designer is strong enough to produce the effects we see. But again, the design argument is only the beginning, and the case is not complete until we add the rest of the material. Besides, if the anthropic principle is valid, then the designer is certainly able to do whatever he wants with the creation—which gets us pretty close to the traditional definition of "omnipotent." That is, a hypothetical definition of omnipotence may involve infinite power—and of course you could never get to that conclusion based on observing the world, since what you observe is always finite. But if you can say something about the laws and properties that make everything work—which is what the anthropic principle does—then you can say that it sure looks like the designer made the universe have whatever laws and properties he wanted it to have. And if such a person should tell us that his power has no limit whatever, as he does in the Bible—well, then, he's the only one who can know, and I don't see any reason to doubt his word.

Now, then: is this argument any good? Well, what might we want to use it for? We might use it as a jumping-off point for a full Christian apologetic, as I outlined above. But what if it doesn't bring people to believe? That doesn't mean the argument isn't any good, since the reasons why people believe what they believe are pretty complicated. People may suppress the truth or prefer their moral darkness (see Rom. 1:18; John 3:19-20). At least, though, it can clear the way and show people that in the call to Christian faith no one is asking them to check their brains at the door.

This leads to a second use for the argument from design: namely, to help believers deal with their doubts. C. S. Lewis put it this way, in his chapter on "Faith" in *Mere Christianity:*

> Now Faith, in the sense in which I am here using the word, is the art of holding on to things your reason has once accepted, in spite of your changing moods. For moods will change, whatever view your reason takes. I know that by experience. Now that I am a Christian I do have moods in which the whole thing looks very improbable: but when I was an atheist I had moods in which Christianity looked terribly probable. This rebellion of your moods against your real self is going to come anyway. That is why Faith is such a necessary virtue: unless you teach your moods "where they get off," you can never be either a sound Christian or even a sound atheist, but just a creature dithering to and fro, with its beliefs really dependent on the weather and the state of its digestion. Consequently one must train the habit of Faith.

And the third use is to strengthen our faith—even when we're not paralyzed by doubt. The stronger our faith—our confidence that God really has spoken to us in the Bible, that he really has brought us into his family through the death and resurrection of Jesus, that we really will live with him in glory forever—then the stronger our joy, and the more fully we give ourselves to faithful obedience to our Lord come what may.

I think the way I have put the argument here is better than the way Paley put it—though of course our debt to Paley is enormous. Paley's way has at least three faults. First, he thought that you could derive a fairly full range of God's attributes from the creation—in particular his goodness and kindness. Paul referred simply to God's "eternal power and divine nature" (Rom. 1:20).

Second, not all of Paley's examples of "design" are very good—some of them are more along the line of "I can't see how this could have come about except by design." But we need something stronger than "I can't see how"; we have to show how it *could not* have.

Third, and most serious theologically, is that Paley seems to have thought that you have to be able to assign a purpose for anything you call designed—including for the whole creation. Now a Christian, using the Bible, might be able to say something about the overarching purposes of everything; but the book of Ecclesiastes makes it clear that no one—not even the pious believer—will know the reason for the events in his own life.

Consider the following verses from Ecclesiastes (italics added):

> (3:11) He has made everything beautiful in its time. Also, he has put eternity into man's heart, yet so that he *cannot find out* what God has done from the beginning to the end.

> (7:14) In the day of prosperity be joyful, and in the day of adversity consider: God has made the one as well as the other, so that man *may not find out* anything that will be after him.

> (8:17) Then I saw all the work of God, that man *cannot find out* the work that is done under the sun. However much man may toil in seeking, he *will not find it out.* Even though a wise man claims to know, he *cannot find it out.*

The author of Ecclesiastes uses the key word "find out" in the sense of "figure out" or "fathom." When he speaks of "man" in these verses, he's referring to *man the pious believer* (that is, not to the unbeliever). The believer who wants to figure out the meaning of what happens in the world is baffled at every turn—he can never really get to the bottom of it.

Someone once asked the great biologist J. B. S. Haldane what characteristics of the Creator we can conclude from a study of his creation, and Haldane answered, "An inordinate fondness for beetles." (In his day they estimated that the order *Coleoptera,* the beetles, has as many as a quarter million species—which today looks like an underestimate.) He was right: just looking at the creation doesn't tell you everything you might like to know about God!

In our doctrine of God's providence, we claim that God rules over everything to accomplish his purposes. But let's be honest: that purposefulness is very hard to see—even in looking backward, we're still only guessing. Why did this or that bad thing—a lost job, or the death of a loved one—happen to me? What was God trying to do there?

As a matter of fact, we don't derive our doctrine of providence from looking at the sum total of events in the world. As C. S. Lewis put it,

> There is, to be sure, one glaringly obvious ground for denying that any moral purpose at all is operative in the universe: namely, the actual course of events in all its wasteful cruelty and apparent indifference, or hostility, to life.

Compare Ecclesiastes 9:2-3:

> It is the same for all, since the same event happens to the righteous and the wicked, to the good and the evil, to the clean and the unclean, to him who sacrifices and him who does not sacrifice. As is the good, so is the sinner; and he who swears is as he who shuns an oath. This is an evil in all that is done under the sun, that the same event happens to all; also the hearts of

> the children of man are full of evil, and madness is in their hearts while they live, and after that they go to the dead.

It looks like events are mindlessly indifferent to what actually makes people different from each other!

Lewis also observed,

> At all times, then, an inference from the course of events in this world to the goodness and wisdom of the Creator would have been equally preposterous; and it was never made.

Or, as Paul Helm said,

> Often there is a sharp disjunction between the view that God is in control, and the seeming chaos and meaninglessness of human lives, and human affairs in general. Is not this chaos a *disproof* of the Christian claim that God rules the universe providentially?

But then Helm goes on to answer his own question:

> It *would* be a disproof if the idea of divine providence were an empirical hypothesis, if it were built up only out of a person's direct experience and based wholly upon it. . . . Rather, for Christians, reliance upon the providence of God, and an understanding of the character of that providence, is based upon what God has revealed in Scripture, and is confirmed in their own and others' experience.

So if we look at it this way, we can see that the way in which nature reveals God becomes part of those experiences that confirm the truth of God's providence: nature is *regular* and stable, yes; but there are also *special,* supernatural events that show that God has this unrelenting interest in relationship with you and me, and that he intends to act on that interest at all times. Any help we can get in remembering this, and living by it, is welcome. Think of what we have said about imposed design: these things remind you that you're not an accident, you're the product of purpose.

William Paley, the country pastor, was well aware of this; as he wrote in his *Natural Theology,*

> It is one thing to assent to a proposition of this sort; another, and a very different thing, to have properly imbibed its influence. I take the case to be this: perhaps almost every man living has a particular train of thought, into

> which his mind glides and falls, when at leisure from the impressions and ideas that occasionally excite it: perhaps, also, the train of thought here spoken of, more than any other thing, determines the character. *It is of the utmost consequence, therefore, that this property of our constitution be well regulated.* . . . In a moral view I shall not, I believe, be contradicted when I say, that if one train of thinking be more desirable than another, it is that which regards the phenomena of nature with a constant reference to a supreme intelligent Author. To have made this the ruling, the habitual sentiment of our minds, is to have laid the foundation of every thing which is religious. *The world thenceforth becomes a temple, and life itself one continued act of adoration. The change is no less than this: that whereas formerly God was seldom in our thoughts, we can now scarcely look upon anything without perceiving its relation to him.*

That's it! How shall we keep our hearts adoring our God? How shall we keep our confidence that, indeed, God not only *can* work but actually *is* working all things together for good for those who love him? How shall we be fervent in prayer, never giving up when it seems like our prayers bounce off the ceiling, and everything just goes on in its own witless way anyhow? How shall we remember that everything in our lives matters to God, and is part of our relationship to him? By attending to the evidence God has given us: by remembering the supernatural deeds he has done in revealing his redemption in the Bible; and the marvelous deeds he has accomplished in our own lives—in putting his Spirit in us, in cleansing us and leading us on to love him and to submit to his discipline. And a crucial part of this attending is mulling over the glory he has revealed in the natural world, and the supernatural design of which it speaks so clearly.

So even if we end up thinking that the design argument doesn't have much place in evangelism (I have shown why I think it does have a place), we still can see why we believers need it so much.

What Place Should Science Play in the Argument Today?

So the design argument has its place, not only in evangelism and apologetics but also in nourishing our Christian faith. But what place should science play in framing the argument?

Looked at from one point of view, the answer to that question is, "Not very much." That is, the power of the design argument comes from its accessibility—it appeals to a whole range of people, sophisticated or not. Part of that appeal comes from its nearness to our everyday experience—and science seems to lead us away from that.

Not only that, but since scientific ideas change so often, what seems solid today might be mush tomorrow. That's another reason why we need to stick to a more everyday or intuitive approach—because these things don't change.

On the other hand, science can help us a lot. It is, after all, scientific research that shows what you need to have a working cell—an information system. The more we know about the natural world, the clearer some of the gaps will become; and we do want to focus on the natural gaps and not get misled by the knowledge gaps.

In other words, science can help to sharpen and clarify our case; and this is all to the good. As J. P. Moreland pointed out, "God is not honored when his people use bad arguments for what may actually be correct conclusions."

Good science can also help when we're faced with claims from skeptics that "science has shown that Christianity is a fable." The better we are acquainted with the actual sciences—and with good critical thinking—the better we can show that the real fables are these skeptical claims.

Many who think intelligent design is right are reluctant to take it too far and apply it as a theistic argument. I am not sure that there's any *necessary* jump from intelligent design to the design argument—but Christians are certainly within their rights to employ the results of intelligent design in developing a design argument.

19

The Human and Social Sciences

In chapter 3 I used the name "human sciences" for the disciplines that study human beings, such as anatomy, physiology, and psychology. I used the term "social sciences" for the disciplines that study how people interact, such as linguistics, textual hermeneutics, anthropology, economics, and sociology.

In this chapter I want to discuss how a Christian should approach these disciplines. I can summarize the points I want to make pretty simply. First, I consider these to be valid as sciences. Second, I also think they are worthy of the attention of Christians—not only for the obvious usefulness, say, of physiology to treating illness or of linguistics to Bible translation, but also for their own merit of satisfying curiosity. And third, these sciences, being so close to our own humanness, will easily make use of premises that have major interaction with key points of our faith.

Maintaining Sound Thinking

The premises that a Christian should be careful to guard, when considering the human and social sciences, include: there is a transcendent reality that human beings can partake of—for example, they can reason truly and they can make decisions in the light of moral absolutes (as we saw in chapter 8). Therefore we must keep in mind the body-soul nexus that makes up human nature. This means that body and soul will have an influence on each other. This also means that human health includes spiritual well-being, and moral transformation to being more like Jesus.

A further premise that we must guard is the way God works to change us. There is a supernatural effect on human beings that clears away their resistance to Christian truth, and that moves them to obey God's commandments, and that works Christ's character into his followers. No merely natural explanations for such things will be enough—human will isn't strong enough to overcome the pull of our pride and resistance to God, nor is human encouragement enough to impel us to character transformation (though strength of will and encouragement from others may play a valuable role).

At the same time we must be clear that our faith does not tell us everything we might like to know about the topics of these sciences: the Bible is not a textbook of anatomy or sociology, for example. There is plenty of room for learning from empirical study—and there is plenty to be learned, even from those who don't share our Christian convictions.

I say this because I have heard a "biblical" Christian counselor argue that there are four basic approaches to relating Christian psychology to the "secular" brand. The first kind he calls "liberal Christian," which is indistinguishable from secular. The second kind he calls "fundamentalist," and it keeps the different parts of life in separate compartments (and probably thinks that nothing but the "spiritual" matters much). The third kind he calls "evangelical," and it attempts to integrate theology and psychology. The fourth, which he favors, is "biblical": the Bible is both our only guide and our only reliable source of information. But his "biblical" approach is unworkable. We always read things in light of our precommitments and our experience of the world, and this applies to the Bible as well. Not only that, but there's no reason to believe that the Bible ever intended to give us all we need for this kind of work. Instead, it supplies us with a basic orientation toward God, and a set of premises by which we approach all our thinking. That is, we don't have the data until we collect it and analyze it. There's no reason why we can't accept the data collection that others will do—so long as we look at it critically. In other words, we can't help but use our experience when we read the Bible and try to obey it—so the real question is whether we do it well.

Let me mention a few examples here before we go on to our more detailed discussions. Every few years another psychological study comes out declaring that spanking is bad for children. A psychologist, John Rosemond, evaluated some of these studies and showed how they were inadequate. He wrote:

> I've seen the research on spanking. In fact, this being a relatively fascinating topic, I dare say I've kept closely abreast of the research. Without exception, it paints an ominous picture. A person who was spanked as a child is more likely to commit violent crimes as an adult, be physically abusive toward his or her spouse and children, suffer from low self-esteem . . . need I go on?

> First, not one study I've seen proves anything. From design to procedure, they are impeachable. Yet this bad science is being used to promote social policy that will allow both the law and the "helping" professional to invade the privacy of the average American family.
>
> But let's make an important distinction: There are spankings, and there are beatings, and they are not one and the same. Studies that purport to prove that children who are spanked are more likely to grow up to beat on other people, however, do not make this distinction. Therefore, the outcomes are skewed by people who suffered unspeakable abuse as kids. No doubt about it, if you're beaten as a child, you're more likely, as an adult, to pass it on. Common sense will tell you that.
>
> But are spankings per se abusive? Not in my book. There's no conclusive evidence that an occasional swat or two to the rear of a child for the purpose of terminating an outrageous or dangerous behavior and securing the child's attention is psychologically damaging. It could be argued that the parent had other options, but I've yet to hear a coherent, non-emotional argument to the effect that this constitutes abuse.

This shows how the researcher's own biases can seriously twist his results: as Rosemond points out, when the researchers lump together abusive beating and morally based spanking, they can't help but get bad results—probably the results they were looking for to begin with. This lumping together is no accident: it reflects the views of the researchers that *any* bodily punishment is the same as any other—it assumes a moral stance, and then uses the research to support that stance. As Rosemond points out, this is bad science.

On the other hand, researchers might be able to establish that some psychological disorders can be controlled with medication. Perhaps some problem in brain chemistry leads to the disorder (or perhaps something else causes the imbalance—that's a tough one to call). But a Christian who takes seriously the ruinous effects of mankind's fall can bring this insight into how he thinks of mental problems.

Another set of examples arises from the way we might want to use studies from the human and social sciences, either to help us defend our ethical standards, or to help us form an ethical position.

In the first case, suppose we want to show people that the biblical standard on faithfulness in marriage is really for their good. We might look for a study that shows that people who are faithful live longer, or are healthier, or have fewer emotional hang-ups, or have less chance of getting various hideous diseases. Well, I have no idea whether such a study exists; and if it did, I would wonder about how it framed its definitions of key terms (such as "faithful" and "healthy," or even "marriage"), and what kinds of tests it used. And suppose the results were not decisive—what then? Well, the moral duty remains the same. And if we're not careful, we could end up giving the impression that the chief benefits of Christian faith are material. It is certainly true that the biblical book of Proverbs often points to the consequences of good and bad behavior—but that's not for the purpose of proving that morality is good. Instead, it's for the purpose of showing that God, whose own nature defines good and bad, rules the world so that his moral approval shines through—eventually; if not here, then hereafter. It also helps the one who has already accepted that the moral code is right, to see that it is also pleasing, so that he can embrace it with his whole being.

As an example of the second case, that of using a study to help us come to a position on some ethical issue, take the matter of the death penalty for deliberate murder. People favor using the death penalty for a variety of reasons. Some think that a murderer has given up his right to life and that the state is obliged to put him to death to display God's own judgment. Some think that the death penalty is good because it helps deter others from committing murder. Suppose we find a study that seems to say that the death penalty doesn't deter: does that settle the ethical issue? Not if deterrence wasn't part of your ethical reasoning. It is becoming common now to cite studies that seem to say that there is racial discrimination in how the death penalty is used in the United States—that blacks get it more often than whites. Well, that may be a reason to call a halt to using the death penalty; it may be a reason for not using it at all; but it doesn't address the basic ethical question of whether the state has the right or even the duty to take the life of murderers.

In other words, we have to recognize that these sciences have limitations when it comes to moral reasoning.

Let's consider three sample areas where our faith and our science can interact. First we'll look at the question of the brain and its relationship to the mind and soul. Second, we'll consider the genetic basis of behavior. And third, we'll think a little about the place of counseling in the Christian life.

THE BRAIN, MIND, AND SOUL

It is common in some circles to say that the mind and the brain are two names for the same thing. Since I have already discussed why this cannot be right—not only from the point of view of the Christian faith but more generally from the philosophical side, to account for rationality—I won't repeat why I think this is ridiculous and unworkable. I think that we can be misled by the idea that to be scientific we have to make measurements; and the main thing we can measure for mental activity is the signals the brain makes. Then we allow ourselves to think that because that's measurable, that's objective—and therefore that's what is really there.

I'm reminded of the time I met a drunk who was looking at the ground under a street lamp. I asked him what he was doing, and he said he was looking for his car keys. I said I'd like to help him, and asked where he had them last. He pointed to a car outside the circle of light and said, "Over there, by my car." When I asked him why he wasn't looking over there, he said, "I'm looking here because the light's better."

Well, just because the light is better, doesn't mean we're going to find the keys; and just because we can measure brain activity but can't measure the mind or soul, doesn't mean we'll find what makes us tick only by measurements.

On the other hand, it helps to remember how closely interwoven the body and soul are, and that the brain is the normal vehicle for the mind to express itself. If I am drunk or tired—a condition of my brain—then my mind likely doesn't work right. And that puts limits on my spiritual attainments. I know of a Christian man who had a serious stroke, which left much of his brain unable to function. He can't read anymore, for example. It's no surprise that his faith has suffered in the whole business, because some of the brain functions that his spiritual life used for its vehicle are no longer there. It's common for the victims of various kinds of brain injuries to lose their ability to make sound judgments.

A Genetic Basis of Behavior

Anyone who has more than one child can recognize how different they are—even, it seems, from birth. One child "sees" math problems in his head, the other can't get the concepts without painful work with pencil and paper. My son is different from my daughter: he makes sounds naturally—like the roaring of an engine or the bursting of bombs—that she never did. We can't find anything in our child-rearing that accounts for these differences; they seem to be hardwired. There are other parts of their personalities that seem to depend a lot on hardwiring but also on how the child is treated: say, one tends to be optimistic, the other pessimistic; one tends to be cuddly, the other is always looking for something to do.

So the idea that certain parts of our behavior are built in seems to go along with daily experience. We can't always tell which parts are due to nature and which to nurture—in most areas it seems like there's always an element of both.

And what about aspects of our moral behavior? Are they influenced by our genes, too? We have heard that some people are genetically more liable to become alcoholics than others; some, so we are told, may be genetically more inclined toward depression, or homosexuality, than others.

This presents us with a conflict: how can such behaviors be *moral* issues if they are governed by physical causes? That is, how can we—or God—hold anyone responsible for behavior that was physically mandated? If my shower takes a few minutes to warm up, I might think the plumber who laid the pipes so close to the outside wall did a bad job—but I'm pretty silly if I blame the water for taking so long!

The trouble with this objection is that it doesn't use the right analogy. Think instead of someone driving a car ahead of you, going slow in the fast lane. It might be that he's going slow because he's just not thinking, and his car could go faster if he drove it properly. That's rude—or at least negligent. On the other hand, maybe his car can't go any faster. You can't blame his car, but you might think that he shouldn't then have put himself in the fast lane. In either case he did have some choice in the matter.

As a Christian—or as a moralist in general—I would oppose claims that genes *determine* behaviors that are supposed to be moral. That is, I look at one's learning style as morally neutral, just as hair color is; but lying is a sin. If anyone is genetically determined to lie, I can't call that determination a sin—but I can still insist that he not put himself in a place where he has to follow its impulse.

Well, fortunately, the evidence doesn't actually favor the idea that these behaviors are genetically *determined*, though it still may turn out that the genes do strongly *dispose* people in certain ways.

From a moral point of view, a genetic predisposition isn't much different from a bad habit learned at an early age: it's part of our sinfulness that God wants to cleanse and heal. It's going to be hard for us to achieve much in the way of moral goodness, but we still have to work at it and not give up. C. S. Lewis, in his chapter "Nice People or New Men" in *Mere Christianity,* has nailed the main issues. He addresses the question, "If Christianity is true why are not all Christians obviously nicer than all non-Christians?" He replies that the right way to see it is that if Christianity is true, then any Christian will be nicer than the same person would be if he were not a Christian—that is, we have to look at the impact of one's Christian faith on the raw material. He argues:

> Christian Miss Bates may have an unkinder tongue than unbelieving Dick Firkin. . . . Miss Bates and Dick, as a result of natural causes and early upbringing, have certain temperaments: Christianity professes to put both temperaments under new management if they will allow it to do so. . . . Everyone knows that what is being managed in Dick Firkin's case is much "nicer" than what is being managed in Miss Bates's. That is not the point. To judge the management of a factory, you must consider not only the output but also the plant. Considering the plant at Factory A it may be a wonder that it turns out anything at all; considering the first-class outfit at Factory B its output, though high, may be a great deal lower than it ought to be. No doubt the good manager at Factory A is going to put in new machinery as soon as he can, but that takes time. In the meantime low output does not prove that he is a failure. . . .
>
> You cannot expect God to look at Dick's placid temper and friendly disposition exactly as we do. They result from natural causes which God Himself creates. Being merely temperamental, they will all disappear if Dick's digestion alters. The niceness, in fact, is God's gift to Dick, not Dick's gift to God. In the same way, God has allowed natural causes, working in a world spoiled by centuries of sin, to produce in Miss Bates the narrow mind and jangled nerves which account for most of her nastiness. He intends, in His own good time, to set that part of her right. . . .
>
> There is either a warning or an encouragement here for every one of us. If you are a nice person—if virtue comes easily to you—beware! Much is expected from those to whom much is given. . . .
>
> But if you are a poor creature—poisoned by a wretched upbringing in some house full of vulgar jealousies and senseless quarrels—saddled, by no choice of your own, with some loathsome sexual perversion—nagged day in and day out by an inferiority complex that makes you snap at your best friends—do not despair. He knows all about it. You are one of the poor whom He blessed. He knows what a wretched machine you are trying to drive. Keep on. Do what you can. One day (perhaps in another world, but perhaps far sooner than that) He will fling it on the scrap-heap and give you a new one. And then you may astonish us all—not least yourself: for you have learned your driving in a hard school.

What Lewis says here applies beyond his immediate apologetic purposes: he shows us how to think about the "raw material" with which we set out on the Christian journey, and keeps us from thinking that the differences in areas such as temperament are unfair. The main thing I would add to his words is to remind Christians that when they are pursuing virtue, they aren't doing it to gain merit with God. Rather, they are expressing their faith in their

Lord, and doing what they can to live pleasingly to him. It's not their moral failures that displease God so much as it is their unwillingness to make the effort to be changed.

In thinking about how behavior might have a genetic basis, we should also reflect on whether the study of animals will shed much light on human behavior. Since the Bible allows us to think of humans as "rational animals," it stands to reason that studying the other animals will tell us something about our animal mechanism—just as it can tell us something about our blood chemistry.

But it seems to me that the help we will get from studies of animals when it comes to moral and social behavior will be pretty limited. I think the discontinuities between us and them are too significant.

COUNSELING AND PSYCHOTHERAPY

By counseling and psychotherapy I mean the task of helping people with their personal and emotional problems and disorders. I think that, in normal usage, "psychotherapy" is seen as the more technical discipline, requiring longer training (and sometimes focusing on serious mental disorders). "Counseling," which may take special training, is often focused on less severe problems—say, helping a couple learn how to communicate in marriage, and heal the effects of their years of failure to do so. Both counseling and psychotherapy draw on the discipline of psychology, which studies how human behavior works.

There are some misconceptions that we should clear away before we can go any further.

First, some think that Christians aren't supposed to have emotional problems—or if they do, the best solution is to read their Bibles and pray more. This viewpoint stems from some positive insights, but is wrongheaded. The positive insights are the idea that living by Christian standards is good for you, and the further idea that we need God's help, which we lay hold of by prayer and through the Bible (not to mention through the church's worship and fellowship), to advance us to genuine well-being.

But the wrongness of the viewpoint comes from its failure to reckon with the fallenness of our human nature, as Lewis described in the previous section, and the failure to allow for the ministry of trained people to help us along the way.

Another misconception is that we are loyal to Christ only if we make the Bible our sole source of guidance, and refuse to learn from anyone who doesn't wear our kind of Christian label—whether they be Christians with different views than ours, or not Christians at all. As I have already said, I think this is a terrible misuse of the Bible itself. The Bible should form our beliefs and values—but it doesn't offer all the data we could ever ask for. How could it do so and still be a manageable book?

A final misconception is on the opposite end of the scale from the first two: the idea that emotional and spiritual matters have no bearing on each other. By this view, our faith doesn't address our emotional side, which is purely the realm of the scientists. But this is wrong because, at the very least, our faith provides us with a way of tapping into spiritual power for change that is beyond what nature provides. This power can give an energy to our wills, and an effect to our moral choices, that is supernatural. But our faith also defines for us what good health is, and sets clear guidelines for us in our choices (like the Ten Commandments), so that we're not left to our own resources. Our faith also shows us what man is really like, and how body and soul interact with each other.

In *Mere Christianity* C. S. Lewis has a chapter called "Morality and Psychoanalysis," which is really a study of how human choices work. But he does say some things about psychoanalysis; let me quote him before I go on to disagree with some of it:

> Since Christian morality claims to be a technique for putting the human machine right, I think you would like to know how it is related to another technique which seems to make a similar claim—namely, psychoanalysis.
>
> Now you want to distinguish very clearly between two things: between the actual medical theories and techniques of the psychoanalysts, and the general philosophical view of the world which Freud and some others have gone on to add to this. The second thing—the philosophy of Freud—is in direct contradiction to Christianity: and also in direct contradiction to the other great psychologist, Jung. And furthermore, when Freud is talking about how to cure neurotics he is speaking as a specialist in his own subject, but when he goes on to talk general philosophy he is speaking as an amateur. It is therefore quite sensible to attend to him with respect in the one case and not in the other—and that is what I do. I am all the readier to do it because I have found that when he is talking off his own subject and on a subject I do know something about (namely, languages) he is very ignorant. But psychoanalysis itself, apart from all the philosophical additions that Freud and others have made to it, is not in the least contradictory to Christianity. . . .
>
> When a man makes a moral choice two things are involved. One is the

> act of choosing. The other is the various feelings, impulses and so on which his psychological outfit presents him with, and which are the raw material of his choice. . . . Now what psychoanalysis undertakes to do is to remove the abnormal feelings, that is, to give the man better raw material for his acts of choice: morality is concerned with the acts of choice themselves.

Lewis gives an example of three men who go to war. One has normal feelings—including fears of danger—which he overcomes by moral effort and becomes brave. The other two have irrational fears, "which no amount of moral effort can do anything about." A psychoanalyst can come along and help these two lads with their irrational fears—that is, he puts them in the position of the first fellow.

> Well, it is just then that the psychoanalytical problem is over and the moral problem begins. Because, now that they are cured, these two men might take quite different lines. The first might say, "Thank goodness I've got rid of all those doo-dahs. Now at last I can do what I always wanted to do—my duty to my country." But the other might say, "Well, I'm very glad that I now feel moderately cool under fire, but, of course, that doesn't alter the fact that I'm still jolly well determined to look after Number One and let the other chap do the dangerous job whenever I can." . . .
>
> The bad psychological material is not a sin but a disease. It does not need to be repented of, but to be cured. . . . Human beings judge one another by their external actions. God judges them by their moral choices. When a neurotic who has a pathological horror of cats forces himself to pick up a cat for some good reason, it is quite possible that in God's eyes he has shown more courage than a healthy man may have done in winning the Victoria Cross [a British medal for exceptional bravery].

While I do think that Lewis has given us some sound advice, I also think he has oversimplified things. (Perhaps the situation in Britain during the Second World War was so different from how it is here and now that he didn't see some of these other factors; or perhaps detailed critique just didn't suit the purposes of radio addresses defending Christian truth.) First, he seems to assume that the techniques of the psychoanalysts—things like the tests they give, or the way they ask questions, or the course of action they prescribe—are neutral. Well, they might be, but then again they might not be. We have to be able to decide whether these techniques depend on beliefs about human nature; for example, if they assume that there are no real moral absolutes, or that man is not fallen, then this could affect their plan of action. Second, and related to the first, is the way the presumed morality of the therapist informs his counsel: it shapes what he thinks of as good, or allowable behavior. For example, can adultery ever "enrich" one's life or marriage (as some therapists have said)? If we accept a transcendent moral code, we will never think that the effects of adultery could ever be called "enriching." Third, this discussion of Lewis's—which is admittedly brief—underestimates the way that goodness and sin can impact emotional life. For example, my "doo-dahs" may result from a bad upbringing, it is true (which means I have been sinned against); but they can also be affected by my own misdeeds, as well as by a human nature badly damaged by the fall. And fourth, Lewis has said nothing about the role that anyone's faith plays in the process of psychological treatment—either the patient's or the therapist's. When counselors have helped me, they have helped me to act on my faith, and to find strength from God, to do the right things.

So Lewis seems perilously close to arguing for a complementarity model for spiritual life and psychotherapy. It doesn't look like that model is quite adequate for everything, although there may in fact be areas where it does apply; but I'll leave it to a competent psychotherapist to rule on that one.

Section IV
Conclusion

20

CULTURE WARS AND WARRIORS

Faith, Science, and the Public Square

IT'S PRETTY COMMON TO hear that we're in a culture war—the traditionalists and the secularists are fighting over who will control the culture. There is a sense in which the image is right: as we will see in the next chapter, there are worldviews that are at odds with each other, and therefore it's no surprise that we find conflict. The image is a dangerous one, though, because it can lead us to look at everything in combatant terms: people who disagree with us become our *enemies,* and we have to *defeat* them. If you are my enemy, and I am a Christian, then—even if you're a Christian too—you must be morally defective.

Three further dangers follow from this warfare imagery. The first is that we can forget that worldviews involve not just philosophical positions but also moral commitments; and that back behind unbelief there lies a demonic enslaver. As Paul put it in Ephesians 6,

> [12] For we do not wrestle against flesh and blood, but against the rulers, against the authorities, against the cosmic powers over this present darkness, against the spiritual forces of evil in the heavenly places. [13] Therefore take up the whole armor of God, that you may be able to withstand in the evil day, and having done all, to stand firm. . . . [18] [Pray] at all times in the Spirit, with all prayer and supplication. To that end keep alert with all perseverance, making supplication for all the saints . . .

There is a spiritual component to this battle; and therefore, all our intellectual efforts must express our faithfulness to Christ and must be bathed in prayer. We must never use the weapons of unbelief—dishonesty, slander, name-calling, and so on. The second danger, related to the first, is that we can forget that the unbeliever is not the person we're fighting *against;* rather, he is the person we are fighting *for:* that is, the purpose of all this is to free people from their slavery to the Devil. The third danger that arises is that we can forget that any Christian—and any Christian church—always has only a partial grasp of a fully Christian worldview; and even those parts that we grasp rightly, we practice only partly. So some of our "warfare" ought to be against our own imperfections!

The warfare image is a biblical one, to be sure; but we will do well to be careful how we use it.

The purpose of this chapter is to address some of the questions that arise from the fact that we Christians live in a society in which the cultural leaders are generally not governed by Christian thinking, and that therefore what they feed us is often at odds with our faith.

DEALING WITH DISAGREEMENTS BETWEEN CHRISTIANS

Christians who want to be true to the Bible will hold to a form of what we can call "creationism." Straightaway that leads to trouble: in the most general sense, a creationist is someone who believes that God created the world, and that therefore the world doesn't exist on its own. A consistent creationist also recognizes that God can "interfere" with his world any time he wants—particularly for the purpose of pursuing a relationship with his creatures. (This is "consistent creationism," because there's no reason to suppose that God has restricted his supernatural deeds to the initial creation.)

Hardly anyone uses this word in its most general sense, however. Usually, "creationism" means "young earth creationism." Young earth creationists take the title for themselves—to them it's an honor. Many of them refer to everyone else as "evolutionary" or "accommodationist"—regardless of what view they take of neo-Darwinism.

It doesn't make much sense to contrast "creation" with "evolution," unless we are clear in our terms. This is a meaningful contrast when "evolution" means "evolution-as-the-big-picture," which is a form of naturalism. But if "evolution" simply means "development," or "change over time," it is not opposed to creation—not without a lot of clarification, anyhow.

Christians often have differences, and they can run deep. They don't agree on whom to baptize, or how Christ is present in the Lord's Supper (they don't even agree on whether to call them "sacraments" or "ordinances"). Sometimes our language about those we disagree with can get pretty colorful. For example, a leading textbook of theology claims that

> the difference between [my church] and [the other church] in the doctrine of baptism is fully and adequately defined by saying that the former believes God's word concerning baptism, the latter not.

Once you have said that, no further discussion is possible. You can't even wonder whether the other guys simply *understand* it differently than you do, and believe according to their understanding: you have to insist that their understanding results from their unbelief.

When it comes to Christians with different views of what the Bible says about the sciences, it's pretty easy to find plenty of claims just like this one—and they're all conversation stoppers. Maybe that's just what the people who say such things want: to rally the troops on "our" side. But that hardly serves the cause of Christ. Even if the other kind of Christian really is wrong, and his wrongness stems from some kind of unbelief, this kind of face-slapping is not likely to make him more willing to listen to your reasoning.

It would help us to talk frankly about our disagreements if we could try to understand what makes the other side tick, and to describe them in terms with which they themselves would agree. Perhaps every conversation has to start with a set of mutually agreed definitions—but then when we talk *about* each other among those on our side, we ought to stick to the same definitions!

So what shall we do about a "Christian" position on something like the age and history of the earth? My experience leads me to think that when Christians hold different views on this subject, they certainly do differ on how they read Genesis 1; but the differences run much deeper than that. To address them we have to delve into such topics as *metaphysics* (what the world is like, and how God interacts with it); *anthropology* (what human nature is like, and how our fallenness affects our thinking); *epistemology* (how do we come to know things, and may we trust what we think we know); and *hermeneutics* (what counts as a sound and authoritative way of interpreting the Bible). These are high-sounding names, I know; but what they deal with matters to everyone you meet.

I think Christians ought to be able to find agreement on some basic core positions in each of these four areas; but perhaps they must first agree on just how to think about thinking in these areas! My aim in this book is to point to how to think these topics through, as much as it is to persuade you of my own viewpoints.

Of course Christians who want to be biblically faithful feel the need to draw the line somewhere—to be able to say what separates genuine belief from error or defection. Churches have their creeds and confessions in order to identify what standards they will hold their official teaching to; but Christian unity will often cross over denominational boundaries. The basis of spiritual unity among Christians is, in my judgment, the "Christian worldview" that I will outline in the next chapter. It will include such elements as the creation of all things from nothing; the uniqueness of man; and the right of Scripture to speak about actual events in space and time and to describe supernatural works of God.

CHRISTIANS IN THE PUBLIC SQUARE

Secular people generally use the title "creationist" for "young earth creationist," too. While for a Christian the title "creationist" (in the general sense) is a badge of honor, for secular people the word drums up associations of rejecting science, of Bible-thumping, of anti-intellectualism. (The film *Inherit the Wind*—a film that is an atrocity against good history writing, by the way—says most of that.) To call someone a "creationist" in the hearing of a secular person, then, is to demean his reputation. As we saw in our discussion of intelligent design, some groups are deliberately connecting "intelligent design" with "creationism," in order to brand design advocates as "religious" and therefore unwelcome in science.

Let me give you an example of someone trying to marginalize Christian belief. In December 1997, William F. Buckley's television program *Firing Line* hosted a debate on the resolution, "The evolutionists should acknowledge creation." The affirmative side included Buckley himself, Phillip Johnson, Michael Behe, and David Berlinski (a mathematician). Those opposed included Barry Lynn (of Americans United for Separation of Church and State), Eugenie Scott (National Center for Science Education), Michael Ruse (a philosopher), and Kenneth Miller (a biology professor at Brown University). Here is what Barry Lynn (a liberal Protestant) said in his opening remarks:

> More importantly, though, we'll demonstrate that the arguments made by the other side are based on fundamentalist religious beliefs or discredited philosophical constructs, or what we sometimes refer to as just plain nonsense. We can't afford, ladies and gentlemen, for this to become too abstract a debate, because creation science advocates from California to Alabama have already duped school boards and thus required children to believe that evolution can somehow be debunked by alternative theories. In so doing, schools are being asked to elevate pseudo-science to the level of genuine science. What's next? Will we find the casting of astrological

> charts replacing telescope observations in high schools? I hope not, but I think that's the direction we might end up going. And indeed, if our children are not as prepared as those in Japan and Europe to understand what science is, to recognize the difference between a scientific question and a religious question, then they frankly will not be able to compete in the extraordinarily well-developing world of the future.

Lynn's comments are themselves just plain nonsense, for a number of reasons. For example, none of the affirmative side were actually "fundamentalists" or "creation science" advocates: Buckley and Behe are Roman Catholics, Johnson a member of a mainline Presbyterian church, and Berlinski was not even explicitly religious at all. Nor in fact is there any logical connection between intelligent design (or just opposition to neo-Darwinism in the case of Berlinski) and astrology. And the notion that creationists are ill-equipped to function well as researchers and engineers defies all the data.

But that's not my focus at this point: what I want you to see is how Lynn is aiming to mold your emotional reaction to his opponents. They're "against science"; they'll "impose their views" on your kids; who knows what else they'll bring into the schools; and your kids won't be as well prepared as kids in other countries. If he's right, you think, then Phil Johnson and company have to be stopped. Lynn's whole speech has nothing to do with anything the other team ever wrote or advocated—I wonder if he's ever read anything by Johnson, Behe, or Berlinski; it's all about making you think that they're dangerous kooks. In such a case it is reasonable for the intelligent design side to draw attention to the rhetorical ploy, and to ask the defenders of neo-Darwinism to justify these claims. (This also shows why we Christians have to favor an education that fosters sound critical thinking and keen awareness of rhetoric.)

Just a little later in that same debate, Eugenie Scott offered her definition of "evolution":

> Let me define evolution the way scientists define evolution and the way we're going to use it on our side of the table. Evolution is used two ways. One is the bigger idea that the present is different from the past, that the universe has had a history, that stars, galaxies, the planet Earth and the plants and animals on it have changed through time. Biological evolution is a subset of the idea of change through time, saying that living things, plants and animals, have shared common ancestors and have descended with modification from those ancestors. Now notice in this definition, I

> talked about what happened. I didn't talk about whodunit, and I didn't talk about how, because those are separate issues. Scientists are very much united on what happened. . . . But how it happened is something that we argue about a lot in science. How important is natural selection, how important are other mechanisms? Whodunit is something that as scientists we can't comment on—as scientists. We can put on our philosopher's hat and comment as individuals, but as scientists we can't deal with ultimate cause. So I think we have to be very clear what we mean by evolution. What they mean by evolution is some sort of a metaphysical system that we do not recognize.

Be sure you see just what Scott has done here. First, she wants you to think that she speaks on behalf of science and scientists—you can see that from how she uses "we." Second, she wants you to think that your religious values—"whodunit" and "ultimate causes"—are safe with her version of science. And third, she uses a harmless definition of evolution that almost no one can be bothered about: if the Johnson crowd are upset about that, well then, let them go away. We're concerned with real science.

I can't say whether Scott intended to deceive with what she said, but you are deceived if you buy it. There's just enough truth to her statement that it sounds plausible—being a physicist doesn't make you more qualified than someone else when it comes to ultimate issues of life's meaning. On the other hand, her definition of "evolution" is way wide of the mark—see our discussion of the different meanings of that word in chapter 16. She has completely left out the actual problem, what I called evolution-as-the-big-picture. What she has described is not actually the problem, at least not for me. The problem is in fact the claim that, whatever the mechanism in the big picture, it can be described as a *natural process,* with *no specific direction or goal* (as in the NABT statement). This kind of "evolution" certainly does make claims about how it happened, and it has religious implications; it certainly does make claims about what God has done or not done, say, in the origin of life and of mankind. And it does so, not on the basis of evidence but in the face of the evidence—in the service of a philosophical system.

I think we will do our best when we keep the discussion focused on these basic issues and not let ourselves get sidetracked on just how much of the other kinds of evolution we're willing to allow for.

And then what should we say when people like Richard Dawkins tell us that, when we object, it's just because our religion tells us to? Well, we commonly want to defend ourselves and show that we're interested in good science and sound thinking; and that's a good and true defense, and I'll take it up in a moment. But let me first point out that we must not allow statements like this to cow us into submission. After all, not every religiously motivated objection is bad. I believe, for example, that you and I and everyone else have souls, and that our lives have meaning, and that there are right and wrong ways to treat other people. A secular view says these things are either false or unknowable, and tricks us into thinking that good science says so too. But I am sure that all the evidence, scientific and otherwise, favors my position. It's no surprise that I won't yield on these basic claims without a struggle.

Further, as a Christian I affirm that both good faith and good science are aiming to say true things about the world. And that's the big issue for me: I want truth to prevail. And I want to make sure that everyone has a fair shot at finding the truth. I believe that in such a climate of fairness Christian faith will come off the winner. So you can hardly blame me, can you, when I insist that honesty be the key feature of public discussion?

But as I said, not every effort to argue against neo-Darwinism is "religious" or "unscientific" (and those two adjectives aren't the same thing!). As a matter of fact, the way that neo-Darwinism is protected in the science classroom reeks of being, not just unscientific, but bad science. And further, it is not illegal in American public schools to present the evidence for and against neo-Darwinism—so long as the presenter confines himself to the evidence. But even then, it's only fair to ask people to come clean about their premises and assumed definitions, since these play a big role in making one theory more plausible than another.

I think every Christian should agree with those who think that better science education is much to be desired; and in fact our Christian schools, home schools, and Christian teachers in the public arena should lead the way. At the same time we have to keep in mind that good science requires sound critical thinking—and we all need lots more of that.

21

LIFE IN A CREATED WORLD

IN THIS CHAPTER I AIM to tie together some of the strands I have spun during the course of this book. How should we believers live in the world that God made?

OUTLINE OF A CHRISTIAN WORLD-AND-LIFE VIEW

The Christian faith cannot be confined to a "religious" compartment in our lives. Rather, it provides us with a way of looking at ourselves and at the world—a way that equips us to live in this world. In fact, if Christianity is true, its world-and-life view ought to equip us to live *better* in this world than any other view can.

But let's first define our terms. A world-and-life view is your basic stance toward the world; and we can express it by questions like these:

Where does the world come from?

Is the world good or bad? (How can we define good or bad?)

What does it mean to be human?

How should people live?

Should all people live by the same standards?

What should we do with our failures to live by these standards?

What is a reliable guide for answering these questions?

What place does God have in it all?

Depending on how you answer these questions, you'll have different ways of answering other questions, such as, "How do these standards affect the way we should speak on public issues, such as government and education?" (In the previous chapter I touched on some of this.)

Now, Christianity claims to have the true answers to these questions. Apologetics focuses on showing that the Christian answers are the right ones.

Even though I put the "God-question" at the end, Christianity starts with God. It is a wise, good, and powerful Creator who made the world by the word of his power; God made mankind to be his friends and to display his own character; God will call all mankind to account for their response to God's purpose; and even though mankind are sinful by the corruption of their wills, God still pursues them with the offer of forgiveness, moral renewal, and friendship. God inspired the Bible as his special word to man, and therefore the Bible speaks truly about the world God made.

The reason we need to start here is so we can be the same person wherever we go: far too often we put our lives into compartments—my religion tells me what to do in church, but then I have to follow other rules at work or at play. But if we follow the Bible, we'll see how God speaks to every aspect of our lives—for our good.

The foundation for a Christian view of the world, and for the scientific study of the world, is what we believe about God's work of creation. Back in chapter 4 we outlined the Christian doctrine of creation: God made all things—

(a) *from nothing*. This means that God, and only God, is self-sufficient: the created world depends on him, but he doesn't depend on it. When he made the world, he made something different than he is, and less than he is.

(b) *by the word of his power*. This means that when God wanted something to be a certain way, he spoke a word and that's just the way it was.

(c) *in the space of six days*. This means that he spread the work of fashioning the world for us over a length of time.

(d) *all very good*. This is what the creation was like at first; we have also seen the sense in which this still applies. Sin and dysfunction are foreign invaders of God's good creation.

(e) *so that it bears his imprint.* The whole creation displays to all of us something of what God is like; it helps us to know and worship him.

We saw that, according to the Bible, God made man in his image—that is, to reflect something of the way God is, to be "an expression or transcription of the eternal, incorporeal creator in terms of temporal, bodily, creaturely existence." As we saw, this tells us why man, unlike the other animals, has the ability to reason, a will to choose what pleases him, language, a moral pointer, the ability to make and enjoy beauty, and the capacity to enter into relationships governed by love and commitment. The sin of Adam and Eve, our first parents, brought guilt and corruption to us all; and our chief good is to have that guilt forgiven and that corruption cleansed. This applies to all mankind.

You can see that a worldview is not the same as specific doctrinal positions—say, whom to baptize and how much water to use. So the "Christian worldview"—at least as I understand it—isn't going to settle for us questions like the age of the earth and so on. Instead, this worldview is something traditional Christians should hold in common, and it provides a way of thinking about their doctrinal issues.

Christianity is directly opposed to other worldviews. The chief options in our culture are what we can call "secular naturalism," "theistic naturalism," and "relativism."

Before I say anything more about these three alternative worldviews, however, let's recognize a few things up front. First, people are usually inconsistent in the way they hold their worldviews: I might act like a secular naturalist when I'm in the lab, a relativist when I defend my ethical failures, and a Christian when I'm in church. You and I may think it's better to pursue greater consistency—but at best that's only a goal, which no one has ever met. Second, we have to recognize that people hold their worldviews in their hearts—which means that the reasons they give might not be *why* they hold what they do. It may be that someone is a Christian because he can't handle life; or that another is a secular naturalist because he's running from God; or that someone else is a theistic naturalist because he doesn't want to make waves; or that still another is a relativist because he hates you for judging him. I have two things to say to that: one, that says nothing about whether the worldview is true; and two, that means we can't rely solely on arguments to help people embrace the Christian worldview. There's no substitute for a gentle and holy Christian character that everyone knows they can rely on in a pinch: that's what shows others our worldview is one to live by.

At the same time, you can see that I think we should offer reasons for holding our worldview: a good worldview needs to be consistent within itself, and it also needs to explain why the things we know about the world (such as our "touchstone truths") are so.

Secular naturalism is the worldview that the world exists on its own, and that God exercises no influence at all on any object or event in the world. By this view, there may in fact be a God, but since he has no effect on our lives or on anything else in the world, he doesn't matter. We have seen already that people who hold this worldview use neo-Darwinism as its support. Various organizations and philosophers are trying to make a rule for all science that it has to be *methodologically naturalistic*—that is, all of its theories have to be fully compatible with the secular naturalistic worldview. We have also seen that there may be ways for that to be honest: for example, to say that there's a gap in our understanding of the world and we don't know why it's there. On the other hand, the pressure is on to paper over these gaps, and to require us to say that it's just a matter of time before we solve them—that is, to *assume* before we get started that the only gaps we find are gaps in our knowledge, with no gaps due to properties.

Theistic naturalism says that nature does not exist on its own—it is God's creation—but that after the initial creation God's main activity is that of keeping the whole show going according to its created properties. Natural processes are not purposeless, but express God's purpose, which he built into the creation at the beginning. Those who hold this view think they have a reason for expecting nothing but knowledge gaps, namely God's abilities as a craftsman. They differ from the secular naturalists in that they generally hold that science and faith are complementary explanations.

The third alternative is *relativism*—the view that there is no such thing as knowledge of the world that applies to all people. By this worldview, you don't *receive* knowledge or meaning, you *make* it; that's why it's called relativism, because your knowledge is relative to who you are. In some versions of relativism you make knowledge based on your own subjectivity, your own feelings. In other versions you make meaning based on the group that you belong to—your culture, or race, or gender. (This is at the heart of what is now called "postmodernism.")

One of the clearest expressions of this worldview came to the fore after the World Trade Center fell down on September 11, 2001. A group of three New York City firefighters—all white men—raised an American flag at

Ground Zero, and someone snapped a photo of the raising. This photo became so famous that a few months later someone decided that we needed to have a statue (like the statue based on the flag-raising on Iwo Jima during World War II). But the statue wasn't going to be a straight image of the photo: the firefighters were to be white, black, and Hispanic. The idea was to allow the figures to represent the population of New York, by having the major ethnic groups in the statue.

Most people I know don't like this: they think that the statue should represent the three guys who actually did the deed. They don't have any trouble feeling that these fellows acted on behalf of us all. But the revision is perfectly consistent with relativism: it doesn't give the historical events any privileged place; it allows the artist to *impose* meaning on the events. And it doesn't accept that there's anything like a universal human nature that would allow a white man to represent a black or Hispanic or Asian man, let alone women.

When it comes to science, relativism might deny that science yields any real knowledge; or it might say that European science will yield different results than Asian science—and that each is valid for its culture. Relativism will deny that science is any kind of search for "truth"—if by truth we mean something that is valid for everyone. Philosophically, relativism will appeal to ideas like those of Thomas Kuhn regarding "paradigms." (You can find my review of Kuhn's famous work, *The Structure of Scientific Revolutions,* in an appendix to this book.)

In this chapter I really can't discuss or evaluate fully any of these alternative worldviews. Christian apologists have developed very fine analyses and refutations for secular naturalism, which has been the chief opponent to Christianity in the modern West; and in dealing with Darwinism and design, I have shown some of the ways we might address that worldview. Many of the arguments against secular naturalism also apply to theistic naturalism. We might add that the Bible doesn't support theistic naturalism either.

To analyze relativism is a lot harder, because this worldview hasn't been a major player until pretty recently—my generation, the baby-boomers, are the ones who have brought it in with a vengeance. (That also means that Christians haven't done enough to understand and answer it.) But further, the kinds of relativism are so diverse that it's hard to cover all of them.

In a book about science, I can point out two arguments that tell against relativism. The first is the universality of science. The only sensible way to talk about "Western science" is to mean the approach to science that Westerners pioneered. There's nothing distinctly "Western" about it beyond that—I went to MIT with people of Chinese, Japanese, African, and Polynesian ancestry (and lots of mixtures, too). Medicine applies to everyone—and if our modern technological medicine falls short, that's because it's too materialistic and not human enough—not because it's Western. There's no such thing as a Western airplane: it either flies or doesn't, and that has nothing to do with who made it but only with whether they did it right.

The second argument is to insist that we come back to our touchstones. Relativism asks me to deny my deepest intuitions about the world—that it exists, that I as a self can make use of transcendent reason to understand the world. I suspect this is one reason why few people in the sciences feel much pull toward relativism as a worldview—though they may pick and choose, of course, when it comes to morals!

I believe that the Christian worldview makes the best account of science: it shows us why science works (the same God who made the world made us to rule it); it shows why we like science (God made us curious); and it shows why science reveals natural gaps (because God has carried out supernatural actions as well as maintaining nature).

PARTICIPATION IN THE SCIENCES FOR CHRISTIANS

The cash value of the last section is that the Christian worldview makes a better home for science than any other worldview does. Here I want to go further, and say that everyone who really embraces the Christian faith should support the sciences wholeheartedly.

Our faith supplies us with four strong motives for loving science.

The first is, *to praise the Creator for his creativity.* God made the world, as we saw, out of his own overflowing goodness. He has so much goodness that any one creature, or multitudes of only one kind of creature, wouldn't be enough to display it. There are so many different elements, different compounds, different plant and animal types, different planets and stars—and the same God made them all to show forth his glory. To study just a little bit of this, knowing that the God who saved me in Christ is the one who made it all, enables me to honor him more fully.

Second, the sciences allow Christians *to enjoy God's goodness as we satisfy our curiosity.* Curiosity is part of the image of God; and though we can get curious about sordid things (human evil), the world God made is not sordid. Christians in recent times have been uncertain about whether the life of the mind is good, or even tolerable; but this is a thoroughly unbiblical aversion.

Third, the sciences allow us *to serve mankind.* The sciences have helped us to harness the powers of nature for the sake of human good—medicine is the obvious example of this. Of course we have used these tools to ruin others, as well; but all that shows is that the natural sciences don't carry the ethics within them. We need consecrated Christians, with hearts formed by Christian teaching, who know how to apply their ethics as well as their intellects to the world God made.

Fourth, the sciences allow us *to answer unbelief.* C. S. Lewis once observed,

> If all the world were Christian, it might not matter if all the world were uneducated. But, as it is, a cultural life will exist outside the Church whether it exists inside or not. To be ignorant and simple now—not able to meet the enemies on their own ground—would be to throw down our weapons, and to betray our uneducated brethren who have, under God, no defence but us against the intellectual attacks of the heathen. Good philosophy must exist, if for no other reason, because bad philosophy needs to be answered. The cool intellect must work not only against cool intellect on the other side, but against the muddy heathen mysticisms which deny intellect altogether. . . .
>
> The learned life then is, for some, a duty.

We have seen throughout this book that unbelievers use the tools of the sciences to "prove" a worldview that opposes the Christian one. As it turns out, such a use is actually a misuse—but it takes some knowledge to be able to see this.

In my experience, Christians have stressed the last two of these motives for loving science, and haven't thought enough about the first two; to allow ourselves to keep on doing so is to lose some key facets of the image of God in us.

How to Give Our Kids a Scientific Education

If we are to claim the world for the Lord Jesus, we must see more of our young people going into the sciences for their careers, and we need to instill in those who have other careers a positive appreciation of the sciences as well as a trained palate for truth and falsehood. This means we must pursue excellence in the way our children are taught the sciences. We parents are shirking our responsibilities if we pass the job along to their schools: instead we have to be models of what we aim for. Let's consider some practical steps for parents to take. (Here I'm not talking at all about whether we should prefer public, private, or home schools; instead I'm talking about the tone we set for our kids in day-to-day life.)

First, we should express curiosity and wonder about the world God made. We can, say, look out our back window and watch the birds and squirrels go about their lives. We can comment on the diversity of habits and foods and dwellings of the different animals. We can talk about airflow as we watch a hawk or crow soar. We can look at the different rocks in the garden and see what they tell us about the prehistory of the region we live in. We can wonder aloud how things work; and we can use toys that teach kids how to build things.

Second, we can go to museums and zoos. They can take us into parts of the universe we can never visit on our own.

The third step comes from the second: many museums and zoos have signs with their exhibits, which make claims that go beyond the evidence, and this means we have to teach and model sound critical thinking. How do we know what we so confidently assert? How do we answer disagreement? Do we allow our children to discuss things with us, to ask us to prove our position with reasons—and do we allow them to take positions that they must support with reasons?

Finally, we should expect achievement from those who teach science to our children. We want them to be qualified in their subjects as well as in the skills of teaching. We should be willing to put money into improving their teaching—paying them properly, helping them to further their education and attend conferences, giving them time to read and study, and hiring enough teachers so that they aren't overworked.

God is magnificent, his world is glorious and fascinating, and we honor him when we use all our abilities to study what he has done. God has no fear that we will uncover reasons for forsaking our faith, as long as we're being truly critical; neither should we.

PSALM 104:31-35

[31] May the glory of the LORD endure forever;
may the LORD rejoice in his works,
[32] who looks on the earth and it trembles,
who touches the mountains and they smoke!
[33] I will sing to the LORD as long as I live;
I will sing praise to my God while I have being.
[34] May my meditation be pleasing to him,
for I rejoice in the LORD.
[35] Let sinners be consumed from the earth,
and let the wicked be no more!
Bless the LORD, O my soul!
Praise the LORD!

PSALM 111

[1] Praise the LORD!
I will give thanks to the LORD with my whole heart,
in the company of the upright, in the congregation.
[2] Great are the works of the LORD,
studied by all who delight in them.
[3] Full of splendor and majesty is his work,
and his righteousness endures forever.
[4] He has caused his wonderful works to be remembered;
the LORD is gracious and merciful.
[5] He provides food for those who fear him;
he remembers his covenant forever.
[6] He has shown his people the power of his works,
in giving them the inheritance of the nations.
[7] The works of his hands are faithful and just;
all his precepts are trustworthy;
[8] they are established forever and ever,
to be performed with faithfulness and uprightness.
[9] He sent redemption to his people;
he has commanded his covenant forever.
Holy and awesome is his name!
[10] The fear of the LORD is the beginning of wisdom;
all those who practice it have a good understanding.
His praise endures forever!

APPENDICES

Appendix A

Notes and Comments on the Chapters

Chapter 1: Introduction

Some helpful popular surveys of the sciences include Robert M. Hazen and James Trefil, *Science Matters: Achieving Scientific Literacy* (New York: Doubleday, 1991); Lawrence Krauss, *The Physics of Star Trek* (New York: HarperCollins, 1995); James Trefil, *101 Things You Don't Know About Science and No One Else Does Either* (Boston: Houghton Mifflin, 1996); John Gribbin, *Almost Everyone's Guide to Science* (London: Phoenix, 1999); Roger Highfield, *Can Reindeer Fly? The Science of Christmas* (London: Metro Books, 1999); Charles Taylor and Stephen Pople, *The Oxford Children's Book of Science* (New York: Oxford University Press, 1995).

The general subject of science and religion has become prominent in recent years, and the John Templeton Foundation has done a great deal to foster interest in it. Some of the most highly regarded writers in this area include Ian Barbour, Arthur Peacocke, and John Polkinghorne—all of whom earned doctorates in the natural sciences before their theological studies. Of these, Polkinghorne is the closest to a traditional Christian, though he still has many points of difference with the Christian tradition. An author who is closer to the tradition is E. L. Mascall, *Christian Theology and Natural Science: Some Questions in Their Relations* (London: Longman, Green, 1956); and a classic from a conservative evangelical author is Bernard Ramm, *The Christian View of Science and Scripture* (Grand Rapids, Mich.: Eerdmans, 1954).

The C. S. Lewis quotation comes from *Mere Christianity,* book iii, chapter 2, "The 'Cardinal Virtues'."

Chapter 2: Science, Faith, and Rationality

G. K. Chesterton, "The Revival of Philosophy—Why?" in *The Common Man* (1950); excerpted in Chesterton, *As I Was Saying: A Chesterton Reader,* Robert Knille, ed. (Grand Rapids, Mich.: Eerdmans, 1985), 82-83.

C. S. Lewis, *"De Futilitate,"* in *Christian Reflections,* Walter Hooper, ed. (Grand Rapids, Mich.: Eerdmans, 1967), 57-71, at 61-62.

J. B. S. Haldane, *Possible Worlds and Other Papers* (Freeport, N.Y.: Books for Libraries Press, 1971 [originally 1928]), 220. This is part of an essay, "When I Am Dead," where Haldane denies personal immortality but explains why "It seems to me unlikely that mind is a mere by-product of matter." C. S. Lewis quoted this in his book *Miracles: A Preliminary Study* (New York: Simon & Schuster, 1996 [2nd edn., 1960]), 24 (chapter 3).

My material on sound thinking has been developed over the years as I have reflected on what my doctoral advisor, Professor Alan Millard of the University of Liverpool, taught me about how to think. The ideas build on Peter Kreeft and Ronald Tacelli, *Handbook of Christian Apologetics* (Downers Grove, Ill.: InterVarsity Press, 1994), 17-20. I have found assistance in Stephen Toulmin, *The Uses of Argument* (Cambridge: Cambridge University Press, 1957); D. A. Carson, *Exegetical Fallacies* (Grand Rapids, Mich.: Baker, 1984); Arthur Gibson, *Biblical Semantic Logic* (New York: St. Martin's Press, 1981); and J. P. Moreland, *Love Your God with All Your Mind: The Role of Reason in the Life of the Soul* (Colorado Springs: NavPress, 1997). And I encourage everyone to see reason at work in the stories about Sherlock Holmes (by A. Conan Doyle) and Father Brown (by G. K. Chesterton).

The overall position on the dependence of science on rationality is well presented in Roger Trigg, *Rationality and Science: Can Science Explain Everything?* (Oxford: Blackwell, 1993). I also recommend Mikael Stenmark, *Rationality in Science, Religion, and Everyday Life* (Notre Dame, Ind.: University of Notre Dame Press, 1995).

I quote J. Gresham Machen from *What Is Faith?* (Edinburgh: Banner of Truth, 1991 [originally 1925]), 13-14.

CHAPTER 3: MUST SCIENCE AND FAITH BE AT ODDS?

General introductions to philosophy of science from an explicitly Christian point of view include J. P. Moreland, *Christianity and the Nature of Science* (Grand Rapids, Mich.: Baker, 1989); Del Ratzsch, *Philosophy of Science: The Natural Sciences in Christian Perspective* (Downers Grove, Ill.: InterVarsity Press, 1986).

In this book I do not have space to cover the history of science and its interaction with Christianity. Some of the materials you should read to get familiar with the issues are: Nancy Pearcey and Charles Thaxton, *The Soul of Science* (Wheaton, Ill.: Crossway, 1994); John H. Brooke, *Science and Religion: Some Historical Perspectives* (Cambridge: Cambridge University Press, 1991); Colin Russell, *Cross-Currents: Interaction Between Science and Faith* (London: Christian Impact, 1995); C. S. Lewis, *The Discarded Image* (Cambridge: Cambridge University Press, 1964); David Lindberg, *The Beginnings of Western Science* (Chicago: University of Chicago Press, 1992); David Lindberg, ed., *Science in the Middle Ages* (Chicago: University of Chicago Press, 1978); David Lindberg and Ronald Numbers, eds., *God and Nature* (Berkeley: University of California Press, 1986); Mark Kalthoff, "God and Creation: An Historical Look at Encounters Between Christianity and Science," in Michael Bauman, ed., *Man and Creation: Perspectives on Science and Theology* (Hillsdale, Mich.: Hillsdale College Press, 1993), 5-29; Colin Russell, "The Conflict Metaphor and Its Social Origins," *Science and Christian Belief* 1:1 (1989), 3-26.

Defining "Science"

A sampling of over-simplified definitions of "science" from respectable sources: "the empirical study of the order of nature" (Ian Barbour, *Religion in an Age of Science* [New York: HarperSanFrancisco, 1990], 3); "the quest to find the immutable and universal laws that govern processes, presuming that there are cause-and-effect relations among the processes" (Neil Postman, *Technopoly* [New York: Alfred A. Knopf, 1994], 148). Paul Helm (*The Providence of God* [Downers Grove, Ill.: InterVarsity Press, 1994], 30) is more careful when he says, "In the natural sciences, a good theory explains the occurrence of certain data, doing so in a simple and economical way, and enabling predictions of the future occurrence of more such data to be made"; but he, like the others, still limits science to the study of regularities. Compare the much more careful survey of possible meanings in David Lindberg, *The Beginnings of Western Science* (Chicago: University of Chicago Press, 1992), 1-4.

Stephen Hawking, *A Brief History of Time: From the Big Bang to Black Holes* (New York: Bantam, 1988), 42.

The first quotation from Sherlock Holmes comes from the story *A Study in Scarlet,* by Arthur Conan Doyle (similar dicta appear in "A Scandal in Bohemia" and "The Adventure of the Second Stain"). The second quotation comes from "The Adventure of the Reigate Squire."

The John Gribbin quotation comes from *Almost Everyone's Guide to Science* (London: Phoenix, 1999), 4.

The survey of the history of the word "science" depends heavily on James

Weisheipl, "The Nature, Scope, and Classification of the Sciences," in David Lindberg, ed., *Science in the Middle Ages* (University of Chicago, 1978), 461-482. The citation of William Whewell comes from the *Oxford English Dictionary* (1933), under "scientist." According to W. F. Bynum, E. J. Browne, and Roy Porter, *Dictionary of the History of Science* (Princeton, N.J.: Princeton University Press, 1984), Whewell first proposed the term in 1833, at a meeting of the British Association for the Advancement of Science.

The C. S. Lewis quotation comes from his essay "The Funeral of a Great Myth," in *Christian Reflections* (Grand Rapids, Mich.: Eerdmans, 1967), 82-93, at 82-83. I cite John Gribbin from his *Almost Everyone's Guide to Science,* 2. The Sherlock Holmes quotation is from *The Sign of Four* (1890), chapter 2.

Sherlock Holmes describes himself as a scientific detective in *The Sign of Four,* chapter 1, while the Father Brown quote comes from *The Secret of Father Brown.* Along these lines, compare what J. Gresham Machen wrote in *What Is Faith?*

> The question is whether a method which ignores the consciousness of sin is really scientific or not; and the answer must be, we think, that it is not (130).

> In any true universal science—a science that would obliterate the artificial departmental boundaries which we have erected for purposes of convenience and as a concession to human limitations—in any true universal science, confidence in personal beings would have a recognized place as a means of obtaining knowledge just as truly as chemical balances or telescopes (235).

Machen thought that science should be subject to the rules of rationality, and not make its own rules.

Defining "Faith"

The National Academy of Science, in its booklet *Teaching About Evolution and the Nature of Science* (Washington, D.C.: National Academy Press, 1998; on the Internet at <http://www.nap.edu>), says that "usually 'faith' refers to beliefs that are accepted without empirical evidence" (chapter 5, "Frequently Asked Questions"). This statement, like that in the Webster's dictionary, was written by someone with no serious contact with a mature believer.

J. Gresham Machen, *What Is Faith?* (Edinburgh: Banner of Truth, 1991 [originally 1925]).

For more discussion of the "heart," see Derek Kidner, *Proverbs* (Tyndale Old Testament Commentary; Downers Grove, Ill.: InterVarsity Press, 1964), on Proverbs 4:23 (68); see also B. O. Banwell, "Heart," in D. R. W. Wood, et al., eds., *New Bible Dictionary* (3rd edn.; Downers Grove, Ill.: InterVarsity Press, 1996), 456. The context of Proverbs 4:23 makes the point clear: the heart is the place where one keeps words for thought (v. 21), and which governs motivations and feelings (vv. 24-27).

On the core content of the faith, we have to be careful just why we want to identify it. On the one hand, I agree with Machen, who dealt with the question of "what are the minimum doctrinal requirements in order that a man may be a Christian?"

> That is a question which I have never answered, and which I have not the slightest intention of answering now. Indeed it is a question which I think no human being can answer. . . .
>
> The very asking of the question often betokens an unfortunate attitude with regard to Christian truth. . . . Some men seem to devote most of their energies to the task of seeing just how little of Christian truth they can get along with (*What Is Faith?* 155, 159).

On the other hand, we might ask, "What is the core content of true faith that unites all Christians, against which specific expressions (such as denominational confessions) can be measured?"—in which case we are asking a sensible question.

The C. S. Lewis quotation comes from *Mere Christianity,* book iii, chapter 11. I quote Pascal from his *Pensées,* A. J. Krailsheimer, ed. (London: Penguin, 1995), no. 174 (no. 270 by the Brunschvicg numbers).

Premises of the Methods of Science

The National Science Teachers Association has posted its position statement, "The Teaching of Evolution" (July 1997) at <http://www.nsta.org/159&id=10>. See also its statement, "The Nature of Science" (July 2000), at <http://www.nsta.org/159&id=22>.

Science and Knowledge

The view of knowledge that I advocate may also be called "critical common sense." The researches of the philosophers have uncovered difficulties, to be sure; but all they've really done is help us to be more "critical" in how we apply our common sense. As Machen put it (*What Is Faith?* 27):

> I am not altogether unaware of the difficulties that beset what may be called the common-sense view of truth; epistemology presents many interesting problems and some puzzling antinomies. But the antinomies of epistemology are like other antinomies which puzzle the human mind; they indicate the limitations of our intellect, but they do not prove that the intellect is not reliable so far as it goes.

The body lice example comes from Darrell Huff, *How to Lie with Statistics* (New York: Norton, 1954), 98-99. (The whole book is good reading for developing critical thinking skills.) The James Trefil citation comes from *101 Things You Don't Know About Science and No One Else Does Either* (Boston: Houghton Mifflin, 1996), 65.

The passage from David Hume comes from his *Enquiry Concerning Human Understanding,* iv.2; and my reply is from *The God of Miracles* (Wheaton, Ill.: Crossway, 2000 / Leicester, U.K.: Inter-Varsity Press, 2001), chapter 10.

Michael Behe, *Darwin's Black Box: The Biochemical Challenge to Evolution* (New York: Free Press, 1996), 240 (italics his). Machen, *What Is Faith?* 29.

Operating Relationships of Faith and Science

Compare how Machen dismisses radical complementarity in *What Is Faith?* (241-242):

> It is highly misleading, therefore, to say that religion and science are separate, and that the Bible is not intended to teach science. No doubt that assertion that the Bible is not intended to teach science does contain an element of truth: it is certainly true that there are many departments of science into which the Bible does not enter; and very possibly it is advantageous to isolate certain departments provisionally and pursue investigations in those departments without for the moment thinking of others. But such an isolation is at the best provisional merely; and ultimately there ought to be a real synthesis of truth. *On principle, it cannot be denied that the Bible does teach certain things about which science has a right to speak.* The matter is particularly clear in the sphere of history.
>
> We shall have to reject, therefore, the easy apologetic for Christianity which simply declares that religion and science belong in independent

> spheres and that science can never conceivably contradict religion. Of course real science can never actually contradict any religion that is true; but to say, before decision of the question whether the religion is true or false, that science cannot possibly contradict it, is to do despite both to religion and to science.

See also his *Christianity and Liberalism* (Grand Rapids, Mich.: Eerdmans, 1996 [originally 1923]), 4-6.

Stephen Jay Gould, *Rocks of Ages* (New York: Ballantine, 1999), is all about his NOMA proposal.

On biblical chronology, see K. A. Kitchen and T. C. Mitchell, "Chronology of the Old Testament," in D. R. W. Wood, et al., eds., *New Bible Dictionary* (3rd edn.; Downers Grove, Ill.: InterVarsity Press, 1996), 185-193.

The sciences may be misused in ethics, as well: for example, in John Stott's commentary on Ephesians 5:18 ("do not get drunk with wine, for that is debauchery"), he cites the famous London preacher D. M. Lloyd-Jones for the argument that since alcohol is a "depressant" it is bad. In the nineteenth century alcohol was called a "stimulant," using the word in a different sense than physiologists use it today. Lloyd-Jones (whose first training was as a medical doctor) has a problem with terms: the technical terms "stimulant" and "depressant" are not the same as the moral use of these words. Not only that, but Lloyd-Jones actually concluded something that is contrary to the Bible (see Ps. 104:15). So this is a misuse of science.

CHAPTER 4: THIS IS MY FATHER'S WORLD

How Many Creation Accounts Does One Religion Need? Literary Relationships of Genesis 1 and 2

I have written a technical paper on this topic, "Discourse Analysis and the Interpretation of Gen 2:4-7," *Westminster Theological Journal* 61 (1999), 269-276, where I give some further bibliography as well. I would also recommend Alviero Niccacci, "Analysis of Biblical Narrative," in R. D. Bergen, ed., *Biblical Hebrew and Discourse Linguistics* (Dallas: Summer Institute of Linguistics, 1994), 175-198, especially 183-189; and my essay on Genesis 1, "Reading Genesis 1:1–2:3 as an Act of Communication: Discourse Analysis and Literal Interpretation," in Joseph Pipa, Jr., and David Hall, eds., *Did God Create in Six Days?* (Taylors, S.C.: Southern Presbyterian Press, 1999), 131-151 (which I will cover in more detail in the next chapter).

Outline of Genesis 1:1–2:3

The idea that the days of Genesis 1 follow a pattern of ordering (days 1-3) and adornment (days 4-6)—one of the key observations behind what is now called the "framework view" that we will examine in the next chapter—is at least as old as the English bishop Robert Grossteste (1168–1253). Thomas Aquinas (1225–1274) also held this idea. See Robert Letham, "'In the Space of Six Days': The Days of Creation from Origen to the Westminster Assembly," *Westminster Theological Journal* 61:2 (1999), 149-174, at 160-163.

What Is Genesis 1:1–2:3 About?

C. S. Lewis, *A Preface to Paradise Lost* (London: Oxford University Press, 1942), 1.

The argument that Genesis 1:1 is a summary of the whole account gets a careful presentation in Bruce Waltke, "The Creation Account in Genesis 1:1-3, Part III: The Initial Chaos Theory and the Precreation Chaos Theory," *Bibliotheca Sacra* 132 (July–September 1975), 216-228. His basic argument is that the phrase "created the heavens and the earth" describes the finished product, as opposed to the initial production of something "without form and void" (v. 2). Besides the arguments given in the text, I would add the following considerations: (a) the verb forms of verses 1-3 show that verses 1-2 are background to verse 3 (see Niccacci, 183); (b) the word order of verse 2 shows its relationship to verse 1: verse 1 ends with "the heavens and the earth," while verse 2 begins with "and the earth"—which in Hebrew has the effect of, "now as for the earth (which I just mentioned)." Therefore Waltke's conclusion that a reading like mine—which he acknowledges to be the standard reading among Jewish and Christian interpreters—"faces such serious objections as to render it untenable," is actually wrong. (Waltke also refers to Wisdom 11:17, but misunderstands it; see my discussion below.)

Is Genesis 1:1–2:3 Supposed to Be a Historical Record?

On the problem of "history," see V. P. Long, *The Art of Biblical History* (Grand Rapids, Mich.: Zondervan, 1994), especially 58-87 (chapter 2, "History and Fiction: What Is History?"). The first definition of "myth" is a paraphrase of the *Oxford English Dictionary* (1933), sense 1. The second definition is a paraphrase from the *Webster's New World College Dictionary* (1999). The schoolchild's definition of "fairy tale" comes from Richard Lederer, *More Anguished English* (New York: Dell, 1993), 6. The Tolkien reference comes from the Epilogue of his essay, "On Fairy Stories," in *The Monsters and the Critics* (Boston: Houghton-Mifflin, 1984) and in *The Tolkien Reader* (New York: Ballantine, 1966).

Does Genesis 1:1 Teach "Creation from Nothing"?

On creation from nothing as a genuinely biblical teaching see Paul Copan, "Is *creatio ex nihilo* a Post-Biblical Invention? An Examination of Gerhard May's Proposal," *Trinity Journal* new series 17 (1996), 77-93.

Three verses from the Apocryphal or Deuterocanonical books also apply to the question of creation from nothing. In 2 Maccabees 7:28-29, a Jewish mother speaks to her son who is about to be martyred under the wicked king Antiochus (ruled the Syrian kingdom, 175–163 B.C.), saying:

> [28] "I beg you, child, to look at the heavens and the earth and see all that is in them; then you will know that *God did not make them out of existing things;* and in the same way the human race came into existence. [29] Do not be afraid of this executioner, but be worthy of your brothers and accept death, so that in the time of mercy I may receive you again with them" (NAB).

This clear affirmation of creation from nothing steeled the boy and his mother for their own sufferings.

The Wisdom of Solomon comes from Alexandria, Egypt, about 100 B.C. The author uses Greek philosophical terms and concepts to show that the Scriptures provide the best philosophy, to commend biblical faith to the Greek world, and to strengthen Jewish thinkers who were drawn to the higher culture. In Wisdom 11:17 we find (RV),

> For thine all-powerful hand,
> *that created the world out of formless matter,*
> lacked not means to send upon them [the Egyptians]
> a multitude of bears, or fierce lions.

When he says "that created the world out of formless matter," he seems to be using a Greek term, "formless matter." Greek philosophers who used this term did not hold to creation from nothing: instead, God formed the world from preexisting formless matter. Is this author following the Greek ideas? I think not, in view of his very biblical statement earlier (9:1), addressing God as "you who have made all things by your word" (NAB). In 11:17 he doesn't say that the formless matter is eternal; as the commentator J. A. F. Gregg remarked, "the use of *create* here is non-committal: it leaves the origin of matter out of sight, and deals merely with the arrangement of matter." This is consistent with the senses of the Greek verb *ktizô* (here translated with "to create") in the general Greek world. See J. A. F. Gregg, *The Wisdom of Solomon* (Cambridge Bible for Schools and Colleges; Cambridge: Cambridge University Press, 1909); see also Joseph Reider, *The Book of Wisdom* (New York: Harper & Brothers, 1957).

Is Genesis 1:1–2:3 a "Scientific" Account of Creation?

The quotations from John Calvin come from his commentary on Genesis (original Latin, 1563), using the Calvin Translation Society English edition (Grand Rapids, Mich.: Baker, 1979; originally 1847), 79, 86. Calvin also believed the science of his day, namely the pre-Copernican model, as he shows (61):

> We indeed are not ignorant, that the circuit of the heavens is finite, and that the earth, like a little globe, is placed in the center.

Such a picture does not enter into his exegesis—though it can't help but affect the way he *imagined* the narratives.

What Does It Mean That the Creation Was "Good"?

On the display of God's goodness in his creatures, compare Thomas Aquinas, *Summa Theologiae,* I.47.1.

What Does This Mean for Us?

C. S. Lewis, *Mere Christianity,* book iii, chapter 1 ("The Three Parts of Morality"); and book ii, chapter 5 ("The Practical Conclusion").

CHAPTER 5: WHAT KIND OF DAYS WERE THOSE, ANYHOW?

On the details of interpreting the days, see the bibliography for chapter 4. Add to this my "How Old Is the Earth? Anthropomorphic Days in Genesis 1:1–2:3," *Presbyterion* 20:2 (Fall 1994), 109-130, which supplies some of the historical references as well.

The Catholic Study Bible (New York: Oxford University Press, 1990), based on the *New American Bible* (1970), aims to be representative of Roman Catholic biblical scholarship. At a more popular level is a book written by a theologically conservative Roman Catholic, Peter Kreeft, *You*

Can Understand the Old Testament (Ann Arbor, Mich.: Servant, 1990), see 21-22.

Actually, it is not clear that the best brains of the Middle Ages did insist on the ordinary day reading. See the survey of Robert Letham, "'In the Space of Six Days': The Days of Creation from Origen to the Westminster Assembly," *Westminster Theological Journal* 61 (1999), 149-174, for extensive documentation. The Catholic Answers website also has excerpts from ancient and medieval authors, showing that they held a variety of views, at <www.catholic.com/library/Creation_and_Genesis.asp>.

On contemporary usage of "literal," see R. W. Burchfield, *The New Fowler's Modern English Usage* (Oxford: Oxford University Press, 2000), 463.

I quote Charles Hodge from his *Systematic Theology* (Grand Rapids, Mich.: Eerdmans, 1981), I:570-571.

An Interpretation That Accounts for All of These Features

Advocates of the ordinary day view often point to the refrain as evidence for their interpretation: namely, they argue that "evening and morning" together imply that we have an ordinary day, because every other time those two terms are used together in the Bible, you have an ordinary day. This argument suffers from the same problem with statistical reasoning that I will discuss below. For one example out of many, see John D. Morris, "How Old Is the Earth According to the Bible?" *Back to Genesis* 74b (Vital Articles on Science and Creation, February 1995); available on the Internet at <icr.org>. Morris says (repeating what he's been told many times, I guess),

> Furthermore, *yom* [Hebrew for "day"] is modified by "evening and morning," which in Hebrew can only mean a literal day.

This sentence is utter nonsense as it stands—perhaps due to the compressed nature of the short essay. But "day" is not "modified" by "evening and morning," as should be clear from my discussion. And there is no "rule" in Hebrew that would make this refer to a "literal" day anyhow.

The Sherlock Holmes story is "The Adventure of Silver Blaze."

Augustine, *Confessions* 13:36 in Henry Chadwick's edition (Oxford: Oxford University Press, 1991); some editions have it as 13:51. Aquinas seems to have the same view of the creation Sabbath and of John 5:17 (compare *Summa Theologiae,* I.73.2-3; I.74.1).

Regarding "ordinary providence" in the creation week: Joseph Pipa, Jr.,

"From Chaos to Cosmos: A Critique of the Non-literal Interpretations of Genesis 1:1–2:3," in Joseph Pipa, Jr., and David Hall, eds., *Did God Create in Six Days?* (Taylors, S.C.: Southern Presbyterian Press, 1999), 153-198, discusses the claim that "ordinary providence" was God's manner of working during the creation week (from M. G. Kline, whose framework view is discussed below) at 161-164. Pipa disagrees with Kline's claim—and so do I. However, I am simply arguing that (1) a special creative act was certainly taking place in 1:11-12; and (2) the explanation Moses gives in 2:5-6 is not the absence of miracle but the ordinary way things work.

What About the Fourth Day?

For more on the details of the fourth day, consult Yehudah Kiel, *Sefer Bere'shit* (*Book of Genesis*) in the Da'at Mikra commentary series (Jerusalem: Mossad Harav Kook, 1997), with its references to the medieval Jewish scholars.

Other Possible Interpretations of the Days

The framework view is the hardest to describe, perhaps because it is really a family of views with a few basic tenets in common. Meredith Kline first advocated it in "Because It Had Not Rained," *Westminster Theological Journal* 20 (1958), 146-157; then in the entry on "Genesis" in D. Guthrie et al., *The New Bible Commentary: Revised* (Grand Rapids, Mich.: Eerdmans, 1970); and in its full development in "Space and Time in the Genesis Cosmogony," *Perspectives on Science and Christian Faith* 48 (1996), 2-15. A clearer description of the Kline-type view comes from M. D. Futato, "Because It Had Rained: A Study of Gen 2:5-7 with Implications for Gen 2:4-25 and Gen 1:1–2:3," *Westminster Theological Journal* 60 (1998), 1-21. Others who have advocated a framework-type view, but with less claim of historicity, include Henri Blocher, *In the Beginning* (Downers Grove, Ill.: InterVarsity Press, 1984); B. K. Waltke, "The Literary Genre of Genesis, Chapter One," *Crux* 27 (1991), 2-10; Umberto Cassuto, *A Commentary on the Book of Genesis* (Jerusalem: Magnes, 1961); M. W. Poole and G. J. Wenham, *Creation or Evolution: A False Antithesis?* (Oxford: Latimer, 1987); and Claus Westermann, *Genesis 1–11: A Commentary* (Minneapolis: Augsburg, 1984).

There are other approaches that I haven't discussed in these pages. They include the "days of revelation" interpretation, where the days are six consecutive days in which God *revealed* the narrative to Moses. This is associated with the British soldier and diplomat P. J. Wiseman, *Creation Revealed in Six Days* (1958); and his son, the well-respected Assyriologist D. J. Wiseman, "Creation Time—What Does Genesis Say?" *Science and Christian Belief* 3:1 (1991), 25-34. I reject it because it does not explain either the picture of God as a workman or the Sabbath commandment. Another is the "days of divine fiat" interpretation, where the days are six consecutive ordinary days in which God said his instructions, while the fulfillment of those instructions took place over long periods of time. In other words, in Genesis 1 only what God *said* took place during the creation week, and the rest would be in parentheses. Recently Alan Hayward has popularized this view in *Creation and Evolution: Rethinking the Evidence from Science and the Bible* (Minneapolis: Bethany, 1995; originally London: SPCK, 1985). I don't see how this can be consistent with the Sabbath commandment, which locates God's work during the six days—and which relies on the analogy between God's work and rest and ours. Another view is the "focus-on-Palestine" view advocated by John Sailhamer in *Genesis Unbound* (Sisters, Ore.: Multnomah, 1996). By this approach, the creation proper is restricted to Genesis 1:1, and then in verse 2 the account shifts to describing the way God prepared Palestine for Israel. In discussing Genesis 2:4-7 I already noted that the word "earth" can refer just to a specific "land," and I employed that in my interpretation of those verses. However, I do not think that possible in the first story, since the "earth" as dry land is contrasted with the seas (1:10). Similarly, the waters of the fifth day include the seas since they contain the great sea creatures (1:21). Also the Sabbath commandment refers to God's making "heaven and earth, the sea and all that is in them," which is quite global.

And finally, there is the "expanding time" view, from the Israeli physicist Gerald Schroeder in *Genesis and the Big Bang* (New York: Bantam, 1991); and *The Science of God* (New York: Free Press, 1997). First, he contends that since the Jewish calendar begins with Adam, we may take the six creation days as separate from this clock. Second, he employs Einstein's relativity theory, under the assumption that the six "days" are days from a different frame of reference than ours on earth, namely from the initial Big Bang (from our frame of reference, the universe is 15 billion years old). Under this scheme, the first day is twenty-four hours from the "beginning of time" perspective, and 8 billion years from ours. The second day, twenty-four hours from the beginning of time perspective, was 4 billion years long from ours. The third day from our vantage point was 2 billion years, the fourth day one billion years, the fifth day half a billion, and the sixth day was a quarter billion years long. To Schroeder's delight, this adds up to 15.75 billion years, the same as the modern cosmologists' calculation. The appeal of this view is that it does not need another meaning for "day," and at the same time harmonizes with modern cosmology. The exegetical difficulty is that it requires a vantage point other than that of earth, which the Genesis account seems to presuppose. Philosophically, it must justify its strong impulse toward harmonization with science (as with the day-age view). Actually, the analogical days view is simpler, and less reliant on harmonization with science.

Many advocates of the ordinary day view are fond of quoting a letter from James Barr to David C. C. Watson, dated April 23, 1984 (cited recently, for example, in Douglas Kelly, *Creation and Change: Genesis 1.1–2.4 in the Light of Changing Scientific Paradigms* [Fearn, Ross-shire, U.K.: Christian Focus, 1997], 50-51). There are several problems with the way ordinary day authors use this quote: to begin with, they only cite a portion of the letter. Here is the full text, with the portion that Kelly cites in italics. (Mr. Steve Jones of Australia obtained a copy of the letter from Answers in Genesis, and kindly sent me a copy of it; he has posted it on the Internet at <http://members.iinet.net.au/~sejones/barrlett.html>.):

THE UNIVERSITY OF OXFORD

23 April 1984

David C. C. Watson, Esq.,
1300 N. Cross
Wheaton Illinois

Dear Mr Watson,

Thank you for your letter. I have thought about your question, and would say that probably, *so far as I know, there is no professor of Hebrew or Old Testament at any world-class university who does not believe that the writer(s) of Genesis 1–11 intended to convey to their readers the ideas that (a) creation took place in a series of six days which were the same as the days of 24 hours we now experience (b) the figures contained in the Genesis genealogies provided by simple addition a chronology from the beginning of the world up to later stages in the biblical story (c) Noah's flood was understood to be world-wide and extinguish all human and animal life except for those in the ark. Or, to put it negatively, the apologetic arguments which suppose the 'days' of creation to be long eras of time, the figures of years not to be chronological, and the flood to be a merely local*

> *Mesopotamian flood, are not taken seriously by any such professors, as far as I know.* The only thing I would say to qualify this is that most professors may avoid much involvement in that sort of argument and so may not say much explicitly about it one way or the other. But I think what I say would represent their position correctly. However, you might find one or two people who would take the contrary point of view and are competent in the languages, in Assyriology, and so on: it's really not so much a matter of technical linguistic competence, as of appreciation of the sort of text that Genesis is.
>
> Perhaps I might mention that I have another book coming out soon, Escaping from Fundamentalism, SCM Press London, which has some discussion of these questions. Westminster Press in Philadelphia are doing the American edition, perhaps with a different title, I don't know. It comes out in this country on 1st June.
>
> Thanks again for your letter and all good wishes,
>
> Yours sincerely
> James Barr [signed]

Before we assess the bit that ordinary day writers usually cite, we must take account of the material that they commonly omit. First, Barr plays down the significance of his testimony when he writes, "The only thing I would say to qualify this is that most professors may avoid much involvement in that sort of argument and so may not say much explicitly about it one way or the other"—which means he's not claiming to have done a survey. Second, he concedes that "you might find one or two people who would take the contrary point of view and are competent in the languages, in Assyriology, and so on"—perhaps referring to Donald Wiseman, a professor of Assyriology at the University of London. And third, he gives the whole game away—as far as the ordinary day view is concerned—when he says, "it's really not so much a matter of technical linguistic competence, as of appreciation of the sort of text that Genesis is." But this is exactly why the ordinary day authors cite Barr's letter: to show that it *is* a matter of technical competence.

And what shall we make of the part that these authors actually do cite? No one should be taken in by their claims. First, there is the appeal to authority: "no professor" takes this seriously, therefore neither should you. The same James Barr began a book on Genesis 3 by claiming that Old Testament scholarship "has long known that the reading of the story as the 'Fall of Man' in the traditional sense, though hallowed by St. Paul's use of it, cannot stand up to examination through a close reading of the Genesis text" (*The Garden of Eden and the Hope of Immortality* [Minneapolis: Fortress, 1992], ix). Few believing Christians would find this a good reason for not following Paul over this alleged consensus of Old Testament scholarship (and see my study of the passage in "What Happened to Adam and Eve? A Literary-Theological Approach to Genesis 3," *Presbyterion* 27:1 [Spring 2001], 12-44). You can't decide any issues by counting noses: you need to look at *reasons* and evaluate *those*.

Second, Barr has made some factual errors. For example, in his point (a) he left out Claus Westermann's commentary on Genesis 1–11, whose German original appeared in 1974. Westermann takes a sort of nonhistorical literary framework view, as I mentioned above. In his point (b) he left out Terence Mitchell of the British Museum and Alan Millard of Liverpool University, whose article "Genealogy" appeared in the 1982 edition of the *New Bible Dictionary* (Leicester, U.K.: InterVarsity Press / Wheaton, Ill.: Tyndale, 1982). Mitchell and Millard give reasons to believe that the work of W. H. Green (discussed in my chapter 7) proves that the genealogies have gaps and are thus not intended to provide material for chronological computations. (I have spoken with other specialists in the Genesis genealogies—some of whom teach at British universities—who agree with Green.)

I have no reason to doubt that Barr wrote truly, that is, to the best of his knowledge; but in view of the problems we can see, to accept his letter as settling anything is to be snookered.

Let's look at another common argument that we frequently find in support of the ordinary day reading: that the "days" in Genesis 1 must be ordinary days because whenever the word "day" has a number with it in the rest of the Old Testament, it is an ordinary day. (See, for example, Kelly, 107; Henry Morris and John Morris, *The Modern Creation Trilogy* [Green Forest, Ark.: Master, 1996], I:43-45.) This argument is unsound, and uses the statistics in an unsound manner.

The statistic cited may in fact be accurate, but statistics alone are not enough to establish an inductive argument (which is what this argument is). We would need, not just a statistic, but also an explanation of *why* the statistic demonstrates a principle. Otherwise this would be an example of the *post hoc ergo propter hoc* ("after this, therefore because of this") fallacy. (Darrell Huff, *How to Lie with Statistics* [New York: Norton, 1954], devotes his chapter 8, "Post Hoc Rides Again," to the matter.)

For a lexical argument such as this one, this explanation would be in terms of the combinational rules of the Hebrew word *yôm* ("day") and the kinds of words with which it is being combined. An example of the right kind of argument from English would be: the English word "house" has several possible meanings, such as (a) "physical structure in which people live," (b) "household," and (c) "lineage." If we modify the word with a color term, such as "red house," we virtually eliminate senses (b) and (c) from consideration (except in very unusual instances that we need not worry about). And it's pretty clear why: we wouldn't ordinarily use a color term to describe any of the other senses. This illustrates what I mean by explaining a statistic with a principle.

For this argument to be good, then, we must propose a combinational rule for the Hebrew word *yôm* ("day") when it is modified by a number. We would then have to show that the rule applies in every case; and to do that we would have to show that it was the *rule,* and not the *context* of the other usages, which secured the interpretation of *yôm.* To do so we would have to compare like with like, that is, we would need a context comparable to that of Genesis 1 where the proposed rule overrode any contextual factors that pointed away from a strictly "literal" understanding of *yôm* (unfortunately I do not know of such a context in the Hebrew Bible).

Further, you'd have to be convinced that a rule like this was even possible in Hebrew (or in any other language); that is to say, you'd have to find some *motivation* for the rule. I myself find it hard to believe that such a rule would be possible. And finally, the most this proposed rule could do, even if it were valid, would be to count against the "day-age" theory, since the other interpretations listed above do not strictly speaking involve "figurative" (a slippery word anyhow) uses of *yôm:* instead, they posit a "literary" use of an ordinary meaning of the word.

Conclusions

For a discussion of the Dutch stalwarts of the late nineteenth and early twentieth centuries, see Max Rogland, "*Ad litteram:* Some Dutch Reformed Theologians on the Creation Days," *Westminster Theological Journal* 63 (2001), 211-233.

CHAPTER 6: OTHER BIBLICAL PASSAGES ABOUT CREATION

Old Testament

C. S. Lewis, *The Screwtape Letters* (London: Geoffrey Bles, 1942), letter 21 (end).

The Sabbath commandment appears in Exodus 20:8-11 and Deuteronomy 5:12-15, with minor differences. The difference that gets the most attention is the fact that while Exodus grounds the commandment in the creation Sabbath, Deuteronomy grounds it in the way God delivered his people from slavery in Egypt. These are not contradictions: the Pentateuch represents the two lists as being spoken on separate occasions, so they need not be identical. Also, we shouldn't make this an either-or proposition, when both-and makes good sense. Exodus 31:12-17 also enjoins Sabbath observance, calling the day (v. 13) "a sign between me and you throughout your generations, that you may know that I, the LORD, sanctify you"—a reference to God's covenant with Israel, which connects it to the deliverance from Egypt. The same passage also calls the Sabbath (v. 17) "a sign forever between me and the people of Israel that in six days the LORD made heaven and earth, and on the seventh day he rested and was refreshed"—a reference to creation. Hence the two ideas, creation and deliverance, belong together. Further, Leviticus 23:3 requires that Sabbath observance include both bodily rest and assembled worship—again connecting creation (bodily rest) and covenant (worship).

Many have sought to relate Psalm 104 to the whole structure of the days in Genesis 1; for an example see Derek Kidner, *Psalms 73–150* (Tyndale Old Testament Commentary; Downers Grove, Ill.: InterVarsity Press, 1973), 368.

For the Old Testament's "primitive" world view, see the nice illustration in W. D. Reyburn, *A Handbook on the Book of Job* (New York: United Bible Societies, 1992), 181. This illustration is surprising for the way it takes pictorial language literalistically: for example, it misses the point of the phenomenological description of the "expanse/canopy" of Genesis 1:6 (not to mention what it does to the "pillars" of the sky and earth). I would level the same criticisms at Paul Seely, "The Geographical Meaning of 'Earth' and 'Seas' in Genesis 1:10," *Westminster Theological Journal* 59 (1997), 231-255.

The quote from Nicholas Wolterstorff comes from his *Divine Discourse* (Cambridge: Cambridge University Press, 1995), 209-210.

On the history of cosmology, see John North, *The Norton History of Astronomy and Cosmology* (New York: Norton, 1995).

CHAPTER 7: IS THE EARTH YOUNG OR OLD?

Did Jesus Think the Creation Period Was Short?

I did not make up this argument from the Gospels. It appears, for example, in Sid Dyer, "The New Testament Doctrine of Creation," in Joseph Pipa, Jr., and David Hall, eds., *Did God Create in Six Days?* (Taylors, S.C.: Southern Presbyterian Press, 1999), 221-242. Dyer cites for support the opinion of

Francis Turretin, a very conservative seventeenth-century Swiss Protestant theologian. I have found that those who accept this argument consider it very important, because in their view to reject it amounts to denying a fundamental doctrine of Christianity, the deity of Christ.

The Genealogies in Genesis

An example of a scholar who reads the genealogies as supplying chronology is James Barr, in the citation of him that I discussed in the notes for chapter 5. (Barr writes as a "liberal," that is, as one who thinks that this interpretation shows why we shouldn't attribute historical truthfulness to the Bible.) Another Old Testament scholar who denies that there are gaps in the genealogies is the Seventh-Day Adventist Gerhard Hasel, in "The Meaning of the Chronogenealogies of Genesis 5 and 11," *Origins* 7:2 (1980), 53-70 (available on the Internet at <www.grisda.org/origins/07053.htm>). I will discuss below why I disagree with Hasel.

Others, who are not Old Testament scholars like Barr and Hasel are, include Henry Morris, *The Genesis Record* (Grand Rapids, Mich.: Baker, 1976), 154 (albeit with caution); Douglas Kelly, *Creation and Change: Genesis 1.1–2.4 in the Light of Changing Scientific Paradigms* (Fearn, Ross-shire, U.K.: Christian Focus, 1997), 139-142; and James Jordan, "The Biblical Chronology Question: An Analysis," *Creation and Social Science Humanities Quarterly* 2:2 (Winter 1979), whom Kelly cites with approval. See also Walter Brown, *In the Beginning: Compelling Evidence for Creation and the Flood* (Phoenix: Center for Scientific Creation, 1995), 192-193.

For my analysis of the genealogies I am heavily in debt to my former student Jeffrey Dryden, who wrote a seminar paper for me on this topic in 1997. I have urged him to publish his work, but now that he is a Ph.D. student in *New* Testament at Cambridge, it is unlikely he'll get to it any time soon. The William Henry Green essay "Primeval Chronology" was first published in *Bibliotheca Sacra* 47 (1890), 285-303; it has been reprinted in Walter Kaiser, *Classical Evangelical Essays in Old Testament Interpretation* (Grand Rapids, Mich.: Baker, 1972), 13-28; and in Robert Newman and Herman Eckelmann, Jr., *Genesis One and the Age of the Earth* (Downers Grove, Ill.: InterVarsity Press, 1977), 105-123. Scholars of the Ancient Near East who accept Green's conclusions include the following contributors to the *New Bible Dictionary* (3rd edn.; Downers Grove, Ill.: InterVarsity Press, 1996): Egyptologist Kenneth Kitchen ("Chronology of the Old Testament," see 187b); Terence Mitchell of the British Museum and Alan Millard, professor of ancient Semitic languages ("Genealogy," see 400a-401a). See also Desmond Alexander, who has extensively studied the genealogies of Genesis, in "Genealogies, Seed, and the Compositional Unity of Genesis," *Tyndale Bulletin* 44:2 (1993), at 262 n. 14.

The essay by Hasel cites some of the above works in order to disagree with them; but I find his arguments quite weak. He points out that the formula used in Genesis 5 and 11 is not simply "A begat B," but (compare how I cite it in the chapter), "When PN_1 had lived *x* years, he fathered PN_2. And PN_1 lived after he fathered PN_2 *y* years, and he fathered other sons and daughters. And all the days of PN_1 were *z* years." He then writes,

> A reduction of this stereotyped literary formula with its inseparable interconnection of line of descent and years before the *birth* of the named son followed by the subsequent years of life to simply "A begat B" is an oversimplification. It distorts drastically the components of the formula. This unwarranted procedure leads Kitchen and other interpreters [e.g. Green and those who follow him] to argue that the line of descent in Genesis 5 and 11 is *discontinuous* (italics added to aid discussion).

The problems with this line of reasoning are many. First, as I have already noted in the chapter, the formula says nothing about how old PN_1 was at the *birth* of PN_2; it says how old PN_1 was when he *fathered* PN_2—Hasel strangely shifted from his correct formula citation ("fathered") to an unwarranted interpretation ("birth"), thus begging the very question he should be proving. Second, the adjective "discontinuous" is a curious choice of word that distorts the meaning of Green's position: the Green view advocates taking the genealogies as describing a continuous line of descent, but as not claiming to list every member of that line. So the better adjective is "selective" or "representative." Third, when Hasel claims that the formula found in Genesis 5 and 11 sets these genealogies off from those found elsewhere, he fails to show how that means that these genealogies would follow different conventions from other genealogies. Indeed, we have to study the other genealogies in both the Bible and the rest of the ancient Near East to get a feel for what those conventions might be—and I would say that you need a great deal of evidence before you set aside the "feel" that scholars like Kitchen, Millard, Mitchell, and Alexander have for such things. Therefore the display of erudition found in Hasel's essay is all to no avail.

The genealogies in Genesis 5 and 11 indicate long lives for the people mentioned. Just how to read these numbers is a separate question from my discussion here; but see the commentaries of V. P. Hamilton, *Genesis 1–17*

(New International Commentary on the Old Testament; Grand Rapids, Mich.: Eerdmans, 1990), 250-254, on the relationship between these and ancient king lists; and G. J. Wenham, *Genesis 1–15* (Word Biblical Commentary; Waco: Word, 1987), 130-134. Wenham does not favor the W. H. Green approach, but doesn't have much discussion. He does call the matter of the ages an "intractable problem," and passes on the suggestion that "these figures are designed to show that though the narrative is dealing with very distant times, it is a sort of history, and that however long men lived, they were mortal."

CHAPTER 8: WHAT A PIECE OF WORK IS MAN!

The Hamlet quotations are from Shakespeare's play *Hamlet;* the first from Act II, scene ii, lines 307 and following; and Act IV, scene v, lines 33 and following. I quote Blaise Pascal from his *Pensées,* A. J. Krailsheimer, ed. (London: Penguin, 1995), no. 200 (no. 347 by the Brunschvicg numbers).

You Are a Human Animal

To whom does "us" refer in Genesis 1:26 ("let *us* make man")? The basic possibilities are: (a) the account originally came from a polytheistic culture, where many gods consulted among themselves, and the Israelites just didn't clean up that part of the story enough when they took it over for their own; (b) God is speaking to his heavenly court, that is, to the host of angels; (c) it is a "we" of self-deliberation (which can open the way for plurality of persons in the Godhead). Only possibilities (b) and (c) are compatible with traditional Christianity, and many able scholars have argued for (b)—among them Franz Delitzsch, Gordon Wenham, and Bruce Waltke. Option (c), however, is surely the one that the text itself supports the best, since: (1) the possessive "our" should refer to the same person as "us" here, and in verse 27 (the fulfillment) man is in God's image, that is, not in the image of anyone else (as also in 5:1); (2) the verbs "make" and "create" in this account only ever have God as their subject throughout, and compare 1:31 and 2:2-3 where God is the only maker/creator; (3) in Genesis 11:7, "let *us* go down and confuse," we have a similar construction, and the one who "goes down" (v. 5) and "scatters" (v. 8) is only said to be God. Further, the advocates of position (b) have offered a number of verses that they say prove that the angels are God's heavenly council, but a careful look at those verses shows that none of them implies that God would make the heavenly court his counselors: compare, for example, Isaiah 6:8, where Isaiah goes up for "us," but it's really just the LORD; Psalm 89:6-8, where none of the heavenly beings is like God in power and authority; 1 Kings 22:19-22, where a lying spirit volunteers to entice Ahab to his death, and there is no reference to "us"; Job 1, where the sons of God present themselves in his presence strictly as his subordinates; Daniel 7:10-13, where thousands upon thousands of heavenly beings attend at God's throne, but only the Ancient of Days and the one like a Son of Man have dominion and authority; Luke 2:9-14, where the angels are messengers of good news of a great joy, but not counselors for God; Revelation 4–5, where the twenty-four elders and the four living creatures surround God's throne and worship, but are not called his counselors.

I know that some object to calling God's arrangement with Adam in 2:15-17 a "covenant," since the text doesn't use that word here. (It does, however, use it in Hosea 6:7, which refers to the events of Genesis 3.) For more discussion see the next chapter; and my "What Happened to Adam and Eve? A Literary-Theological Approach to Genesis 3," *Presbyterion* 27:1 (Spring 2001), 12-44, at 21-22.

The passage from Laura Ingalls Wilder comes from her book *The Long Winter* (New York: HarperCollins, 1968 [originally 1940]), 12-13. The citation from Epictetus comes from his *Discourses,* I.iii.3; and that from Aristotle comes from his *Nicomachean Ethics,* I.vii.12-13 (see also I.xiii.9-20).

Body and Soul

My discussion of body and soul is deeply indebted to John Murray, *Collected Writings* (Edinburgh: Banner of Truth Trust, 1984), 2:14-46. See also John Cooper, *Body, Soul and Life Everlasting* (Grand Rapids, Mich.: Eerdmans, 1989), who advocates "holistic dualism" (although often his exegesis is really unsatisfying); Thomas Aquinas, *Summa Theologiae* I.75-78; and James Barr, *The Garden of Eden and the Hope of Immortality* (Minneapolis: Augsburg/Fortress, 1993), 36-47, for an incisive analysis of "Hebrew 'totality thinking' and the soul" (this is the kind of work in which Barr really shines, showing the faulty word study method and conclusions of much of twentieth-century "Biblical theology").

For a helpful introduction to proper word study method, see Moisés Silva, *Biblical Words and Their Meaning* (Grand Rapids, Mich.: Zondervan, 1994 [1st edn., 1983]). See also D. A. Carson, *Exegetical Fallacies* (Grand Rapids, Mich.: Baker, 1984), chapter 1.

The citation from C. S. Lewis, *Screwtape Letters,* is from Letter 8.

The Apocrypha (or Deuterocanonical books) show the same range of usage and ideas as the Hebrew Old Testament, including the areas that I have adduced in favor of dualism: for example, we find body as distinct from soul or spirit in Wisdom 9:15; 2 Maccabees 6:30; 15:30; the soul or spirit leaves the body at death in Wisdom 15:8; 16:14; Tobit 3:6; Sirach (Ecclesiasticus) 38:23; Baruch 2:17; and 2 Maccabees 7:22-23 (where it also *enters* the body in the mother's womb); and the soul and spirit are names for the same thing in Wisdom 15:11; 16:14.

The *Oxford English Dictionary* (1971 edn.) includes, under its entry for "pineal," a quotation from Thomas Reid's *Essays on the Intellectual Powers of Man* (1785), II.iv.99: "Des Cartes, observing that the pineal gland is the only part of the brain that is single, was determined by this to make that gland the soul's habitation."

The citations from C. S. Lewis, *Mere Christianity,* are from book iii, chapter 9 ("Charity"); and from book ii, chapter 5 ("The Practical Conclusion").

The Image of God

Important bibliography on the image of God, besides the manuals of theology, includes James Barr, "The Image of God in the Book of Genesis—A Study of Terminology," *Bulletin of the John Rylands Library* 51 (1968), 11-26; David Clines, "The Image of God in Man," *Tyndale Bulletin* 19 (1968), 53-103; J. M. Miller, "In the 'Image' and 'Likeness' of God," *Journal of Biblical Literature* 91 (1972), 289-304; J. F. A. Sawyer, "The Meaning of *betselem elohim* ('in the Image of God') in Genesis I-XI," *Journal of Theological Studies* new series 25:2 (1974), 418-426; Raymond Van Leeuwen, "Form, Image," in W. A. VanGemeren, ed., *New International Dictionary of Old Testament Theology and Exegesis* (Grand Rapids, Mich.: Zondervan, 1997), 4:643-648; and the painstakingly detailed Gunnlaugur A. Jónsson, *The Image of God: Genesis 1:26-28 in a Century of Old Testament Research* (Coniectanea Biblica, OT Series 26; Lund, Sweden: Almqvist & Wiksell, 1988). Jónsson concludes that the representative view is not only the right one but also the most common one among Old Testament scholars; he mentions a few scholars who take the relational view, and calls this the only tenable alternative. He does note that neither Sawyer nor Barr in the articles cited side with either of these two (and Sawyer seems to favor the resemblance view).

Some of the historical factors that seem to have produced the shift away from *being* to *doing* include the way Biblical criticism seemed to undermine the historical reliability of biblical texts; and those who wanted to use the Bible religiously had to find some other resting place than its historical claims (which have to do with being). They began to say that the Bible is *theology*, not *history*, and thus to find its focus on man's "religious" life as opposed to his interaction with the world. I do not attack this philosophical trend, which I disagree with, in my defense of the resemblance view, because that would be to commit the genetic fallacy: one's view must stand or fall on its ability to cover the data, not on whether its advocates hold a philosophy I don't accept. There are many today who would affirm the truthfulness of the Bible but would also reject the resemblance view—mostly because many advocates of the resemblance view have seen human reason as the chief part of our likeness to God, and this seems to leave out the moral and relational side of life. (A common way to express this idea is to call the resemblance view "static" and the relational view "dynamic.") But I reply that (1) the objectors think of reason as cold analysis, and I don't think the resemblance people have used it in so narrow a sense; and (2) even if some advocates of a view are out of balance, that doesn't mean that the view itself can't be fixed.

A valuable work from a theologian is Herman Bavinck, *In the Beginning: Foundations of Creation Theology* (Grand Rapids, Mich.: Baker, 1999; English translation from the Dutch *Gereformierde Dogmatiek,* 2nd edn., 4 vols., 1906–1911). Bavinck is in general agreement with the positions outlined in the present work regarding the image of God and man's body-soul composition. On the other hand, we have the work by the theologian A. Hoekema, *Created in God's Image* (Grand Rapids, Mich.: Eerdmans, 1986), which argues for what he calls a *functional* view of the image, which is basically a combination of the relational and representative views (although he does allow the resemblance view in a way, but not as the foundation for the functions). Hoekema's discussion is odd for a number of reasons. First, although he presents himself as an heir to Bavinck, he doesn't really interact with Bavinck's arguments for the resemblance view. Second, Hoekema lacks the exegetical care found in Bavinck, as well as reference to important recent exegetical works such as the articles from Barr and Sawyer mentioned above. And third, Hoekema is parochial, apparently limiting his scope to North American Reformed Christians with strong Dutch ties—not only does he fail to take account of sources from, say, English-speaking Presbyterians, he even neglects the compendium of his own heritage by H. Heppe, *Reformed Dogmatics* (Grand Rapids, Mich.: Baker, 1978; English translation of 1935 German edition), not to mention the resources of the wider church. In contrast, Bavinck—a Dutch Reformed theologian from the late nineteenth and early twentieth centuries—is quite catholic in his scope.

The survey of passages could include the two references to the image of God in the Apocrypha/Deuterocanonical books, but I have not included them in the main chapter because there are some textual and interpretive issues that are a quicksand I wanted to avoid in this kind of study. However, I will here point out that both of these passages fall into our category (a), mankind as made in God's image. In Wisdom of Solomon 2:23, we read that "God created man for incorruption, and made him an image of his own eternity" (other texts read "of his own proper nature"). Then Sirach (or Ecclesiasticus) 17:3 tells us that God "endowed [mankind] with strength like his own" [other texts: "strength proper to them"], "and made them after his image." Even if you don't accept these books as canonical, you should acknowledge that the way they reflect the best of intertestamental Jewish thinking should serve as evidence for what is likely to be a "natural" reading of the Old Testament material. In this case, these passages go best with the resemblance view: that is, the image of God in man describes properties of man that are like properties in God.

If, as some think, the personification of Wisdom in the Old Testament (as in Proverbs 8) is the background for the Gospel of John calling Christ the Word of God (1:1-18), then the book of Wisdom may be a rest stop in the journey; it calls Wisdom "an unspotted mirror of the working of God, and an image of his goodness" (7:26, RV). This would then be part of the background for the New Testament reference to Christ as the "image of God."

The word for "image" in Hebrew is *tselem* (Greek *eikon*), and "likeness" is *demut* (Greek *homoiosis*). A couple of problematic uses of *tselem* are Psalm 39:6 (v. 7 in Hebrew) and 73:20. In Psalm 39:6, "surely a man goes about *as a shadow,*" the word "shadow" may instead be "a lifeless statue," or it may be "a mere semblance." In Psalm 73:20 "their *phantoms*" may be instead "their very semblances." (Consult Francis Brown, S. R. Driver, and C. A. Briggs, *A Hebrew and English Lexicon of the Old Testament* [Oxford: Clarendon, 1951], 853b-854a.) Other examples of *demut* ("likeness") in comparisons include Ezekiel 1:5, 10, 13, 16, 22, 26, 28; 8:2; 10:1, 10, 21, 22; Psalm 58:4 (Hebrew v. 5): in many cases the term is translated with "like."

Outside of the Bible, the Aramaic equivalents for both our words "image" and "likeness" appear on a remarkable statue found in 1979 at Tell Fekheriyeh in northeast Syria. The statue was put up in the ninth century B.C. (800s B.C.), and has an Assyrian inscription and an Aramaic paraphrase. The Aramaic refers to the statue as a "likeness" in lines 1 and 15, and an "image" in line 12. This agrees quite well with the pattern we find in the biblical material itself. Publications on this inscription include A. Abou-Assaf, P. Bordreuil, and A. R. Millard, *La statue de Tell Fekherye* (Paris: Editions Recherche sur les Civilisations, 1982); A. R. Millard and P. Bordreuil, "A Statue from Syria with Assyrian and Aramaic Inscriptions," *Biblical Archaeologist* 45:3 (Summer 1982), 135-141; S. A. Kaufman, "Reflections on the Assyrian-Aramaic Bilingual from Tell Fakhariyeh," *Maarav* 3:2 (1982), 137-175; and V. Sasson, "The Aramaic Text of the Tell Fakhriyah Assyrian-Aramaic Bilingual Inscription," *Zeitschrift für die Alttestamentliche Wissenschaft* 97:1 (1985), 86-103.

The discussion in the chapter agrees with Sawyer's conclusion (426), "Every human being has in him some almost tangible resemblance to God, whereby he is distinguished from all other creatures."

I quote Derek Kidner from his Tyndale Commentary on Genesis (Downers Grove, Ill.: InterVarsity Press, 1967), on Genesis 1:26. See also C. John Collins, *Homonymous Verbs in Biblical Hebrew: An Investigation of the Role of Comparative Philology* (University of Liverpool Ph.D. thesis, 1988), 137-138.

The Possibility of Science

As we think about how the biblical worldview paves the way for science, we come to realize that this is what explains the things we typically observe, namely that things act consistently according to their natures. Stephen Hawking, in *A Brief History of Time* (Toronto: Bantam, 1988), 171-172, claims that:

> The earliest theoretical attempts to describe and explain the universe involved the idea that events and natural phenomena were controlled by spirits with human emotions who acted in a very humanlike and unpredictable manner. These spirits inhabited natural objects, like rivers and mountains, including celestial bodies, like the sun and moon. They had to be placated and their favors sought in order to ensure the fertility of the soil and the rotation of the seasons. Gradually, however, it must have been noticed that there were certain regularities: the sun always rose in the east and set in the west, whether or not a sacrifice had been made to the sun god. Further, the sun, the moon, and the planets followed precise paths across the sky that could be predicted in advance with considerable accuracy. The sun and moon might still be gods, but they were gods who obeyed strict laws, apparently without any exceptions, if one discounts stories like that of the sun stopping for Joshua.

I think that this accurately reflects the popular view of the history of science. I also think that it is not factually correct—either as to the ancient beliefs or to the history of science. First, Hawking has assumed that a form of animism is the earliest kind of human belief—and that needs to be proven. Second, he has assumed that in such animistic systems there is limited possibility for "scientific" explanation. That is clearly not true, so long as we have a sufficiently reasonable notion of "science": for example, any tribe that survives in its environment does so because its members have learned how to make use of the natural properties of the environment—in making tools and weapons, in avoiding dangerous animals, and so on. Third, the animistic systems with which I am familiar—from the ancient Mediterranean world—view the gods as controlling natural events by exploiting (or overruling) the natural properties of things, such as by sending a rainstorm, which means that those things can still be understood. Therefore the question is not whether there are deities that use nature for their purposes, but whether those purposes are benign. What we know as Western science didn't develop because people noticed and studied regularities; it developed because people came to believe that the world was made and ruled by a rational and good Creator, who made a reliable and intelligible world. Now there were important Greek philosophers who rejected the "primitive" or animistic view of nature that Hawking describes; but it was the church's appropriation of these philosophers' methods within the context of a theological worldview that gave rise to science as we know it (other factors, such as favorable economic conditions, of course came into play). And since Hawking mentioned the incident of the sun stopping in Joshua 10, we have to note that theologically—as we will discuss in a later chapter—God's support of natural processes *is* divine activity; and the "interventions" or "miracles" are not violations or suspensions of natural properties, but *additions* due to intelligent agency (and thus not at all capricious).

CHAPTER 9: THE GLORIOUS RUIN

God's Arrangement with Adam and Eve

I have addressed many of the exegetical issues concerning God's relationship with Adam and Eve in the Garden, the two trees, and the first sin in, "What Happened to Adam and Eve? A Literary-Theological Approach to Genesis 3," *Presbyterion* 27:1 (Spring 2001), 12-44.

The other common possible ways to interpret "the tree of knowing good and evil" are: (1) it bestows moral autonomy (the humans make their own rules for good and bad); (2) it is a way of gaining knowledge of everything (that is, since "good and evil" are polar opposites, the expression includes everything in between, which is everything); (3) it is a symbol of sexual experience (since "know" can be used as a euphemism for that, as in Genesis 4:1); and (4) the tree is a symbol for cultural advancement (from primitive to civilized). None of these works very well, however: we can dismiss option (2) because it doesn't match with what God says in 3:22—the humans *don't* know everything. Option (3) is absurd, because in the first place the tree isn't about "knowledge" but about "knowledge of good and evil," and in the second place because sexual differences and reproduction are part of the good creation (1:28; 2:18-25). And option (4) doesn't make any sense: why would God want to keep cultural advancement away from his creatures? (Besides, Genesis 3 doesn't say anything about it anyhow!) That leaves option (1) as the strongest contender against the one I prefer. However, the humans do not achieve moral autonomy in the passage: they disobey God's command and suffer his judgment for it. Further, this option doesn't account for the evidence of the way these expressions are used elsewhere in the Bible.

The quotation from C. S. Lewis comes from *Mere Christianity,* iii:4 ("Morality and Psychoanalysis").

The G. K. Chesterton quotation originally appeared in his book *The Thing: Why I Am a Catholic* (1929); I found it in Robert Knille, ed., *As I Was Saying: A Chesterton Reader* (Grand Rapids, Mich.: Eerdmans, 1985), 160.

Is Science Possible for Fallen Man?

The quotation from Benjamin Warfield is from his essay, "A Review of Herman Bavinck's *De Zekerheid des Geloofs,*" in Warfield, *Selected Shorter Works* (Phillipsburg, N.J.: Presbyterian & Reformed, 1973), II:106-123, especially 117-119.

CHAPTER 10: HOW "FALLEN" IS NATURE?

The "Curses" in Genesis 3

For a full grammatical discussion of Genesis 3:15, see my essay, "A Syntactical Note (Genesis 3:15): Is the Woman's Seed Singular or Plural?" in *Tyndale Bulletin* 48:1 (1997), 139-148. Many have noticed that the Septuagint (Greek version from the third century B.C.) uses a masculine pronoun *he* to refer back to the noun *seed* ("offspring"), which in Greek is neuter; this is for the purpose of stressing that they saw the verse as prophesying a particular individual. I have added to this argument by noticing that the Hebrew noun *seed* follows a pattern when it means "offspring": when it means "offspring in general" it uses plural pronouns, and when it means "a particular offspring" it uses singular ones. The Hebrew pronouns in "*he* shall bruise your head, and you shall bruise *his* heel" are singular.

The idea of "cursing the ground" could be present in Genesis 4:11, if we interpret it as "you are more cursed than the ground"; but no major translation does that. They normally agree with ESV, "you are cursed from the ground."

What Did Lions Eat Before Man's Fall?

For a commentary on Psalm 104, see Derek Kidner, *Psalms 73–150* (Tyndale Old Testament Commentary; Downers Grove, Ill.: InterVarsity Press, 1973), 367-373. Kidner mentions the possible links with the Egyptian Hymn to the Sun of the "heretic king" Akhenaten (died about 1362 B.C.).

The best handbook for interpreting biblical prophecy is an old one: Patrick Fairbairn, *The Interpretation of Prophecy* (Edinburgh: Banner of Truth, 1964 [originally 1865]). Fairbairn articulates his principles in pages 1-201, with pages 83-181 on "The Prophetic Style and Diction."

The C. S. Lewis quotation is from *The Problem of Pain* (London: Geoffrey Bles, 1940), at the end of the chapter on "Animal Pain."

An essay in general agreement with my conclusions is John C. Munday, Jr., "Creature Mortality: From Creation or the Fall?" *Journal of the Evangelical Theological Society* 35:1 (1992), 51-68. Austin Farrer critiques the view of his friend C. S. Lewis, that animal predation is the result of Satanic influence before the fall, in "The Christian Apologist," in Jocelyn Gibb, ed., *Light on C. S. Lewis* (London: Geoffrey Bles, 1965), 23-43, at 41-42.

Young earth creationists consider animal death a part of the problem of evil, and think that it is incompatible with the original goodness of creation. For example, see Paul Nelson and John Mark Reynolds, "Young Earth Creationism," in J. P. Moreland and John Mark Reynolds, eds., *Three Views on Creation and Evolution* (Grand Rapids, Mich.: Zondervan, 1999), 41-75, especially 42, 44, 47-48.

While I was writing this chapter, I attended a lecture on dinosaurs for home-school parents and children given by a young earth creationist. He showed the mouth of a *Tyrannosaurus rex* and asked the kids what they thought it ate. Most of the children said "meat." He told them they needed to use their Scriptural glasses, and not their ordinary sight. Behind this advice is the premise that the Bible asks us to *deny* what our senses and common sense are shouting at us—a premise that is deeply troubling. I know of no reason to think that this is what the Bible intends to do—instead it gives us the spiritual knowledge and humility to interpret what we see by God's purposes. When you look at a lion, or weasel, or a *T. rex* skeleton, you are looking at a well-designed predator; and Scripture enables you to rejoice in the God who designed them so well (as well as to mourn over your own sinfulness that keeps you from exercising the proper dominion over such creatures).

Often we find unbelievers offering as an argument against our view of God's good design in his world, the problem posed by animals eating other animals. It is fascinating to note that the classic statement of the design argument, William Paley's *Natural Theology,* which appeared in 1802—and says nothing about young or old earth—discusses the "Goodness of the Deity" in chapter 26. He argued that venomous animals and beasts of prey are actually a part of the *good* provision of God! This shows that we cannot say that the Christian tradition assigns all such things to the fall of man and the corruption of creation.

CHAPTER 11: HOW DOES GOD RULE THE WORLD?

I have treated many of the issues in this chapter in my book, *The God of Miracles: An Exegetical Examination of God's Action in the World* (Wheaton, Ill.: Crossway, 2000 / Leicester, U.K.: Inter-Varsity Press [United Kingdom], 2001); this also has a pretty full bibliography.

The Traditional Christian Picture of God's Providence

For the sake of keeping my presentation simple, I have treated providence as having two parts: maintaining the goodness of creation, and governing it all to holy and wise ends. Theologians often break maintenance down into two parts: *preservation,* that is, keeping created things in existence with their properties; and *concurrence,* that is, confirming the interactions of causal properties. As I discuss in *The God of Miracles,* I am happy with this theological tradition; but the ideas matter more than the terms do, so I won't much care whether we make preservation and concurrence separate, or if we group them together under what I have called "maintenance," so long as we mean the same things.

The technical word for the inner workings of events is *metaphysics*—the discipline that studies what the world is like, how its parts interact, and what role God plays in it all. By this we can say that the different categories for "ordinary" and "special" providences distinguish events based either on their metaphysics or on their effect on the people involved. C. S. Lewis, in *Miracles: A Preliminary Study* (2nd edn.; New York: Macmillan, 1960), has an appendix where he discusses "special providences." He prefers to group things by their metaphysics—and though I am sympathetic to this, I can see the usefulness of the subjective effect categories as well. Here is what I wrote in chapter 9 of *The God of Miracles,* footnote 22:

> I do not want to deny what C. S. Lewis said in *Miracles,* . . . appendix B, "On 'Special Providences'": "It seems to me, therefore, that we must abandon the idea that there is any special class of events (apart from miracles) which can be distinguished as 'specially providential.' Unless we are to abandon the conception of Providence altogether, and with it the belief in efficacious prayer, it follows that all events are equally providential. If God directs the course of events at all then he directs the movement of every atom at every moment." This is correct as to the metaphysics; but it is convenient to have a category to designate those events in which God's supervision becomes in some sense visible to the pious. In the section in chapter 10 on the problem of evil, we will see that Scripture teaches us to expect that in ordinary providence God's purposiveness is *not* discernible by even the best of believers.

The Biblical Evidence

The reference to Eeyore comes from the Winnie the Pooh story, "In Which Tigger Comes to the Forest and Has Breakfast," in *The House at Pooh Corner,* by A. A. Milne. This tale—like *all* the Pooh tales—is a gold mine of instruction. Tigger asserts that it is his nature to like honey, just as Pooh does, and finds out by tasting it that he is wrong (empirical method!); he then claims to like acorns, as Piglet does, and discovers again that he is wrong; next he claims to like thistles, whereupon Pooh takes him to Eeyore, who delights in them. Again Tigger finds out that he is wrong. Finally, he learns that Kanga's Extract of Malt (strengthening medicine for Roo) is just the thing: "So *that's* what Tiggers like!" Each animal in the Forest has his own nature, and a food that is suited to that nature.

I cite Derek Kidner from his *Psalms 73–150* (Tyndale Old Testament Commentary; Downers Grove, Ill.: InterVarsity Press, 1973), 372.

Definitions That Restate the Biblical View of Providence

The definitions of "natural" and "supernatural" come from my *God of Miracles,* chapter 9 ("Theological Conclusions"). For a reference point, my notion of "supernatural event" is very close to Blaise Pascal's definition of a "miracle": "an effect which exceeds the natural power of the means which are employed for it; and what is not a miracle is an effect which does not exceed the natural power of the means which are employed for it." See Blaise Pascal, *Pensées,* A. J. Krailsheimer, ed. (London: Penguin, 1995), no. 891 (no. 804 by the Brunschvicg numbers). This is also similar to Paul Gwynne's definition of "special divine action" in *Special Divine Action: Key Issues in the Contemporary Debate* (Rome: Gregorian University Press, 1996), 24: "God brings it about that some particular outcome is different from what it would have been had only natural, created factors been operative."

I cite C. S. Lewis from *Miracles: A Preliminary Study* (2nd edn.; New York: Macmillan, 1960), the opening sentence of chapter 2. Lewis's explanatory footnote seems to have escaped the notice of the fussy souls:

> This definition is not that which would be given by many theologians. I am adopting it not because I think it an improvement upon theirs but because, being crude and "popular," it enables me most easily to treat those questions which "the common reader" probably has in mind when he takes up a book on Miracles.

In other words, the popular and analogical definition suits his communicative purpose quite well.

In my comments on the conditions for finding supernatural events—namely God's pursuit of relationship with man—I have purposely *not* addressed the question of whether anyone since the biblical apostles was a miracle worker or an authoritative spokesman for God. These are important questions, and they divide Christians from Christians; but I don't need to settle that in order to make the point I am after.

Other Views: Are They Truer to the Bible?

The occasionalist author on Psalm 104 is H. J. Kraus, in his commentary on the Psalms (Continental Commentary; Minneapolis: Augsburg, 1989 [German original, 1978]), 304. He in turn cites Gerhard von Rad, "The Reality of God," in *God at Work in Israel* (Nashville: Abingdon, 1980), 116.

The providentialist biologist is R. J. Berry, in "The Virgin Birth of Christ," *Science and Christian Belief* 8:2 (1996), 101-110; the quotation comes from *Science and Christian Belief* 9:1 (1997), 77, in Berry's reply to P. Addinall's response to his 1996 article. In the original article, Berry suggests that if we were to find a natural mechanism for the conception of Jesus, that would not decrease the "miraculous" nature of the event—and thus you can see that he is using the word "miraculous" to mean something like "special, amazing," rather than "supernatural." (I warned you that the word "miracle" can lead to trouble!) I have also used Colin Brown's entry on "Miracle, Wonder, Sign," in Brown, ed., *New International Dictionary of New Testament Theology* (Exeter, U.K.: Paternoster, 1976), vol. 2, 620-635, at 628.

The *NBD* article is M. H. Cressey, "Miracles," in N. Hillyer et al., eds., The *New Bible Dictionary* (Leicester, U.K.: Inter-Varsity Press, 1982), 782a-784a; quotations are from 782, "Miracles and the Natural Order."

For a book-length discussion and refutation of open theism, see Bruce Ware, *God's Lesser Glory* (Wheaton, Ill.: Crossway, 2000).

The C. S. Lewis passage on Deism is in *Prayer: Letters to Malcolm* (London: Geoffrey Bles, 1964), letter 10.

Providence and Science

The Lewis comment about Joseph comes from *Miracles,* chapter 7.

The Paul Helm quotes come from Paul Helm, *The Providence of God* (Downers Grove, Ill.: InterVarsity Press, 1994), 82 and 89. Other writers have referred to the hiddenness of the "causal joint" between God and the creation (Austin Farrer's term). On his page 46, Helm virtually defines "providence" as "that great matrix of causes and effects through which God governs the world."

Chapter 12: God Reveals Himself in His World

Defining Terms

A recent work from a biblical scholar (who is nevertheless not a traditional Christian) is James Barr, *Biblical Faith and Natural Theology* (Oxford: Clarendon, 1993). He discusses some of the different uses of the term "natural theology" in his chapter 1, pages 1-20. One of Barr's chief goals seems to be to show that the way that many in the twentieth century have come to consider natural theology as anti-biblical (following Karl Barth), is itself unbiblical. Along the way, however, he takes his swings at traditional Christians as well. I would love to see a detailed review from a traditional Christian who is biblically informed.

For the cardinal and theological virtues, see C. S. Lewis, *Mere Christianity,* iii:2 ("The Cardinal Virtues"). See also Thomas Aquinas, *Summa Theologiae,* I-II, questions 61-62. The idea of the four cardinal virtues is quite an old one, going back at least to the Greek philosopher Plato (about 427–327 B.C., taught in Athens); see David Winston, *The Wisdom of Solomon* (Anchor Bible Commentary; Garden City, N.Y.: Doubleday, 1979), on Wisdom 8:7 ("the fruits of her [Wisdom's] works are virtues; for she teaches moderation and prudence, justice and fortitude, and nothing else in life is more useful for men than these," NAB). Support for this way of thinking comes from Umberto Cassuto's *Commentary on Exodus* (Jerusalem: Magnes, 1983): in his introduction to the Ten Commandments (Ex. 20:1-17) he shows that there is ethical common property between the Ten Commandments and pagan ethics—as well as new material in Israel's code, derived from Israel's unique theology. See also Jay Budziszewski, *Written on the Heart* (Downers Grove, Ill.: InterVarsity Press, 1997).

Natural Revelation in the Old Testament

I cite Derek Kidner from his *Psalms 1–72* (Tyndale Old Testament Commentary; Downers Grove, Ill.: InterVarsity Press, 1973). The Psalm 8 quote comes from page 67.

Besides the psalms that use nature as a vehicle for worship, there are of course many that incorporate *images* from the world of nature to describe God: for example, in 36:5-6 God's steadfast love and faithfulness go beyond the skies, his righteousness is like the mountains, and his judgments are like the great deep.

On the apologetic strategy of the Wisdom of Solomon, see John J. Collins, "Natural Theology and Biblical Tradition: The Case of Hellenistic Judaism," *Catholic Biblical Quarterly* 60:1 (1998), 1-15; Derek Kidner, *The Wisdom of Proverbs, Job, and Ecclesiastes* (Downers Grove, Ill.: InterVarsity Press, 1985), 149-157.

For a detailed discussion of the relationship between Proverbs and the Egyptian material, see John Ruffle, "The *Teaching of Amenemope* and Its Connection with the Book of Proverbs," *Tyndale Bulletin* 28 (1977), 29-68; and for a summary, see Kidner, *The Wisdom of Proverbs, Job, and Ecclesiastes*, 44-45.

Natural Revelation in the New Testament

Important bibliography for discussion of the New Testament passages about natural revelation, aside from the commentaries on Acts and Romans, include: Michael Green, *Evangelism in the Early Church* (Grand Rapids, Mich.: Eerdmans, 1970); Bertil Gärtner, *The Areopagus Speech and Natural*

Revelation (Uppsala, Sweden: Gleerup, 1955); David DeSilva, "Paul and the Stoa: A Comparison," *Journal of the Evangelical Theological Society* 38:4 (1995), 549-564; Bruce Winter, "In Public and in Private: Early Christians and Religious Pluralism," in A. D. Clarke and B. W. Winter, eds., *One God, One Lord: Christianity in a World of Religious Pluralism* (Grand Rapids, Mich.: Baker, 1992), 125-148; and "On Introducing Gods to Athens: An Alternative Reading of Acts 17:18-20," *Tyndale Bulletin* 47:1 (1996), 71-90; N. Clayton Croy, "Hellenistic Philosophies and the Preaching of the Resurrection (Acts 17:18, 32)," *Novum Testamentum* 39:1 (1997), 21-39; Michel Gourges, "La littérature profane dans le discours d'Athens (*Ac* 17, 16-31): Un dossier fermé?" *Revue Biblique* 109:2 (2002), 241-260; and James Barr, *Biblical Faith and Natural Theology.*

Among the many commentaries on these books, I find the most help in K. Lake and H. J. Cadbury's commentary on Acts, vols. 4 and 5 of F. J. Foakes-Jackson and K. Lake, *The Beginnings of Christianity* (Grand Rapids, Mich.: Baker, 1965 [originally 1932]); F. F. Bruce's commentary on the Greek text of Acts (London: Tyndale Press, 1951); and his commentary on Acts (New International Commentary on the New Testament; Grand Rapids, Mich.: Eerdmans, 1988); C. K. Barrett's commentary on Acts 1-14 (International Critical Commentary; Edinburgh: T & T Clark, 1994); John Murray's commentary on Romans (New International Commentary on the New Testament; Grand Rapids, Mich.: Eerdmans, 1959); C. E. B. Cranfield's commentary on Romans (International Critical Commentary; Edinburgh: T & T Clark, 1975); J. D. G. Dunn's commentary on Romans 1–8 (Word Biblical Commentary; Waco: Word, 1988); and Douglas Moo's commentary on Romans (New International Commentary on the New Testament; Grand Rapids, Mich.: Eerdmans, 1996).

I cite Michael Green on Acts 17:30 from his *Evangelism in the Early Church,* 128.

James Barr takes the position that Paul's main polemic in Acts 17 is against idolatry—a point Paul would have had in common with the philosophers. He says (*Biblical Faith and Natural Theology,* 33), "Paul's speech is distinctly friendly to Greek thought and displays no polemic in principle against it" and (35) "the Areopagites, Stoics, and Epicureans of Paul's time in Athens did not for a moment suppose that a statue of wood or metal *was* an actual deity to be worshipped." However, while it is true that Paul does establish points of contact, this is for the sake of setting out the metaphysical side. The Stoics would have found Paul's message more congenial than the Epicureans did, as I have argued. Croy's essay examines the views of first-century Epicureans and Stoics and concludes that Luke means us to infer that, by and large, the Epicureans were the ones who sneered, while the Stoics wanted to hear more.

More examples of "power made known by being expressed" in Paul include: Rom. 9:17; 15:13, 19; 1 Cor. 1:18, 24; 2:4-5; 6:14; 2 Cor. 4:7; 6:7; 12:9; 13:4; Eph. 3:16; Phil. 3:10; 2 Tim. 1:7.

See Josephus, *Against Apion,* ii.167, 190-192. For the Stoics' appeal to design, see DeSilva, 562.

I have avoided critical review of the commentaries on Romans in my discussion of 2:14-16, but some is in order here. Cranfield takes the reference to Gentiles in verse 14 as denoting Gentile *Christians* (following Barth), but this cannot be: it would be a very obscure way of referring to them, and Christians are not said not to have law. These verses do not suggest that such people are *justified* by their doings; they rather explain the universality of the law so that not even Gentiles, to whom no special revelation came, can plead ignorance (see also Moo). That is, the "Gentiles" of verse 14 are those who never received the covenantal revelation of God.

We should also be clear that "the work of the law as written on their hearts" (v. 15) is different from "the law written on their hearts" (Heb. 8:10, citing Jer. 31:33), which describes spiritual rebirth. As Moo suggests, "Paul is almost certainly pressing into service a widespread Greek tradition to the effect that all human beings possess an 'unwritten' or 'natural' law—an innate moral sense of 'right and wrong'."

A fruitful area for further study would be the relationship of Paul's approach, not just to the Wisdom of Solomon but also to Josephus's apologetic and to developments in Greek philosophical thought of the time. In his *Life,* 12, Josephus the Pharisee describes Pharisaism as "similar to the sect which Greeks call Stoic." In his more important *Against Apion* he found common ground with the better Greek philosophers such as Pythagoras, Anaxagoras, Plato (whom he also criticizes, in ii.192, 223-224), Aristotle, and the Stoics. For example, in ii.168 he says, "Pythagoras, Anaxagoras, Plato, the Stoics who succeeded him, and indeed all the philosophers appear to have similar views [to those expressed by Moses] concerning the nature of God." He also condemns the Epicureans for their denial of providence (ii.180).

The C. S. Lewis quote comes from his essay, "On Ethics," in *Christian Reflections* (Grand Rapids, Mich.: Eerdmans, 1967), 44-56 (from 46-47).

I cite Jay Budziszewski from his *Written on the Heart,* 185.

Science, Natural Revelation, and Apologetics

One area in which the sciences could help us, but haven't, is in the study of universals of human behavior. Unfortunately, the human sciences are dominated by a relativistic mindset that denies universals. Steven Pinker—no friend to Christian faith—makes just this point in *The Language Instinct* (London: Penguin / New York: HarperCollins, 1995), chapter 13, "Mind Design." Pinker describes, for example, the way Margaret Mead was taken in by Samoan teenagers who were pulling her leg. He then discusses mental features that seem to be common to all mankind. These common features can tie in to the Christian apologetic.

An objection to the existence of "natural law" is the observation that not everyone holds to it; this commonly comes from the people called "postmodern." For example, Stanley Fish, writing in the *New York Times* for October 15, 2001, said:

> Postmodernism maintains only that there can be no independent standard for determining which of many rival interpretations of an event is the true one. The only thing postmodern thought argues against is the hope of justifying our response to the attacks [of September 11, 2001] in universal terms that would be persuasive to everyone, including our enemies. Invoking the abstract notions of justice and truth to support our cause wouldn't be effective anyway because our adversaries lay claim to the same language. (No one declares himself to be an apostle of injustice.)

But this objection opposes only the version of natural law theory that supposes that all adults living acknowledge the same moral code—a version that does not exist; that is, Fish attacks a straw man. In fact, later in the same essay Fish gives away the game when he writes,

> We have not seen the face of evil; we have seen the face of an enemy who comes at us with a full roster of grievances, goals and strategies.

The enemy's grievances are the key: they are a sense of having been on the receiving end of violated justice. Those who support the terrorists of September 11, 2001, appeal to these grievances that they hold against the West. Fish supports the Reuters News Agency, which banned the use of the word "terrorist" to describe the suicide bombers of September 11, because, as they said, "one man's terrorist is another man's freedom fighter." But the evil consists in allowing these grievances to produce implacable hatred, and in directing their anger at people who never did anything to them. So they may portray themselves as freedom fighters, but they are not pursuing freedom. Further, we generally recognize that there is such a thing as moral education, which can change one's moral compass (such has happened in this case); there is also such a thing as the dulling of one's conscience (which also seems to have happened here). Therefore it is no argument against some kind of natural law, that some people can put themselves into a frame of soul in which they reject its demands.

Let me end by quoting what one of my colleagues, David Jones (an ethicist), wrote me about Fish's essay:

> "One man's terrorist is another man's freedom fighter." Right. And one man's serial rapist is another man's invincible lover.

CHAPTER 13: CARING FOR GOD'S WORLD

I want to acknowledge my daughter's help in the biblical research and thought for this chapter, and in insightful comments that improved it considerably. She loves the world God made.

For a sympathetic account of James Watt's service, see Ron Arnold, *At the Eye of the Storm: James Watt and the Environmentalists* (Chicago: Regnery Gateway, 1982). At 74-87 Arnold describes Watt's appearance before Congress and the highly biased press reports of it.

Valuable reading on the topic of this chapter includes Michael B. Barkey, ed., *Environmental Stewardship in the Judeo-Christian Tradition: Jewish, Catholic, and Protestant Wisdom on the Environment* (Grand Rapids, Mich.: Acton Institute, 2000), with its own bibliography; Colin Russell, *The Earth, Humanity and God* (London: University College of London Press, 1994).

The World Still Serves Man

The Francis Bacon quote is from *Novum Organum Scientiarum,* book ii, aphorism 52.

As to Matthew 12:11-12, we can compare what Josephus (A.D. 37–95) wrote in his *Antiquities of the Jews* (book iv, chapter 8, section 30, italics added):

> It is not lawful to pass by any beast that is in distress, when in a storm it is fallen down in the mire, but to endeavor to preserve it, *as having a sympathy with it in its pain.*

Josephus may be referring to Exodus 23:4-5 and Deuteronomy 22:4, which enjoin an Israelite to assist his neighbor's beast when it is in trouble, but he has drawn out the spirit of the law with his reference to "sympathy." We may contrast this, as a matter of fact, with the views at Qumran (the Jewish sect that produced the Dead Sea Scrolls, from around the time of Jesus), which forbade rescuing animals on the Sabbath!

On Deuteronomy 22:6-7, see Christopher Wright, *Deuteronomy* (New International Biblical Commentary; Peabody, Mass.: Hendrickson, 1996), 241. He suggests that the rationale for the law is "the conservationist principle of preserving a source of food supply for the future by not consuming it all at the present. Long term prudence should set limits to short term greed." That may be so, but I suspect that there is something more to it: namely, to eat the mother and the eggs together can dull the spirit of compassion. (This is Adam Clarke's view.) I think this gains support from what Gordon Wenham, *Leviticus* (New International Commentary on the Old Testament; Grand Rapids, Mich.: Eerdmans, 1979), says on 296 (regarding Lev. 22:28):

> More than mere sentimentality seems to underlie this law. It is in conformity with other laws such as that forbidding men to take a bird and its eggs (Deut. 22:6-7), or to cook a kid in its mother's milk (Exod. 23:19; 34:26; Deut. 14:21), or wantonly to destroy trees (Deut. 20:19-20). Noah was commissioned to gather a pair of each kind of animal to preserve life from the all-destroying flood (Gen. 6:19-20; 7:2-3). Every Israelite was expected to do his part in conservation by avoiding wanton destruction of the God-given creation.

See also Wright, *Deuteronomy,* 230 (regarding 20:19-20). In any case such laws put a brake on human greed and shortsightedness.

The material on beauty and animals in the Psalms depends heavily on C. S. Lewis, *Reflections on the Psalms* (London: Geoffrey Bles, 1958), chapter 8.

Ethical Considerations for the Environment

The citation from William Still is from *Letters of William Still* (Edinburgh: Banner of Truth, 1984), 58-59.

I would like to see someone study this subject from an apologetic standpoint. For example, Colin Tudge, in *The Varieties of Life: A Survey and Celebration of All the Creatures That Ever Lived* (Oxford: Oxford University Press, 2000), ends his book (note the suggestive subtitle!) with a section on "Why Conserve?" (623-627). He considers economic arguments, aesthetic ones, and finally ethical ones, and concludes, "I do not believe that there is a 'good' reason that will satisfy everybody—or even one that many people will find convincing." He criticizes the "Jewish-Christian-Islamic" religions—those that most clearly embrace the notion of an omnipotent Creator—because "the Ten Commandments of Moses do not tell us to take care of wild creatures." Instead, God gave "us" dominion, "which people through the ages have interpreted in a wide variety of ways, and often to justify insouciance."

We are left, then, with an appeal to emotion. He justifies such an appeal by pointing to David Hume (1711–1776), who claimed that "in the end, all ethical positions are rooted in emotion, and that moral philosophers merely find arguments to support whatever attitude they hold in the first place." Hume's is an absurd position, and I don't know how anyone could live with it. Tudge can't live with it, as he shows when he writes,

> The moral task for each of us is to explore our own feelings, refine our own emotional responses, and then follow our convictions. . . . [Saving the varieties of creatures] has to be worth doing. I cannot demonstrate that it has to be done, and neither can anyone else. But it is hard to think of anything more worthwhile.

When Tudge appeals to "refining our emotional responses," he must mean that there is some standard by which we can evaluate our responses, something higher than what we feel now (or else he's spouting nonsense, which I don't think he's doing). He then insists that it is "worthwhile"; in other words, there is something that gives this task worth, not just for Colin Tudge, but also for the rest of us.

I agree with Tudge in the worthiness of the project. But I find it sad that he has had a genuine moral experience (a sense of obligation to something good), and can't find a name for it or a philosophy that will explain it. It's also too bad that he hasn't really understood the Bible (as explained in my chapter). Christians can say where this moral sense comes from, how to refine it and measure it against competing claims, and what we must do for our guilt of having disobeyed it.

CHAPTER 14: SCIENCE, PROVIDENCE, AND MIRACLE

Rudolph Bultmann, "The New Testament and Mythology," *Kerygma and Myth* (New York: Harper & Row, 1961), 5. Robert W. Funk, Roy Hoover, and the Jesus Seminar, *The Five Gospels: The Search for the Authentic Words of Jesus* (New York: Macmillan, 1993), 2. The very liberal Episcopal bishop

John Shelby Spong expressed virtually the same sentiment when the 1998 Lambeth Conference took a traditional line against blessing homosexual unions and ordaining homosexuals as clergy. It was conservative bishops from Africa, Asia, and Latin America who led the way. Spong said of the Africans,

> They've moved out of animism into a very superstitious kind of Christianity. They've yet to face the intellectual revolution of Copernicus and Einstein that we've had to face in the developing world. That's just not on their radar screen.

When told that African and Caribbean bishops might be upset by his remarks, he replied:

> That's too bad: I'm not going to cease being a twentieth-century person for fear of offending someone in the Third World.

(Cited in *World* magazine, September 12, 1998, 20, from an interview in the Church of England newspaper, July 10, 1998.)

We should be clear about what this means: by this way of seeing the modern scientific outlook, that outlook has the right to tell us both what we may believe about God and Jesus, and also what we may consider to be moral behavior.

Modern Science and the Supernatural

I dealt with many of the objections to the traditional Christian view of God's providence in my *God of Miracles* (Wheaton, Ill.: Crossway, 2000 / Leicester, U.K.: Inter-Varsity Press [United Kingdom], 2001), especially in chapter 10, "Is the Biblical Picture Viable Today?" I have also dealt with the "God-of-the-gaps" problem in my paper, "Miracles, Intelligent Design, and God-of-the-Gaps," a paper presented at the Gifford Bequest International Conference on Natural Theology, Aberdeen, Scotland, 26-29 May, 2000—and now published in *Perspectives on Science and Christian Faith* 55:1 (March 2003), 22-29.

Douglas Geivett and Gary Habermas, *In Defense of Miracles* (Downers Grove, Ill.: InterVarsity Press, 1997); and C. S. Lewis, *Miracles: A Preliminary Study* (2nd edn.; New York: Macmillan, 1960).

Science and Reliable Natural Properties

For my description of quantum mechanics I wouldn't dream of making up my own summary from my days in university. Instead my description draws especially on John Polkinghorne, *The Quantum World* (London: Penguin, 1986); Robert M. Hazen and James Trefil, *Science Matters: Achieving Scientific Literacy* (New York: Doubleday, 1991), 65-74; and Nancy Pearcey and Charles Thaxton, *The Soul of Science: Christian Faith and Natural Philosophy* (Wheaton, Ill.: Crossway, 1994), 187-221.

In the main text I haven't said much about how to assess the probabilistic side of quantum mechanics, but I've given reasons why I don't think it matters. However, Paul Gwynne, *Special Divine Action: Key Issues in the Contemporary Debate (1965–1995)* (Rome: Gregorian University Press, 1996), lists five possible meanings of "chance" on page 210:

a. *Epistemological chance,* which means that we do not, or can not, know what caused something—but it doesn't mean that there is no cause.

b. *Mathematical chance,* which simply refers to a statistical calculation such as the "chance" of getting heads on a coin toss.

c. *Existential chance,* which refers to a meaningful coincidence that surprises us—such as meeting a long lost friend at the grocery store in a crowded city.

d. *Physical chance,* which refers to quantum level events whose causes our science cannot peer into.

e. *Metaphysical chance,* which means that an event has no cause at all.

In these terms, there is no agreement as to which kind of chance is involved in the uncertainty principle. In any case it is philosophy, not physical science, that governs which of these we think most likely.

Gwynne also discusses the appeal to uncertainty and indeterminacy for miracles and human freedom on pages 212-221, and offers a mild critique—*too* mild, I think.

Chaos Theory

I cite James Trefil's chaos example from his *101 Things You Don't Know About Science and No One Else Does Either* (Boston: Houghton Mifflin, 1996), 50-52; see also Hazen and Trefil, *Science Matters,* 18-19.

Providence and the Problem of Evil

The first paragraph in the C. S. Lewis quote is from *"De Futilitate,"* in *Christian Reflections* (Grand Rapids, Mich.: Eerdmans, 1967), 57-71, at 69; the second is from *The Problem of Pain* (New York: Macmillan, 1962), chapter 1. See also his essay on "Historicism" in *Christian Reflections* on the futility of inferring the divine purpose from our limited knowledge of the actual course of events.

I quote J. I. Packer from *Knowing God* (Downers Grove, Ill.: InterVarsity Press, 1973), chapter 10 ("God's Wisdom and Ours"). Packer's view is virtually identical to that found in J. Stafford Wright's article "The Interpretation of Ecclesiastes," first published in *Evangelical Quarterly* 18 (1946), 18-34; reprinted in W. Kaiser, ed., *Classical Evangelical Essays in Old Testament Interpretation* (Grand Rapids, Mich.: Baker, 1972), 133-150; and in R. B. Zuck, ed., *Reflecting with Solomon* (Grand Rapids, Mich.: Baker, 1994), 17-30. Packer told me that he and Stafford Wright came to their conclusions independently. The unpublished M.A. thesis of Betsy Thomas, *Coherence in Ecclesiastes: A Consideration of Plot Development* (Covenant Theological Seminary, 1997), which employs the tools of discourse analysis, puts this interpretation on a very solid footing.

CHAPTER 15: HOW OLD IS THE EARTH?

Cosmology and the Big Bang

For the Big Bang, see John Polkinghorne, *The Faith of a Physicist* (Minneapolis: Fortress, 1996), 71-73; and Ian Barbour, *Religion in an Age of Science* (New York: HarperSanFrancisco, 1990), 125-128. Historical material is available in the very readable *Norton History of Astronomy and Cosmology* by John North (New York: Norton, 1995), especially 522-541 (North includes references to the ideological and personal factors involved); and very colorfully in Stephen Hawking's *Brief History of Time* (Toronto: Bantam, 1988).

When it comes to linking the cosmological theory of the Big Bang with the origin and development of life on earth, the National Science Teachers Association commits the sin badly in its position paper on the teaching of evolution (available on the Internet at <www.nsta.org/159&id=10>). They say,

> Evolution in the broadest sense can be defined as the idea that the universe has a history: that change through time has taken place. If we look today at the galaxies, stars, the planet Earth, and the life on planet Earth, we see

> that things today are different from what they were in the past: galaxies, stars, planets, and life forms have evolved. Biological evolution refers to the scientific theory that living things share ancestors from which they have diverged: Darwin called it "descent with modification." There is abundant and consistent evidence from astronomy, physics, biochemistry, geochronology, geology, biology, anthropology and other sciences that evolution has taken place.

Among other things, they are equivocating on the word "evolution" if they want to apply it to both cosmology and biology: the biological theory, as we shall see later, presupposes development as a strictly natural process. Further, it is not true—at least in my judgment—that the kinds of evidence in the different sciences they mention all have the same force or logical validity. It does not follow that if we accept one or more—say cosmology and geology—we must accept the lot. We must allow each to stand or fall on its own merits.

Geology and the History of the Earth

A general textbook on geology is Brian Skinner and Stephen Porter, *The Dynamic Earth: An Introduction to Physical Geology* (New York: John Wiley & Sons, 1992); see also C. M. R. Fowler, *The Solid Earth: An Introduction to Geophysics* (Cambridge: Cambridge University Press, 1990). I have also profited from A. G. Unklesbay and J. D. Vineyard, *Missouri Geology: Three Billion Years of Volcanoes, Seas, Sediments, and Erosion* (Columbia: University of Missouri Press, 1992); David Alt and Donald Hyndman, *Northwest Exposures: A Geologic Story of the Northwest* (Missoula, Mont.: Mountain Press, 1995); and Elizabeth Orr and William Orr, *The Geology of the Pacific Northwest* (New York: McGraw-Hill, 1996). A helpful history of geology is A. Hallam, *The Great Geological Controversies* (Oxford: Oxford University Press, 1992). The leading spokesman for mainstream geology on the age of the earth is G. Brent Dalrymple, *The Age of the Earth* (Stanford, Calif.: Stanford University Press, 1991). Dalrymple has examined the views of young earth creationists in *Radiometric Dating, Geologic Time, and the Age of the Earth: A Reply to "Scientific" Creationism* (U.S. Geological Survey Open File Report 86-110, 986). On the Internet you can find William Newman, *Geologic Time* (U.S. Geological Survey, 1997), at pubs.usgs.gov/gip/geotime/contents.html.

A Christian who accepts the standard geological theories about the earth is Davis Young, *Christianity and the Age of the Earth* (Grand Rapids, Mich.:

Zondervan, 1982). (Young's father was the famous conservative Old Testament scholar, E. J. Young.)

For the other side, I have interviewed a number of scientific representatives of young earth creationism, and have also visited the web site of the Institute of Creation Research (www.icr.org), where many resources on flood geology are available. Among these are Steven Austin et al., *Catastrophic Plate Tectonics: A Global Flood Model of Earth History,* originally presented at the Third International Conference on Creationism, Pittsburgh, Pa., July 18-23, 1994 (www.icr.org/research/as/platetectonics.html). See also Steven Austin, "Ten Misconceptions About the Geologic Column," *Impact* 137 (November 1984); "Grand Canyon Lava Flows: A Survey of Isotope Dating Methods," *Impact* 178 (April 1988); "Excessively Old 'Ages' for Grand Canyon Lava Flows," *Impact* 224 (February 1992); and John Woodmorappe, "Studies in Creationism and Flood Geology," *Impact* 238 (April 1993), which is a survey of Woodmorappe's own writings, which have been combined into a single volume, *Studies in Flood Geology.* See also Walt Brown, *In the Beginning: Compelling Evidence for Creation and the Flood* (Phoenix: Center for Scientific Creation, 1995): this is influential because it is widely read, but several of the young earth creationists I interviewed warned me against it, one of them saying, "the geology is just very poor, as Brown is an engineer, not a geologist."

J. P. Moreland and John Mark Reynolds edited *Three Views on Creation and Evolution* (Grand Rapids, Mich.: Zondervan, 1999). The young earth section, by Paul Nelson and John Mark Reynolds, says very little about geology or cosmology.

The account of Lake Missoula and the channeled scablands of eastern Washington comes from Alt and Hyndman, *Northwest Exposures,* 381-389. The quote comes from 382, with italics added.

The material on the age of the earth comes from Dalrymple, *The Age of the Earth.* A summary of the process of dating can be found in Newman, *Geologic Time,* in the chapter on "Age of the Earth."

Realism, Anti-Realism, and Appearance of Age

The quotations from Nelson and Reynolds come from pages 51 and 99. They defend appeal to appearance of age on pages 51-53. You can find the Answers in Genesis paper, "Arguments We Think Creationists Should NOT Use," on the Internet at <http://www.answersingenesis.org/Home/Area/faq/dont_use.asp>. The book by John Byl is *God and Cosmos: A Christian View of Time, Space, and the Universe* (Edinburgh: Banner of Truth, 2001); see my review in *Presbyterion* 29:1 (Spring 2003), 56-59.

The Sherlock Holmes quotation comes from *A Study in Scarlet* (1887), chapter 14 ("The Conclusion"). See also what Holmes says in the story "The Boscombe Valley Mystery," when Lestrade asks Holmes how he knows that a particular stone was the murder weapon: "The grass was growing under it. It had only lain there a few days. There was no sign of a place whence it had been taken. It corresponds with the injuries. There is no sign of any other weapon." Holmes may reason this way, only if historical inferences are valid.

Many young earth creationists try to combine my options 2 and 4—namely, appeal to reinterpreted physical evidence along with appearance of age to cover anything that won't yield to reinterpretation. It is not entirely clear to me whether Nelson and Reynolds follow this line, or instead offer them as options—or if they've given much thought as to whether the two are compatible. You can find the haphazard mixing of both approaches, with a dash of option 3 (skepticism about historical inferences) in the textbook by George Mulfinger and Donald Snyder, *Earth Science for Christian Schools* (Greenville, S.C.: Bob Jones University Press, 2000): see chapters 12 ("Science, Faith, and Reason"); 13C ("The Earth's History"); and 20C ("The 'Ice Age'").

Is the Big Bang the Same as the Absolute Beginning?

As an example of a theologian who denies that creation from nothing is a historical doctrine, see David Kelsey, "The Doctrine of Creation from Nothing," in Ernan McMullin, ed., *Evolution and Creation* (Notre Dame, Ind.: University of Notre Dame Press, 1985), 176-196. Kelsey considers the exegetical basis of *historical* creation from nothing to be precariously grounded in Genesis 1:1: "The exegetical controversy about this text is unresolved and perhaps unresolvable" (186). See, however, my discussion in chapters 4 and 6 for a better treatment of the "exegetical controversy"; I take the view that the controversy *is* resolvable provided we follow the exegetical rules. Ian Barbour, *Religion in an Age of Science* (New York: HarperSanFrancisco, 1990), 128-135, is similar to Kelsey.

For most of the text of Aquinas, see Peter Kreeft, *A Summa of the Summa* (San Francisco: Ignatius, 1990), 197-203. The Kreeft quotation is from 197 n. 15. The McMullin quotation comes from Ernan McMullin, "How Should Cosmology Relate to Theology?" in A. R. Peacocke, ed., *The Sciences and Theology in the Twentieth Century* (Notre Dame, Ind.: University of Notre Dame Press, 1981), 39 (cited in Kelsey, 190).

Stephen Hawking, *A Brief History of Time,* 122-141. William Lane Craig, "Cosmos and Creator," *Origins and Design* 17:2 (1996), 18-28; at 20-23 he critiques Hawking. Craig's mathematical example, at 27-28 n. 22, comes originally from Paul Dirac (1902–1984), as told in John Barrow, *The World Within the World* (Oxford: Oxford University Press, 1988), 254. See also Hugh Ross, "Astronomical Evidences for a Personal, Transcendent God," in J. P. Moreland, ed., *The Creation Hypothesis* (Downers Grove, Ill.: InterVarsity Press, 1994), 141-172, especially at 154-159, for more defense of the Big Bang as a singularity.

Robert Hazen and James Trefil *Science Matters: Achieving Scientific Literacy* (New York: Doubleday, 1991, 155. See also James Trefil, *101 Things You Don't Know About Science and No One Else Does Either* (Boston: Houghton Mifflin, 1996), 9-11. Craig critiques this approach in "Cosmos and Creator," 20.

Are the Geologists Wrong?

John Whitcomb and Henry Morris, *The Genesis Flood* (Philadelphia: Presbyterian & Reformed, 1961), 452. See the discussion in Davis Young, *Christianity and the Age of the Earth,* 137-148. See Walt Brown, *In the Beginning: Compelling Evidence for Creation and the Flood* (Phoenix: Center for Scientific Creation, 1995), 130: "Only processes observable today and acting at the present rates can be used to explain past events. . . . Uniformitarianism was intended to banish the global flood."

The quotation from Davis Young comes from his *Christianity and the Age of the Earth,* 143.

The articles by Steven Austin, mentioned already, are, "Grand Canyon Lava Flows: A Survey of Isotope Dating Methods," *Impact* 178 (April 1988); and "Excessively Old 'Ages' for Grand Canyon Lava Flows," *Impact* 224 (February 1992). Dalrymple's pamphlet, "Some Comments and Observations on Steven Austin's 'Grand Canyon Dating Project'," was dated March 10, 1992, and privately circulated. See also Davis Young, *Christianity and the Age of the Earth,* 93-116.

Note that Dalrymple had said in his 1986 USGS Open File Report (4),

> A favorite claim of creation "scientists" is that geologists have somehow devised the geologic time-scale and an ancient age for the Earth in order to provide adequate time for the biologists' theory of evolution [with references]. The idea that the theory of evolution and the age of the Earth are the result of a conspiracy is absurd. I have no reason whatever to want the

> age of the Earth to be any more or less than it happens to be. I would take great delight in proving that the Earth is only 10,000 years old if it were possible to do so. As for the biologists, they are entirely on their own—they will have to make do with whatever we geologists are able to discover about the age and history of the Earth. If there is a conspiracy of "evolutionists," neither I nor my colleagues were invited to join.

What Dalrymple claims about geologists seems to fit what I am able to learn about the history of geology. This statement further shows that calling all advocates of old-earth theories "evolutionists" is counterproductive: it suggests that the theories exist in order to support Darwinism, and this is both historically false and needlessly belittling to the integrity of other disciplines.

The Anthropic Principle

On the anthropic principle, see Hugh Ross, "Astronomical Evidences for a Personal, Transcendent God," in J. P. Moreland, ed., *The Creation Hypothesis* (Downers Grove, Ill.: InterVarsity Press, 1994), 141-172, especially at 160-170, for an impressive list of finely tuned parameters. See also Ian Barbour, *Religion in an Age of Science* (New York: HarperSanFrancisco, 1990), 135-16, 144-148. The material from Paul Davies is collected in Alan Hayward, *Creation and Evolution: Rethinking the Evidence from Science and the Bible* (Minneapolis: Bethany, 1995; originally London: SPCK, 1985), 58-65. See also William Lane Craig, "Cosmos and Creator," *Origins and Design* 17:2 (1996), 18-28; at 23-24 he discusses the anthropic principle.

CHAPTER 16: WHERE DO ANIMALS COME FROM?

What Does Darwinism Claim?

To get an authoritative description of the theory of evolution, to which everyone agrees, is actually quite difficult. In this chapter I have relied heavily on John Maynard Smith, *The Theory of Evolution* (Cambridge: Cambridge University Press, 1993).

The National Association of Biology Teachers (NABT) issued a "Statement on Teaching Evolution," which is posted on the web at <http://www.nabt.org/Evolution.html>. (It was last updated in August 2000.) The National Science Teachers Association's (NSTA) position statement, "The Teaching of Evolution" (July 1997), is posted at

<http://www.nsta.org/159&id=10>. I quote from the Internet editions of these statements.

How Did Darwinism Develop?

I have drawn some of the details of the historical survey from articles in W. F. Bynum, E. J. Browne, and Roy Porter, eds., *Dictionary of the History of Science* (Princeton, N.J.: Princeton University Press, 1984). I will cite Darwin's *Origin* from Charles Darwin, *The Origin of Species* (Harvard Classics, vol. 11; New York: Collier, 1909), which is the sixth edition of 1872 (the first edition came out in 1859).

Few today give much time to the Lamarckian view of the inheritance of acquired characteristics, because we now think that inheritance comes through genes. These were unknown to Lamarck, since the work of Gregor Mendel (1822–1889) in the 1860s—rediscovered around 1900—came so much later than Lamarck. In the modern context, one would have to show that acquired characteristics affect the genetic make-up of a living thing, and that the effects can be passed on to the young. Even if one showed this, however, it wouldn't be true Lamarckism, since it would lack many of Lamarck's own philosophical ideas, such as the notion of the power of life.

The 1871 Darwin letter comes from Francis Darwin, *The Life and Letters of Charles Darwin* (New York: Appleton, 1887), ii:202 (footnote): it is addressed to Joseph Hooker, and dated February 1871. For a quotation see Stephen C. Meyer, *Of Clues and Causes: A Methodological Interpretation of Origin of Life Studies* (University of Cambridge Ph.D. dissertation, October 1990), 152-153. Meyer's page 251 has a facsimile of Darwin's handwritten letter. It is also quoted in Charles Thaxton, Walter Bradley, and Roger Olsen, *The Mystery of Life's Origin: Reassessing Current Theories* (New York: Philosophical Library, 1984), 12.

How Does Neo-Darwinism Impact Christian Faith?

Charles Hodge, *Systematic Theology* (Grand Rapids, Mich.: Eerdmans, 1981; originally 1871–1873); and *What Is Darwinism?* (Grand Rapids, Mich.: Baker, 1994; originally 1874). The historical information on the 1873 meeting of the Evangelical Alliance comes from Philip Schaff and S. Irenaeus Prime, eds., *History, Essays, Orations, and Other Documents of the Sixth General Conference of the Evangelical Alliance, Held in New York, October 2-12, 1873* (New York: Harper & Brothers, 1874), 318 and 320. See also Mark Noll and David Livingstone's editorial introduction to Hodge's *What*

Is Darwinism? and Jonathan Wells, *Charles Hodge's Critique of Darwinism: An Historical-Critical Analysis of Concepts Basic to the 19th Century Debate* (Lewiston, N.Y.: Edwin Mellen, 1988).

The quotation from Howard Van Till comes from his "Basil, Augustine, and the Doctrine of Creation's Functional Integrity," *Science and Christian Belief* 8 (1996), 21-38. Van Till is a very outspoken advocate of theistic neo-Darwinism, and of a complementarity model for science and faith interaction. Another source, which is, in my judgment, much more careful than Van Till (and much more concerned to stay within traditional Christianity), is Michael Poole and Gordon Wenham, *Creation or Evolution: A False Antithesis?* (Oxford: Latimer, 1987). Poole is a physicist and Wenham is a highly regarded Old Testament scholar.

As to the supernaturalist reading of Genesis 1, note also that the Wisdom of Solomon takes the same view, where the divine "word" is the supernatural agent in creation and other miracles (9:1; 16:12; 18:15).

The Darwin quotation about separate creation comes from chapter 6 of the *Origin* (page 180 of my edition). The quotation from Ian Barbour comes from his *Religion in an Age of Science* (New York: HarperSanFrancisco, 1990), 154. See also the NSTA position statement, "The Teaching of Evolution," which I have cited earlier, under the heading "Creationism."

On Linnaeus see R. W. Burckhardt, "Evolution," in Bynum, Browne, and Porter, eds., *Dictionary of the History of Science,* 131b—which also mentions Benoit de Maillet (1656–1738) and Comte de Buffon (1707–1788) as thinking that new forms had come into existence during the earth's history; and Nancy Pearcey and Charles Thaxton, *The Soul of Science: Christian Faith and Natural Philosophy* (Wheaton, Ill.: Crossway, 1994), 102-103.

The Hebrew word translated "kind" is *mîn,* which means something like "category" or "variety." It would be a mistake to think that it is a technical term here, with as narrow a meaning as "species." See Mark Futato, *mîn* (no. 4786), in Willem VanGemeren, ed., *The New International Dictionary of Old Testament Theology and Exegesis* (Grand Rapids, Mich.: Zondervan, 1997), 2:934-935; and Paul Seely, "The Basic Meaning of *mîn,* 'Kind'," *Science and Christian Belief* 9:1 (1997), 47-56. Both conclude that the word classifies creatures in terms of their appearance.

The Darwin quotation about man's gradual ascent comes from the last chapter of the *Origin* (page 505 of my edition). The Barbour quotation comes from *Religion in an Age of Science,* 154. The quotation from Gerald Bray comes from *A Christian Theological Language* (Latimer Studies 32; Oxford: Latimer, 1989), 24.

I cite J. Oliver Buswell from his *Systematic Theology of the Christian Religion* (Grand Rapids, Mich.: Zondervan, 1962), I:159. Note also Psalm 103:14 (using ESV margin): "for he knows how we are *formed;* he remembers that we are *dust":* this certainly looks back to Genesis 2:7, and again someone may say that it is further evidence for a more "natural" process of formation. But since the verse refers to the weakness of our time-bound human nature, I don't see how it can help in this discussion.

Is Neo-Darwinism Credible?

My list of the evidences for evolution is based on reading in the authors on the subject; see also the second paragraph of the NABT "Statement on Teaching Evolution," and the bullet points that follow the fifth paragraph; and Robert Hazen and James Trefil, *Science Matters: Achieving Scientific Literacy* (New York: Doubleday, 1991), 251-252.

The description of "evolution" comes from Geoffrey Zubay, *Genetics* (Menlo Park, Calif.: Benjamin Cummings, 1987), 829.

Richard Dawkins, *The Blind Watchmaker: Why the Evidence of Evolution Reveals a Universe Without Design* (New York: Norton, 1987), 1, 6 (don't miss the significance of the subtitle). Since 1995 Dawkins has held the endowed Charles Simonyi Chair of Public Understanding of Science at Oxford University. He spends much of his time as a science popularizer.

An example of granting a special privilege to evolutionary theory is in the NSTA position statement, which says that in the schools

> Policy makers and administrators should not mandate policies requiring the teaching of creation science, or related concepts such as so-called "intelligent design," "abrupt appearance," and "arguments against evolution."

I don't know how this is compatible with their later claim that "evolution, as in any aspect of science, is continually open to and subject to experimentation and questioning."

According to my *Webster's New World College Dictionary* (4th edn., 1999), *Archaeopteryx* was "a reptilian bird of the Jurassic Period [about 208 million to 144 million years ago], that had teeth and feathers, a lizardlike tail, and well-developed wings." It has been often cited as an example of how birds arose from the reptiles. For detail, see Colin Tudge, *The Varieties of Life: A Survey and Celebration of All the Creatures That Ever Lived* (Oxford: Oxford University Press, 2000), 521-524. Tudge says (524),

> Old-fashioned taxonomists were wont to say that *Archaeopteryx* was the ancestor of all later birds, but . . . it really is most unlikely that one or other of the known skeletons was, in fact, the particular ancestor. It is much safer to suggest that *Archaeopteryx* and all other birds shared a common ancestor that was itself a bird—and which, in fact, was probably very like *Archaeopteryx* as the sister group of all other birds, leaving open the option that it *might* be their ancestor.

The quote from G. G. Simpson comes from his article "The History of Life," in Sol Tax, ed., *The Evolution of Life* (Chicago: University of Chicago Press, 1960), 118-180, at 149. It was cited in Michael Denton, *Evolution: A Theory in Crisis* (Bethesda, Md.: Adler & Adler, 1986), 165. I have drawn on Denton's chapter 8, "The Fossil Record" (157-198); and chapter 9, "Bridging the Gaps" (199-232), for my discussion.

For further critique of the evidence for neo-Darwinism, see Jonathan Wells, *Icons of Evolution: Science or Myth? Why Much of What We Teach About Evolution Is Wrong* (Washington, D.C.: Regnery, 2000).

Hazen and Trefil, *Science Matters,* 251 and then 247. John Maynard Smith tries to get around the problem of life's origin by redefining what "life" is. In *The Theory of Evolution* (109) he says,

> If we are to discuss the origin of life, we must adopt some definition of living. . . . Fortunately Darwin's theory of natural selection provides us with a satisfactory definition. We shall regard as alive any population of entities which has the property of multiplication, heredity and variation.

Then (113-114) he writes,

> The most plausible conjecture we can make is that the first living things, on the definition given at the start of this chapter, were replicating polynucleotide molecules. . . . It may seem odd to regard such replicating molecules as alive. . . .
>
> The thesis put forward in the last section amounts to the claim that the first living things were naked genes.

A number of problems arise from this move, however. The first is that, since he invoked Darwin's theory to supply the definition, he can't use the definition to prove that Darwin's theory is true. The second is that the definition doesn't match what we usually think of as "live"—it doesn't include, for example, metabolism. The third is that it still doesn't solve the problem of where the information processing system came from to begin with. And finally, it has to be clear to everyone that it only gains its credibility from its prior commitment to a *naturalistic* account come what may. In fact, Smith ends his chapter with, "This chapter has necessarily been speculative" (120). That, I think, qualifies as an understatement. It seems to me that these authors, whether they know it or not, agree with what Cyril Ponnamperuma wrote in *Nature* 201 (1965), 337:

> Life is only a special and complicated property of matter, and . . . *au fond* [at bottom] there is no difference between a living organism and lifeless matter.

The C. S. Lewis quote comes from *The Problem of Pain* (New York: Macmillan, 1962), chapter 2. The insight that natural process producing an information system is a self-contradiction comes from Stephen Meyer, "The Origin of Life and the Death of Materialism," *Intercollegiate Review* 31:2 (Spring 1996), 24-43, at 39. The issue of information is well-discussed in Pearcey and Thaxton, *The Soul of Science,* 221-248. Thaxton, Bradley, and Olson, *The Mystery of Life's Origin,* also discuss the thermodynamic difficulties with the chemical reactions needed to make the first cell—but I think the information argument is the stronger of the two.

The Paul Helm quotation comes from his book *The Providence of God* (Contours of Christian Theology; Downers Grove, Ill.: InterVarsity Press, 1994), 221. See also Stephen R. L. Clark, *From Athens to Jerusalem: The Love of Wisdom and the Love of God* (Oxford: Clarendon, 1984):

> Accordingly, I cannot coherently believe in the standard account of human evolution, for the following reasons. . . .
>
> Firstly: the existence of consciousness is incomprehensible if we are merely complex, self-replicating kinetic systems selected for their inclusive genetic fitness over some four thousand million years. Consciousness, the subjectivity of being, can play no part in the evolutionary story. It is enough that creatures 'behave' in certain ways, as programmed automata might do. There will be those who claim that the only sort of 'consciousness' that has any real existence is behavioural consciousness, not a subjective reality but a type of public behaviour. The man, the dog, the robot is 'conscious' if it is awake, 'awake' if it responds to certain stimuli in certain distinctive ways. My own judgement is that this discounts a known reality, and renders it impossible to think of scientific or other research as remotely rational. To be genuinely conscious is a necessary condition for experiencing the moral obligations implicit in the intellectual enterprise. [See page 11, where he shows that to claim something is true is to claim that you *ought* to believe

> it—that is, it's a moral claim.] Accordingly, a story which renders the most obvious of facts incomprehensible cannot be acceptable. . . .
>
> Secondly, even if neo-Darwinian evolution had thrown up conscious beings, it could not be expected to produce creatures with a capacity for understanding the workings of the universe. . . . It is not enough to reply that surprising things do happen, that evolution has thrown up a world-spanning intelligence as a by-product of the practical cleverness and linguistic ability which gave our ancestors a genetic advantage. For we do not know that it has done so: we do not have good reason to think that our abilities do match reality unless we have good reason to think that creatures like us would have such abilities. The neo-Darwinian story gives us good reason to think the opposite.
>
> Accordingly, the neo-Darwinian account of our history is not one that we can coherently believe: if we attempt to follow through its implications we find that it gives us no right to believe in the theories we form about the world, including the neo-Darwinian story itself (28-30). . . .
>
> I should re-emphasize that any merely materialistic or naturalistic metaphysician must have considerable difficulty in accommodating any rules of evidence. If what I think is the echo or epiphenomenon merely of material processes, so that my thought is what it is because my neural chemistry is what it is, it seems very difficult to see how that thought can be one that I ought to have or ought not to have (96-97).

In my terms, Clark is invoking touchstone truths—which the neo-Darwinist story would undermine, and therefore so much the worse for neo-Darwinism.

Clark has not invented a straw man, by the way: witness the words of Francis Crick (one of the discoverers of the Watson-Crick double-helix model of DNA), in his book *The Astonishing Hypothesis: The Scientific Search for the Soul* (New York: Simon & Schuster, 1994), 3:

> The Astonishing Hypothesis is that "You," your joys and your sorrows, your memories and your ambitions, your sense of personal identity and free will, are in fact no more than the behavior of a vast assembly of nerve cells and their associated molecules.

Now, Crick is a reductionist as well as a materialist: hence everything is just chemistry and physics in the final analysis. Not all neo-Darwinians are the same—but that, I think, is because they are inconsistent with their biological theory, which only allows natural and material causes to act in the production of life, the universe, and everything.

The John Maynard Smith quotations come from page 343, and then 24-

25, of his *Theory of Evolution* (1993 edn.). For evidence from the linguists, compare Victoria Fromkin and Robert Rodman, *An Introduction to Language* (3rd edn.; New York: Holt, Rhinehart and Winston, 1983), 26-28, 341-342, 359-360 (the 5th edn., 1993, still has the same overall conclusions). The recent work of Stephen Pinker (professor of cognitive sciences at MIT), *The Language Instinct* (New York: Harper-Collins / London: Penguin, 1995), actually supports this inference. In his chapter 11 he shows that language is uniquely human, and deals with the claims for apes. He then offers an evolutionary explanation of how this came about (342-369 / 375-406). But his explanation consists of just the kind of "I can imagine a scenario" guesses as we ordinarily find from other Darwinists. (For example, see 365 / 401-402, and look at all the *could*'s in the explanatory paragraph.) Then consider his claim (366 / 403):

> The languages of children, pidgin speakers, immigrants, tourists, aphasics, telegrams, and headlines show that there is a vast continuum of viable language systems varying in efficiency and expressive power, exactly what the theory of natural selection requires.

He says this in order to explain how language could have evolved gradually, as Darwinism would have it. The trouble with such examples, though, is that these kinds of communications function only because there's already a functioning language community—that is, they're a stripped down version of a living language, rather than living languages being souped up versions of these. Pinker pays no mind to the fact that language use in humans is tied to rationality. It is hard to avoid the impression that he finds these arguments persuasive because of a prior commitment to evolution-as-the-big-picture, and to a naturalistic world: see how he says (360 / 396):

> Darwin is history's most important biologist because he showed how such "organs of extreme perfection and complication" could arise from the purely physical process of natural selection.
>
> And here is the key point. Natural selection is not just a scientifically respectable alternative to divine creation. It is the *only* alternative that can explain the evolution of a complex organ like the eye.

We might also note that the fact that language and reason are universal to humans shows that we all come from the same source—that is, the once-popular view of "polygenetic" origins of humans (that is, that different types of humans arose from separate stocks) is surely false, as the Bible would have led us to believe. See further Pinker's chapter 13, which describes human universals as an analogy to the recognized language universals.

Evolution and "Progress"

The citation of J. B. S. Haldane is from his book *Possible Worlds and Other Papers* (Freeport, N.Y.: Books for Libraries Press, 1971 [originally 1928]), 30 (in an essay entitled "Darwinism To-day"). C. S. Lewis discussed the "myth" in "The Funeral of a Great Myth," in *Christian Reflections* (Grand Rapids, Mich.: Eerdmans, 1967), 82-93; and "Is Theology Poetry?" in *The Weight of Glory and Other Addresses* (New York: Simon & Schuster, 1996 [originally 1980]), 90-106. For more of his views on the influences of nineteenth-century myth on the acceptance of scientific theories, see the Epilogue of Lewis, *The Discarded Image: An Introduction to Medieval and Renaissance Literature* (Cambridge: Cambridge University Press, 1964), 216-223.

CHAPTER 17: IS INTELLIGENT DESIGN A DUMB IDEA?

Charles Thaxton, Walter Bradley, and Roger Olsen, *The Mystery of Life's Origin: Reassessing Current Theories* (New York: Philosophical Library, 1984). Michael Denton, *Evolution: A Theory in Crisis* (Bethesda, Md.: Adler & Adler, 1986). Phillip Johnson, *Darwin on Trial* (Downers Grove, Ill.: InterVarsity Press, 1990). Michael Behe, *Darwin's Black Box: The Biochemical Challenge to Evolution* (New York: Free Press, 1996). William Dembski, *Intelligent Design: The Bridge Between Science and Theology* (Downers Grove, Ill.: InterVarsity Press, 1999). See also the special issue of the journal *Rhetoric and Public Affairs* on the intelligent design argument, 1:4 (Winter 1998), with essays pro and con; and see the special issue of the journal *Touchstone: A Journal of Mere Christianity* on intelligent design, 12:4 (July–August 1999).

Critics include Robert Pennock, *The Tower of Babel: The Evidence Against the New Creationism* (Cambridge, Mass.: MIT Press, 1999); Howard Van Till, a professor of physics at Calvin College, in many essays; and numerous reviews of Behe (by both Christians and anti-Christians). See also Malcolm A. Jeeves and R. J. Berry, *Science, Life, and Christian Belief* (Grand Rapids, Mich.: Baker, 1998).

William F. Buckley's PBS program *Firing Line* hosted a debate on intelligent design in December 1997. Those in favor of intelligent design were Behe and Johnson, as well as David Berlinski (a mathematician), and Buckley himself. Those opposed were Michael Ruse (a philosopher), Eugenie Scott (of the National Center for Science Education, an organization dedicated to protecting and promoting Darwinism in the public schools), Kenneth Miller (a biologist at Brown University), and Barry Lynn (a liberal clergyman, with Americans United for the Separation of Church and State).

When I refer to the National Association of Biology Teachers, I mean their "Statement on Teaching Evolution," which was last updated in August 2000, and is posted on the Internet at <http://www.nabt.org/Evolution.html>. You can find the National Science Teachers Association's (NSTA) position statement, "The Teaching of Evolution" (July 1997), at <http://www.nsta.org/159&id=10>. The National Academy of Sciences has two booklets available, both in print and on the Internet: *Science and Creationism: A View from the National Academy of Sciences* (Washington, D.C.: National Academy Press, 1999); and *Teaching About Evolution and the Nature of Science* (Washington, D.C.: National Academy Press, 1998). Both are posted on the Internet at <http://www.nap.edu>; and I quote from the Internet editions of these booklets.

The NAS makes it clear where they stand on the matter of design when they list in the recommended readings for *Science and Creationism* the book by Richard Dawkins, *Climbing Mount Improbable* (New York: Norton, 1996), calling it "an authoritative and elegant account of the evolutionary explanation of the 'design' of organisms." Dawkins considers all instances of design to be mere appearance, which good science will remove. They further list Pennock's *Tower of Babel,* saying, "a philosopher of science analyzes the newer 'intelligent design' theory and 'theistic science' creationism."

I delivered an early version of the material in this chapter at a Veritas Forum held at Ohio State University, April 12, 1999. Other presenters were Michael Behe and Philip Hefner (a theologian at the University of Chicago). The format was for Behe to present his basic ideas, and then to have two theologians interact with them—Hefner in opposition, myself in support. We then had a panel discussion with three members of the university faculty, two of whom (an ecologist and a philosopher married to a microbiologist) were dead set against Behe, while one was supportive (a biochemist specializing in human nutrition). Interestingly enough, however, they all affirmed the accuracy of the science in *Darwin's Black Box.* They also confirmed my contention that the assertion that all gaps are just gaps in knowledge is by faith, and not an empirical inference.

An example of a young earth creationist group that is critical of Intelligent Design is Answers in Genesis. At their website, <www.answersingenesis.org>, you can find essays such as "It's Intelligent, but Is That Good Enough?" and "The New Anti-Darwinism: Joys and Dangers."

The quotation of Stephen Jay Gould comes from his book *The Panda's Thumb* (New York: Norton, 1980), 20-21.

The quotation of C. S. Lewis is from *The Problem of Pain* (New York: Macmillan, 1962), 28.

Those who believe that theistic evolution is theologically superior to any form of intelligent design are saying that God *must* have made a world with all its capacities built into it, or else he's not a fully skilled Designer. Therefore they must say that all gaps are gaps due to ignorance only, and that in due course they will be—or, at least in theory, may be—filled in by scientific study. I have given my reasons for thinking that this is a misreading of the biblical account of creation; I have also argued that it's philosophically wrong, since it involves a contradiction in terms (such as the idea that a natural process could produce thinking creatures like us). It also violates a fundamental principle of rationality: as the Christian philosopher Paul Helm put it, "It is not appropriate to argue, *a priori,* what God will and will not do with and in the physical creation, but—as with any contingent matter of fact—it is necessary to investigate what God has done" (Paul Helm, *The Providence of God* [Contours of Christian Theology; Downers Grove, Ill.: InterVarsity Press, 1994], 76). That is, don't theorize that God *must* have made the world without gaps; go out and see if he did!

For a discussion of the legal situation in the United States, see David K. DeWolf, Stephen C. Meyer, and Mark E. DeForrest, *Intelligent Design in Public School Science Curricula: A Legal Guidebook* (Dallas: Foundation for Thought and Ethics, 1999).

I cite G. K. Chesterton from *The Everlasting Man* (Garden City, N.Y.: Doubleday, 1955 [1925]), 27.

The quotation from Haldane (1892–1964) comes from J. B. S. Haldane, *Possible Worlds and Other Papers* (Freeport, N.Y.: Books for Libraries Press, 1971 [originally 1928]), 220; and is quoted in C. S. Lewis, *Miracles: A Preliminary Study* (New York: Simon & Schuster, 1996 [2nd edn., 1960]), 24 (chapter 3). Haldane shows up in a number of Lewis's writings as an energetic advocate of scientific naturalism; see Roger Lancelyn Green and Walter Hooper, *C. S. Lewis: A Biography* (Glasgow: Collins, 1979), 163, 173, 217.

The NAS, *Teaching About Evolution and the Nature of Science,* tells us that evolutionary theory is important because of its great practical benefits: it explains why various pests, such as bacteria and rats, are becoming immune to the chemicals we've used to get rid of them; it tells us about the relationships between wild and domesticated plants and animals and their natural enemies; and it helps us locate fossil fuels. But as a matter of fact, none of these has much to do with neo-Darwinism or evolution-as-the-big-picture. They have to do with small-scale changes, and say nothing about how organisms can *gain* information (some of the immunities, for example, result from *deleting* the functions of genes, not from *adding* new ones). They have confused the neutral kind of evolution with the big-picture kind; and they have not shown how these examples, any more than the finch beak examples I mentioned in the previous chapter, really prove the big-picture kind.

William Dembski, *The Design Inference: Eliminating Chance Through Small Probabilities* (Cambridge: Cambridge University Press, 1998; originally a University of Illinois at Chicago Ph.D. thesis, 1996).

I can note here a number of other objections to intelligent design that I didn't include in the main chapter. For example, it is common to find authors who say that creation beliefs or intelligent design do not belong in the science classroom because they are not testable or falsifiable: for example, the NAS in *Science and Creationism* says,

> Creationism, intelligent design, and other claims of supernatural intervention in the origin of life or of species are not science because they are not testable by the methods of science.

The trouble with that statement is that the NAS authors think that these views have in fact been shown false; for example, in the same booklet they say,

> Science cannot comment on the role that supernatural forces might play in human affairs. But scientific investigations have concluded that the same forces responsible for the evolution of all other life forms on earth can account for the evolution of human beings.

The NAS people are trying to have it both ways.

The decision of Judge William R. Overton in the Arkansas creation law case sets out some criteria for whether some theory is scientific:

> More precisely, the essential characteristics of science are:
>
> (1) It is guided by natural law;
> (2) It has to be explanatory by reference to natural law;
> (3) It is testable against the empirical world;
> (4) Its conclusions are tentative, i.e., are not necessarily the final word; and
> (5) It is falsifiable.

Now, I don't think that these criteria will stand up under serious scrutiny from the history of science or from the philosophy of science. But in any case, suppose we accept these criteria for now: so what? This does not insist that there are no gaps due to properties, only that the science doesn't say why those gaps are there. Further, it's not clear that the Big Bang theory, as it's usually stated, actually meets criterion 2, since no one has any idea what *natural* cause there could be for it (and that's why you get so many astronomers saying it's supernatural for all we know). And I'd like to see someone try to apply criterion 4 to neo-Darwinism in a public forum! See William R. Overton, "Decision of the Court," in Ashley Montagu, ed., *Science and Creationism* (Oxford: Oxford University Press, 1984), 365-397, at 380.

CHAPTER 18: SCIENCE AND THE ARGUMENT FROM DESIGN

A valuable resource for this chapter is Jay Wesley Richards, "Proud Obstacles and a Reasonable Hope: The Apologetic Value of Intelligent Design," *Touchstone* 12:4 (July–August 1999), 29-32.

What Is the Argument from Design?

I cite Thomas Aquinas, *Summa Theologiae,* I.2.3, using the translation of the English Dominican Fathers. This is available in Peter Kreeft, *Summa of the Summa* (San Francisco: Ignatius, 1990), 69. I cite William Paley from *Natural Theology* (New York: American Tract Society, no date given [originally 1802]), chapter 23.

Some may doubt whether Paul in Romans 1:19-20 is really advocating a "design argument." After all, they say, he's only saying that you can perceive the universe as God's creation—he doesn't say that you can perceive that God has *shaped* the universe for a purpose. But I think that Paul does in fact point this way, especially when he speaks of God's "eternal *power*" being perceived. Josephus (A.D. 37–95), in his work *Against Apion* (2:167), describes God as "known to us by his *power*" (using the same word as Paul); in context, this refers to power expressed in God's works of creation, rather than in redemptive-historical miracles (2:190-192): "We see his works, the light, the heaven, the earth, the sun and the moon, the waters, the generations of animals, the production of fruits. . . ." Similarly, Paul commonly uses this word "power" to mean "power made evident by being used": Rom. 1:4, 16; 9:17; 15:13, 19; 1 Cor. 1:18, 24; 2:4-5; 6:14; 2 Cor. 4:7; 6:7; 12:9; 13:4; Eph. 3:16; Phil. 3:10; 2 Tim. 1:7. Thus it looks like Paul actually meant that God's power is visible to all from the way the world is—including the elements of design or craftsmanship.

For Aquinas's five ways, see Kreeft, *Summa of the Summa,* 61-70; see also Peter Kreeft and Ronald Tacelli, *Handbook of Christian Apologetics* (Downers Grove, Ill.: InterVarsity Press, 1994), 48-58.

What Is the History of This Kind of Argument?

For historical background on the design argument, see Robert H. Hurlbutt, III, *Hume, Newton, and the Design Argument* (Lincoln: University of Nebraska Press, 1965), on which I depend heavily for Plato, Aristotle, Stoics, and Newton; Thomas McPherson, *The Argument from Design* (London: Macmillan, 1972); D. L. LeMahieu, *The Mind of William Paley* (Lincoln: University of Nebraska Press, 1976); David Livingstone, "The Idea of Design: The Vicissitudes of a Key Concept in the Princeton Response to Darwin," *Scottish Journal of Theology* 37 (1984), 329-357; and David Burbridge, "William Paley Confronts Erasmus Darwin: Natural Theology and Evolutionism in the Eighteenth Century," *Science and Christian Belief* 10 (1998), 49-71.

The works of David Hume include, *Enquiries Concerning the Human Understanding and Concerning the Principles of Morals,* edited by L. A. Selby-Bigge (Oxford University Press, 1902 [originally 1777]); *Dialogues Concerning Natural Religion* (New York: Hafner, 1948 [originally 1779]).

Elliott Sober, *Philosophy of Biology* (Boulder, Colo.: Westview, 1993).

The Aquinas quotation comes from his *Summa Theologiae,* I.2.3, objection 2 (my rendering of the Latin). The quotation from Carl Sagan is from his "Introduction" to Stephen Hawking, *A Brief History of Time: From the Big Bang to Black Holes* (Toronto: Bantam, 1988), x. Darwin is cited from Francis Darwin, *The Life and Letters of Charles Darwin* (New York: Appleton, 1887), ii:105-106.

George Gaylord Simpson, *The Meaning of Evolution* (New Haven, Conn.: Yale University Press, 1967), 345. I quote Michael Behe from his review of Robert Pennock, *Tower of Babel: The Evidence Against the New Creationism* (Cambridge, Mass.: MIT Press, 1999), in *The Weekly Standard,* June 7, 1999, 35.

Is the Argument Any Good?

I know that there is a huge disagreement among Christians over the proper place of *argument* in the process of coming to Christian faith. Some object to it, because they think that this means we are subjecting the Bible to human assessment. For them, we simply have to take the Bible as our starting point for all thinking. In reply to this view, I don't know what else to say except that this is not what the apostles did (see Acts 17, and the discussion of it in an earlier chapter). Others think that argument and evidence are all there is. This fails because it doesn't account for the way unbelievers may suppress the truth (Rom. 1:18), and because it doesn't account for assurance: "I believe that Jesus *probably* rose from the dead" is a far cry from the kind of joy and peace you find in the Bible.

I don't see how either of these approaches makes much sense on its own. David Hume said, "A wise man proportions his belief to the evidence" (in his *Enquiry Concerning the Human Understanding,* x.1), and applies it to religious believing. But I don't think that this is a general rule of thought; the rule to follow depends on what we're thinking about. You see, Christian belief is about a call to a *personal* relationship with our Maker; and therefore we have to think about the rules for interpersonal relationships. If you applied Hume's rule to your own relationships, you wouldn't have any—because you'd never trust anyone! Relationships are based on experience and testimony, which lay a groundwork for trust; but you always, as it were, have to take a chance if you want to keep it going, and you expect that further experience will confirm your initial trust. Think of marriage: who can ever know enough about someone else to *prove,* in the Humean sense, that the step of total self-giving is sane? But who can ever have a happy marriage without such a step?

I think that Benjamin Warfield put it well when he wrote in his essay "On Faith in Its Psychological Aspects," *Biblical and Theological Studies* (Philadelphia: Presbyterian & Reformed, 1968), 375-403 (originally in *Princeton Theological Review* 9 [1911], 537-566):

> "Faith" then emerges as the appropriate name of those acts of mental consent in which the element of trust is prominent. . . .
>
> It is the nature of trust to seek a personal object on which to repose, and it is only natural, therefore, that what we call religious faith does not reach its height in assent to propositions of whatever religious content and however well fitted to call out religious trust, but comes to its rights only when it rests with adoring trust on a person. . . .
>
> But evidence cannot produce belief, faith, except in a mind open to this evidence, and capable of receiving, weighing, and responding to it. . . .
>
> There may stand in the way of the proper and objectively inevitable effect of the evidence, the subjective nature or condition to which the evidence is addressed. This is the ground of responsibility for belief, faith; it

> is not merely a question of evidence but of subjectivity; and subjectivity is the other name for personality. . . .
>
> These things being so, it is easy to see that the sinful heart—which is enmity towards God—is incapable of that supreme act of trust in God—or rather of entrusting itself to God, its Savior—which has absorbed into itself the term "faith" in its Christian connotation. . . . The solution [the Christian revelation] offers is frankly to allow the impossibility of "faith" to the sinful heart and to attribute it, therefore, to the gift of God. Not, of course, as if this gift were communicated to man in some mechanical manner, which would ignore or do violence to his psychological constitution or to the psychological nature of the act of faith. The mode of the divine giving of faith is represented rather as involving the creation by God the Holy Spirit of a capacity for faith under the evidence submitted. . . . In this its highest exercise faith thus, though in a true sense the gift of God, is in an equally true sense man's own act, and bears all the character of faith as it is exercised by unrenewed man in its lower manifestations.

Another way of rejecting arguments like this one is to quote the observation that Blaise Pascal made in his *Pensées* (no. 463 in Krailsheimer's English translation, and no. 243 in the Brunschvicg system):

> It is a remarkable fact that no canonical author has ever used nature to prove God. They all try to make people believe in him. David, Solomon, etc., never said: "There is no such thing as a vacuum, therefore God exists." They must have been cleverer than the cleverest of their successors, all of whom have used proofs from nature. This is very noteworthy.

It's hard to know just where Pascal intended to go with this, since the *Pensées* were the notes for an apologetic work that he never lived to write. Perhaps he meant the "metaphysical proofs" of the sort that Aquinas summarized, which are so far from ordinary human experience (see his *Pensée* no. 190/543). But, in view of the discussions in this chapter and in chapter 12, we can't accept the statement at face value. It is certainly true that these "philosophical arguments" (I prefer to speak of *arguments* rather than *proofs*) don't get you to the experience Pascal describes in the *Pensée* he kept sewn into his coat pocket, no. 913:

> The year of grace 1654.
>
> Monday, 23 November . . .
> From about half past ten in the evening until half past midnight.

> Fire
> "God of Abraham, God of Isaac, God of Jacob," not of philosophers and scholars.
> Certainty, certainty, heartfelt, joy, peace.
> God of Jesus Christ.
> God of Jesus Christ.
> Joy, joy, joy, tears of joy.

But this is just what I have said in distinguishing between the *metaphysical* part and the *experiential* part of the Christian message. It also points out the trouble with talking of "belief in God"—it depends on what you mean by "belief." You are not a Christian if you stop with acknowledging that there is a Creator; you have to go on to embrace this Creator's gracious offer of life and forgiveness as the Bible offers it to you—and that's why the design argument must never stand on its own. In other words, you need to *go beyond it,* not *do without it.*

In the notes to chapter 14 I mentioned the support for this way of reading Ecclesiastes, namely J. Stafford Wright, "The Interpretation of Ecclesiastes," first published in *Evangelical Quarterly* 18 (1946), 18-34; reprinted in W. Kaiser, ed., *Classical Evangelical Essays in Old Testament Interpretation* (Grand Rapids, Mich.: Baker, 1972), 133-150; and in R. B. Zuck, ed., *Reflecting with Solomon* (Grand Rapids, Mich.: Baker, 1994), 17-30. See also J. I. Packer, *Knowing God* (Downers Grove, Ill.: InterVarsity Press, 1973), chapter 10 ("God's Wisdom and Ours").

The first C. S. Lewis quote is from *"De Futilitate,"* in *Christian Reflections* (Grand Rapids, Mich.: Eerdmans, 1967), 57-71, at 69; the second is from *The Problem of Pain* (New York: Macmillan, 1962), chapter 1. The Paul Helm citation is from *The Providence of God* (Downers Grove, Ill.: InterVarsity press, 1994), 223. The William Paley quotation comes from the final chapter of *Natural Theology.*

What Place Should Science Play in the Argument Today?

J. P. Moreland, *Love Your God with All Your Mind: The Role of Reason in the Life of the Soul* (Colorado Springs: NavPress, 1997), 107.

CHAPTER 19: THE HUMAN AND SOCIAL SCIENCES

A useful foil for much of what I argue in this chapter is Malcolm A. Jeeves and R. J. Berry, *Science, Life, and Christian Belief* (Grand Rapids, Mich.: Baker, 1998). Jeeves is an experimental psychologist, while Berry is a geneticist. They fail to recognize the reality of the soul, and how people participate in transcendence. They also follow a naturalistic view of human origins.

On the other hand, see C. Stephen Evans, *Preserving the Person: A Look at the Human Sciences* (Downers Grove, Ill.: InterVarsity Press, 1977).

I have found that many who report on the human and social sciences have a superficial understanding of how to reason from statistics. I recommend Darrell Huff, *How to Lie with Statistics* (New York: Norton, 1954); and Neil Postman, *Technopoly: The Surrender of Culture to Technology* (New York: Alfred A. Knopf, 1992).

Several chapters in C. S. Lewis's *Mere Christianity* give us some helpful advice in the areas that I touch on in this chapter. They include "Social Morality" (iii:3); "Morality and Psychoanalysis" (iii:4); and "Nice People or New Men" (iv:10). See also William Kirk Kilpatrick, *Psychological Seduction: The Failure of Modern Psychology* (Nashville: Nelson, 1983)—which isn't a rejection of all psychology but an exposé of secularized psychology and its disastrous impact on the contemporary church.

For a bracing scientific (and basically naturalistic) presentation of some of the issues I discuss in this chapter, see the following sections in James Trefil, *101 Things You Don't Know About Science and No One Else Does Either* (Boston: Houghton Mifflin, 1996): "Will We Ever Understand Consciousness?" (15-17); "How Much of Human Behavior Depends on Genes?" (21-23); "Can We Monitor the Living Brain?" (27-29); "How Does the Brain 'See'?" (214-216); "What Is the Connection Between Mind and Brain?" (217-219); "The Molecular Origins of Human Beings" (270-272); and "How Did We Get to Be So Smart?" (273-275).

Consider, for example, Trefil's essay "How Much of Human Behavior Depends on Genes?" He subtitles it, "Or Nature vs. Nurture, *Tabula rasa* vs, Original Sin, Predestination vs. Free Will." This mixing of categories—original sin, as traditionally understood by Christians, is not the same as genetic determinism (though it may impact it)—shows a larger confusion that appears again and again in this short article. For example, he fails utterly to distinguish between different categories of behavior: for example, lying is a *moral* behavior, while mental retardation is not—it's instead a *disorder* of the mechanism. He further tells us, "Extensive studies of animals, from fruit flies to rats, showed clear genetic influences on behaviors such as learning and mating. . . . New techniques developed in studies of inbred rats give us hope that before too long we will be able to sort out genetic and environmental influences in these more complex situations." But what reason do we have to suppose that we have any right to extrapolate these studies to apply them to humans? Trefil says nothing about what makes humans distinct. In "Can We Monitor the Living Brain" he claims, "Everything that makes you human—your thoughts, your dreams, your creative impulses—comes from a region of the brain." This is materialism, working as a premise rather than as a conclusion.

The real problem with these essays is that they take a naturalistic and materialistic worldview and act as if that is necessary for the discussion to be properly "scientific." As a matter of fact, that worldview is not adequate for the data that he mentions in these essays—which tells against the scientific validity of the worldview. Sadly, Trefil is unaware of these issues.

The John Rosemond material comes from his column, "An Occasional Swat Is Not Abuse," in the *St. Louis Post-Dispatch,* September 16, 1993. The byline tells us that Rosemond "is a family psychologist in private practice in North Carolina." His website is <www.rosemond.com>.

For more on Proverbs see Derek Kidner, *The Wisdom of Proverbs, Job, and Ecclesiastes* (Downers Grove, Ill.: InterVarsity Press, 1985), chapter 2.

CHAPTER 20: CULTURE WARS AND WARRIORS

For a more fair history of the 1925 Scopes trial in Dayton, Tennessee, see Edward Larson, *Summer for the Gods: The Scopes Trial and America's Continuing Debate over Science and Religion* (Cambridge, Mass.: Harvard University Press, 1997).

The quotations from *Firing Line* come from the transcript of the program of December 4, 1997 (FLS #203/PBS #203), 4-5. The tape and transcript are available from:

Producers Incorporated for Television
2700 Cypress Street
Columbia, SC 29205
803/799-3449

Richard Dawkins makes this kind of claim in lots of places; consider, for example, his preface to the 1996 edition of his *Blind Watchmaker.*

For another good example of the way religion can be marginalized, see the National Science Teachers Association position statement on teaching evolution; they bracket "creation science" together with "intelligent design theory" as "synonyms." They then go on to say,

> Explanations on how the natural world changed based on myths, personal beliefs, religious values, mystical inspiration, superstition, or authority may be personally useful and socially relevant, but they are not scientific.

By saying these views are "not scientific," they are also saying that rational people need not consider them.

CHAPTER 21: LIFE IN A CREATED WORLD

Outline of a Christian World-and-Life View

An important work in the history of detailing the Christian view of the world is James Orr, *The Christian View of God and the World* (Edinburgh: Andrew Elliott, 1897).

For discussions and analyses of relativism in its various forms, see Peter Kreeft and Ronald Tacelli, *Handbook of Christian Apologetics* (Downers Grove, Ill.: InterVarsity Press, 1994), chapter 15 ("Objective Truth"). More technically, see Roger Trigg, *Rationality and Science: Can Science Explain Everything?* (Oxford: Blackwell, 1993); and Mikael Stenmark, *Rationality in Science, Religion, and Everyday Life* (Notre Dame, Ind.: University of Notre Dame Press, 1995). Steven Pinker deals with it from a secular naturalist perspective in *The Language Instinct* (London: Penguin / New York: HarperCollins, 1995), chapter 13 ("Mind Design"). See also Gene Edward Veith, *Postmodern Times: A Christian Guide to Contemporary Thought and Culture* (Wheaton, Ill.: Crossway, 1994). A proponent of postmodernism is Richard Rorty, and he speaks for himself in Stephen Louthan, "On Religion—A Discussion with Richard Rorty, Alvin Plantinga and Nicholas Wolterstorff," *Christian Scholars Review* 26:2 (Winter 1996), 177-183; in the same issue Nancey Murphy has "Philosophical Resources for Postmodern Evangelical Theology," 184-220. Craig Bartholomew gives an overview in "Post/Late-Modernity as the Context of Christian Scholarship Today," *Themelios* 22:2 (January 1997), 25-38; see also Stan Wallace, "Discerning and Defining the Essentials of Postmodernism," *The Real Issue* 16:3 (March 1998), 5-8; William Dembski, "The Fallacy of Contextualism," *Themelios* 20:3 (1995), 8-11; Jay Wesley Richards, "The Logic of Tolerance," *Princeton Theological Review* 4:2 (May 1997), 2-12; and Dennis McCallum, "The Postmodern Puzzle: When There Are No Absolute Truths and No Rules of Logic, How Do We Defend the Gospel?" *The Real Issue* 16:3 (March 1998), 1, 9-14.

Participation in the Sciences for Christians

The C. S. Lewis quotation comes from his essay "Learning in War-time" in *The Weight of Glory and Other Addresses* (New York: Simon & Schuster, 1996 [originally 1980]). The essay, which was originally a talk given to Christian students in Oxford during the Second World War, really makes the case for why a learned career is worthwhile for a Christian (and not just during wartime). I highly recommend it.

APPENDIX B

Other Resources

In this appendix I want to point you to resources for further study, in addition to what I have already given you in these notes.

INTERNET

The following websites carry material that touches on the topics in this book, and have links to other sites:

<www.arn.org>, the Access Research Network—generally intelligent design

<www.discovery.org/crsc>, the Center for Science and Culture (Discovery Institute), a Seattle-based think tank with key essays on intelligent design

<www.origins.org>, Christian Leadership Ministries (the university faculty ministry of Campus Crusade for Christ)

<www.reasons.org>, Reasons to Believe, the ministry of Hugh Ross

<www.icr.org>, Institute for Creation Research, young earth creationists promoting "creation science"

<www.answersingenesis.org>, Answers in Genesis, a strongly young earth creationist group

<www.asa3.org>, American Scientific Affiliation, an association of Christians in the sciences (primarily North America)

<www.ncseweb.org>, National Center for Science Education, an organization devoted to promoting neo-Darwinism as good science (especially in schools)

<www.metanexus.net>, Metanexus, affiliated with the John Templeton Foundation and its interest in science and religion

JOURNALS

Two journals that represent the "mere Christianity" perspective I have followed here are *First Things* and *Touchstone*. They often have articles dealing with the heart of the Christian faith, defending the truthfulness of our faith, and Christian witness in the public square.

The following journals are concerned with issues of science and faith, from differing perspectives:

- *Perspectives on Science and Christian Faith,* published by the American Scientific Affiliation, an organization of predominantly evangelical Christians in the sciences. The articles arise from a wide variety of perspectives, the most common being the intelligent design and complementarity views.

- *Science and Christian Belief,* published by the British group Christians in Science—a sort of British counterpart to the American Scientific Affiliation, though much wider in its theological diversity. Most of the articles express the complementarity view.

- *Origins and Design,* a journal devoted to intelligent design.

- *Zygon,* a journal for faith-science dialogue—although most of the articles consist of naturalistic sciences telling the theologians what they should teach.

Other journals that often carry articles of interest are *Faith and Philosophy, Philosophia Christi, Christian Scholars Review, Religious Studies,* and the "web-zine" *Boundless* (www.boundless.org).

APPENDIX C

Thomas Kuhn and Paradigms: A Review Essay

INTRODUCTION

In this essay I aim to review the theories that Thomas Kuhn presented in his book *The Structure of Scientific Revolutions.*[1] This is worth our attention for several reasons. First, Kuhn's book is a "classic" in the ironic sense: a book that everyone praises but few have read. Second, that book is where we get some of our contemporary buzzwords such as "paradigm." Third, Kuhn's views are often cited in defense of postmodern relativism. And fourth, a number of Christian writers have pressed Kuhn's ideas into the service of Christian apologetics, especially in the area of science and faith.[2] If we are to weigh these claims carefully, we must weigh Kuhn's work itself.

Ian Barbour points out:[3]

> The fundamental components of modern science are: (1) particular observations and experimental data, and (2) general concepts and theories. How are theories related to data?

How are theories related to data? That is of course the crucial question. In 1962 Thomas Kuhn, who had started out as a theoretical physicist but became a historian and philosopher of science, published the first edition of his famous book *The Structure of Scientific Revolutions.* He wrote against the background of the "Baconian" view of science, as a critique of that view. We could summarize the "Baconian" view of science thus:[4]

---

[1] Thomas Kuhn, *The Structure of Scientific Revolutions* (Chicago: University of Chicago Press, 1970 [1st edn., 1962]). All quotations are from the second edition.

[2] For example, R. J. Rushdoony, *The Mythology of Science* (Nutley, N.J.: Craig, 1967); Douglas Kelly, *Creation and Change: Genesis 1.1–2.4 in the Light of Changing Scientific Paradigms* (Fearn, Ross-shire, U.K.: Christian Focus, 1997); and David Hall, "The Evolution of Mythology: Classic Creation Survives as the Fittest Among Its Critics and Revisers," in Joseph Pipa, Jr., and David Hall, eds., *Did God Create in Six Days?* (Taylors, S.C.: Southern Presbyterian Press, 1999), 267-305.

[3] Ian Barbour, *Religion in an Age of Science* (San Francisco: HarperSanFrancisco, 1990), 31.

[4] From Del Ratzsch, *Philosophy of Science* (Downers Grove, Ill.: InterVarsity Press, 1986), 22 (verb tenses adapted).

> Scientists begin by collecting observational data in some purely objective manner, free of all prejudices on the topic being investigated, having no prior preferences concerning what theory should be correct, and not hampered by any surreptitious philosophical or religious presuppositions. They then organize their data in some naturally perspicuous way, again without any smuggled presuppositions or constraints. Then, by a process known as induction, the correct generalizations and explanatory principles emerge out of the organized data.
>
> . . . At no point do presuppositions, philosophical predispositions, religious principles or any subjective constraints enter in. In this method the three basic characteristics attributed to science are to be absolutely preserved. [1] The lack of any presuppositions or a priori restraints on the process guarantees its objectivity. [2] Basing the entire process on empirical data alone guarantees its empiricality. [3] And the process is to be rigorously rational in depending only on the logical process of induction.

Positivism is this view of science coupled with the absolute prohibition of any discussion of metaphysics, including the supernatural.

Kuhn's work is famous because of its term "paradigm," and his argument that *science* does not function independently of *scientists:* their precommitments are intertwined with their theories.[5] Postmodernism tends to take this even further: since all our knowing is done by humans with worldview commitments, our knowing is relative only—it is common to say, "all data are theory-laden." So you never know anything in itself, but only as your paradigm interprets it—whether it be a rock, a text, an ethical maxim, or God.

PRESENTATION OF KUHN'S THEORIES

We will first let Kuhn speak for himself. I have added italics for emphasis where necessary.

(a) Kuhn defines and discusses the terms "paradigms" and "normal science":

[5] Historically, the idea itself was not original to Kuhn, as he himself acknowledged. In fact, C. S. Lewis applied these ideas to scientific theories—particularly cosmology and evolutionary biology—in the "Epilogue" of *The Discarded Image: An Introduction to Medieval and Renaissance Literature* (Cambridge: Cambridge University Press, 1964), 216-223. His word "model" corresponds to what Kuhn would call a "paradigm," and he compares the Medieval to the modern models. He says, "there is no question of the old Model's being shattered by the inrush of new phenomena. The truth would seem to be the reverse; that when changes in the human mind produce a sufficient disrelish of the old Model and a sufficient hankering for some new one, phenomena to support that new one will obediently turn up. . . . We can no longer dismiss the change of Models as a simple progression from error to truth. No Model is a catalogue of ultimate realities, and none is a mere fantasy. . . . [N]ature gives most of her evidence in answer to the questions we ask her" (Lewis, 221, 222, 223).

> In this essay, '*normal science*' means research firmly based upon one or more past scientific achievements, achievements that some particular scientific community acknowledges for a time as supplying the foundation for its further practice. . . . [Some scientific texts got to be classics because they] served for a time implicitly to define the legitimate problems and methods of a research field for succeeding generations of practitioners. They were able to do so because they shared two essential characteristics: [1] Their achievement was sufficiently unprecedented to attract an enduring group of adherents away from competing modes of scientific activity. [2] Simultaneously, it was sufficiently open-ended to leave all sorts of problems for the redefined group of practitioners to solve. Achievements that share these two characteristics I shall henceforth refer to as '*paradigms*' (10).

> One of the things a scientific community acquires with a paradigm is a *criterion for choosing problems* that, while the paradigm is taken for granted, can be assumed to have solutions. To a great extent these are the only problems that the community will admit as scientific or encourage its members to undertake. . . . In short, consciously or not, the decision to employ a particular piece of apparatus and to use it in a particular way carries an *assumption that only certain sorts of circumstances will arise* (37, 59).

> In much of the book the term 'paradigm' is used in two different senses. On the one hand, it stands for the entire constellation of beliefs, values, techniques, and so on shared by the members of a given community. On the other, it denotes one sort of element in that constellation (175, in the "Postscript" of the 2nd. edn.).

(b) Kuhn describes the historical pattern by which communities exchange one paradigm for another, which he calls a "paradigm shift": normal science encounters phenomena that the paradigm does not seem to be able to explain—which Kuhn calls "anomalies." Scientists may ignore these anomalies, or they can find in them a cause for concern. If the anomalies cause concern, they might be solved within the existing paradigm; or someone might propose another paradigm that accounts for these phenomena, and it gains general acceptance. Under Kuhn's explanation, science does not "progress" by accumulating theories and experiments; instead it moves by *shifting paradigms:*

> We have therefore to ask what it is that makes an anomaly seem worth concerted scrutiny, and to that there is *probably no fully general answer* (82).

> Once it has achieved the status of paradigm, a scientific theory is declared invalid only if an alternate candidate is available to take its place. . . . *The decision to reject one paradigm is always simultaneously the decision to accept another* (77).[6]

> Scientific revolutions are here taken to be those *non-cumulative developmental episodes* in which an older paradigm is replaced in whole or in part by an incompatible new one (92).

> As in political revolutions, so in paradigm choice—there is *no higher standard than the assent of the relevant community* (94).

(c) One feature of paradigms is that they are independent of one another, and not subject to critique from outside the paradigm, since the paradigm governs how one actually sees the phenomenon; Kuhn expresses this by calling paradigms "incommensurable":

> Paradigms are not corrigible by normal science at all. Instead, . . . normal science ultimately leads only to the recognition of anomalies and to crises. And these are terminated, not by deliberation and interpretation, but by a relatively *sudden and unstructured event like the gestalt switch* (122).

> As a result of those crises and of other intellectual changes besides, Galileo *saw the swinging stone quite differently* [from the scientists before him] (123, speaking of the change in theories describing pendulum motion).

> Testing occurs as part of the competition between two rival paradigms for the allegiance of the scientific community. . . . If, as I have already urged, there can be *no scientifically or empirically neutral system of language or concepts,* then the proposed construction of alternate tests and theories must proceed from within one or another paradigm-based tradition (145-146).

---

[6] Kuhn never clarifies whether he thinks this is just a descriptive statement of what has in fact happened, or a prescription for scientific rationality. I often hear it cited as the latter. However, an anecdote will show that this cannot be prescriptive for rationality. Once when my sister was visiting my family, she was driving her children in her car, following ours. My son, who was about two, said from the back seat, "Yo-yo up pee." We thought he was referring to his cousin Laura, whom he called "Lolo." After all, the phonetic shift from "l" to "y" is attested in children of that age—at least in mine. We knew that "pee" meant "please." But we had no idea what a request for Laura to be up could possibly mean; and I did not think the "l" to "y" shift applied here. Would we have been rational in supposing that nevertheless it must be the right interpretation, because we had no alternative? I think not; nor do I think Kuhn's observation ought to be elevated to a higher level than the merely descriptive. (Later we discovered that our son was asking for the *radio* ["yo-yo"] to be turned up, because he likes classical music.)

> The competition between paradigms is *not* the sort of battle that can be *resolved by proofs* (148).

(d) Kuhn describes a paradigm shift in terms that religious people—especially the more fideistic ones—have typically used to describe evangelism and conversion:

> Before [adherents of different paradigms] can hope to communicate fully, one group or the other must experience the *conversion* that we have been calling a paradigm shift. . . . The *transfer of allegiance* from paradigm to paradigm is a *conversion experience* that cannot be forced. . . . To say . . . that paradigm change cannot be *justified by proof,* is not to say that no *arguments* are relevant. . . . Though some scientists . . . may resist indefinitely, most of them can be *reached*. . . . A decision of that kind [to embrace a new paradigm] can only be made *on faith* (150, 151, 152, 158).
>
> These are the arguments, rarely made explicit, that appeal to the individual's sense of the appropriate or the aesthetic—the new theory is said to be "neater," "more suitable," or "simpler" than the old (155).

(e) In support of his explanation Kuhn draws an analogy with psychological experiments that seem to show that people see what they expect to see, and commonly overlook what does not fit the pattern they expect.[7] Everyday experience is consistent with these experiments, up to a point: for example, once when my wife came home from shopping she asked me to get the maple syrup from the trunk of the car; I went out expecting to find one bottle, and that's all I saw in the trunk. When I came inside, she asked me what happened to the other bottle; and when I went out to the car again, there it was in plain sight!

An example of a "paradigm shift" would be the change in astronomical theories, from the medieval Ptolemaic (geo-centric, with stars embedded in concentric spheres, etc.),[8] to the post-Copernican (earth and planets go around the sun; universal gravitation explains their motion).

---

[7] See, for example, 113, 126 ("modern psychological experimentation is rapidly proliferating phenomena with which that theory [namely a theory of neutral observation] can scarcely deal") 128. At 62-63 Kuhn summarizes one of these experiments: people were shown playing cards, most of which were normal. But a few of the cards were funny, switching the color: for example, there might be a *black* four of hearts (not red). The funny cards were usually identified as normal—that is, the subjects "saw" the black four of hearts as the four of spades or as the four of hearts (apparently seeing it as red). After a while, though, most subjects caught on and correctly identified the cards.

[8] The modern idea that the medieval picture was ignorant or superstitious (as I was taught in school) is the result of historical ignorance on the part of moderns. For a sympathetic description of the older model, compare Lewis, *Discarded Image,* chapter v.

INSIGHTS FROM KUHN'S ANALYSIS

What are some of the advantages to clear thinking that come from Kuhn's analysis? First, it was part of the opposition to positivism, and anything that helps to demolish that philosophy is welcome. Second, Kuhn's theory brings to the forefront the way our precommitments interact with the data; thus it opens up the possibility that moral and religious factors come into play in *all* acts of knowing, including scientific ones—and this interplay is not necessarily bad. Indeed, it challenges the notion that, say, the only "objective" or "scientific" students of a religion are those not committed to it: "objectivity" of this sort does not exist, nor is it desirable.[9]

How good it would be if the scientists themselves were to reflect on this! As Kuhn himself observed,

> It is, I think, in periods of acknowledged crisis that scientists have turned to philosophical analysis as a device for unlocking the riddles of their field. Scientists have not generally needed or wanted to be philosophers (88).[10]

> The depreciation of historical fact is deeply, and probably functionally, ingrained in the ideology of the scientific profession, the same profession that places the highest of all values upon factual details of other sorts (138).

And hence we find a Christian philosopher, Del Ratzsch, saying:[11]

> Within the newer picture of science, it is in principle rationally permissible to assess scientific theories in part on grounds of whether or not such theories conflict with well-grounded theological principles. Even some secular philosophers of science now admit that.

These ideas apply more generally, too (as Kuhn himself warrants, page 208): for example, in modern studies of the Old Testament, there is a paradigm that insists that in ancient Israel there were certain annual festivals, which may or may not correspond to the festivals mentioned in Deuteronomy. This paradigm presupposes continuity between Israelite practice and the practice found in ancient Babylon, which did have these festivals. This has led many scholars who write on the Psalms to spend a lot of effort

---

[9] For example, in South Carolina a professor of religion was prohibited from teaching a class on the New Testament, because he was a Christian, and hence would not have the proper "detachment." But this kind of "neutrality" is moonshine; nor is it necessary for critical study.

[10] As a matter of fact, this is historically inaccurate except in the modern period. The older term for what we call a "scientist" was "natural philosopher."

[11] Del Ratzsch, "Science," in D. J. Atkinson and D. H. Field, eds., *New Dictionary of Christian Ethics and Pastoral Theology* (Leicester, U.K.: Inter-Varsity Press, 1995), 763.

trying to figure out which of these hypothetical festivals a particular psalm belongs to, and in what function. To refute the work of one of these scholars, say, regarding Psalm 2, one really needs to critique the paradigm at least as much as his detailed work on the psalm.

And finally, Kuhn helps to explain why people from very different cultures seem often to be talking past each other, and why some arguments do not seem to work: the logic that seems so clear to me may owe its clarity to my paradigm.

Critique of Kuhn's Analysis

Kuhn's ideas do not, in my experience, win much favor with practitioners of the natural sciences (except in the most superficial way); but they are popular with nonscientists—including religionists who want to explain perceived conflicts between science and faith by critiquing the paradigm or presuppositions of scientists (appealing, say, to Bible texts such as 2 Cor. 4:3-4).[12] However, we should not give uncritical acceptance to such appeals to Kuhn. His overall theory suffers from several important defects, which limit its ability both to support postmodernism and to undergird a simplistic apologetic-by-dismissal.

(a) The theory is not based on exhaustive historical study—Kuhn is neither deep in what he does cover, nor broad in covering other areas—and hence does not deal with any possible counterexamples. A counterexample would be the comparative philology movement in Old Testament studies: advocates of that "paradigm" were obligated to show that they were satisfying certain criteria of accuracy in describing cognate languages, and of explanatory adequacy for the Old Testament, and the critique of James Barr did them in.[13]

(b) Kuhn shows little or no recognition of a *hierarchy* of precommitments (worldviews, paradigms, sub-paradigms).[14] He does not recognize that, for example, both before and after the advent of quantum mechanics, researchers shared such common assumptions as that the world is intelligible and that mathematics provides a good tool for describing reality. That is, Kuhn does not sufficiently grapple with the notion that there are criteria higher on the

[12] Rushdoony, *Mythology of Science,* 85-93, does just this, wedding his reading of Kuhn to his version of Cornelius Van Til's presuppositionalism.

[13] James Barr, *Comparative Philology and the Text of the Old Testament* (Oxford: Oxford University Press, 1968).

[14] On page 175, in the Postscript, Kuhn acknowledges his equivocation with the term "paradigm." On page 93 appears a paragraph that makes clear that a "paradigm" is not the same as "shared metaphysical and methodological commitments," though Kuhn himself did not make this explicit.

scale of commitments, by which we can evaluate a proposed paradigm—things such as empirical adequacy, simplicity, internal consistency, and fruitfulness for further research.[15] For example, the "annual festival" paradigm I mentioned earlier has some pretty severe problems, not the least of which is the lack of evidence from the Old Testament itself and the nature of the assumption that Israel simply *must* have had the same religious structure as Babylon.

(c) Similarly, Kuhn says that no rational critique of rival paradigms is allowed:

> When paradigms enter, as they must, into a debate about paradigm choice, their role is necessarily circular. Each group uses its own paradigm to argue in that paradigm's defense (94).

But this decouples "science" from "rationality"; indeed, it seems to favor only one-way influence, from precommitments to perception of the external world (actually, at other times Kuhn speaks as if it *is* possible for external world data to influence one's paradigm). It is a long shot from saying "people often behave irrationally, even in science" to "people *always and necessarily* do." By Kuhn's argument, for example, I am not allowed to critique Richard Dawkins, who said in a lecture at Washington University in St. Louis (March 12, 1997), "The vertebrate eye *must* have developed slowly: we don't need evidence for this, it *must* be true, because the alternative is the fully functioning complex eye initially in place" (slightly paraphrased). Here Dawkins is treating the data as if their only function is to *support* the theory, never to *question* it; and Kuhn would forbid us from declaring this to be what we intuitively feel it to be, irrational.

(d) Kuhn is anti-realistic:

> We may . . . have to relinquish the notion, explicit or implicit, that changes of paradigm carry scientists and those who learn from them closer and closer to the truth (170, compare 206).[16]

However, in this Kuhn suffers from a serious self-contradiction: namely, he must assume some kind of scientific realism if he is to base his arguments on psychological experiments, as he does—that is, he assumes that these

[15] Compare Barbour, *Religion in an Age of Science,* 34-35.

[16] Kelly, *Creation and Change,* 138, betrays a colossal misunderstanding when he cites Kuhn in favor of the following conclusion: "If truth is on their side, however, their explanation will eventually supplant the older, majority paradigm." But "truth" in this sense plays little or nor role in Kuhn's picture.

experiments allow us to make *true* generalizations about human perception. Besides, these experiments seem to suggest that when people finally *do* see the things they had overlooked, they begin to be able to see them where they had missed them before; in other words, the new "paradigm" is actually *better* adapted for seeing what is there. Besides, most people have had the experience of perceptions being corrected by feedback: perhaps we have initially in poor light thought an object on the ground was an animal, and we were surprised as we got closer that it did not run away, only to find out it was just a rock or log seen from an odd angle.[17]

(e) Kuhn wants to establish his own position as a *paradigm* for historical research (145)—but he also claims to say something true about what actually happens: that is, he supplies no *self*-critique. He does not consider the possibility that his own theory is self-contradictory: that is, it is an empirically based inference, and hence by his criteria not entitled to be called "true."[18]

For additional critique of Kuhn's scheme, see Barry Gholson and Peter Barker, "Kuhn, Lakatos, and Laudan: Applications in the History of Physics and Psychology," *American Psychologist* 40:7 (July 1985), 755-769.

Does Kuhn Support Constructivism?

We might try to consider whether Kuhn's valid insights support the postmodern or constructivist assertion that the paradigm structure of an individual or community determines perception in such a way that members of different groups actually have incommensurable perceptions of the world—that, for instance, "It's a guy thing, you wouldn't understand it" is a universal truth. What would need to be true for us to accept such a claim? To begin with, Kuhn's theories cannot be accepted without critique, as indicated above. In particular, the theory suffers badly if applied to itself. But also, it makes nothing of the efforts of countless people—including, but not limited to, missionaries—to do precisely what the constructivist says they cannot do: that is, to communicate across cultural paradigms, and to persuade people to adopt new ideological positions. Some, at least, seem to think the effort was successful.[19] That is to say, the social constructivist application is neither logically consistent nor empirically adequate.

Besides, we might add, it cannot explain why Amelia Bedelia is funny.

---

[17] Remember also the syrup-in-the-trunk example given earlier: once my perceptive apparatus was revised, I was better equipped to see what was actually there.

[18] This happens generally with constructivist (or paradigm-relative) theories: compare William Dembski, "The Fallacy of Contextualism," *Themelios* 20:3 (1995), 8-11.

[19] Consider also Stephen Pinker's "universal human" in chapter 13 of *The Language Instinct* (New York: HarperPerennial, 1995), a direct rejection of the relativism so predominant among anthropologists.

In this series of children's books, Amelia Bedelia is always interpreting instructions from within the framework of her own world—her "paradigm"—*and we readers know she is wrong.* When asked to draw the drapes, for example, she takes a sketchpad and makes a drawing. Constructivism would rise to her defense, telling the rest of us that our laughter shows that we are "outside the paradigm," with no right to pass judgment, much less to laugh.

Scientifically, Kuhn's ideas are at their most plausible when applied to things we cannot experience directly, such as cosmology, quantum mechanics, relativity, and the origin and development of life. Our explanations of these things are a network of inferences, and hence based on things we have to take for granted; empirical testing of them is always *indirect.* With other things, such as animal eating habits, we have direct observational access and we *do* know more today than our ancestors did, say, about what kinds of snake a mongoose will kill.

In reply to the constructivist, who contends that we do not really "know" things in the external world except through the mediation of our paradigms, I would argue that a lot depends on just what we mean by the word "know." The modernist said that "to know something objectively" means "to know without personal involvement, and exhaustively." The postmodern critique has shown that we cannot exclude our precommitments from the knowing process, and of course we all know that we will not live long enough to be sure that we know *completely.* Full-blown postmodernism then concludes that we never really "know" objectively. Now this usage is contrary to what the word "know" means in ordinary language, where it means "know well enough for successful agency." I think we should stay close to the ordinary usage of words if we can, and keep our meaning transparent. There is no reason why we have to think that we do not know something unless we know it exhaustively. We know "well enough" for successful agency.

And there is no reason to believe that this kind of knowing is *strictly* paradigm-relative. For instance, when the first settlers came to North America over the Bering Strait, they encountered a category of little black animals, many with white stripes or spots, which defend themselves by spraying a foul-smelling musk. These people, I have no doubt, quickly learned what to do when the animal took up its position to spray (run away). When European settlers came to the same continent, they also met these little animals; they learned a name from some descendants of those earlier settlers, *segongw,* and brought it into English as *skunk.* Now there is no doubt that the Europeans had a very different social paradigm; but they also learned quickly what to do when a skunk took up its spraying position. And nothing changes, even if you have the modern view that this animal shares a common ancestor with not only weasels but all carnivores—indeed with all mammals, including ourselves. Postmodern relativism fails to account for agency, and therefore should again fall victim to the criteria for a good theory. We saw earlier that a good theory should not contradict itself, and constructivism does; now we must ask it to be empirically adequate, and find that it is not: it does not describe or account for our actual behavior in the world.

Paradigms and Apologetic Critique of Scientific Theories

In this essay I am not discussing the philosophy of apologetics, or reviewing the different schools of apologetics. But I can make a few general observations about how we might apply Kuhn's ideas to the apologetic enterprise. It follows from what I have argued so far that Christians have no warrant to dismiss scientific theories on the basis of "paradigm-projection," simply because they do not like the results.[20] We need a more delicate analysis, which I can only outline here.

If I encounter a conclusion I do not agree with, I should recognize that an inference is the result of (1) *data* or raw facts; (2) *premises* or things taken for granted by the reasoner; (3) *terms* that may or may not be clear and well-defined, and that may or may not be used equivocally; and (4) *logic,* the process of arranging conclusions in a step-by-step sequence.[21] A disagreement may mean that I and my author do not share the same body of "raw data" (for example, I think the verb is past tense, he thinks it is future);[22] or we do not take the same things for granted (for example, "baby boomers" take it as given that "tradition" is bad, or at least suspect, while someone like C. S. Lewis certainly would not). Or possibly we either mean different things by the terms or else do not use them consistently; or one or both of us has made

[20] When Rushdoony, *Mythology of Science,* 88-93, cites Kuhn to support his position on the place of worldview commitments in science, he is making the same mistake that I have criticized Kuhn for: he does not adequately account for a hierarchy of precommitments, in which a paradigm is lower down than a worldview.

[21] Compare V. P. Long, *The Art of Biblical History* (Grand Rapids, Mich.: Zondervan, 1994), 194-198, for a helpful discussion of argument structure.

[22] Some will say, of course, that different precommitments can lead to differing assessments of just what constitutes a "raw datum." I do not intend to dispute this; but that just means we push this analysis back a few levels. A Greek verb in the indicative is either a future form or it is not, for example. The skink on my back patio either ate an earwig or it did not. Not to see this is not to have a different paradigm but to be ignorant of the topic of discussion.

a logical error in our chain of reasoning. To handle disagreement with someone, then, I have to make explicit these factors that underlie his position and my own. As the Old Testament scholar E. L. Greenstein put it,[23]

> I can get somewhere when I challenge the deductions you make from your fundamental assumptions. But I can get nowhere if I think I am challenging your deductions when in fact I am differing from your assumptions, your presuppositions, your premises, your beliefs.

If I am sensible I should be willing to subject my own assumptions and terms to evaluation for their merits.

In such a process, indeed, the various premises of the contending parties need to be made explicit and warranted. And these premises may include, not simply cognitive positions (for example, that a mammal must have four legs), but also worldview issues and heart commitments. V. P. Long, in his *Art of Biblical History,* shows great sensitivity to these factors in articulating his apologetic. For another example, the Christian philosopher Alvin Plantinga discusses why he feels it important to oppose Darwinism but is content with Big Bang cosmology:[24] besides the fact that Bible scholars whom he trusts tell him that it is possible to read the Bible in such a way as to allow for an old universe, there is the worldview commitment (and not simply a paradigm) underlying the theories. Big Bang theory does not gain its credibility by imposing a naturalistic metaphysic on the world, while Darwinism does. That is to say, the premises of Darwinism are unacceptable (and its proponents usually do not warrant them); and these premises severely limit critical evaluation of the data, terms, and chains of reasoning.[25]

From this discussion we can see why a scientific paradigm, like a worldview, plays an important role in the forming of an inference: they both enter into the premises, and generally affect the definition of terms; and they thus will affect what data are observed or counted as relevant. But there are several mistakes to avoid: for example, conflating "paradigm" and "worldview"; supposing that *all* data are paradigm-relative; thinking that exposure

---

[23] E. L. Greenstein, "The Role of Theory in Biblical Criticism," *Proceedings of the Ninth World Congress of Jewish Studies: Jerusalem, August 4-12, 1985* (Jerusalem: World Union of Jewish Studies, 1986), 167-174, at 167; cited from Long, *Art of Biblical History,* 172.

[24] Alvin Plantinga, "When Faith and Reason Clash: Evolution and the Bible," *Christian Scholar's Review* 21:1 (September 1991), 8-32; and "Evolution, Neutrality, and Antecedent Probability: A Reply to McMullin and Van Till," in the same issue, 80-109.

[25] The writings of, say, Douglas Kelly or David Hall, cited above, show little awareness of these factors.

of an underlying paradigm or worldview in itself constitutes refutation of an argument.[26]

In such discussions there are aspects of our common humanity that can be used as touchstones for our higher-order thinking—for evaluating our premises and paradigms—such as the fact that we exist, and that we can reason validly.[27] But simply dismissing a paradigm does not persuade anyone—indeed, it denies the possibility of persuasion. In understanding all of this Kuhn's theories help us to be aware of the unstated factors, though they do not adequately explain how they work.

[26] Indeed, the apologetic by worldview critique can easily fall into what is called the "genetic fallacy" (rejecting an idea because it comes from an unsavory source): to say "you only think that because you are a socialist" does not settle anything about whether the actual thought is *true*. (See C. S. Lewis, "'Bulverism'; or, The Foundation of 20th Century Thought," in *God in the Dock* [Walter Hooper, ed., Grand Rapids, Mich.: Eerdmans, 1970], 271-277.) This is just what Richard Dawkins does in the preface to the 1996 edition of his *Blind Watchmaker* (New York: Norton, 1996), where he dismisses advocates of "intelligent design" because their motivation is "religious" (despite anything they might say, implying he thinks they are dishonest as well), and thereby excluded from consideration by rational people. I am not, of course, suggesting that all worldview critiques are instances of this fallacy, or that the misuse of worldview critique by some apologists is in any way an argument against a *proper* worldview critique. Far from it: I want to show where such critique has an important place, provided it is used properly.

[27] That is to say, we require our premises to satisfy the criteria of empirical adequacy, simplicity, internal consistency, and fruitfulness for further research mentioned above. This is apparently what J. P. Moreland calls a "particularist" position in *Love Your God with All Your Mind* (Colorado Springs: NavPress, 1997), 140. I prefer to think of it as "critical common sense."

General Index

Scripture Index